PowerXL Air Fryer Grill Cookbook

500

Easy and Savory Recipes for Air Fryer Grill to Grill, Air Fry, Bake, Broil and More

Hamilton Moenciny

Table of Content

Chapter 3 Wraps and Sandwiches 28

Chapter 4 Vegetables 35

Chapter 5 Appetizers and Snacks 55

Chapter 8 Fish and Seafood .. 109

Chapter 12 Casseroles, Frittatas, and Quiches 156

Chapter 13 Rotisserie 162

Introduction

PowerXL Air Fryer Grill Cookbook explains the recipes you could use PowerXL Air Fryer Grill to make. It describes recipes that could change your favorite foods into healthy cuisines with plenty flavor. The cookbook discusses their features, nutritional value, benefits and their modes of preparation.

The good news is that the recipes in this cookbook are incredibly simple, straightforward and easy to follow. It includes clear chapters and concise sections that highlight various cooking methods, menu ideas, and common ingredients, with recipes that not only work but also give you the opportunity to impress your family, friends and guests.

If you want to know how to use PowerXL Air fryer grill to prepare any kind of meal, you are on the right page, as this witty cookbook provides set-up guidelines, care and maintenance tips, and go-to grilling techniques for your favourite recipes. PowerXL Air Fryer Grill Cookbook also serves as a comprehensive guidebook to make any meal with the provision of recipes and their preparation methods. This cookbook is a key to unlock the door on how to take care of your scarce working time, and it presents to you a whole new life through tastiest and easiest ways.

In this cookbook for daily cooking, the author shares 500 recipes you would love to incorporate into your life. Each recipe is written with a simple yet convenient way to prepare each meal so you could always have a healthy meal on your table any day in the year. If you want a gift for your friend or relative who is a budding chef or loves cooking and sharing food recipes, then PowerXL Air Fryer Grill Cookbook is the practical and go-to resource gift. On the other hand, if you have a busy lifestyle or you want a homeguide to your kitchen, then PowerXL Air Fryer Grill Cookbook is the answer for you to enjoy healthy meals at home, as it is a collection of recipes and kitchen tips which strike a balance of healthiness, excitement and nourishment. Another thing is that the recipes are fast and affordable, and they include ingredients that are budget-friendly and could be found easily in any supermarket. This cookbook has 10 categories of recipes - from staples to breakfast, vegetables to holiday specials - and all of them are accessible to any cook irrespective of their level.

PowerXL Air Fryer Grill Cookbook is easy to understand, and you do not need any prior knowledge to successfully prepare your favorite meals. An amazing thing about this cookbook is that it contains no fussy extra methods, no difficult-to-find ingredients and nothing you will not be able to master - everything you need is in this cookbook. What more? Read, enjoy and learn.

PowerXL Air Fryer Grill is a grill that sears, sizzles and air fry crisps. The cooking power of this outdoor grill and its 450° nonstick grill delivers awesome grill flavour/marks conveniently to your countertops any day and at any time.

PowerXL Air Fryer Grill is 12.5" × 10", and it has 8 piece deluxe accessory set. This ultimate meal making machine which has 8-in-1 functionality, and it has an indoor grill and hairdryer which is 7 times more spearheaded air. PowerXL Air Fryer Grill has a nonstick griddle pan, baking pan, stainless steel mesh fry basket, muffin/egg pan, nonstick grill grate, drip tray, rotisserie spit and a recipe book.

Also, there is a circulation of super heated cyclonic air at extra speed around each side of food for tender, even cooking inside and extra golden crisping outside.

Benefits of Using PowerXL Air Fryer Grill

- Did you forget to defrost your dinner? PowerXL Air Fryer Grill is your answer, as you could cook or transform your frozen foods to a nicely char-grilled in few minutes right out of the freezer. With this fryer grill, you could cook ingredient as soon as possible, and you could give your cuisines a golden, crispy finish.

- Also, you could virtually grill without any smoke on your countertop at any time.

- Faster cooking: The most interesting thing about this fryer grill is that it could air fry up to 40% faster than a conventional oven. In 20 minutes, you could prepare a full meal. You could cook an entire 10 lb chicken, grill six huge burgers, rotisserie kebabs, bake desserts, and more.

- Furthermore, there are intuitive pre-sets which are made available for you to cook to perfect doneness without having to guess. The pre-sets include: grill, air fry / grill, air fry, broil, pizza/bake, toast/bagel, rotisserie, reheat or program your own time and temperature.

- Easy cleaning: The dishwasher safe parts are very easy to clean. The parts include: mesh fry basket, nonstick grill and griddle pans, muffin/egg pan, muffin/egg pan, stainless steel cooking rack.

- Air fry: Less or no oil required up to 70% fewer calories from fat.

Safety Tips to Operate PowerXL Air Fryer Grill

1. **Read the PowerXL Air Fryer Grill manual**

   The PowerXL Air Fryer Grill contains information about your safety and how to use a PowerXL Air Fryer Grill properly. Read the instructions carefully before you start to use the PowerXL Air Fryer Grill.

2. Do not overfill the baskets because doing that could make foods not to cook eventually or the food might fail to reach the appropriate temperature. When you overfill the fryer basket, it could affect the browning process.

3. **Do not leave the PowerXL Air Fryer Grill plugged in when it is not in use.**

   This is a safe practice to prevent bumping on a button suddenly.

4. **Do not burn your countertops or yourself by touching any of the hot elements with your bare hands.**

5. **Keep the area around your fryer grill clean**

   Even with every sense of caution around a fryer, you might be unable to prevent oil from escaping and getting into surrounding areas like the floor. It is therefore vital that you maintain your fryer grill area throughout the day. You could invest in non-slip mats with holes to ensure a slip-resistant floor whenever your kitchen is too busy for a regular cleaning.

6. **Do not put your air fryer on your stove**

   Avoid putting your air fryer on the stove. If you suddenly turn on your stove, you might melt your air fryer, and this could cause a serious fire outbreak.

7. **Check your food**

   While you cook your meal, you need to check it so that it will not burn. You could also use a timer so that you will know the time to shake, flip or check the food.

8. **Do not use any plastic around your fryer**

   One thing you need to be cautious of is that hot oil has the ability to melt any plastic quickly. It is thus essential that when you filter or change oil manually, you should use any steel appropriate equipment.

9. **Keep a fire extinguisher nearby**

   Without any iota of doubt, hot oil could cause fire, and the dangerous thing about oil fires is that they cannot be extinguished with water. Hence, it is crucial that you have a fire extinguisher which is nearby and could be easily accessed.

1.Balsamic Dressing

Prep time: 5 minutes | Cook time: 0 minutes | Makes 1 cup

2 tablespoons Dijon mustard
¼ cup balsamic
vinegar
¾ cup olive oil

1. Put all ingredients in a jar with a tight-fitting lid. Put on the lid and shake vigorously until thoroughly combined. Refrigerate until ready to use and shake well before serving.

2.Pico de Gallo

Prep time: 5 minutes | Cook time: 0 minutes | Serves 2

3 large tomatoes, chopped
½ small red onion, diced
⅛ cup chopped fresh cilantro
3 garlic cloves, chopped
2 tablespoons chopped pickled jalapeño pepper
1 tablespoon lime juice
¼ teaspoon pink Himalayan salt (optional)

1. In a medium bowl, combine all the ingredients and mix with a wooden spoon.

3.Cashew Ranch Dressing

Prep time: 15 minutes | Cook time: 0 minutes | Serves 12

1 cup cashews, soaked in warm water for at least 1 hour
½ cup water
2 tablespoons freshly squeezed lemon juice
1 tablespoon vinegar
1 teaspoon garlic powder
1 teaspoon onion powder
2 teaspoons dried dill

1. In a food processor, combine the cashews, water, lemon juice, vinegar, garlic powder, and onion powder. Blend until creamy and smooth. Add the dill and pulse a few times until combined.

4.Cashew Pesto

Prep time: 10 minutes | Cook time: 0 minutes | Makes 1 cup

¼ cup raw cashews
Juice of 1 lemon
2 garlic cloves
$^1/_3$ red onion (about 2 ounces / 56 g in total)
1 tablespoon olive oil
4 cups basil leaves, packed
1 cup wheatgrass
¼ cup water
¼ teaspoon salt

1. Put the cashews in a heatproof bowl and add boiling water to cover. Soak for 5 minutes and then drain.
2. Put all ingredients in a blender and blend for 2 to 3 minutes or until fully combined.

5.Ginger Sweet Sauce

Prep time: 5 minutes | Cook time: 5 minutes | Makes $^2/_3$ cup

3 tablespoons ketchup
2 tablespoons water
2 tablespoons maple syrup
1 tablespoon rice vinegar
2 teaspoons peeled
minced fresh ginger root
2 teaspoons soy sauce (or tamari, which is a gluten-free option)
1 teaspoon cornstarch

1. In a small saucepan over medium heat, combine all the ingredients and stir continuously for 5 minutes, or until slightly thickened. Enjoy warm or cold.

6.Hummus

Prep time: 5 minutes | Cook time: 0 minutes | Serves 2

1 (19-ounce / 539-g) can chickpeas, drained and rinsed
¼ cup tahini
3 tablespoons cold water
2 tablespoons freshly squeezed lemon juice
1 garlic clove
½ teaspoon turmeric powder
⅛ teaspoon black pepper
Pinch of pink Himalayan salt

1. Combine all the ingredients in a food processor and blend until smooth.

7.Peanut-Lime Dressing

Prep time: 5 minutes | Cook time: 0 minutes | Serves 8

1 cup lite coconut milk
¼ cup freshly squeezed lime juice
¼ cup creamy peanut butter
2 tablespoons low-sodium soy sauce or tamari
3 garlic cloves, minced
1 tablespoon grated fresh ginger

1. Place all the ingredients in a food processor or blender and process until completely mixed and smooth.
2. It's delicious served over grilled chicken or tossed with noodles and green onions.

8.Creamy Ranch Dressing

Prep time: 5 minutes | Cook time: 0 minutes | Serves 8

1 cup plain Greek yogurt
¼ cup chopped fresh dill
2 tablespoons chopped fresh chives
Zest of 1 lemon
1 garlic clove, minced
½ teaspoon sea salt
⅛ teaspoon freshly cracked black pepper

1. Mix together the yogurt, dill, chives, lemon zest, garlic, sea salt, and pepper in a small bowl and whisk to combine.
2. Serve chilled.

9.Creamy Coconut Lime Dressing

Prep time: 5 minutes | Cook time: 0 minutes | Makes about 1 cup

8 ounces (227 g) plain coconut yogurt
2 tablespoons chopped fresh parsley
2 tablespoons freshly squeezed lemon juice
1 tablespoon snipped fresh chives
½ teaspoon salt
Pinch freshly ground black pepper

1. Stir together the coconut yogurt, parsley, lemon juice, chives, salt, and pepper in a medium bowl until completely mixed.
2. Transfer to an airtight container and refrigerate until ready to use.
3. This dressing perfectly pairs with spring mix greens, grilled chicken, or even your favorite salad.

10.Garlic Lime Tahini Dressing

Prep time: 5 minutes | Cook time: 0 minutes | Makes about ¾ cup

⅓ cup tahini
3 tablespoons filtered water
2 tablespoons freshly squeezed lime juice
1 tablespoon apple cider vinegar
1 teaspoon lime zest
1½ teaspoons raw honey
¼ teaspoon garlic powder
¼ teaspoon salt

1. Whisk together the tahini, water, vinegar, lime juice, lime zest, honey, salt, and garlic powder in a small bowl until well emulsified.
2. Serve immediately, or refrigerate in an airtight container for to 1 week.

11.Fresh Mixed Berry Vinaigrette

Prep time: 15 minutes | Cook time: 0 minutes | Makes about 1½ cups

1 cup mixed berries, thawed if frozen
½ cup balsamic vinegar
⅓ cup extra-virgin olive oil
2 tablespoons freshly squeezed lemon or lime juice
1 tablespoon lemon or lime zest
1 tablespoon Dijon mustard
1 tablespoon raw honey or maple syrup
1 teaspoon salt
½ teaspoon freshly ground black pepper

1. Place all the ingredients in a blender and purée until thoroughly mixed and smooth.
2. You can serve it over a bed of greens, grilled meat, or fresh fruit salad.

12.Lemon Dijon Vinaigrette

Prep time: 5 minutes | Cook time: 0 minutes | Makes about 6 tablespoons

¼ cup extra-virgin olive oil
1 garlic clove, minced
2 tablespoons freshly squeezed lemon juice
1 teaspoon Dijon mustard
½ teaspoon raw honey
¼ teaspoon salt
¼ teaspoon dried basil

1. Place all the ingredients in a mason jar. Cover and shake vigorously until thoroughly mixed and well emulsified.
2. Serve chilled.

13. Chimichurri

Prep time: 15 minutes | Cook time: 0 minutes | Makes 2 cups

1 cup minced fresh parsley	fresh oregano leaves
½ cup minced fresh cilantro	1 teaspoon fine Himalayan salt
¼ cup minced fresh mint leaves	1 cup olive oil or avocado oil
¼ cup minced garlic (about 6 cloves)	½ cup red wine vinegar
2 tablespoons minced	Juice of 1 lemon

1. Thoroughly mix the parsley, cilantro, mint leaves, garlic, oregano leaves, and salt in a medium bowl. Add the olive oil, vinegar, and lemon juice and whisk to combine.
2. Store in an airtight container in the refrigerator and shake before using.
3. You can serve the chimichurri over vegetables, poultry, meats, and fish. It also can be used as a marinade, dipping sauce, or condiment.

14. Cashew Vodka Sauce

Prep time: 15 minutes | Cook time: 5 minutes | Makes 3 cups

¾ cup raw cashews	1 tablespoon arrowroot powder
¼ cup boiling water	1 teaspoon salt
1 tablespoon olive oil	1 tablespoon nutritional yeast
4 garlic cloves, minced	1¼ cups marinara sauce
1½ cups unsweetened almond milk	

1. Put the cashews in a heatproof bowl and add boiling water to cover. Let soak for 10 minutes. Drain the cashews and place them in a blender. Add ¼ cup boiling water and blend for 1 to 2 minutes or until creamy. Set aside.
2. In a small saucepan, heat the olive oil over medium heat. Add the garlic and sauté for 2 minutes until golden. Whisk in the almond milk, arrowroot powder, and salt. Bring to a simmer. Continue to simmer, whisking frequently, for about 5 minutes or until the sauce thickens.
3. Carefully transfer the hot almond milk mixture to the blender with the cashews. Blend for 30 seconds to combine, then add the nutritional yeast and marinara sauce. Blend for 1 minute or until creamy.

15. Kale and Almond Pesto

Prep time: 15 minutes | Cook time: 0 minutes | Makes about 1 cup

2 cups chopped kale leaves, rinsed well and stemmed	squeezed lemon juice
½ cup toasted almonds	2 teaspoons lemon zest
2 garlic cloves	1 teaspoon salt
3 tablespoons extra-virgin olive oil	½ teaspoon freshly ground black pepper
3 tablespoons freshly	¼ teaspoon red pepper flakes

1. Place all the ingredients in a food processor and pulse until smoothly puréed.
2. It tastes great with the eggs, salads, soup, pasta, cracker, and sandwiches.

16. Marinara Sauce

Prep time: 15 minutes | Cook time: 30 minutes | Makes 3 cups

¼ cup extra-virgin olive oil	can crushed tomatoes
1 small onion, chopped (about ½ cup)	½ teaspoon dried oregano
3 garlic cloves, minced	½ teaspoon dried basil
2 tablespoons minced or puréed sun-dried tomatoes (optional)	¼ teaspoon red pepper flakes
1 (28-ounce / 794-g)	1 teaspoon kosher salt or ½ teaspoon fine salt

1. Place the oil into a medium saucepan over medium heat. When the oil shimmers, add the onion and garlic. Cook, stirring frequently, for 2 to 3 minutes, or until the onion has started to soften. Add the sun-dried tomatoes (if using) and cook for 1 minute, or until fragrant. Add the crushed tomatoes and stir to combine, scraping the bottom of the pot if there is anything stuck. Stir in the oregano, basil, red pepper flakes, and salt.
2. Bring to a simmer and cover the saucepan. Cook, stirring occasionally, for about 30 minutes.
3. Turn off the heat and let the sauce cool for about 10 minutes. Taste and adjust the seasoning, adding more salt if necessary. Refrigerate in an airtight container for up to a week or freeze for 4 to 6 weeks if not using right away.

17. Asian Sauce

Prep time: 15 minutes | Cook time: 0 minutes | Makes 1 cup

¼ cup low-sodium chicken or vegetable stock
¼ cup rice vinegar
¼ cup hoisin sauce
3 tablespoons soy sauce

1 teaspoon chili-garlic sauce or sriracha (or more to taste)
1 tablespoon minced or pressed garlic
1 tablespoon minced or grated ginger

1. In a small bowl, whisk together all the ingredients or place in a jar with a tight-fitting lid and shake to combine.

18. Basic Rice

Prep time: 3 minutes | Cook time: 35 minutes | Makes 4 cups

1 cup long-grain white rice
1 tablespoon unsalted butter, melted, or 1 tablespoon extra-

virgin olive oil
2 cups water
1 teaspoon kosher salt or ½ teaspoon fine salt

1. Rinse the rice well under cold water and let drain.
2. Place the butter in a baking pan and add the rice. Stir it to coat with the fat, then pour in the water and add the salt. Stir to dissolve the salt.
3. Place the pan on the bake position. Select Bake, set temperature to 325ºF (163ºC), and set time to 35 minutes.
4. After 20 minutes, remove the pan from the grill and stir the rice. Return the pan to the grill and continue cooking. After 10 more minutes, check the rice again. It should be mostly cooked through, and the water should be absorbed. If not, continue cooking for a few more minutes.
5. When cooking is complete, remove the pan from the grill and cover with aluminum foil. Let sit for 10 minutes, then gently fluff the rice with a fork. Serve immediately, or let cool for 20 minutes, then refrigerate in an airtight container.

19. Red Enchilada Sauce

Prep time: 15 minutes | Cook time: 0 minutes | Makes 2 cups

3 large ancho chiles, stems and seeds removed, torn into pieces
1½ cups very hot water
2 garlic cloves, peeled and lightly smashed
2 teaspoons kosher

salt or 1 teaspoon fine salt
½ teaspoon dried oregano
½ teaspoon ground cumin
1½ teaspoons sugar
2 tablespoons wine vinegar

1. Place the chile pieces in the hot water and let sit for 10 to 15 minutes.
2. Pour the chiles and water into a blender jar and add the garlic, salt, oregano, cumin, sugar, and vinegar. Blend until smooth.

20. Teriyaki Sauce

Prep time: 5 minutes | Cook time: 0 minutes | Makes ¾ cup

½ cup soy sauce
3 tablespoons honey
1 tablespoon rice vinegar
1 tablespoon rice wine

or dry sherry
2 teaspoons minced fresh ginger
2 garlic cloves, smashed

1. In a small bowl, whisk together all the ingredients.

21. Caesar Dressing

Prep time: 5 minutes | Cook time: 0 minutes | Serves ²/₃ cup

1 teaspoon anchovy paste
¼ teaspoon minced or pressed garlic
¼ teaspoon kosher salt or ⅛ teaspoon

fine salt
1 egg
2 tablespoons freshly squeezed lemon juice
½ cup extra-virgin olive oil

1. Place all the ingredients in the order listed in a tall narrow container. Place the blade of the immersion blender in the bottom of the container. Turn the blender on and slowly bring it up to the top of the ingredients, repeating if necessary to thoroughly emulsify the dressing.

22. Southwestern Seasoning

Prep time: 5 minutes | Cook time: 0 minutes | Makes ¾ cup

3 tablespoons paprika
3 tablespoons ancho chile powder
2 teaspoons cayenne
2 tablespoons freshly ground black pepper
2 teaspoons cumin

1 tablespoon granulated garlic
1 tablespoon granulated onion
2 tablespoons dried oregano

1. Place all the ingredients in a small bowl and whisk to combine. Store in an airtight container in the pantry.

23. Shawarma Seasoning

Prep time: 5 minutes | Cook time: 0 minutes | Makes 1 tablespoon

1 teaspoon cumin
1 teaspoon smoked paprika
¼ teaspoon kosher salt or ⅛ teaspoon fine salt
¼ teaspoon turmeric

¼ teaspoon allspice
¼ teaspoon cinnamon
¼ teaspoon freshly ground black pepper
¼ teaspoon red pepper flakes

1. In a small bowl, combine all the ingredients. Store in an airtight container in the pantry.

24. Roasted Mushrooms

Prep time: 8 minutes | Cook time: 30 minutes | Makes 1½ cups

1 pound (454 g) button or cremini mushrooms, washed, stems trimmed
¼ cup water
1 teaspoon kosher

salt or ½ teaspoon fine salt
3 tablespoons unsalted butter, cut into pieces, or extra-virgin olive oil

1. Place a large piece of aluminum foil in the baking pan. Cut the mushrooms into quarters or thick slices and place them in the middle of the foil. Spread them out into a single layer as much as possible. Pour the water over them, then sprinkle with the salt and add the butter. Seal the foil, fully enclosing the mushrooms.
2. Place the pan on the roast position. Select Roast, set temperature to 325°F (163°C), and set time to 15 minutes.
3. After 15 minutes, remove the pan from the grill. Carefully place the foil packet on a cutting board and open it up. Pour the mushrooms and liquid from the foil into the baking pan.
4. Place the pan on the roast position. Select Roast, set temperature to 350°F (177°C), and set time to 15 minutes.
5. After about 10 minutes, remove the pan from the grill and stir the mushrooms. The liquid should be evaporating. Return the pan to the grill and continue cooking.
6. When cooking is complete, the liquid will be mostly gone and the mushrooms will have begun to brown, anywhere from 5 to 15 more minutes. Use immediately or refrigerate in an airtight container up to 5 days.

25. Polenta (Grits)

Prep time: 3 minutes | Cook time: 65 minutes | Makes 4 cups

1 cup polenta or grits (not instant or quick cook)
2 cups milk
2 cups chicken or vegetable stock

1 teaspoon kosher salt or ½ teaspoon fine salt
2 tablespoons unsalted butter, cut into 4 pieces

1. Place the grits in a baking pan. Add the milk, stock, salt, and butter and stir gently.
2. Place the pan on the bake position. Select Bake, set temperature to 325°F (163°C), and set time to 1 hour, 5 minutes.
3. After 15 minutes, remove the pan from the grill and stir the polenta. Return the pan to the grill and continue cooking.
4. After 30 minutes, remove the pan again and stir the polenta. Return the pan to the grill and continue cooking. After another 15 minutes (1 hour total), remove the pan from the grill. The polenta should be soft and creamy, with all the liquid absorbed. If necessary, continue cooking for 5 to 10 minutes more.
5. When cooking is complete, remove the pan from the grill. Serve, or let cool to room temperature, then cover and refrigerate for up to 3 days.

Chapter 2 Breakfasts

26.Honey-Lime Glazed Grilled Fruit Salad

Prep time: 10 minutes | Cook time: 4 minutes | Serves 4

½ pound (227 g) strawberries, washed, hulled and halved
1 (9-ounce / 255-g) can pineapple chunks, drained, juice reserved
2 peaches, pitted and sliced
6 tablespoons honey, divided
1 tablespoon freshly squeezed lime juice

1. Place the grill plate on the grill position. Select Grill, set the temperature to 450ºF (232ºC), and set the time to 4 minutes.
2. Combine the strawberries, pineapple, and peaches in a large bowl with 3 tablespoons of honey. Toss to coat evenly.
3. Place the fruit on the grill plate. Gently press the fruit down to maximize grill marks. Grill for 4 minutes without flipping.
4. Meanwhile, in a small bowl, combine the remaining 3 tablespoons of honey, lime juice, and 1 tablespoon of reserved pineapple juice.
5. When cooking is complete, place the fruit in a large bowl and toss with the honey mixture. Serve immediately.

27.Mushroom and Onion Frittata

Prep time: 10 minutes | Cook time: 10 minutes | Serves 4

4 large eggs
¼ cup whole milk
Sea salt, to taste
Freshly ground black pepper, to taste
½ bell pepper, seeded
and diced
½ onion, chopped
4 cremini mushrooms, sliced
½ cup shredded Cheddar cheese

1. In a medium bowl, whisk together the eggs and milk. Season with the salt and pepper. Add the bell pepper, onion, mushrooms, and cheese. Mix until well combined.
2. Place the baking pan on the bake position. Select Bake, set the temperature to 400ºF (204ºC), and set the time to 10 minutes.
3. Pour the egg mixture into the baking pan, spreading evenly.
4. Bake for 10 minutes, or until lightly golden.

28.Sourdough Croutons

Prep time: 5 minutes | Cook time: 6 minutes | Makes 4 cups

4 cups cubed sourdough bread, 1-inch cubes
1 tablespoon olive oil
1 teaspoon fresh
thyme leaves
¼ teaspoon salt
Freshly ground black pepper, to taste

1. Combine all ingredients in a bowl.
2. Place the crisper tray on the air fry position. Select Air Fry, set the temperature to 400ºF (204ºC), and set the time to 6 minutes.
3. Toss the bread cubes and transfer to the crisper tray. Air fry for 6 minutes, shaking the crisper tray once or twice while they cook.
4. Serve warm.

29.Cornflakes Toast Sticks

Prep time: 10 minutes | Cook time: 6 minutes | Serves 4

2 eggs
½ cup milk
⅛ teaspoon salt
½ teaspoon pure vanilla extract
¾ cup crushed cornflakes
6 slices sandwich bread, each slice cut into 4 strips
Maple syrup, for dipping
Cooking spray

1. Place the crisper tray on the air fry position. Select Air Fry, set the temperature to 390ºF (199ºC), and set the time to 6 minutes.
2. In a small bowl, beat together the eggs, milk, salt, and vanilla.
3. Put crushed cornflakes on a plate or in a shallow dish.
4. Dip bread strips in egg mixture, shake off excess, and roll in cornflake crumbs.
5. Spray both sides of bread strips with oil.
6. Put bread strips in crisper tray in a single layer.
7. Air fry for 6 minutes or until golden brown.
8. Repeat steps 5 and 6 to air fry remaining French toast sticks.
9. Serve with maple syrup.

30.Spinach Omelet

Prep time: 10 minutes | Cook time: 10 minutes | Serves 1

1 teaspoon olive oil	cheese
3 eggs	¼ cup chopped
Salt and ground black	spinach
pepper, to taste	1 tablespoon chopped
1 tablespoon ricotta	parsley

1. Grease the baking pan with olive oil.
2. Place the baking pan on the bake position. Select Bake, set the temperature to 330ºF (166ºC), and set the time to 10 minutes.
3. In a bowl, beat the eggs with a fork and sprinkle salt and pepper.
4. Add the ricotta, spinach, and parsley and then transfer to the baking pan.
5. Bake for 10 minutes or until the egg is set.
6. Serve warm.

31.Ham and Corn Muffins

Prep time: 10 minutes | Cook time: 6 minutes | Makes 8 muffins

¾ cup yellow cornmeal	2 tablespoons canola oil
¼ cup flour	½ cup milk
1½ teaspoons baking powder	½ cup shredded sharp Cheddar cheese
¼ teaspoon salt	½ cup diced ham
1 egg, beaten	

1. Place the baking pan on the bake position. Select Bake, set the temperature to 390ºF (199ºC), and set the time to 6 minutes.
2. In a medium bowl, stir together the cornmeal, flour, baking powder, and salt.
3. Add the egg, oil, and milk to dry ingredients and mix well.
4. Stir in shredded cheese and diced ham.
5. Divide batter among 8 parchment paper-lined muffin cups.
6. Put 4 filled muffin cups in the pan. Bake for 5 minutes.
7. Reduce temperature to 330ºF (166ºC) and bake for 1 minute or until a toothpick inserted in center of the muffin comes out clean.
8. Repeat steps 6 and 7 to bake remaining muffins.
9. Serve warm.

32.Fast Coffee Donuts

Prep time: 5 minutes | Cook time: 6 minutes | Serves 6

¼ cup sugar	¼ cup coffee
½ teaspoon salt	1 tablespoon
1 cup flour	aquafaba
1 teaspoon baking	1 tablespoon
powder	sunflower oil

1. In a large bowl, combine the sugar, salt, flour, and baking powder.
2. Add the coffee, aquafaba, and sunflower oil and mix until a dough is formed. Leave the dough to rest in and the refrigerator.
3. Place the crisper tray on the air fry position. Select Air Fry, set the temperature to 400ºF (204ºC), and set the time to 6 minutes.
4. Remove the dough from the fridge and divide up, kneading each section into a doughnut.
5. Put the doughnuts in the crisper tray. Air fry for 6 minutes.
6. Serve immediately.

33.Bacon and Egg Stuffed Peppers

Prep time: 10 minutes | Cook time: 15 minutes | Serves 4

1 cup shredded Cheddar cheese	4 large eggs
4 slices bacon, cooked and chopped	Sea salt, to taste
4 bell peppers, seeded and tops removed	Freshly ground black pepper, to taste
	Chopped fresh parsley, for garnish

1. Place the crisper tray on the air fry position. Select Air Fry, set the temperature to 390ºF (199ºC), and set the time to 15 minutes.
2. Meanwhile, divide the cheese and bacon between the bell peppers. Crack one of the eggs into each bell pepper, and season with salt and pepper.
3. Place each bell pepper in the crisper tray. Air fry for 10 to 15 minutes, until the egg whites are cooked and the yolks are slightly runny.
4. Remove the peppers from the crisper tray, garnish with parsley, and serve.

34.Lush Vegetable Omelet

Prep time: 10 minutes | Cook time: 13 minutes | Serves 2

2 teaspoons canola oil
4 eggs, whisked
3 tablespoons plain milk
1 teaspoon melted butter
1 red bell pepper, seeded and chopped
1 green bell pepper, seeded and chopped
1 white onion, finely chopped
½ cup baby spinach leaves, roughly chopped
½ cup Halloumi cheese, shaved
Kosher salt and freshly ground black pepper, to taste

1. Place the baking pan on the bake position. Select Bake, set the temperature to 350ºF (177ºC), and set the time to 13 minutes.
2. Grease the baking pan with canola oil.
3. Put the remaining ingredients in the baking pan and stir well.
4. Bake for 13 minutes.
5. Serve warm.

35.Cheesy Breakfast Casserole

Prep time: 10 minutes | Cook time: 14 minutes | Serves 4

6 slices bacon
6 eggs
Salt and pepper, to taste
Cooking spray
½ cup chopped green bell pepper
½ cup chopped onion
¾ cup shredded Cheddar cheese

1. Place the bacon in a skillet over medium-high heat and cook each side for about 4 minutes until evenly crisp. Remove from the heat to a paper towel-lined plate to drain. Crumble it into small pieces and set aside.
2. Whisk the eggs with the salt and pepper in a medium bowl.
3. Place the baking pan on the bake position. Select Bake, set the temperature to 400ºF (204ºC), and set the time to 8 minutes.
4. Spritz the baking pan with cooking spray.
5. Place the whisked eggs, crumbled bacon, green bell pepper, and onion in the prepared pan. Bake for 6 minutes.
6. Scatter the Cheddar cheese all over and bake for 2 minutes more.
7. Allow to sit for 5 minutes and serve on plates.

36.Spinach with Scrambled Eggs

Prep time: 10 minutes | Cook time: 10 minutes | Serves 2

2 tablespoons olive oil
4 eggs, whisked
5 ounces (142 g) fresh spinach, chopped
1 medium tomato, chopped
1 teaspoon fresh
lemon juice
½ teaspoon coarse salt
½ teaspoon ground black pepper
½ cup of fresh basil, roughly chopped

1. Grease the baking pan with the oil, tilting it to spread the oil around.
2. Place the baking pan on the bake position. Select Bake, set the temperature to 280ºF (138ºC), and set the time to 10 minutes.
3. In the pan, mix the remaining ingredients, apart from the basil leaves, whisking well until everything is completely combined.
4. Bake for 10 minutes.
5. Top with fresh basil leaves before serving.

37.Grilled Sausage Mix

Prep time: 5 minutes | Cook time: 22 minutes | Serves 4

8 mini bell peppers
2 heads radicchio, each cut into 6 wedges
Canola oil, for brushing
Sea salt, to taste
Freshly ground black pepper, to taste
6 breakfast sausage links
6 hot or sweet Italian sausage links

1. Place the grill plate on the grill position. Select Grill, set the temperature to 450ºF (232ºC), and set the time to 22 minutes.
2. Brush the bell peppers and radicchio with the oil. Season with salt and black pepper.
3. Place the bell peppers and radicchio on the grill plate; Grill for 10 minutes, without flipping.
4. Meanwhile, poke the sausages with a fork or knife and brush them with some of the oil.
5. After 10 minutes, remove the vegetables and set aside. Decrease the temperature to LOW. Place the sausages on the grill plate; Grill for 6 minutes.
6. Flip the sausages. Grill for 6 minutes more. Remove the sausages from the grill plate.
7. Serve the sausages and vegetables on a large cutting board or serving tray.

38. Sausage and Cheese Quiche

Prep time: 5 minutes | Cook time: 25 minutes | Serves 4

12 large eggs	sugar-free breakfast
1 cup heavy cream	sausage
Salt and black pepper,	2 cups shredded
to taste	Cheddar cheese
12 ounces (340 g)	Cooking spray

1. Coat a casserole dish with cooking spray.
2. Place the casserole dish on the bake position. Select Bake, set the temperature to 375ºF (191ºC), and set the time to 25 minutes.
3. Beat together the eggs, heavy cream, salt and pepper in a large bowl until creamy. Stir in the breakfast sausage and Cheddar cheese.
4. Pour the sausage mixture into the prepared casserole dish. Place the dish directly in the pan. Bake for 25 minutes, or until the top of the quiche is golden brown and the eggs are set.
5. Remove from the grill and let sit for 5 to 10 minutes before serving.

39. Crustless Broccoli Quiche

Prep time: 5 minutes | Cook time: 10 minutes | Serves 4

1 cup broccoli florets	¾ cup heavy cream
¾ cup chopped	½ teaspoon salt
roasted red peppers	Freshly ground black
1¼ cups grated	pepper, to taste
Fontina cheese	Cooking spray
6 eggs	

1. Spritz the baking pan with cooking spray.
2. Place the baking pan on the air fry position. Select Air Fry, set the temperature to 325ºF (163ºC), and set the time to 10 minutes.
3. Add the broccoli florets and roasted red peppers to the pan and scatter the grated Fontina cheese on top.
4. In a bowl, beat together the eggs and heavy cream. Sprinkle with salt and pepper. Pour the egg mixture over the top of the cheese. Wrap the pan in foil.
5. Air fry for 8 minutes. Remove the foil and continue to cook another 2 minutes until the quiche is golden brown.
6. Rest for 5 minutes before cutting into wedges and serve warm.

40. English Pumpkin Egg Bake

Prep time: 10 minutes | Cook time: 10 minutes | Serves 2

2 eggs	1 tablespoon sugar
½ cup milk	1 cup pumpkin purée
2 cups flour	1 teaspoon cinnamon
2 tablespoons cider	powder
vinegar	1 teaspoon baking
2 teaspoons baking	soda
powder	1 tablespoon olive oil

1. Place the baking pan on the bake position. Select Bake, set the temperature to 300ºF (149ºC), and set the time to 10 minutes.
2. Crack the eggs into a bowl and beat with a whisk. Combine with the milk, flour, cider vinegar, baking powder, sugar, pumpkin purée, cinnamon powder, and baking soda, mixing well.
3. Grease the baking pan with oil. Add the mixture to the pan. Bake for 10 minutes.
4. Serve warm.

41. Mushroom and Squash Toast

Prep time: 10 minutes | Cook time: 10 minutes | Serves 4

1 tablespoon olive oil	sliced
1 red bell pepper, cut	2 tablespoons
into strips	softened butter
2 green onions, sliced	4 slices bread
1 cup sliced button or	½ cup soft goat
cremini mushrooms	cheese
1 small yellow squash,	

1. Brush the crisper tray with the olive oil.
2. Place the crisper tray on the air fry position. Select Air Fry, set the temperature to 350ºF (177ºC), and set the time to 7 minutes.
3. Put the red pepper, green onions, mushrooms, and squash inside the crisper tray and give them a stir. Air fry for 7 minutes or the vegetables are tender, shaking the crisper tray once throughout the cooking time.
4. Remove the vegetables and set them aside.
5. Spread the butter on the slices of bread and transfer to the crisper tray, butter-side up. Air fry for 3 minutes.
6. Remove the toast from the grill and top with goat cheese and vegetables. Serve warm.

42.Grilled Egg and Arugula Pizza

Prep time: 10 minutes | Cook time: 8 minutes | Serves 2

2 tablespoons all-purpose flour, plus more as needed
½ store-bought pizza dough (about 8 ounces / 227 g)
1 tablespoon canola oil, divided
1 cup fresh ricotta cheese
4 large eggs
Sea salt, to taste
Freshly ground black pepper, to taste
4 cups arugula, torn
1 tablespoon extra-virgin olive oil
1 teaspoon freshly squeezed lemon juice
2 tablespoons grated Parmesan cheese

1. Place the grill plate on the grill position. Select Grill, set the temperature to 450ºF (232ºC), and set the time to 7 minutes.
2. Dust a clean work surface with flour. Place the dough on the floured surface and roll it into a 9-inch round of even thickness. Dust your rolling pin and work surface with additional flour, as needed, to ensure the dough does not stick.
3. Brush the surface of the rolled-out dough evenly with ½ tablespoon of canola oil. Flip the dough over and brush with the remaining ½ tablespoon oil. Poke the dough with a fork 5 or 6 times across its surface to prevent air pockets from forming during cooking.
4. Place the dough on the grill plate. Grill for 4 minutes.
5. After 4 minutes, flip the dough, then spoon teaspoons of ricotta cheese across the surface of the dough, leaving a 1-inch border around the edges.
6. Crack one egg into a ramekin or small bowl. This way you can easily remove any shell that may break into the egg and keep the yolk intact. Imagine the dough is split into four quadrants. Pour one egg into each. Repeat with the remaining 3 eggs. Season the pizza with salt and pepper.
7. Continue cooking for the remaining 3 to 4 minutes until the egg whites are firm.
8. Meanwhile, in a medium bowl, toss together the arugula, oil, and lemon juice, and season with salt and pepper.
9. Transfer the pizza to a cutting board and let it cool. Top it with the arugula mixture, drizzle with olive oil, if desired, and sprinkle with Parmesan cheese. Cut into pieces and serve.

43.Mushroom and Artichoke Frittata

Prep time: 10 minutes | Cook time: 15 minutes | Serves 6

2 tablespoons unsalted butter, melted
¼ cup chopped onion
1 cup coarsely chopped artichoke hearts (drained if canned; thawed if frozen)
8 eggs
½ teaspoon kosher salt or ¼ teaspoon
fine salt
¼ cup whole milk
¾ cup shredded Mozzarella cheese, divided
½ cup Roasted Mushrooms
¼ cup grated Parmesan cheese
¼ teaspoon freshly ground black pepper

1. Brush the baking pan with the butter. Add the onion and artichoke hearts and toss to coat with the butter.
2. Place the pan on the roast position. Select Roast, set temperature to 375ºF (191ºC), and set time to 12 minutes.
3. While the vegetables cook, whisk the eggs with the salt in a medium bowl. Let sit for a minute or two, then add the milk and whisk again. The eggs should be thoroughly mixed with no streaks of white remaining, but not foamy. Stir in ½ cup of Mozzarella cheese.
4. After the vegetables have cooked for 5 minutes, remove the pan. Spread the mushrooms over the vegetables. Pour the egg mixture over the vegetables. Stir gently just to distribute the vegetables evenly. Return the pan to the grill and resume cooking for 5 to 7 minutes, or until the edges are set. The center will still be quite liquid. (If the frittata begins to form large bubbles on the bottom, use a silicone spatula to break the bubbles and let the air out so the frittata flattens out again.)
5. Place the pan on the broil position. Select Broil, set temperature to 400ºF (204ºC), and set time to 3 minutes.
6. After 1 minute, remove the pan and sprinkle the remaining ¼ cup of Mozzarella and the Parmesan cheese over the frittata. Return the pan to the grill and continue cooking for the remaining 2 minutes.
7. When cooking is complete, the cheese should be melted, with the top completely set but not browned. Sprinkle the black pepper over the frittata.

44.Cinnamon Toast with Strawberries

Prep time: 15 minutes | Cook time: 10 minutes | Serves 4

1 (15-ounce / 425-g) can full-fat coconut milk, refrigerated overnight
½ tablespoon powdered sugar
1½ teaspoons vanilla extract, divided
1 cup halved strawberries
1 tablespoon maple syrup, plus more for garnish
1 tablespoon brown sugar, divided
¾ cup lite coconut milk
2 large eggs
½ teaspoon ground cinnamon
2 tablespoons unsalted butter, at room temperature
4 slices challah bread

1. Turn the chilled can of full-fat coconut milk upside down (do not shake the can), open the bottom, and pour out the liquid coconut water. Scoop the remaining solid coconut cream into a medium bowl. Using an electric hand mixer, whip the cream for 3 to 5 minutes, until soft peaks form.
2. Add the powdered sugar and ½ teaspoon of the vanilla to the coconut cream, and whip it again until creamy. Place the bowl in the refrigerator.
3. Place the grill plate on the grill position. Select Grill, set the temperature to 450ºF (232ºC), and set the time to 15 minutes.
4. Combine the strawberries with the maple syrup and toss to coat evenly. Sprinkle evenly with ½ tablespoon of the brown sugar.
5. In a large shallow bowl, whisk together the lite coconut milk, eggs, the remaining 1 teaspoon of vanilla, and cinnamon.
6. Place the strawberries on the grill plate. Gently press the fruit down to maximize grill marks. Grill for 4 minutes without flipping.
7. Meanwhile, butter each slice of bread on both sides. Place one slice in the egg mixture and let it soak for 1 minute. Flip the slice over and soak it for another minute. Repeat with the remaining bread slices. Sprinkle each side of the toast with the remaining ½ tablespoon of brown sugar.
8. After 4 minutes, remove the strawberries from the grill and set aside. Decrease the temperature to 400ºF (204ºC). Place the bread on the grill plate; Grill for 4 to 6 minutes until golden and caramelized. Check often to ensure desired doneness.
9. Place the toast on a plate and top with the strawberries and whipped coconut cream. Drizzle with maple syrup, if desired.

45.Egg and Sausage Stuffed Breakfast Pockets

Prep time: 15 minutes | Cook time: 23 minutes | Serves 4

1 (6-ounce / 170-g) package ground breakfast sausage, crumbled
3 large eggs, lightly beaten
⅓ cup diced red bell pepper
⅓ cup thinly sliced scallions (green part only)
Sea salt, to taste
Freshly ground black pepper, to taste
1 (16-ounce / 454-g) package pizza dough
All-purpose flour, for dusting
1 cup shredded Cheddar cheese
2 tablespoons canola oil

1. Place the baking pan on the roast position. Select Roast, set the temperature to 375ºF (191ºC), and set the time to 15 minutes.
2. Place the sausage directly in the pan. Roast for 10 minutes, checking the sausage every 2 to 3 minutes, breaking apart larger pieces with a wooden spoon.
3. After 10 minutes, pour the eggs, bell pepper, and scallions into the pan. Stir to evenly incorporate with the sausage. Let the eggs roast for the remaining 5 minutes, stirring occasionally. Transfer the sausage and egg mixture to a medium bowl to cool slightly. Season with salt and pepper.
4. Place the crisper tray on the air fry position. Select Air Fry, set the temperature to 350ºF (177ºC), and set the time to 8 minutes.
5. Meanwhile, divide the dough into four equal pieces. Lightly dust a clean work surface with flour. Roll each piece of dough into a 5-inch round of even thickness. Divide the sausage-egg mixture and cheese evenly among each round. Brush the outside edge of the dough with water. Fold the dough over the filling, forming a half circle. Pinch the edges of the dough together to seal in the filling. Brush both sides of each pocket with the oil.
6. Place the breakfast pockets in the crisper tray. Air fry for 6 to 8 minutes, or until golden brown.

46. PB&J

Prep time: 5 minutes | Cook time: 6 minutes | Serves 4

½ cup cornflakes, crushed
¼ cup shredded coconut
8 slices oat nut bread or any whole-grain, oversize bread
6 tablespoons peanut butter
2 medium bananas, cut into ½-inch-thick slices
6 tablespoons pineapple preserves
1 egg, beaten
Cooking spray

1. Place the crisper tray on the air fry position. Select Air Fry, set the temperature to 360ºF (182ºC), and set the time to 6 minutes.
2. In a shallow dish, mix the cornflake crumbs and coconut.
3. For each sandwich, spread one bread slice with 1½ tablespoons of peanut butter. Top with banana slices. Spread another bread slice with 1½ tablespoons of preserves. Combine to make a sandwich.
4. Using a pastry brush, brush top of sandwich lightly with beaten egg. Sprinkle with about 1½ tablespoons of crumb coating, pressing it in to make it stick. Spray with cooking spray.
5. Turn sandwich over and repeat to coat and spray the other side. Place the sandwiches in the crisper tray.
6. Air fry for 6 minutes or until coating is golden brown and crispy.
7. Cut the cooked sandwiches in half and serve warm.

47. Buttermilk Biscuits

Prep time: 5 minutes | Cook time: 5 minutes | Makes 12 biscuits

2 cups all-purpose flour, plus more for dusting the work surface
1 tablespoon baking powder
¼ teaspoon baking soda
2 teaspoons sugar
1 teaspoon salt
6 tablespoons cold unsalted butter, cut into 1-tablespoon slices
¾ cup buttermilk

1. Spray the crisper tray with olive oil.
2. Place the crisper tray on the bake position. Select Bake, set the temperature to 360ºF (182ºC), and set the time to 5 minutes.
3. In a large mixing bowl, combine the flour, baking powder, baking soda, sugar, and salt and mix well.
4. Using a fork, cut in the butter until the mixture resembles coarse meal.
5. Add the buttermilk and mix until smooth.
6. Dust more flour on a clean work surface. Turn the dough out onto the work surface and roll it out until it is about ½ inch thick.
7. Using a 2-inch biscuit cutter, cut out the biscuits. Put the uncooked biscuits in the greased crisper tray in a single layer.
8. Bake for 5 minutes. Transfer the cooked biscuits from the grill to a platter.
9. Cut the remaining biscuits. Bake the remaining biscuits.
10. Serve warm.

48. Chicken Breakfast Sausages

Prep time: 15 minutes | Cook time: 8 to 12 minutes | Makes 8 patties

1 Granny Smith apple, peeled and finely chopped
2 tablespoons apple juice
2 garlic cloves, minced
1 egg white
⅓ cup minced onion
3 tablespoons ground almonds
⅛ teaspoon freshly ground black pepper
1 pound (454 g) ground chicken breast

1. Place the crisper tray on the air fry position. Select Air Fry, set the temperature to 330ºF (166ºC), and set the time to 12 minutes.
2. Combine all the ingredients except the chicken in a medium mixing bowl and stir well.
3. Add the chicken breast to the apple mixture and mix with your hands until well incorporated.
4. Divide the mixture into 8 equal portions and shape into patties. Arrange the patties in the crisper tray. You may need to work in batches depending on the size of your crisper tray.
5. Air fry for 8 to 12 minutes, or until a meat thermometer inserted in the center of the chicken reaches at least 165ºF (74ºC).
6. Remove from the grill to a plate and repeat with the remaining patties.
7. Let the chicken cool for 5 minutes and serve warm.

49. Banana Bread

Prep time: 10 minutes | Cook time: 22 minutes | Makes 3 loaves

3 ripe bananas, mashed
1 cup sugar
1 large egg
4 tablespoons (½ stick) unsalted butter, melted
1½ cups all-purpose flour
1 teaspoon baking soda
1 teaspoon salt

1. Coat the insides of 3 mini loaf pans with cooking spray.
2. In a large mixing bowl, mix the bananas and sugar.
3. In a separate large mixing bowl, combine the egg, butter, flour, baking soda, and salt and mix well.
4. Add the banana mixture to the egg and flour mixture. Mix well.
5. Divide the batter evenly among the prepared pans.
6. Place the loaf pans on the bake position. Select Bake, set the temperature to 310ºF (154ºC), and set the time to 22 minutes.
7. Bake for 22 minutes. Insert a toothpick into the center of each loaf; if it comes out clean, they are done.
8. When the loaves are cooked through, remove the pans from the grill. Turn out the loaves onto a wire rack to cool.
9. Serve warm.

50. Mixed Berry Dutch Baby Pancake

Prep time: 10 minutes | Cook time: 12 to 16 minutes | Serves 4

1 tablespoon unsalted butter, at room temperature
1 egg
2 egg whites
½ cup 2% milk
½ cup whole-wheat pastry flour
1 teaspoon pure vanilla extract
1 cup sliced fresh strawberries
½ cup fresh raspberries
½ cup fresh blueberries

1. Place the baking pan on the bake position. Select Bake, set the temperature to 330ºF (166ºC), and set the time to 16 minutes.
2. Grease the baking pan with the butter.
3. Using a hand mixer, beat together the egg, egg whites, milk, pastry flour, and vanilla in a medium mixing bowl until well incorporated.
4. Pour the batter into the pan. Bake for 12 to 16 minutes, or until the pancake puffs up in the center and the edges are golden brown.
5. Allow the pancake to cool for 5 minutes and serve topped with the berries.

51. Banana Churros with Oatmeal

Prep time: 15 minutes | Cook time: 15 minutes | Serves 2

For the Churros:

1 large yellow banana, peeled, cut in half lengthwise, then cut in half widthwise
2 tablespoons whole-wheat pastry flour
⅛ teaspoon sea salt
2 teaspoons oil (sunflower or melted coconut)
1 teaspoon water
Cooking spray
1 tablespoon coconut sugar
½ teaspoon cinnamon

For the Oatmeal:

¾ cup rolled oats
1½ cups water

To make the churros

1. Put the 4 banana pieces in a medium-size bowl and add the flour and salt. Stir gently. Add the oil and water. Stir gently until evenly mixed. You may need to press some coating onto the banana pieces.
2. Spray the crisper tray with the oil spray. Put the banana pieces in the crisper tray and air fry for 5 minutes. Remove, gently turn over, and air fry for another 5 minutes or until browned.
3. In a medium bowl, add the coconut sugar and cinnamon and stir to combine. When the banana pieces are nicely browned, spray with the oil and place in the cinnamon-sugar bowl. Toss gently with a spatula to coat the banana pieces with the mixture.

To make the oatmeal

1. While the bananas are cooking, make the oatmeal. In a medium pan, bring the oats and water to a boil, then reduce to low heat. Simmer, stirring often, until all the water is absorbed, about 5 minutes. Put the oatmeal into two bowls.
2. Top the oatmeal with the coated banana pieces and serve immediately.

52. Asparagus and Cheese Strata

Prep time: 10 minutes | Cook time: 14 to 19 minutes | Serves 4

6 asparagus spears, cut into 2-inch pieces
1 tablespoon water
2 slices whole-wheat bread, cut into ½-inch cubes
4 eggs
3 tablespoons whole milk
2 tablespoons chopped flat-leaf parsley
½ cup grated Havarti or Swiss cheese
Pinch salt
Freshly ground black pepper, to taste
Cooking spray

1. Place the baking pan on the bake position. Select Bake, set the temperature to 330ºF (166ºC), and set the time to 19 minutes.
2. Add the asparagus spears and 1 tablespoon of water in the baking pan. Bake for 3 to 5 minutes until crisp-tender. Remove the asparagus from the pan and drain on paper towels. Spritz the pan with cooking spray.
3. Place the bread and asparagus in the pan.
4. Whisk together the eggs and milk in a medium mixing bowl until creamy. Fold in the parsley, cheese, salt, and pepper and stir to combine. Pour this mixture into the baking pan.
5. Bake for 11 to 14 minutes, or until the eggs are set and the top is lightly browned.
6. Let cool for 5 minutes before slicing and serving.

53. Potato Bread Rolls

Prep time: 15 minutes | Cook time: 20 minutes | Serves 5

5 large potatoes, boiled and mashed
Salt and ground black pepper, to taste
½ teaspoon mustard seeds
1 tablespoon olive oil
2 small onions, chopped
2 sprigs curry leaves
½ teaspoon turmeric powder
2 green chilis, seeded and chopped
1 bunch coriander, chopped
8 slices bread, brown sides discarded

1. Place the crisper tray on the air fry position. Select Air Fry, set the temperature to 400ºF (204ºC), and set the time to 15 minutes.
2. Put the mashed potatoes in a bowl and sprinkle on salt and pepper. Set to one side.
3. Fry the mustard seeds in olive oil over a medium-low heat in a skillet, stirring continuously, until they sputter.
4. Add the onions and cook until they turn translucent. Add the curry leaves and turmeric powder and stir. Cook for a further 2 minutes until fragrant.
5. Remove the skillet from the heat and combine with the potatoes. Mix in the green chilies and coriander.
6. Wet the bread slightly and drain of any excess liquid.
7. Spoon a small amount of the panato mixture into the center of the bread and enclose the bread around the filling, sealing it entirely. Continue until the rest of the bread and filling is used up. Brush each bread roll with some oil and transfer to the crisper tray.
8. Air fry for 15 minutes, gently shaking the crisper tray at the halfway point to ensure each roll is cooked evenly.
9. Serve immediately.

54. Coconut Brown Rice Porridge with Dates

Prep time: 5 minutes | Cook time: 23 minutes | Serves 1 or 2

½ cup cooked brown rice
1 cup canned coconut milk
¼ cup unsweetened shredded coconut
¼ cup packed dark brown sugar
4 large Medjool dates, pitted and roughly chopped
½ teaspoon kosher salt
¼ teaspoon ground cardamom
Heavy cream, for serving (optional)

1. Place the baking pan on the bake position. Select Bake, set the temperature to 375ºF (191ºC), and set the time to 23 minutes.
2. Place all the ingredients except the heavy cream in the baking pan and stir until blended.
3. Bake for 23 minutes until the porridge is thick and creamy. Stir the porridge halfway through the cooking time.
4. Remove from the grill and ladle the porridge into bowls.
5. Serve hot with a drizzle of the cream, if desired.

55. Soufflé

Prep time: 10 minutes | Cook time: 22 minutes | Serves 4

$^1/_3$ cup butter, melted
¼ cup flour
1 cup milk
1 ounce (28 g) sugar
4 egg yolks
1 teaspoon vanilla
extract
6 egg whites
1 teaspoon cream of tartar
Cooking spray

1. In a bowl, mix the butter and flour until a smooth consistency is achieved.
2. Pour the milk into a saucepan over medium-low heat. Add the sugar and allow to dissolve before raising the heat to boil the milk.
3. Pour in the flour and butter mixture and stir rigorously for 7 minutes to eliminate any lumps. Make sure the mixture thickens. Take off the heat and allow to cool for 15 minutes.
4. Place the baking pan on the bake position. Select Bake, set the temperature to 320ºF (160ºC), and set the time to 15 minutes.
5. Spritz 6 soufflé dishes with cooking spray.
6. Put the egg yolks and vanilla extract in a separate bowl and beat them together with a fork. Pour in the milk and combine well to incorporate everything.
7. In a smaller bowl mix the egg whites and cream of tartar with a fork. Fold into the egg yolks-milk mixture before adding in the flour mixture. Transfer equal amounts to the 6 soufflé dishes.
8. Put the dishes in the pan. Bake for 15 minutes.
9. Serve warm.

56. Olives, Kale, and Pecorino Baked Eggs

Prep time: 5 minutes | Cook time: 10 to 12 minutes | Serves 2

1 cup roughly chopped kale leaves, stems and center ribs removed
¼ cup grated pecorino cheese
¼ cup olive oil
1 garlic clove, peeled
3 tablespoons whole almonds
Kosher salt and freshly ground black pepper, to taste
4 large eggs
2 tablespoons heavy cream
3 tablespoons chopped pitted mixed olives

1. Place the kale, pecorino, olive oil, garlic, almonds, salt, and pepper in a small blender and blitz until well incorporated.
2. Place the baking pan on the bake position. Select Bake, set the temperature to 300ºF (149ºC), and set the time to 12 minutes.
3. One at a time, crack the eggs in the baking pan. Drizzle the kale pesto on top of the egg whites. Top the yolks with the cream and swirl together the yolks and the pesto.
4. Bake for 10 to 12 minutes, or until the top begins to brown and the eggs are set.
5. Allow the eggs to cool for 5 minutes. Scatter the olives on top and serve warm.

57. Apple and Walnut Muffins

Prep time: 15 minutes | Cook time: 10 minutes | Makes 8 muffins

1 cup flour
$^1/_3$ cup sugar
1 teaspoon baking powder
¼ teaspoon baking soda
¼ teaspoon salt
1 teaspoon cinnamon
¼ teaspoon ginger
¼ teaspoon nutmeg
1 egg
2 tablespoons
pancake syrup, plus 2 teaspoons
2 tablespoons melted butter, plus 2 teaspoons
¾ cup unsweetened applesauce
½ teaspoon vanilla extract
¼ cup chopped walnuts
¼ cup diced apple

1. Place the baking pan on the bake position. Select Bake, set the temperature to 330ºF (166ºC), and set the time to 10 minutes.
2. In a large bowl, stir together the flour, sugar, baking powder, baking soda, salt, cinnamon, ginger, and nutmeg.
3. In a small bowl, beat egg until frothy. Add syrup, butter, applesauce, and vanilla and mix well.
4. Pour egg mixture into dry ingredients and stir just until moistened.
5. Gently stir in nuts and diced apple.
6. Divide batter among 8 parchment paper-lined muffin cups.
7. Put 4 muffin cups in the baking pan. Bake for 10 minutes.
8. Repeat with remaining 4 muffins or until toothpick inserted in center comes out clean.
9. Serve warm.

58. Cheesy Hash Brown Casserole

Prep time: 15 minutes | Cook time: 30 minutes | Serves 4

3½ cups frozen hash browns, thawed
1 teaspoon salt
1 teaspoon freshly ground black pepper
3 tablespoons butter, melted
1 (10.5-ounce / 298-g) can cream of chicken soup
½ cup sour cream
1 cup minced onion
½ cup shredded sharp Cheddar cheese
Cooking spray

1. Put the hash browns in a large bowl and season with salt and black pepper. Add the melted butter, cream of chicken soup, and sour cream and stir until well incorporated. Mix in the minced onion and cheese and stir well.
2. Place the baking pan on the bake position. Select Bake, set the temperature to 325ºF (163ºC), and set the time to 30 minutes.
3. Spray the baking pan with cooking spray.
4. Spread the hash brown mixture evenly into the baking pan.
5. Bake for 30 minutes until browned.
6. Cool for 5 minutes before serving.

59. Breakfast Tater Tot Casserole

Prep time: 5 minutes | Cook time: 17 to 19 minutes | Serves 4

4 eggs
1 cup milk
Salt and pepper, to taste
12 ounces (340 g) ground chicken sausage
1 pound (454 g) frozen tater tots, thawed
¾ cup grated Cheddar cheese
Cooking spray

1. Whisk together the eggs and milk in a medium bowl. Season with salt and pepper to taste and stir until mixed. Set aside.
2. Place a skillet over medium-high heat and spritz with cooking spray. Place the ground sausage in the skillet and break it into smaller pieces with a spatula or spoon. Cook for 3 to 4 minutes until the sausage starts to brown, stirring occasionally. Remove from heat and set aside.
3. Place the baking pan on the bake position. Select Bake, set the temperature to 400ºF (204ºC), and set the time to 15 minutes.
4. Coat the baking pan with cooking spray.
5. Arrange the tater tots in the baking pan. Bake for 15 minutes. Stir in the egg mixture and cooked sausage. Bake for another 6 minutes.
6. Scatter the cheese on top of the tater tots. Continue to bake for 2 to 3 minutes more until the cheese is bubbly and melted.
7. Let the mixture cool for 5 minutes and serve warm.

60. Grit and Ham Fritters

Prep time: 15 minutes | Cook time: 20 minutes | Serves 6 to 8

4 cups water
1 cup quick-cooking grits
¼ teaspoon salt
2 tablespoons butter
2 cups grated Cheddar cheese, divided
1 cup finely diced ham
1 tablespoon chopped chives
Salt and freshly ground black pepper, to taste
1 egg, beaten
2 cups panko bread crumbs
Cooking spray

1. Bring the water to a boil in a saucepan. Whisk in the grits and ¼ teaspoon of salt, and cook for 7 minutes until the grits are soft. Remove the pan from the heat and stir in the butter and 1 cup of the grated Cheddar cheese. Transfer the grits to a bowl and let them cool for 10 to 15 minutes.
2. Stir the ham, chives and the rest of the cheese into the grits and season with salt and pepper to taste. Add the beaten egg and refrigerate the mixture for 30 minutes.
3. Put the panko bread crumbs in a shallow dish. Measure out ¼-cup portions of the grits mixture and shape them into patties. Coat all sides of the patties with the panko bread crumbs, patting them with the hands so the crumbs adhere to the patties. You should have about 16 patties. Spritz both sides of the patties with cooking spray.
4. Place the crisper tray on the air fry position. Select Air Fry, set the temperature to 400ºF (204ºC), and set the time to 12 minutes.
5. Place the fritters in the crisper tray. Air fry for 8 minutes. Using a flat spatula, flip the fritters over and air fry for another 4 minutes.
6. Serve hot.

61.Avocado Quesadillas

Prep time: 10 minutes | Cook time: 11 minutes | Serves 4

4 eggs
2 tablespoons skim milk
Salt and ground black pepper, to taste
Cooking spray
4 flour tortillas
4 tablespoons salsa
2 ounces (57 g) Cheddar cheese, grated
½ small avocado, peeled and thinly sliced

1. Place the baking pan on the bake position. Select Bake, set the temperature to 270ºF (132ºC), and set the time to 8 minutes.
2. Beat together the eggs, milk, salt, and pepper.
3. Spray the baking pan lightly with cooking spray and add egg mixture.
4. Bake for 8 minutes, stirring every 1 to 2 minutes, until eggs are scrambled to the liking. Remove and set aside.
5. Spray one side of each tortilla with cooking spray. Flip over.
6. Divide eggs, salsa, cheese, and avocado among the tortillas, covering only half of each tortilla.
7. Fold each tortilla in half and press down lightly. Increase the temperature of the grill to 390ºF (199ºC).
8. Put 2 tortillas in crisper tray and air fry for 3 minutes or until cheese melts and outside feels slightly crispy. Repeat with remaining two tortillas.
9. Cut each cooked tortilla into halves. Serve warm.

62.Bacon and Egg Bread Cups

Prep time: 10 minutes | Cook time: 8 to 12 minutes | Serves 4

4 (3-by-4-inch) crusty rolls
4 thin slices Gouda or Swiss cheese mini wedges
5 eggs
2 tablespoons heavy cream
3 strips precooked bacon, chopped
½ teaspoon dried thyme
Pinch salt
Freshly ground black pepper, to taste

1. Place the baking pan on the bake position. Select Bake, set the temperature to 330ºF (166ºC), and set the time to 12 minutes.
2. On a clean work surface, cut the tops off the rolls. Using your fingers, remove the insides of the rolls to make bread cups, leaving a ½-inch shell. Place a slice of cheese onto each roll bottom.
3. Whisk together the eggs and heavy cream in a medium bowl until well combined. Fold in the bacon, thyme, salt, and pepper and stir well.
4. Scrape the egg mixture into the prepared bread cups.
5. Place the bread cups directly in the pan. Bake for 8 to 12 minutes, or until the eggs are cooked to your preference.
6. Serve warm.

63.Spinach and Egg Florentine

Prep time: 10 minutes | Cook time: 12 minutes | Serves 4

3 cups frozen spinach, thawed and drained
¼ teaspoon kosher salt or ⅛ teaspoon fine salt
4 ounces (113 g) ricotta cheese
2 tablespoons heavy (whipping) cream
2 garlic cloves, minced
⅛ teaspoon freshly ground white or black pepper
2 teaspoons unsalted butter, melted
3 tablespoons grated Parmesan or similar cheese
½ cup panko bread crumbs
4 large eggs

1. In a medium bowl, stir together the spinach, salt, ricotta, cream, garlic, and pepper.
2. In a small bowl, stir together the butter, cheese, and panko. Set aside.
3. Scoop the spinach mixture into four even circles in the baking pan.
4. Place the pan on the roast position. Select Roast, set temperature to 375ºF (191ºC), and set time to 15 minutes.
5. After 8 minutes, remove the pan. The spinach should be bubbling. With the back of a large spoon, make indentations in the spinach for the eggs. Crack the eggs into the indentations and sprinkle the panko mixture over the surface of the eggs.
6. Return the pan to the grill and continue cooking. After 5 minutes, check the eggs. If the eggs are done to your liking, remove the pan. If not, continue cooking.
7. When cooking is complete, remove the pan from the grill. Serve the eggs with toasted English muffins, if desired.

64. Western Omelet

Prep time: 5 minutes | Cook time: 18 to 21 minutes | Serves 2

¼ cup chopped bell pepper, green or red
¼ cup chopped onion
¼ cup diced ham
1 teaspoon butter
4 large eggs
2 tablespoons milk
⅛ teaspoon salt
¾ cup shredded sharp Cheddar cheese

1. Place the baking pan on the air fry position. Select Air Fry, set the temperature to 390ºF (199ºC), and set the time to 6 minutes.
2. Put the bell pepper, onion, ham, and butter in the baking pan and mix well.
3. Air fry for 1 minute. Stir and continue to cook for an additional 4 to 5 minutes until the veggies are softened.
4. Meanwhile, whisk together the eggs, milk, and salt in a bowl.
5. Pour the egg mixture over the veggie mixture.
6. Reduce the grill temperature to 360ºF (182ºC) and bake for 13 to 15 minutes more, or until the top is lightly golden browned and the eggs are set.
7. Scatter the omelet with the shredded cheese. Bake for another 1 minute until the cheese has melted.
8. Let the omelet cool for 5 minutes before serving.

65. Spinach, Leek and Cheese Frittata

Prep time: 10 minutes | Cook time: 20 to 23 minutes | Serves 2

4 large eggs
4 ounces (113 g) baby bella mushrooms, chopped
1 cup (1 ounce / 28-g) baby spinach, chopped
½ cup (2 ounces / 57-g) shredded Cheddar cheese
¹⁄₃ cup (from 1 large) chopped leek, white part only
¼ cup halved grape tomatoes
1 tablespoon 2% milk
¼ teaspoon dried oregano
¼ teaspoon garlic powder
½ teaspoon kosher salt
Freshly ground black pepper, to taste
Cooking spray

1. Place the baking pan on the bake position. Select Bake, set the temperature to 300ºF (149ºC), and set the time to 23 minutes.
2. Lightly spritz the baking pan with cooking spray.
3. Whisk the eggs in a large bowl until frothy. Add the mushrooms, baby spinach, cheese, leek, tomatoes, milk, oregano, garlic powder, salt, and pepper and stir until well blended. Pour the mixture into the prepared baking pan.
4. Bake for 20 to 23 minutes, or until the center is puffed up and the top is golden brown.
5. Let the frittata cool for 5 minutes before slicing to serve.

66. Nut and Seed Muffins

Prep time: 15 minutes | Cook time: 10 minutes | Makes 8 muffins

½ cup whole-wheat flour, plus 2 tablespoons
¼ cup oat bran
2 tablespoons flaxseed meal
¼ cup brown sugar
½ teaspoon baking soda
½ teaspoon baking powder
¼ teaspoon salt
½ teaspoon cinnamon
½ cup buttermilk
2 tablespoons melted butter
1 egg
½ teaspoon pure vanilla extract
½ cup grated carrots
¼ cup chopped pecans
¼ cup chopped walnuts
1 tablespoon pumpkin seeds
1 tablespoon sunflower seeds
Cooking spray

Special Equipment:

16 foil muffin cups, paper liners removed

1. Place the baking pan on the bake position. Select Bake, set the temperature to 330ºF (166ºC), and set the time to 10 minutes.
2. In a large bowl, stir together the flour, bran, flaxseed meal, sugar, baking soda, baking powder, salt, and cinnamon.
3. In a medium bowl, beat together the buttermilk, butter, egg, and vanilla. Pour into flour mixture and stir just until dry ingredients moisten. Do not beat.
4. Gently stir in carrots, nuts, and seeds.
5. Double up the foil cups so you have 8 total and spritz with cooking spray.
6. Put 4 foil cups in the pan and divide half the batter among them.
7. Bake for 10 minutes, or until a toothpick inserted in center comes out clean.
8. Repeat step 7 to bake remaining 4 muffins.
9. Serve warm.

67.Maple Walnut Pancake

Prep time: 10 minutes | Cook time: 20 minutes | Serves 4

3 tablespoons melted butter, divided
1 cup flour
2 tablespoons sugar
1½ teaspoons baking powder
¼ teaspoon salt
1 egg, beaten
¾ cup milk
1 teaspoon pure vanilla extract
½ cup roughly chopped walnuts
Maple syrup or fresh sliced fruit, for serving

1. Place the baking pan on the bake position. Select Bake, set the temperature to 330ºF (166ºC), and set the time to 20 minutes.
2. Grease the baking pan with 1 tablespoon of melted butter.
3. Mix together the flour, sugar, baking powder, and salt in a medium bowl. Add the beaten egg, milk, the remaining 2 tablespoons of melted butter, and vanilla and stir until the batter is sticky but slightly lumpy.
4. Slowly pour the batter into the greased baking pan and scatter with the walnuts.
5. Bake for 20 minutes until golden brown and cooked through.
6. Let the pancake rest for 5 minutes and serve topped with the maple syrup or fresh fruit, if desired.

68.Banana and Oat Bread Pudding

Prep time: 10 minutes | Cook time: 16 to 20 minutes | Serves 4

2 medium ripe bananas, mashed
½ cup low-fat milk
2 tablespoons maple syrup
2 tablespoons peanut butter
1 teaspoon vanilla
extract
1 teaspoon ground cinnamon
2 slices whole-grain bread, cut into bite-sized cubes
¼ cup quick oats
Cooking spray

1. Spritz the baking pan lightly with cooking spray.
2. Place the baking pan on the air fry position. Select Air Fry, set the temperature to 350ºF (177ºC), and set the time to 20 minutes.
3. Mix the bananas, milk, maple syrup, peanut butter, vanilla, and cinnamon in a large mixing bowl and stir until well incorporated.

4. Add the bread cubes to the banana mixture and stir until thoroughly coated. Fold in the oats and stir to combine.
5. Transfer the mixture to the baking pan. Wrap the baking pan in aluminum foil.
6. Air fry for 10 to 12 minutes until heated through.
7. Remove the foil and cook for an additional 6 to 8 minutes, or until the pudding has set.
8. Let the pudding cool for 5 minutes before serving.

69.Egg and Avocado Burrito

Prep time: 10 minutes | Cook time: 3 to 5 minutes | Serves 4

4 low-sodium whole-wheat flour tortillas
Filling:
1 hard-boiled egg, chopped
2 hard-boiled egg whites, chopped
1 ripe avocado, peeled, pitted, and chopped
1 red bell pepper, chopped
1 (1.2-ounce / 34-g) slice low-sodium, low-fat American cheese, torn into pieces
3 tablespoons low-sodium salsa, plus additional for serving (optional)

Special Equipment:
4 toothpicks (optional), soaked in water for at least 30 minutes

1. Place the crisper tray on the air fry position. Select Air Fry, set the temperature to 390ºF (199ºC), and set the time to 5 minutes.
2. Make the filling: Combine the egg, egg whites, avocado, red bell pepper, cheese, and salsa in a medium bowl and stir until blended.
3. Assemble the burritos: Arrange the tortillas on a clean work surface and place ¼ of the prepared filling in the middle of each tortilla, leaving about 1½-inch on each end unfilled. Fold in the opposite sides of each tortilla and roll up. Secure with toothpicks through the center, if needed.
4. Transfer the burritos to the crisper tray. Air fry for 3 to 5 minutes, or until the burritos are crisp and golden brown.
5. Allow to cool for 5 minutes and serve with salsa, if desired.

70.Fried Potatoes with Peppers and Onions

Prep time: 10 minutes | Cook time: 35 minutes | Serves 4

1 pound (454 g) red potatoes, cut into ½-inch dices
1 large red bell pepper, cut into ½-inch dices
1 large green bell pepper, cut into ½-inch dices
1 medium onion, cut into ½-inch dices
1½ tablespoons extra-virgin olive oil
1¼ teaspoons kosher salt
¾ teaspoon sweet paprika
¾ teaspoon garlic powder
Freshly ground black pepper, to taste

1. Place the crisper tray on the air fry position. Select Air Fry, set the temperature to 350ºF (177ºC), and set the time to 35 minutes.
2. Mix together the potatoes, bell peppers, onion, oil, salt, paprika, garlic powder, and black pepper in a large mixing and toss to coat.
3. Transfer the panato mixture to the crisper tray. Air fry for 35 minutes, or until the potatoes are nicely browned. Shake the crisper tray three times during cooking.
4. Remove from the crisper tray to a plate and serve warm.

71.Veggie Frittata

Prep time: 10 minutes | Cook time: 8 to 12 minutes | Serves 4

½ cup chopped red bell pepper
⅓ cup grated carrot
⅓ cup minced onion
1 teaspoon olive oil
1 egg
6 egg whites
¹/₃ cup 2% milk
1 tablespoon shredded Parmesan cheese

1. Place the baking pan on the bake position. Select Bake, set the temperature to 350ºF (177ºC), and set the time to 12 minutes.
2. Mix together the red bell pepper, carrot, onion, and olive oil in the baking pan and stir to combine.
3. Bake for 4 to 6 minutes, or until the veggies are soft. Stir once during cooking.
4. Meantime, whisk together the egg, egg whites, and milk in a medium bowl until creamy.
5. When the veggies are done, pour the egg mixture over the top. Scatter with the Parmesan cheese.
6. Bake for an additional 4 to 6 minutes, or until the eggs are set and the top is golden around the edges.
7. Allow the frittata to cool for 5 minutes before slicing and serving.

72.Tomato-Corn Frittata with Avocado Dressing

Prep time: 10 minutes | Cook time: 20 minutes | Serves 2 or 3

½ cup cherry tomatoes, halved
Kosher salt and freshly ground black pepper, to taste
6 large eggs, lightly beaten
½ cup corn kernels, thawed if frozen
¼ cup milk
1 tablespoon finely chopped fresh dill
½ cup shredded Monterey Jack cheese

Avocado Dressing:

1 ripe avocado, pitted and peeled
2 tablespoons fresh lime juice
¼ cup olive oil
1 scallion, finely chopped
8 fresh basil leaves, finely chopped

1. Put the tomato halves in a colander and lightly season with salt. Set aside for 10 minutes to drain well. Pour the tomatoes into a large bowl and fold in the eggs, corn, milk, and dill. Sprinkle with salt and pepper and stir until mixed.
2. Place the baking pan on the bake position. Select Bake, set the temperature to 300ºF (149ºC), and set the time to 20 minutes.
3. Pour the egg mixture into the baking pan. Bake for 15 minutes.
4. Scatter the cheese on top. Increase the grill temperature to 315ºF (157ºC) and continue to cook for another 5 minutes, or until the frittata is puffy and set.
5. Meanwhile, make the avocado dressing: Mash the avocado with the lime juice in a medium bowl until smooth. Mix in the olive oil, scallion, and basil and stir until well incorporated.
6. Let the frittata cool for 5 minutes and serve alongside the avocado dressing.

73.Crouton Casserole

Prep time: 10 minutes | Cook time: 12 minutes | Serves 6

3 large eggs
1 cup whole milk
¼ teaspoon kosher salt or ⅛ teaspoon fine salt
1 tablespoon pure maple syrup
1 teaspoon vanilla
¼ teaspoon cinnamon
3 cups (1-inch) stale bread cubes (3 to 4 slices)
1 tablespoon unsalted butter, at room temperature

1. In a medium bowl, whisk the eggs until the yolks and whites are completely mixed. Add the milk, salt, maple syrup, vanilla, and cinnamon and whisk to combine. Add the bread cubes and gently stir to coat with the egg mixture. Let sit for 2 to 3 minutes so the bread absorbs some of the custard, then gently stir again.
2. Grease the bottom of the baking pan with the butter. Pour the bread mixture into the pan, spreading it out evenly.
3. Place the pan on the roast position. Select Roast, set temperature to 350ºF (177ºC), and set time to 12 minutes.
4. After about 10 minutes, remove the pan and check the casserole. The top should be browned and the middle of the casserole just set. If more time is needed, return the pan to the grill and continue cooking.
5. When cooking is complete, serve warm with additional butter and maple syrup, if desired.

74.Cashew Granola

Prep time: 5 minutes | Cook time: 12 minutes | Serves 6

3 cups old-fashioned rolled oats
2 cups raw cashews or mixed raw nuts (such as pecans, walnuts, almonds)
1 cup unsweetened coconut chips
½ cup honey
¼ cup vegetable oil, extra-virgin olive oil, or walnut oil
⅓ cup packed light brown sugar
¼ teaspoon kosher salt or ⅛ teaspoon fine salt
1 cup dried cranberries (optional)

1. Place the oats, nuts, coconut, honey, oil, brown sugar, and salt in a large bowl and mix until well combined. Spread the mixture in an even layer in the baking pan.
2. Place the pan on the bake position. Select Bake, set temperature to 325ºF (163ºC), and set time to 12 minutes.
3. After 5 to 6 minutes, remove the pan and stir the granola, return the pan to the grill, and continue cooking.
4. When cooking is complete, remove the pan. Let the granola cool to room temperature, then stir in the cranberries, if using. If not serving right away, store in an airtight container at room temperature.

75.Corned Beef Hash

Prep time: 10 minutes | Cook time: 12 minutes | Serves 4

2 medium Yukon Gold potatoes, peeled, cut into ¼-inch cubes (about 3 cups)
1 medium onion, chopped (about 1 cup)
⅓ cup diced red bell pepper
3 tablespoons vegetable oil
½ teaspoon dried thyme
½ teaspoon kosher salt or ¼ teaspoon fine salt, divided
½ teaspoon freshly ground black pepper, divided
¾ pound (340 g) corned beef, cut into ¼-inch pieces
4 large eggs

1. In a large bowl, mix the potatoes, onion, red pepper, oil, thyme, ¼ teaspoon of salt, and ¼ teaspoon of pepper. Spread the vegetables in the baking pan in an even layer.
2. Place the pan on the roast position. Select Roast, set temperature to 375ºF (191ºC), and set time to 25 minutes.
3. After 15 minutes, remove the pan from the grill and add the corned beef. Stir the mixture to incorporate the corned beef. Return the pan to the grill and continue cooking for 5 minutes.
4. After 5 minutes (20 minutes total), remove the pan from the grill. Using a large spoon, create 4 circles in the hash to hold the eggs. Gently crack an egg into each circle; season eggs with remaining ¼ teaspoon of salt and ¼ teaspoon of pepper. Return the baking pan to the grill. Continue cooking for 3 to 8 minutes, depending on how you like your eggs (3 to 4 minutes for runny yolks; 8 minutes for firm yolks).
5. When cooking is complete, remove the pan from the grill. Serve immediately.

76.Cinnamon Rolls

Prep time: 10 minutes | Cook time: 25 minutes | Makes 18 rolls

2 teaspoons cinnamon
1/3 cup light brown sugar
1 (9-by-9-inch) frozen puff pastry sheet, thawed

All-purpose flour, for dusting
6 teaspoons (2 tablespoons) unsalted butter, melted, divided

1. In a small bowl, mix together the cinnamon and brown sugar.
2. Unfold the puff pastry on a lightly floured surface. Using a rolling pin, press the folds together and roll the dough out in one direction so that it measures about 9 by 11 inches. Cut it in half to form two squat rectangles of about 5½ by 9 inches.
3. Brush 2 teaspoons of butter over each pastry half, and then sprinkle with 2 generous tablespoons of the cinnamon sugar. Pat it down lightly with the palm of your hand to help it adhere to the butter.
4. Starting with the 9-inch side of one rectangle and using your hands, carefully roll the dough into a cylinder. Repeat with the other rectangle. To make slicing easier, refrigerate the rolls for 10 to 20 minutes.
5. Using a sharp knife, slice each roll into nine 1-inch pieces. Transfer the rolls to the center of the baking pan. They should be very close to each other, but not quite touching. For neater rolls, turn the outside rolls so that the seam is to the inside. Drizzle the remaining 2 teaspoons of butter over the rolls and sprinkle with the remaining cinnamon sugar.
6. Place the pan on the bake position. Select Bake, set temperature to 350ºF (177ºC), and set time to 25 minutes.
7. When cooking is complete, remove the pan and check the rolls. They should be puffed up and golden brown. If the rolls in the center are not quite done, return the pan to the grill for another 3 to 5 minutes. If the outside rolls are dark golden brown before the inside rolls are done, you can remove those with a small spatula before returning the pan to the grill.
8. Let the rolls cool for a couple of minutes, then transfer them to a rack to cool completely.

77.Bacon and Broccoli Bread Pudding

Prep time: 15 minutes | Cook time: 48 minutes | Serves 2 to 4

½ pound (227 g) thick cut bacon, cut into ¼-inch pieces
3 cups brioche bread, cut into ½-inch cubes
2 tablespoons butter, melted
3 eggs
1 cup milk

½ teaspoon salt
Freshly ground black pepper, to taste
1 cup frozen broccoli florets, thawed and chopped
1½ cups grated Swiss cheese

1. Place the crisper tray on the air fry position. Select Air Fry, set the temperature to 400ºF (204ºC), and set the time to 10 minutes.
2. Put the bacon in the crisper tray. Air fry for 8 minutes until crispy, shaking the crisper tray a few times to help it cook evenly. Remove the bacon and set it aside on a paper towel.
3. Air fry the brioche bread cubes for 2 minutes to dry and toast lightly.
4. Butter a cake pan. Combine all the remaining ingredients in a large bowl and toss well. Transfer the mixture to the buttered cake pan, cover with aluminum foil and refrigerate the bread pudding overnight, or for at least 8 hours.
5. Remove the cake pan from the refrigerator an hour before you plan to bake and let it sit on the countertop to come to room temperature.
6. Place the cake pan on the bake position. Select Bake, set the temperature to 330ºF (166ºC), and set the time to 40 minutes.
7. Place the covered cake pan directly in the pan. Fold the ends of the aluminum foil over the top of the pan. Bake for 20 minutes. Remove the foil and bake for an additional 20 minutes. If the top browns a little too much before the custard has set, simply return the foil to the pan. The bread pudding has cooked through when a skewer inserted into the center comes out clean.
8. Serve warm.

78.Posh Orange Rolls

Prep time: 15 minutes | Cook time: 8 minutes | Makes 8 rolls

3 ounces (85 g) low-fat cream cheese
1 tablespoon low-fat sour cream or plain yogurt
2 teaspoons sugar
¼ teaspoon pure vanilla extract
¼ teaspoon orange extract
1 can (8 count) organic crescent roll dough
¼ cup chopped walnuts
¼ cup dried cranberries
¼ cup shredded, sweetened coconut
Butter-flavored cooking spray

Orange Glaze:

½ cup powdered sugar
1 tablespoon orange juice
¼ teaspoon orange extract
Dash of salt

1. Cut a circular piece of parchment paper slightly smaller than the bottom of the crisper tray. Set aside.
2. In a small bowl, combine the cream cheese, sour cream or yogurt, sugar, and vanilla and orange extracts. Stir until smooth.
3. Place the crisper tray on the air fry position. Select Air Fry, set the temperature to 300ºF (149ºC), and set the time to 8 minutes.
4. Separate crescent roll dough into 8 triangles and divide cream cheese mixture among them. Starting at wide end, spread cheese mixture to within 1 inch of point.
5. Sprinkle nuts and cranberries evenly over cheese mixture.
6. Starting at wide end, roll up triangles, then sprinkle with coconut, pressing in lightly to make it stick. Spray tops of rolls with butter-flavored cooking spray.
7. Put parchment paper in crisper tray, and place 4 rolls on top, spaced evenly.
8. Air fry for 8 minutes, until rolls are golden brown and cooked through.
9. Repeat steps 7 and 8 to air fry remaining 4 rolls. You should be able to use the same piece of parchment paper twice.
10. In a small bowl, stir together ingredients for glaze and drizzle over warm rolls. Serve warm.

79.Chocolate Banana Bread with White Chocolate

Prep time: 10 minutes | Cook time: 30 minutes | Serves 4

¼ cup cocoa powder
6 tablespoons plus 2 teaspoons all-purpose flour, divided
½ teaspoon kosher salt
¼ teaspoon baking soda
1½ ripe bananas
1 large egg, whisked
¼ cup vegetable oil
½ cup sugar
3 tablespoons buttermilk or plain yogurt (not Greek)
½ teaspoon vanilla extract
6 tablespoons chopped white chocolate
6 tablespoons chopped walnuts

1. Place the baking pan on the bake position. Select Bake, set the temperature to 310ºF (154ºC), and set the time to 30 minutes.
2. Mix together the cocoa powder, 6 tablespoons of the flour, salt, and baking soda in a medium bowl.
3. Mash the bananas with a fork in another medium bowl until smooth. Fold in the egg, oil, sugar, buttermilk, and vanilla, and whisk until thoroughly combined. Add the wet mixture to the dry mixture and stir until well incorporated.
4. Combine the white chocolate, walnuts, and the remaining 2 tablespoons of flour in a third bowl and toss to coat. Add this mixture to the batter and stir until well incorporated. Pour the batter into the baking pan and smooth the top with a spatula.
5. Bake for 30 minutes. Check the bread for doneness: If a toothpick inserted into the center of the bread comes out clean, it's done.
6. Remove from the grill and allow to cool on a wire rack for 10 minutes before serving.

80. Blueberry Cake

Prep time: 8 minutes | Cook time: 10 minutes | Serves 8

1½ cups Bisquick or similar baking mix
¼ cup granulated sugar (use $^1/_3$ cup for a sweeter cake)
¾ cup whole milk
2 large eggs
1 teaspoon vanilla extract
½ teaspoon lemon zest (optional)
Cooking oil spray
2 cups blueberries
1 tablespoon butter, melted (optional)
½ cup syrup (optional)
2 tablespoons confectioners' sugar (optional)

1. In a medium bowl, whisk together the baking mix and sugar. In a small bowl, whisk together the milk, eggs, vanilla, and lemon zest (if using). Add the wet ingredients to the dry ingredients and stir just until combined (the mixture will be a little bit lumpy).
2. Spray the baking pan with cooking oil spray, then place a square of parchment paper in the pan. Spray the parchment with cooking oil spray. Pour the batter into the pan and spread it out evenly. (It's okay if it doesn't go all the way into the corners; it will spread.) Sprinkle the blueberries evenly over the top.
3. Place the pan on the bake position. Select Bake, set temperature to 375ºF (191ºC), and set time to 10 minutes.
4. When cooking is complete, the pan cake should be pulling away from the edges of the pan and the top should be just starting to turn golden brown.
5. If serving as pancakes, let the cake cool for a minute, then cut into 16 squares and serve with butter and syrup.
6. If serving as "muffins," brush the top of the cake with the melted butter. Let the cake cool for 3 to 4 minutes, then dust with the confectioners' sugar. Slice and serve.

81. Apple Turnovers

Prep time: 15 minutes | Cook time: 20 minutes | Serves 4

1 cup diced apple (about 1 medium apple)
1 tablespoon brown sugar
¼ teaspoon cinnamon
⅛ teaspoon allspice
1 teaspoon freshly squeezed lemon juice
1 teaspoon all-purpose flour, plus more for dusting
½ package (1 sheet) frozen puff pastry, thawed
1 large egg, beaten
2 teaspoons granulated sugar

1. In a medium bowl, stir together the apple, brown sugar, cinnamon, allspice, lemon juice, and flour.
2. Lightly flour a cutting board. Unfold the puff pastry sheet onto the board. Using a rolling pin, gently roll the dough to smooth out the folds, seal any tears, and form it into a square. Cut the dough into four squares.
3. Scoop a quarter of the apple mixture into the center of each puff pastry square and spread it evenly in a triangle shape over half the pastry, leaving a border of about ½ inch around the edges of the pastry. Fold the pastry diagonally over the filling to form triangles. With a fork, crimp the edges to seal them. Place the turnovers in the baking pan, spacing them evenly.
4. Cut two or three small slits in the top of each turnover. Brush with the egg. Sprinkle evenly with the granulated sugar.
5. Place the pan on the bake position. Select Bake, set temperature to 350ºF (177ºC), and set time to 20 minutes.
6. After 10 to 12 minutes, remove the pan from the grill. Check the pastries; if they are browning unevenly, rotate the pan. Return the pan to the grill and continue cooking.
7. When cooking is complete, remove the pan from the grill. The turnovers should be golden brown and the filling bubbling. Let cool for about 10 minutes before serving (the filling will be very hot).

Chapter 3 Wraps and Sandwiches

82.Lamb and Feta Hamburgers

Prep time: 15 minutes | Cook time: 16 minutes | Makes 4 burgers

1½ pounds (680 g) ground lamb
¼ cup crumbled feta
1½ teaspoons tomato paste
1½ teaspoons minced garlic
1 teaspoon ground dried ginger
1 teaspoon ground

coriander
¼ teaspoon salt
¼ teaspoon cayenne pepper
4 kaiser rolls or hamburger buns, split open lengthwise, warmed
Cooking spray

1. Spritz the crisper tray with cooking spray.
2. Place the crisper tray on the air fry position. Select Air Fry, set the temperature to 375ºF (191ºC), and set the time to 16 minutes.
3. Combine all the ingredients, except for the buns, in a large bowl. Coarsely stir to mix well.
4. Shape the mixture into four balls, then pound the balls into four 5-inch diameter patties.
5. Arrange the patties in the crisper tray and spritz with cooking spray. Air fry for 16 minutes or until well browned. Flip the patties halfway through.
6. Assemble the buns with patties to make the burgers and serve immediately.

83.Montreal Steak and Seeds Burgers

Prep time: 15 minutes | Cook time: 10 minutes | Serves 4

1 teaspoon cumin seeds
1 teaspoon mustard seeds
1 teaspoon coriander seeds
1 teaspoon dried minced garlic
1 teaspoon dried red pepper flakes
1 teaspoon kosher

salt
2 teaspoons ground black pepper
1 pound (454 g) 85% lean ground beef
2 tablespoons Worcestershire sauce
4 hamburger buns
Mayonnaise, for serving
Cooking spray

1. Spritz the crisper tray with cooking spray.

2. Place the crisper tray on the air fry position. Select Air Fry, set the temperature to 350ºF (177ºC), and set the time to 10 minutes.
3. Put the seeds, garlic, red pepper flakes, salt, and ground black pepper in a food processor. Pulse to coarsely ground the mixture.
4. Put the ground beef in a large bowl. Pour in the seed mixture and drizzle with Worcestershire sauce. Stir to mix well.
5. Divide the mixture into four parts and shape each part into a ball, then bash each ball into a patty.
6. Arrange the patties in the crisper tray. Air fry for 10 minutes or until the patties are well browned. Flip the patties with tongs halfway through.
7. Assemble the buns with the patties, then drizzle the mayo over the patties to make the burgers. Serve immediately.

84.Tuna Muffin Sandwich

Prep time: 8 minutes | Cook time: 4 to 8 minutes | Serves 4

1 (6-ounce / 170-g) can chunk light tuna, drained
¼ cup mayonnaise
2 tablespoons mustard
1 tablespoon lemon juice

2 green onions, minced
3 English muffins, split with a fork
3 tablespoons softened butter
6 thin slices Provolone or Muenster cheese

1. Place the baking pan on the bake position. Select Bake, set the temperature to 390ºF (199ºC), and set the time to 4 minutes.
2. In a small bowl, combine the tuna, mayonnaise, mustard, lemon juice, and green onions. Set aside.
3. Butter the cut side of the English muffins. Place in the baking pan, butter-side up.
4. Bake for 2 to 4 minutes, or until light golden brown. Remove the muffins from the grill.
5. Top each muffin with one slice of cheese and return to the grill. Bake for 2 to 4 minutes or until the cheese melts and starts to brown.
6. Remove the muffins from the grill, top with the tuna mixture, and serve.

85.Cheesy Greens Sandwich

Prep time: 15 minutes | Cook time: 10 to 13 minutes | Serves 4

1½ cups chopped mixed greens
2 garlic cloves, thinly sliced
2 teaspoons olive oil

2 slices low-sodium low-fat Swiss cheese
4 slices low-sodium whole-wheat bread
Cooking spray

1. Place the baking pan on the air fry position. Select Air Fry, set the temperature to 400ºF (204ºC), and set the time to 5 minutes.
2. In the baking pan, mix the greens, garlic, and olive oil. Air fry for 4 to 5 minutes, stirring once, until the vegetables are tender. Drain, if necessary.
3. Make 2 sandwiches, dividing half of the greens and 1 slice of Swiss cheese between 2 slices of bread. Lightly spray the outsides of the sandwiches with cooking spray. Transfer to the pan.
4. Bake for 6 to 8 minutes, turning with tongs halfway through, until the bread is toasted and the cheese melts.
5. Cut each sandwich in half and serve.

86.Cabbage and Pork Gyoza

Prep time: 10 minutes | Cook time: 10 minutes per batch | Makes 48 gyozas

1 pound (454 g) ground pork
1 small head Napa cabbage (about 1 pound / 454 g), sliced thinly and minced
½ cup minced scallions
1 teaspoon minced fresh chives
1 teaspoon soy sauce

1 teaspoon minced fresh ginger
1 tablespoon minced garlic
1 teaspoon granulated sugar
2 teaspoons kosher salt
48 to 50 wonton or dumpling wrappers
Cooking spray

1. Make the filling: Combine all the ingredients, except for the wrappers in a large bowl. Stir to mix well.
2. Unfold a wrapper on a clean work surface, then dab the edges with a little water. Scoop up 2 teaspoons of the filling mixture in the center.
3. Make the gyoza: Fold the wrapper over to filling and press the edges to seal. Pleat the edges if desired. Repeat with remaining wrappers and fillings.

4. Spritz the crisper tray with cooking spray.
5. Place the crisper tray on the air fry position. Select Air Fry, set the temperature to 360ºF (182ºC), and set the time to 10 minutes.
6. Arrange the gyozas in the crisper tray and spritz with cooking spray. Air fry for 10 minutes or until golden brown. Flip the gyozas halfway through. Work in batches to avoid overcrowding.
7. Serve immediately.

87.Classic Sloppy Joes

Prep time: 10 minutes | Cook time: 17 to 19 minutes | Makes 4 large sandwiches or 8 sliders

1 pound (454 g) very lean ground beef
1 teaspoon onion powder
$1/_3$ cup ketchup
¼ cup water
½ teaspoon celery seed
1 tablespoon lemon juice
1½ teaspoons brown sugar

1¼ teaspoons low-sodium Worcestershire sauce
½ teaspoon salt (optional)
½ teaspoon vinegar
⅛ teaspoon dry mustard
Hamburger or slider buns, for serving
Cooking spray

1. Place the crisper tray on the roast position. Select Roast, set the temperature to 390ºF (199ºC), and set the time to 12 minutes.
2. Spray the crisper tray with cooking spray.
3. Break raw ground beef into small chunks and pile into the crisper tray. Roast for 5 minutes. Stir to break apart and roast for 3 minutes. Stir and roast for 2 to 4 minutes longer, or until meat is well done.
4. Remove the meat from the grill, drain, and use a knife and fork to crumble into small pieces.
5. Give your crisper tray a quick rinse to remove any bits of meat.
6. Place all the remaining ingredients, except for the buns, in the baking pan and mix together. Add the meat and stir well.
7. Adjust the temperature to 330ºF (166ºC). Bake for 5 minutes. Stir and bake for 2 minutes.
8. Scoop into buns. Serve hot.

88.Cream Cheese Wontons

Prep time: 5 minutes | Cook time: 6 minutes | Serves 4

2 ounces (57 g) cream cheese, softened	16 square wonton wrappers
1 tablespoon sugar	Cooking spray

1. Spritz the crisper tray with cooking spray.
2. Place the crisper tray on the air fry position. Select Air Fry, set the temperature to 350ºF (177ºC), and set the time to 6 minutes.
3. In a mixing bowl, stir together the cream cheese and sugar until well mixed. Prepare a small bowl of water alongside.
4. On a clean work surface, lay the wonton wrappers. Scoop ¼ teaspoon of cream cheese in the center of each wonton wrapper. Dab the water over the wrapper edges. Fold each wonton wrapper diagonally in half over the filling to form a triangle.
5. Arrange the wontons in the crisper tray. Spritz the wontons with cooking spray. Air fry for 6 minutes, or until golden brown and crispy. Flip once halfway through to ensure even cooking.
6. Divide the wontons among four plates. Let rest for 5 minutes before serving.

89.Turkey Sliders with Chive Mayo

Prep time: 10 minutes | Cook time: 15 minutes | Serves 6

12 burger buns
Cooking spray
For the Turkey Sliders:

¾ pound (340 g) turkey, minced	chopped scallions
1 tablespoon oyster sauce	1 tablespoon chopped fresh cilantro
¼ cup pickled jalapeno, chopped	1 to 2 cloves garlic, minced
2 tablespoons	Sea salt and ground black pepper, to taste

For the Chive Mayo:

1 tablespoon chives	Zest of 1 lime
1 cup mayonnaise	1 teaspoon salt

1. Place the crisper tray on the air fry position. Select Air Fry, set the temperature to 365ºF (185ºC), and set the time to 15 minutes.
2. Spritz the crisper tray with cooking spray.
3. Combine the ingredients for the turkey sliders in a large bowl. Stir to mix well. Shape the mixture into 6 balls, then bash the balls into patties.
4. Arrange the patties in the crisper tray and spritz with cooking spray. Air fry for 15 minutes or until well browned. Flip the patties halfway through.
5. Meanwhile, combine the ingredients for the chive mayo in a small bowl. Stir to mix well.
6. Smear the patties with chive mayo, then assemble the patties between two buns to make the sliders. Serve immediately.

90.Crispy Crab and Cream Cheese Wontons

Prep time: 10 minutes | Cook time: 10 minutes per batch | Serves 6 to 8

24 wonton wrappers, thawed if frozen
Cooking spray
For the Filling:

5 ounces (142 g) lump crabmeat, drained and patted dry	1½ teaspoons toasted sesame oil
4 ounces (113 g) cream cheese, at room temperature	1 teaspoon Worcestershire sauce
2 scallions, sliced	Kosher salt and ground black pepper, to taste

1. Spritz the crisper tray with cooking spray.
2. Place the crisper tray on the air fry position. Select Air Fry, set the temperature to 350ºF (177ºC), and set the time to 10 minutes.
3. In a medium-size bowl, place all the ingredients for the filling and stir until well mixed. Prepare a small bowl of water alongside.
4. On a clean work surface, lay the wonton wrappers. Scoop 1 teaspoon of the filling in the center of each wrapper. Wet the edges with a touch of water. Fold each wonton wrapper diagonally in half over the filling to form a triangle.
5. Arrange the wontons in the crisper tray. Spritz the wontons with cooking spray. Work in batches, 6 to 8 at a time. Air fry for 10 minutes, or until crispy and golden brown. Flip once halfway through.
6. Serve immediately.

91. Cheesy Shrimp Sandwich

Prep time: 10 minutes | Cook time: 5 to 7 minutes | Serves 4

1¼ cups shredded Colby, Cheddar, or Havarti cheese
1 (6-ounce / 170-g) can tiny shrimp, drained
3 tablespoons mayonnaise
2 tablespoons minced green onion
4 slices whole grain or whole-wheat bread
2 tablespoons softened butter

1. Place the crisper tray on the air fry position. Select Air Fry, set the temperature to 400ºF (204ºC), and set the time to 7 minutes.
2. In a medium bowl, combine the cheese, shrimp, mayonnaise, and green onion, and mix well.
3. Spread this mixture on two of the slices of bread. Top with the other slices of bread to make two sandwiches. Spread the sandwiches lightly with butter. Transfer to the crisper tray.
4. Air fry for 5 to 7 minutes, or until the bread is browned and crisp and the cheese is melted.
5. Cut in half and serve warm.

92. Pork Momos

Prep time: 20 minutes | Cook time: 10 minutes per batch | Serves 4

2 tablespoons olive oil
1 pound (454 g) ground pork
1 shredded carrot
1 onion, chopped
1 teaspoon soy sauce
16 wonton wrappers
Salt and ground black pepper, to taste

1. Place the crisper tray on the air fry position. Select Air Fry, set the temperature to 320ºF (160ºC), and set the time to 10 minutes.
2. Heat the olive oil in a nonstick skillet over medium heat until shimmering.
3. Add the ground pork, carrot, onion, soy sauce, salt, and ground black pepper and sauté for 10 minutes or until the pork is well browned and carrots are tender.
4. Unfold the wrappers on a clean work surface, then divide the cooked pork and vegetables on the wrappers. Fold the edges around the filling to form momos. Nip the top to seal the momos.
5. Arrange the momos in the crisper tray and spritz with cooking spray. Air fry for 10 minutes or until the wrappers are lightly browned. Work in batches to avoid overcrowding.
6. Serve immediately.

93. Sweet Potato and Black Bean Burritos

Prep time: 15 minutes | Cook time: 1 hour | Makes 6 burritos

2 sweet potatoes, peeled and cut into a small dice
1 tablespoon vegetable oil
Kosher salt and ground black pepper, to taste
6 large flour tortillas
1 (16-ounce / 454-g) can refried black beans, divided
1½ cups baby spinach, divided
6 eggs, scrambled
¾ cup grated Cheddar cheese, divided
¼ cup salsa
¼ cup sour cream
Cooking spray

1. Place the crisper tray on the air fry position. Select Air Fry, set the temperature to 400ºF (204ºC), and set the time to 10 minutes.
2. Put the sweet potatoes in a large bowl, then drizzle with vegetable oil and sprinkle with salt and black pepper. Toss to coat well.
3. Place the sweet potatoes in the crisper tray. Air fry for 10 minutes or until lightly browned. Shake the crisper tray halfway through.
4. Unfold the tortillas on a clean work surface. Divide the black beans, spinach, sweet potatoes, scrambled eggs, and cheese on top of the tortillas.
5. Fold the long side of the tortillas over the filling, then fold in the shorter side to wrap the filling to make the burritos.
6. Work in batches, wrap the burritos in the aluminum foil and put in the crisper tray.
7. Adjust the temperature to 350ºF (177ºC). Air fry for 20 minutes. Flip the burritos halfway through.
8. Remove the burritos from the grill and put back to the grill. Spritz with cooking spray and air fry for 5 more minutes or until lightly browned. Repeat with remaining burritos.
9. Remove the burritos from the grill and spread with sour cream and salsa. Serve immediately.

94. Chicken and Yogurt Taquitos

Prep time: 15 minutes | Cook time: 12 minutes | Serves 4

1 cup cooked chicken, shredded	Mozzarella cheese
¼ cup Greek yogurt	Salt and ground black pepper, to taste
¼ cup salsa	4 flour tortillas
1 cup shredded	Cooking spray

1. Spritz the crisper tray with cooking spray.
2. Place the crisper tray on the air fry position. Select Air Fry, set the temperature to 380ºF (193ºC), and set the time to 12 minutes.
3. Combine all the ingredients, except for the tortillas, in a large bowl. Stir to mix well.
4. Make the taquitos: Unfold the tortillas on a clean work surface, then scoop up 2 tablespoons of the chicken mixture in the middle of each tortilla. Roll the tortillas up to wrap the filling.
5. Arrange the taquitos in the crisper tray and spritz with cooking spray.
6. Air fry for 12 minutes or until golden brown and the cheese melts. Flip the taquitos halfway through.
7. Serve immediately.

95. Turkey, Leek, and Pepper Hamburger

Prep time: 10 minutes | Cook time: 20 minutes | Serves 4

1 cup leftover turkey, cut into bite-sized chunks	1 heaping tablespoon fresh cilantro, chopped
1 leek, sliced	1 teaspoon hot paprika
1 Serrano pepper, deveined and chopped	¾ teaspoon kosher salt
2 bell peppers, deveined and chopped	½ teaspoon ground black pepper
2 tablespoons Tabasco sauce	4 hamburger buns
½ cup sour cream	Cooking spray

1. Place the baking pan on the bake position. Select Bake, set the temperature to 385ºF (196ºC), and set the time to 20 minutes.
2. Spritz the baking pan with cooking spray.
3. Mix all the ingredients, except for the buns, in a large bowl. Toss to combine well.
4. Pour the mixture in the baking pan. Bake for 20 minutes, or until the turkey is well browned and the leek is tender.
5. Assemble the hamburger buns with the turkey mixture and serve immediately.

96. Bacon and Bell Pepper Sandwich

Prep time: 10 minutes | Cook time: 6 minutes | Serves 4

$\frac{1}{3}$ cup spicy barbecue sauce	1 yellow bell pepper, sliced
2 tablespoons honey	3 pita pockets, cut in half
8 slices cooked bacon, cut into thirds	1¼ cups torn butter lettuce leaves
1 red bell pepper, sliced	2 tomatoes, sliced

1. Place the crisper tray on the roast position. Select Roast, set the temperature to 350ºF (177ºC), and set the time to 6 minutes.
2. In a small bowl, combine the barbecue sauce and the honey. Brush this mixture lightly onto the bacon slices and the red and yellow pepper slices.
3. Put the peppers into the crisper tray. Roast for 4 minutes. Then shake the crisper tray, add the bacon, and roast for 2 minutes or until the bacon is browned and the peppers are tender.
4. Fill the pita halves with the bacon, peppers, any remaining barbecue sauce, lettuce, and tomatoes, and serve immediately.

97. Eggplant Hoagies

Prep time: 15 minutes | Cook time: 12 minutes | Makes 3 hoagies

6 peeled eggplant slices (about ½ inch thick and 3 inches in diameter)	6 tablespoons grated Parmesan cheese
¼ cup jarred pizza sauce	3 Italian sub rolls, split open lengthwise, warmed
	Cooking spray

1. Spritz the crisper tray with cooking spray.
2. Place the crisper tray on the air fry position. Select Air Fry, set the temperature to 350ºF (177ºC), and set the time to 10 minutes.
3. Arrange the eggplant slices in the crisper tray and spritz with cooking spray.
4. Air fry for 10 minutes or until lightly wilted and tender. Flip the slices halfway through.
5. Divide and spread the pizza sauce and cheese on top of the eggplant slice. Increase the temperature to 375ºF (191ºC). Air fry for 2 more minutes or until the cheese melts.
6. Assemble each sub roll with two slices of eggplant and serve immediately.

98.Veggie Pita Sandwich

Prep time: 10 minutes | Cook time: 9 to 12 minutes | Serves 4

1 baby eggplant, peeled and chopped
1 red bell pepper, sliced
½ cup diced red onion
½ cup shredded carrot
1 teaspoon olive oil

$^1/_3$ cup low-fat Greek yogurt
½ teaspoon dried tarragon
2 low-sodium whole-wheat pita breads, halved crosswise

1. Place the baking pan on the roast position. Select Roast, set the temperature to 390ºF (199ºC), and set the time to 10 minutes.
2. In the pan, stir together the eggplant, red bell pepper, red onion, carrot, and olive oil. Roast for 7 to 9 minutes, stirring once, until the vegetables are tender. Drain if necessary.
3. In a small bowl, thoroughly mix the yogurt and tarragon until well combined.
4. Stir the yogurt mixture into the vegetables. Stuff one-fourth of this mixture into each pita pocket.
5. Place the sandwiches in the baking pan. Bake for 2 to 3 minutes, or until the bread is toasted.
6. Serve immediately.

99.Chicken Pita Sandwich

Prep time: 10 minutes | Cook time: 9 to 11 minutes | Serves 4

2 boneless, skinless chicken breasts, cut into
1-inch cubes
1 small red onion, sliced
1 red bell pepper, sliced
$^1/_3$ cup Italian salad dressing, divided

½ teaspoon dried thyme
4 pita pockets, split
2 cups torn butter lettuce
1 cup chopped cherry tomatoes

1. Place the crisper tray on the bake position. Select Bake, set the temperature to 380ºF (193ºC), and set the time to 11 minutes.
2. Place the chicken, onion, and bell pepper in the crisper tray. Drizzle with 1 tablespoon of the Italian salad dressing, add the thyme, and toss.
3. Bake for 9 to 11 minutes, or until the chicken is 165ºF (74ºC) on a food thermometer, stirring once during cooking time.
4. Transfer the chicken and vegetables to a bowl and toss with the remaining salad dressing.
5. Assemble sandwiches with the pita pockets, butter lettuce, and cherry tomatoes. Serve immediately.

100.Thai Pork Sliders

Prep time: 10 minutes | Cook time: 14 minutes | Makes 6 sliders

1 pound (454 g) ground pork
1 tablespoon Thai curry paste
1½ tablespoons fish sauce
¼ cup thinly sliced scallions, white and green parts

2 tablespoons minced peeled fresh ginger
1 tablespoon light brown sugar
1 teaspoon ground black pepper
6 slider buns, split open lengthwise, warmed
Cooking spray

1. Spritz the crisper tray with cooking spray.
2. Place the crisper tray on the air fry position. Select Air Fry, set the temperature to 375ºF (191ºC), and set the time to 14 minutes.
3. Combine all the ingredients, except for the buns in a large bowl. Stir to mix well.
4. Divide and shape the mixture into six balls, then bash the balls into six 3-inch-diameter patties.
5. Arrange the patties in the crisper tray and spritz with cooking spray. Air fry for 14 minutes or until well browned. Flip the patties halfway through.
6. Assemble the buns with patties to make the sliders and serve immediately.

101.Cheesy Potato Taquitos

Prep time: 5 minutes | Cook time: 6 minutes per batch | Makes 12 taquitos

2 cups mashed potatoes
½ cup shredded Mexican cheese

12 corn tortillas
Cooking spray

1. Line the baking pan with parchment paper.
2. Place the baking pan on the air fry position. Select Air Fry, set the temperature to 400ºF (204ºC), and set the time to 6 minutes.
3. In a bowl, combine the potatoes and cheese until well mixed. Microwave the tortillas on high heat for 30 seconds, or until softened. Add some water to another bowl and set alongside.
4. On a clean work surface, lay the tortillas. Scoop 3 tablespoons of the panato mixture in the center of each tortilla. Roll up tightly and secure with toothpicks if necessary.
5. Arrange the filled tortillas, seam side down, in the prepared baking pan. Spritz the tortillas with cooking spray.
6. Air fry for 6 minutes, or until crispy and golden brown, flipping once halfway through the cooking time. You may need to work in batches to avoid overcrowding.
7. Serve hot.

Chapter 4 Vegetables

102. Black Bean and Tomato Chili

Prep time: 15 minutes | Cook time: 23 minutes | Serves 6

1 tablespoon olive oil
1 medium onion, diced
3 garlic cloves, minced
1 cup vegetable broth
3 cans black beans, drained and rinsed
2 cans diced tomatoes
2 chipanle peppers, chopped
2 teaspoons cumin
2 teaspoons chili powder
1 teaspoon dried oregano
½ teaspoon salt

1. Over a medium heat, fry the garlic and onions in the olive oil for 3 minutes.
2. Add the remaining ingredients, stirring constantly and scraping the bottom to prevent sticking.
3. Place the baking pan on the bake position. Select Bake, set the temperature to 400ºF (204ºC), and set the time to 20 minutes.
4. Take the baking pan and place the mixture inside. Put a sheet of aluminum foil on top.
5. Bake for 20 minutes.
6. When ready, plate up and serve immediately.

103. Garlic Roasted Asparagus

Prep time: 5 minutes | Cook time: 10 minutes | Serves 4

1 pound (454 g) asparagus, woody ends trimmed
2 tablespoons olive oil
1 tablespoon balsamic vinegar
2 teaspoons minced garlic
Salt and freshly ground black pepper, to taste

1. Place the crisper tray on the roast position. Select Roast, set the temperature to 400ºF (204ºC), and set the time to 10 minutes.
2. In a large shallow bowl, toss the asparagus with the olive oil, balsamic vinegar, garlic, salt, and pepper until thoroughly coated.
3. Arrange the asparagus in the crisper tray. Roast for 10 minutes until crispy. Flip the asparagus with tongs halfway through the cooking time.
4. Serve warm.

104. Spicy Cabbage

Prep time: 5 minutes | Cook time: 7 minutes | Serves 4

1 head cabbage, sliced into 1-inch-thick ribbons
1 tablespoon olive oil
1 teaspoon garlic powder
1 teaspoon red pepper flakes
1 teaspoon salt
1 teaspoon freshly ground black pepper

1. Place the crisper tray on the roast position. Select Roast, set the temperature to 350ºF (177ºC), and set the time to 7 minutes.
2. Toss the cabbage with the olive oil, garlic powder, red pepper flakes, salt, and pepper in a large mixing bowl until well coated.
3. Arrange the cabbage in the crisper tray. Roast for 7 minutes until crisp. Flip the cabbage with tongs halfway through the cooking time.
4. Remove from the crisper tray to a plate and serve warm.

105. Rosemary Roasted Potatoes

Prep time: 5 minutes | Cook time: 20 to 22 minutes | Serves 4

1½ pounds (680 g) small red potatoes, cut into 1-inch cubes
2 tablespoons olive oil
2 tablespoons minced fresh rosemary
1 tablespoon minced garlic
1 teaspoon salt, plus additional as needed
½ teaspoon freshly ground black pepper, plus additional as needed

1. Place the crisper tray on the roast position. Select Roast, set the temperature to 400ºF (204ºC), and set the time to 22 minutes.
2. Toss the panato cubes with the olive oil, rosemary, garlic, salt, and pepper in a large bowl until thoroughly coated.
3. Arrange the panato cubes in the crisper tray in a single layer. Roast for 20 to 22 minutes until the potatoes are tender. Shake the crisper tray a few times during cooking for even cooking.
4. Remove from the crisper tray to a plate. Taste and add additional salt and pepper as needed.

106. Baked Potatoes with Yogurt and Chives

Prep time: 5 minutes | Cook time: 35 minutes | Serves 4

4 (7-ounce / 198-g) russet potatoes, rinsed	½ cup 2% plain Greek yogurt
Olive oil spray	¼ cup minced fresh chives
½ teaspoon kosher salt, divided	Freshly ground black pepper, to taste

1. Place the crisper tray on the bake position. Select Bake, set the temperature to 400ºF (204ºC), and set the time to 35 minutes.
2. Pat the potatoes dry and pierce them all over with a fork. Spritz the potatoes with olive oil spray. Sprinkle with ¼ teaspoon of the salt.
3. Put the potatoes in the crisper tray. Bake for 35 minutes, or until a knife can be inserted into the center of the potatoes easily.
4. Remove from the crisper tray and split open the potatoes. Top with the yogurt, chives, the remaining ¼ teaspoon of salt, and finish with the black pepper. Serve immediately.

107. Simple Ratatouille

Prep time: 15 minutes | Cook time: 16 minutes | Serves 2

2 Roma tomatoes, thinly sliced	minced
1 zucchini, thinly sliced	2 tablespoons olive oil
2 yellow bell peppers, sliced	2 tablespoons herbes de Provence
2 garlic cloves,	1 tablespoon vinegar
	Salt and black pepper, to taste

1. Place the baking pan on the roast position. Select Roast, set the temperature to 390ºF (199ºC), and set the time to 16 minutes.
2. Place the tomatoes, zucchini, bell peppers, garlic, olive oil, herbes de Provence, and vinegar in a large bowl and toss until the vegetables are evenly coated. Sprinkle with salt and pepper and toss again. Pour the vegetable mixture into the pan.
3. Roast for 8 minutes. Stir and continue roasting for 8 minutes until tender.
4. Let the vegetable mixture stand for 5 minutes before removing and serving.

108. Buttered Broccoli with Parmesan

Prep time: 5 minutes | Cook time: 4 minutes | Serves 4

1 pound (454 g) broccoli florets	unsalted butter, melted
1 medium shallot, minced	2 teaspoons minced garlic
2 tablespoons olive oil	¼ cup grated Parmesan cheese
2 tablespoons	

1. Place the crisper tray on the roast position. Select Roast, set the temperature to 360ºF (182ºC), and set the time to 4 minutes.
2. Combine the broccoli florets with the shallot, olive oil, butter, garlic, and Parmesan cheese in a medium bowl and toss until the broccoli florets are thoroughly coated.
3. Arrange the broccoli florets in the crisper tray in a single layer. Roast for 4 minutes until crisp-tender.
4. Serve warm.

109. Crusted Brussels Sprouts with Sage

Prep time: 5 minutes | Cook time: 15 minutes | Serves 4

1 pound (454 g) Brussels sprouts, halved	1 tablespoon paprika
1 cup bread crumbs	2 tablespoons canola oil
2 tablespoons grated Grana Padano cheese	1 tablespoon chopped sage

1. Line the crisper tray with parchment paper.
2. Place the crisper tray on the roast position. Select Roast, set the temperature to 400ºF (204ºC), and set the time to 15 minutes.
3. In a small bowl, thoroughly mix the bread crumbs, cheese, and paprika. In a large bowl, place the Brussels sprouts and drizzle the canola oil over the top. Sprinkle with the bread crumb mixture and toss to coat.
4. Place the Brussels sprouts in the crisper tray. Roast for 15 minutes, or until the Brussels sprouts are lightly browned and crisp. Shake the crisper tray a few times during cooking to ensure even cooking.
5. Transfer the Brussels sprouts to a plate and sprinkle the sage on top before serving.

110. Cauliflower Steaks with Ranch Dressing

Prep time: 10 minutes | Cook time: 15 minutes | Serves 2

1 head cauliflower, stemmed and leaves removed	pepper, to taste
¼ cup canola oil	1 cup shredded Cheddar cheese
½ teaspoon garlic powder	Ranch dressing, for garnish
½ teaspoon paprika	4 slices bacon, cooked and crumbled
Sea salt, to taste	2 tablespoons chopped fresh chives
Freshly ground black	

1. Cut the cauliflower from top to bottom into two 2-inch "steaks"; reserve the remaining cauliflower to cook separately.
2. Place the grill plate on the grill position. Select Grill, set the temperature to 450°F (232°C), and set the time to 15 minutes.
3. Meanwhile, in a small bowl, whisk together the oil, garlic powder, and paprika. Season with salt and pepper. Brush each steak with the oil mixture on both sides.
4. Place the steaks on the grill plate. Grill for 10 minutes.
5. After 10 minutes, flip the steaks and top each with ½ cup of cheese. Continue to grill until the cheese is melted, about 5 minutes.
6. When cooking is complete, place the cauliflower steaks on a plate and drizzle with the ranch dressing. Top with the bacon and chives.

111. Potatoes with Zucchinis

Prep time: 10 minutes | Cook time: 45 minutes | Serves 4

2 potatoes, peeled and cubed	thickly
4 carrots, cut into chunks	Salt and ground black pepper, to taste
1 head broccoli, cut into florets	¼ cup olive oil
4 zucchinis, sliced	1 tablespoon dry onion powder

1. Place the baking pan on the bake position. Select Bake, set the temperature to 400°F (204°C), and set the time to 45 minutes.
2. In the baking pan, add all the ingredients and combine well.
3. Bake for 45 minutes, ensuring the vegetables are soft and the sides have browned before serving.

112. Fast and Easy Asparagus

Prep time: 5 minutes | Cook time: 5 minutes | Serves 4

1 pound (454 g) fresh asparagus spears, trimmed	1 tablespoon olive oil
	Salt and ground black pepper, to taste

1. Place the crisper tray on the air fry position. Select Air Fry, set the temperature to 375°F (191°C), and set the time to 5 minutes.
2. Combine all the ingredients and transfer to the crisper tray.
3. Air fry for 5 minutes or until soft.
4. Serve hot.

113. Bean and Corn Stuffed Peppers

Prep time: 15 minutes | Cook time: 32 minutes | Serves 6

6 red or green bell peppers, seeded, ribs removed, and top ½-inch cut off and reserved	enchilada sauce
	½ teaspoon chili powder
4 garlic cloves, minced	¼ teaspoon ground cumin
1 small white onion, diced	½ cup canned black beans, rinsed and drained
2 (8½-ounce / 241-g) bags instant rice, cooked in microwave	½ cup frozen corn
	½ cup vegetable stock
1 (10-ounce / 284-g) can red or green	1 (8-ounce / 227-g) bag shredded Colby Jack cheese, divided

1. Chop the ½-inch portions of reserved bell pepper and place in a large mixing bowl. Add the garlic, onion, cooked instant rice, enchilada sauce, chili powder, cumin, black beans, corn, vegetable stock, and half the cheese. Mix to combine.
2. Place the baking pan on the roast position. Select Roast, set the temperature to 350°F (177°C), and set the time to 32 minutes.
3. Spoon the mixture into the peppers, filling them up as full as possible. If necessary, lightly press the mixture down into the peppers to fit more in.
4. Place the peppers, upright, in the pan. Roast for 30 minutes.
5. After 30 minutes, sprinkle the remaining cheese over the top of the peppers. Roast for the remaining 2 minutes.
6. When cooking is complete, serve immediately.

114. Grilled Mozzarella Eggplant Stacks

Prep time: 10 minutes | Cook time: 14 minutes | Serves 4

1 eggplant, sliced ¼-inch thick
2 tablespoons canola oil
2 beefsteak or heirloom tomatoes, sliced ¼-inch thick
12 large basil leaves
½ pound (227 g) buffalo Mozzarella, sliced ¼-inch thick
Sea salt, to taste

1. Place the grill plate on the grill position. Select Grill, set the temperature to 450ºF (232ºC), and set the time to 14 minutes.
2. Meanwhile, in a large bowl, toss the eggplant and oil until evenly coated.
3. Place the eggplant on the grill plate. Grill for 8 to 12 minutes, until charred on all sides.
4. After 8 to 12 minutes, top the eggplant with one slice each of tomato and Mozzarella. Grill for 2 minutes, until the cheese melts.
5. When cooking is complete, remove the eggplant stacks from the grill. Place 2 or 3 basil leaves on top of half of the stacks. Place the remaining eggplant stacks on top of those with basil so that there are four stacks total. Season with salt, garnish with the remaining basil, and serve.

115. Grilled Vegetable Pizza

Prep time: 10 minutes | Cook time: 10 minutes | Serves 2

2 tablespoons all-purpose flour, plus more as needed
½ store-bought pizza dough (about 8 ounces / 227 g)
1 tablespoon canola oil, divided
½ cup pizza sauce
1 cup shredded Mozzarella cheese
½ zucchini, thinly sliced
½ red onion, sliced
½ red bell pepper, seeded and thinly sliced

1. Place the grill plate on the grill position. Select Grill, set the temperature to 450ºF (232ºC), and set the time to 7 minutes.
2. Dust a clean work surface with the flour.
3. Place the dough on the floured surface and roll it into a 9-inch round of even thickness. Dust your rolling pin and work surface with additional flour, as needed, to ensure the dough does not stick.
4. Evenly brush the surface of the rolled-out dough with ½ tablespoon of oil. Flip the dough over and brush the other side with the remaining ½ tablespoon of oil. Poke the dough with a fork 5 or 6 times across its surface to prevent air pockets from forming while it cooks.
5. Place the dough on the grill plate. Grill for 4 minutes.
6. After 4 minutes, flip the dough, then spread the pizza sauce evenly over it. Sprinkle with the cheese, and top with the zucchini, onion, and pepper.
7. Continue cooking for the remaining 2 to 3 minutes until the cheese is melted and the veggie slices begin to crisp.
8. When cooking is complete, let cool slightly before slicing.

116. Arugula and Broccoli Salad

Prep time: 10 minutes | Cook time: 12 minutes | Serves 4

2 heads broccoli, trimmed into florets
½ red onion, sliced
1 tablespoon canola oil
2 tablespoons extra-virgin olive oil
1 tablespoon freshly squeezed lemon juice
1 teaspoon honey
1 teaspoon Dijon mustard
1 garlic clove, minced
Pinch red pepper flakes
¼ teaspoon fine sea salt
Freshly ground black pepper, to taste
4 cups arugula, torn
2 tablespoons grated Parmesan cheese

1. Place the grill plate on the grill position. Select Grill, set the temperature to 450ºF (232ºC), and set the time to 12 minutes.
2. In a large bowl, combine the broccoli, sliced onions, and canola oil and toss until coated.
3. Place the vegetables on the grill plate. Grill for 8 to 12 minutes, until charred on all sides.
4. Meanwhile, in a medium bowl, whisk together the olive oil, lemon juice, honey, mustard, garlic, red pepper flakes, salt, and pepper.
5. When cooking is complete, combine the roasted vegetables and arugula in a large serving bowl. Drizzle with the vinaigrette, and sprinkle with the Parmesan cheese.

117. Spicy Cauliflower Roast

Prep time: 15 minutes | Cook time: 20 minutes | Serves 4

Cauliflower:

5 cups cauliflower florets
3 tablespoons vegetable oil
½ teaspoon ground cumin
½ teaspoon ground coriander
½ teaspoon kosher salt

Sauce:

½ cup Greek yogurt or sour cream
¼ cup chopped fresh cilantro
1 jalapeño, coarsely chopped
4 cloves garlic, peeled
½ teaspoon kosher salt
2 tablespoons water

1. Place the crisper tray on the roast position. Select Roast, set the temperature to 400ºF (204ºC), and set the time to 20 minutes.
2. In a large bowl, combine the cauliflower, oil, cumin, coriander, and salt. Toss to coat.
3. Put the cauliflower in the crisper tray. Roast for 20 minutes, stirring halfway through the roasting time.
4. Meanwhile, in a blender, combine the yogurt, cilantro, jalapeño, garlic, and salt. Blend, adding the water as needed to keep the blades moving and to thin the sauce.
5. At the end of roasting time, transfer the cauliflower to a large serving bowl. Pour the sauce over and toss gently to coat. Serve immediately.

118. Italian Baked Tofu

Prep time: 5 minutes | Cook time: 10 minutes | Serves 2

1 tablespoon soy sauce
1 tablespoon water
$1/_3$ teaspoon garlic powder
$1/_3$ teaspoon onion powder
$1/_3$ teaspoon dried oregano
$1/_3$ teaspoon dried basil
Black pepper, to taste
6 ounces (170 g) extra firm tofu, pressed and cubed

1. In a large mixing bowl, whisk together the soy sauce, water, garlic powder, onion powder, oregano, basil, and black pepper. Add the tofu cubes, stirring to coat, and let them marinate for 10 minutes.
2. Place the baking pan on the bake position. Select Bake, set the temperature to 390ºF (199ºC), and set the time to 10 minutes.
3. Arrange the tofu in the baking pan. Bake for 10 minutes until crisp. Flip the tofu halfway through the cooking time.
4. Remove from the crisper tray to a plate and serve.

119. Honey-Glazed Roasted Veggies

Prep time: 15 minutes | Cook time: 20 minutes | Makes 3 cups

Glaze:

2 tablespoons raw honey
2 teaspoons minced garlic
¼ teaspoon dried marjoram
¼ teaspoon dried basil
¼ teaspoon dried oregano
⅛ teaspoon dried sage
⅛ teaspoon dried rosemary
⅛ teaspoon dried thyme
½ teaspoon salt
¼ teaspoon ground black pepper

Veggies:

3 to 4 medium red potatoes, cut into 1- to 2-inch pieces
1 small zucchini, cut into 1- to 2-inch pieces
1 small carrot, sliced into ¼-inch rounds
1 (10.5-ounce / 298-g) package cherry tomatoes, halved
1 cup sliced mushrooms
3 tablespoons olive oil

1. Place the crisper tray on the roast position. Select Roast, set the temperature to 380ºF (193ºC), and set the time to 15 minutes.
2. Combine the honey, garlic, marjoram, basil, oregano, sage, rosemary, thyme, salt, and pepper in a small bowl and stir to mix well. Set aside.
3. Place the red potatoes, zucchini, carrot, cherry tomatoes, and mushroom in a large bowl. Drizzle with the olive oil and toss to coat.
4. Pour the veggies into the crisper tray. Roast for 15 minutes, shaking the crisper tray halfway through.
5. When ready, transfer the roasted veggies to the large bowl. Pour the honey mixture over the veggies, tossing to coat.
6. Spread out the veggies in the baking pan and place in the grill.
7. Increase the temperature to 390ºF (199ºC) and roast for an additional 5 minutes, or until the veggies are tender and glazed. Serve warm.

120.Mascarpone Mushrooms

Prep time: 10 minutes | Cook time: 15 minutes | Serves 4

Vegetable oil spray
4 cups sliced mushrooms
1 medium yellow onion, chopped
2 cloves garlic, minced
¼ cup heavy whipping cream or half-and-half
8 ounces (227 g) mascarpone cheese
1 teaspoon dried thyme
1 teaspoon kosher salt
1 teaspoon black pepper
½ teaspoon red pepper flakes
4 cups cooked konjac noodles, for serving
½ cup grated Parmesan cheese

1. Place the baking pan on the bake position. Select Bake, set the temperature to 350ºF (177ºC), and set the time to 15 minutes.
2. Spray the baking pan with vegetable oil spray.
3. In a medium bowl, combine the mushrooms, onion, garlic, cream, mascarpone, thyme, salt, black pepper, and red pepper flakes. Stir to combine. Transfer the mixture to the prepared pan.
4. Bake for 15 minutes, stirring halfway through the baking time.
5. Divide the pasta among four shallow bowls. Spoon the mushroom mixture evenly over the pasta. Sprinkle with Parmesan cheese and serve.

121.Summer Squash and Zucchini Salad

Prep time: 10 minutes | Cook time: 20 minutes | Serves 4

1 zucchini, sliced lengthwise about ¼-inch thick
1 summer squash, sliced lengthwise about ¼-inch thick
½ red onion, sliced
4 tablespoons canola oil, divided
2 portobello mushroom caps, trimmed with gills removed
2 ears corn, shucked
2 teaspoons freshly squeezed lemon juice
Sea salt, to taste
Freshly ground black pepper, to taste

1. Place the grill plate on the grill position. Select Grill, set the temperature to 450ºF (232ºC), and set the time to 25 minutes.
2. Meanwhile, in a large bowl, toss the zucchini, squash, and onion with 2 tablespoons of oil until evenly coated.
3. Arrange the zucchini, squash, and onions on the grill plate. Grill for 6 minutes.
4. After 6 minutes, flip the squash. Grill for 6 to 9 minutes more.
5. Meanwhile, brush the mushrooms and corn with the remaining 2 tablespoons of oil.
6. When cooking is complete, remove the zucchini, squash, and onions and swap in the mushrooms and corn. Grill for the remaining 10 minutes.
7. When cooking is complete, remove the mushrooms and corn, and let cool.
8. Cut the kernels from the cobs. Roughly chop all the vegetables into bite-size pieces.
9. Place the vegetables in a serving bowl and drizzle with lemon juice. Season with salt and pepper, and toss until evenly mixed.

122.Tofu, Carrot and Cauliflower Rice

Prep time: 10 minutes | Cook time: 22 minutes | Serves 4

½ block tofu, crumbled
1 cup diced carrot
½ cup diced onions
Cauliflower:
3 cups cauliflower rice
½ cup chopped broccoli
½ cup frozen peas
2 tablespoons soy sauce
1 tablespoon minced ginger
2 garlic cloves, minced
1 tablespoon rice vinegar
1½ teaspoons toasted sesame oil
2 tablespoons soy sauce
1 teaspoon turmeric

1. Place the baking pan on the roast position. Select Roast, set the temperature to 370ºF (188ºC), and set the time to 22 minutes.
2. Mix together the tofu, carrot, onions, soy sauce, and turmeric in the pan and stir until well incorporated.
3. Roast for 10 minutes.
4. Meanwhile, in a large bowl, combine all the ingredients for the cauliflower and toss well.
5. Remove the pan and add the cauliflower mixture to the tofu and stir to combine.
6. Return the pan to the grill and continue roasting for 12 minutes, or until the vegetables are cooked to your preference.
7. Cool for 5 minutes before serving.

123. Balsamic Mushroom Sliders with Pesto

Prep time: 10 minutes | Cook time: 8 minutes | Serves 4

8 small portobello mushrooms, trimmed with gills removed
2 tablespoons canola oil
2 tablespoons

balsamic vinegar
8 slider buns
1 tomato, sliced
½ cup pesto
½ cup micro greens

1. Place the grill plate on the grill position. Select Grill, set the temperature to 400ºF (204ºC), and set the time to 8 minutes.
2. Brush the mushrooms with the oil and balsamic vinegar.
3. Place the mushrooms, gill-side down, on the grill plate. Grill for 8 minutes until the mushrooms are tender.
4. When cooking is complete, remove the mushrooms from the grill, and layer on the buns with tomato, pesto, and micro greens.

124. Corn and Potato Chowder

Prep time: 15 minutes | Cook time: 50 minutes | Serves 4

4 ears corn, shucked
2 tablespoons canola oil
1½ teaspoons sea salt, plus additional to season the corn
½ teaspoon freshly ground black pepper, plus additional to season the corn
3 tablespoons

unsalted butter
1 small onion, finely chopped
2½ cups vegetable broth
1½ cups milk
4 cups diced potatoes
2 cups half-and-half
1½ teaspoons chopped fresh thyme

1. Place the grill plate on the grill position. Select Grill, set the temperature to 450ºF (232ºC), and set the time to 12 minutes.
2. Brush each ear of corn with ½ tablespoon of oil. Season the corn with salt and pepper to taste.
3. Place the corn on the grill plate. Grill for 6 minutes.
4. After 6 minutes, flip the corn. Continue cooking for the remaining 6 minutes.
5. When cooking is complete, remove the corn and let cool. Cut the kernels from the cobs.
6. In a food processor, purée 1 cup of corn kernels until smooth.
7. In a large pan over medium-high heat, melt the butter. Add the onion and sauté until soft, 5 to 7 minutes. Add the broth, milk, and potatoes. Bring to a simmer and cook until the potatoes are just tender, 10 to 12 minutes. Stir in the salt and pepper.
8. Stir in the puréed corn, remaining corn kernels, and half-and-half. Bring to a simmer and cook, stirring occasionally, until the potatoes are cooked through, for 15 to 20 minutes.
9. Using a panato masher or immersion blender, slightly mash some of the potatoes. Stir in the thyme, and additional salt and pepper to taste.

125. Vegetarian Meatballs

Prep time: 15 minutes | Cook time: 18 minutes | Serves 3

½ cup grated carrots
½ cup sweet onions
2 tablespoons olive oil
1 cup rolled oats
½ cup roasted cashews
2 cups cooked chickpeas
Juice of 1 lemon

2 tablespoons soy sauce
1 tablespoon flax meal
1 teaspoon garlic powder
1 teaspoon cumin
½ teaspoon turmeric

1. Place the baking pan on the roast position. Select Roast, set the temperature to 350ºF (177ºC), and set the time to 6 minutes.
2. Mix together the carrots, onions, and olive oil in the pan and stir to combine.
3. Roast for 6 minutes.
4. Meanwhile, put the oats and cashews in a food processor or blender and pulse until coarsely ground. Transfer the mixture to a large bowl. Add the chickpeas, lemon juice, and soy sauce to the food processor and pulse until smooth. Transfer the chickpea mixture to the bowl of oat and cashew mixture.
5. Remove the carrots and onions from the pan to the bowl of chickpea mixture. Add the flax meal, garlic powder, cumin, and turmeric and stir to incorporate.
6. Scoop tablespoon-sized portions of the veggie mixture and roll them into balls with your hands. Transfer the balls to the crisper tray in a single layer.
7. Increase the temperature to 370ºF (188ºC) and bake for 12 minutes until golden through. Flip the balls halfway through the cooking time.
8. Serve warm.

126.Creamy and Cheesy Spinach

Prep time: 10 minutes | Cook time: 15 minutes | Serves 4

Vegetable oil spray	cream cheese, diced
1 (10-ounce / 283-g) package frozen spinach, thawed and squeezed dry	½ teaspoon ground nutmeg
½ cup chopped onion	1 teaspoon kosher salt
2 cloves garlic, minced	1 teaspoon black pepper
4 ounces (113 g)	½ cup grated Parmesan cheese

1. Place the baking pan on the bake position. Select Bake, set the temperature to 350ºF (177ºC), and set the time to 15 minutes.
2. Spray the baking pan with vegetable oil spray.
3. In a medium bowl, combine the spinach, onion, garlic, cream cheese, nutmeg, salt, and pepper. Transfer to the prepared pan.
4. Bake for 10 minutes. Open and stir to thoroughly combine the cream cheese and spinach.
5. Sprinkle the Parmesan cheese on top. Bake for 5 minutes, or until the cheese has melted and browned.
6. Serve hot.

127.Cheesy Asparagus and Potato Platter

Prep time: 5 minutes | Cook time: 26 to 30 minutes | Serves 5

4 medium potatoes, cut into wedges	trimmed
Cooking spray	2 tablespoons olive oil
1 bunch asparagus,	Salt and pepper, to taste
Cheese Sauce:	
¼ cup crumbled cottage cheese	grain mustard
¼ cup buttermilk	Salt and black pepper, to taste
1 tablespoon whole-	

1. Place the crisper tray on the roast position. Select Roast, set the temperature to 400ºF (204ºC), and set the time to 30 minutes.
2. Spritz the crisper tray with cooking spray.
3. Put the potatoes in the crisper tray. Roast for 20 to 22 minutes, until golden brown. Shake the crisper tray halfway through the cooking time.
4. When ready, remove the potatoes from the crisper tray to a platter. Cover the potatoes with foil to keep warm. Set aside.
5. Place the asparagus in the crisper tray and drizzle with the olive oil. Sprinkle with salt and pepper.
6. Roast for 6 to 8 minutes, shaking the crisper tray once or twice during cooking, or until the asparagus is cooked to your desired crispiness.
7. Meanwhile, make the cheese sauce by stirring together the cottage cheese, buttermilk, and mustard in a small bowl. Season with salt and pepper.
8. Transfer the asparagus to the platter of potatoes and drizzle with the cheese sauce. Serve immediately.

128.Sesame-Thyme Whole Maitake Mushrooms

Prep time: 5 minutes | Cook time: 15 minutes | Serves 2

1 tablespoon soy sauce	woods) mushrooms
2 teaspoons toasted sesame oil	½ teaspoon flaky sea salt
3 teaspoons vegetable oil, divided	½ teaspoon sesame seeds
1 garlic clove, minced	½ teaspoon finely chopped fresh thyme leaves
7 ounces (198 g) maitake (hen of the	

1. Place the crisper tray on the roast position. Select Roast, set the temperature to 300ºF (149ºC), and set the time to 15 minutes.
2. Whisk together the soy sauce, sesame oil, 1 teaspoon of vegetable oil, and garlic in a small bowl.
3. Arrange the mushrooms in the crisper tray in a single layer. Drizzle the soy sauce mixture over the mushrooms. Roast for 10 minutes.
4. Flip the mushrooms and sprinkle the sea salt, sesame seeds, and thyme leaves on top. Drizzle the remaining 2 teaspoons of vegetable oil all over. Roast for an additional 5 minutes.
5. Remove the mushrooms from the crisper tray to a plate and serve hot.

129.Hearty Roasted Veggie Salad

Prep time: 5 minutes | Cook time: 20 minutes | Serves 2

1 potato, chopped
1 carrot, sliced diagonally
1 cup cherry tomatoes
½ small beetroot, sliced
¼ onion, sliced
½ teaspoon turmeric
½ teaspoon cumin
¼ teaspoon sea salt
2 tablespoons olive oil, divided
A handful of arugula
A handful of baby spinach
Juice of 1 lemon
3 tablespoons canned chickpeas, for serving
Parmesan shavings, for serving

1. Place the crisper tray on the roast position. Select Roast, set the temperature to 370ºF (188ºC), and set the time to 20 minutes.
2. Combine the potato, carrot, cherry tomatoes, beetroot, onion, turmeric, cumin, salt, and 1 tablespoon of olive oil in a large bowl and toss until well coated.
3. Arrange the veggies in the crisper tray. Roast for 20 minutes, shaking the crisper tray halfway through.
4. Let the veggies cool for 5 to 10 minutes in the crisper tray.
5. Put the arugula, baby spinach, lemon juice, and remaining 1 tablespoon of olive oil in a salad bowl and stir to combine. Mix in the roasted veggies and toss well.
6. Scatter the chickpeas and Parmesan shavings on top and serve immediately.

130.Mozzarella Broccoli Calzones

Prep time: 10 minutes | Cook time: 24 minutes | Serves 4

1 head broccoli, trimmed into florets
2 tablespoons extra-virgin olive oil
1 store-bought pizza dough (about 16 ounces / 454 g)
2 to 3 tablespoons all-purpose flour, plus more for dusting
1 egg, beaten
2 cups shredded Mozzarella cheese
1 cup ricotta cheese
½ cup grated Parmesan cheese
1 garlic clove, grated
Grated zest of 1 lemon
½ teaspoon red pepper flakes
Cooking oil spray

1. Place the crisper tray on the air fry position. Select Air Fry, set the temperature to 390ºF (199ºC), and set the time to 12 minutes.
2. Meanwhile, in a large bowl, toss the broccoli and olive oil until evenly coated.
3. Add the broccoli to the crisper tray. Air fry for 6 minutes.
4. While the broccoli is cooking, divide the pizza dough into four equal pieces. Dust a clean work surface with the flour. Place the dough on the floured surface and roll each piece into an 8-inch round of even thickness. Dust your rolling pin and work surface with additional flour, as needed, to ensure the dough does not stick. Brush a thin coating of egg wash around the edges of each round.
5. After 6 minutes, shake the crisper tray. Place the crisper tray back in the grill to resume cooking.
6. Meanwhile, in a medium bowl, combine the Mozzarella, ricotta, Parmesan cheese, garlic, lemon zest, and red pepper flakes.
7. After cooking is complete, add the broccoli to the cheese mixture. Spoon one-quarter of the mixture onto one side of each dough. Fold the other half over the filling, and press firmly to seal the edges together. Brush each calzone all over with the remaining egg wash.
8. Coat the crisper tray with cooking spray and place the calzones in the crisper tray. air fry for 10 to 12 minutes, until golden brown.

131.Honey-Glazed Baby Carrots

Prep time: 5 minutes | Cook time: 12 minutes | Serves 4

1 pound (454 g) baby carrots
2 tablespoons olive oil
1 tablespoon honey
1 teaspoon dried dill
Salt and black pepper, to taste

1. Place the crisper tray on the roast position. Select Roast, set the temperature to 350ºF (177ºC), and set the time to 12 minutes.
2. Place the carrots in a large bowl. Add the olive oil, honey, dill, salt, and pepper and toss to coat well.
3. Arrange the carrots in the crisper tray. Roast for 12 minutes, until crisp-tender. Shake the crisper tray once during cooking.
4. Serve warm.

132.Chermoula Beet Roast

Prep time: 15 minutes | Cook time: 25 minutes | Serves 4

Chermoula:

1 cup packed fresh cilantro leaves	1 teaspoon ground coriander
½ cup packed fresh parsley leaves	½ to 1 teaspoon cayenne pepper
6 cloves garlic, peeled	Pinch of crushed saffron (optional)
2 teaspoons smoked paprika	½ cup extra-virgin olive oil
2 teaspoons ground cumin	Kosher salt, to taste

Beets:

3 medium beets, trimmed, peeled, and cut into 1-inch chunks	chopped fresh cilantro 2 tablespoons
2 tablespoons	chopped fresh parsley

1. In a food processor, combine the cilantro, parsley, garlic, paprika, cumin, coriander, and cayenne. Pulse until coarsely chopped. Add the saffron, if using, and process until combined. With the food processor running, slowly add the olive oil in a steady stream; process until the sauce is uniform. Season with salt.
2. Place the crisper tray on the roast position. Select Roast, set the temperature to 375ºF (191ºC), and set the time to 25 minutes.
3. In a large bowl, drizzle the beets with ½ cup of the chermoula to coat. Arrange the beets in the crisper tray. Roast for 25 minutes, or until the beets are tender.
4. Transfer the beets to a serving platter. Sprinkle with the chopped cilantro and parsley and serve.

133.Rosemary Roasted Squash with Cheese

Prep time: 5 minutes | Cook time: 20 minutes | Serves 2

1 pound (454 g) butternut squash, cut into wedges	Salt, to salt
	1 cup crumbled goat cheese
2 tablespoons olive oil	1 tablespoon maple syrup
1 tablespoon dried rosemary	

1. Place the crisper tray on the roast position. Select Roast, set the temperature to 350ºF (177ºC), and set the time to 20 minutes.
2. Toss the squash wedges with the olive oil, rosemary, and salt in a large bowl until well coated.
3. Transfer the squash wedges to the crisper tray, spreading them out in as even a layer as possible.
4. Roast for 10 minutes. Flip the squash and roast for another 10 minutes until golden brown.
5. Sprinkle the goat cheese on top and serve drizzled with the maple syrup.

134.Hearty Thai Vegetable Mix

Prep time: 10 minutes | Cook time: 8 minutes | Serves 4

1 small head Napa cabbage, shredded, divided	sauce
	2 tablespoons freshly squeezed lime juice
8 ounces (227 g) snow peas	2 tablespoons brown sugar
1 medium carrot, cut into thin coins	2 teaspoons red or green Thai curry paste
1 red or green bell pepper, sliced into thin strips	1 cup frozen mango slices, thawed
1 tablespoon vegetable oil	1 serrano chile, seeded and minced
1 tablespoon sesame oil	½ cup chopped roasted peanuts or cashews
2 tablespoons soy	

1. Place half the Napa cabbage in a large bowl. Add the snow peas, carrot, and bell pepper. Drizzle with the vegetable oil and toss to coat. Place in the baking pan in an even layer.
2. Place the pan on the roast position. Select Roast, set temperature to 375ºF (191ºC), and set time to 8 minutes.
3. While the vegetables cook, in a small bowl, whisk together the sesame oil, soy sauce, lime juice, brown sugar, and curry paste.
4. When cooking is complete, the vegetables should be crisp-tender. If necessary, continue cooking for a minute or two longer. Remove the pan from the grill and place the vegetables back in the bowl. Add the mango slices, chile, and the remaining Napa cabbage. Add the dressing and toss to coat.
5. Serve topped with the nuts.

135. Spinach and Zucchini Rolls

Prep time: 15 minutes | Cook time: 18 minutes | Serves 6

3 large zucchinis
2½ teaspoons kosher salt or 1¼ teaspoons fine salt, divided
1½ cups cooked chopped spinach
1½ cups whole milk ricotta cheese
½ cup freshly grated Parmesan cheese
1½ cups shredded Mozzarella, divided
1 large egg, lightly beaten
1 teaspoon Italian seasoning or ½ teaspoon each dried basil and oregano
Freshly ground black pepper
Cooking oil spray
1½ cups Marinara Sauce or store-bought variety

1. Cut off the ends of the zucchini and peel several strips off one side to make a flat base. Use a large Y-shaped peeler or sharp cheese plane to cut long slices about ⅛-inch thick. When you get to a point where you can't get any more slices, set that zucchini aside and start on the next. You need 8 good slices per squash, for a total of 24 slices (a few extra never hurts). Save the rest of the zucchini pieces for another recipe, such as the Ratatouille Casserole.
2. Salt one side of the zucchini slices with 1 teaspoon of kosher salt. Place the slices salted-side down on a rack placed over a baking sheet. Salt the other sides with another teaspoon of kosher salt. Let the slices sit for 10 minutes, or until they start to exude water (you'll see it beading up on the surface of the slices and dripping onto the baking sheet).
3. While the zucchini sits, In a medium bowl, combine the spinach, ricotta, Parmesan cheese, ¾ cup of Mozzarella, egg, Italian seasoning, remaining ½ teaspoon of kosher salt, and pepper.
4. Spray the baking pan with cooking oil spray.
5. Rinse the zucchini slices off and blot them dry with a paper towel. Spread about 2 tablespoons of the ricotta mixture evenly along each zucchini slice. Roll up the slice and place each seam-side down on the prepared baking pan. Place the rolls so they touch, working from the center of the pan out toward the edges. Repeat with remaining zucchini slices and filling. Top the rolls with the marinara sauce and sprinkle with the remaining ¾ cup of Mozzarella.
6. Place the pan on the roast position. Select Roast, set temperature to 375ºF (191ºC), and set time to 18 minutes.
7. After about 15 minutes, check the rolls. They are done when the cheese is melted and beginning to brown, and the filling is bubbling. If necessary, continue cooking for another 3 to 4 minutes.
8. When cooking is complete, remove the pan from the grill. Serve.

136. Roasted Asparagus with Eggs

Prep time: 10 minutes | Cook time: 12 minutes | Serves 4

2 pounds (907 g) asparagus, trimmed
3 tablespoons extra-virgin olive oil, divided
1 teaspoon kosher salt or ½ teaspoon fine salt, divided
1 pint cherry tomatoes
4 large eggs
¼ teaspoon freshly ground black pepper

1. Place the asparagus in the baking pan. Drizzle with 2 tablespoons of olive oil and use tongs (or your hands) to toss the asparagus to coat it with the oil. Sprinkle with ½ teaspoon of kosher salt.
2. Place the pan on the roast position. Select Roast, set temperature to 375ºF (191ºC), and set time to 12 minutes.
3. While the asparagus is cooking, place the tomatoes in a medium bowl and drizzle with the remaining 1 tablespoon of olive oil. Toss to coat.
4. After 6 minutes, remove the pan from the grill. Using tongs, toss the asparagus; it should be starting to get crisp at the tips. Spread the asparagus evenly in the center of the pan. Add the tomatoes around the perimeter of the pan. Return the pan to the grill and continue cooking.
5. After 2 minutes, remove the pan from the grill.
6. Carefully crack the eggs over the asparagus, being careful to space them out so they aren't touching. Sprinkle the eggs with the remaining ½ teaspoon of kosher salt and the pepper. Return the pan to the grill and continue cooking. Cook for another 3 to 7 minutes, depending on how you like your eggs.
7. When cooking is complete, use a large spatula to transfer an egg with the asparagus underneath to plates. Spoon the tomatoes onto the plates.

137.Pizza Margherita

Prep time: 15 minutes | Cook time: 12 minutes | Serves 4

1 pound (454 g) store-bought pizza dough
2 tablespoons extra-virgin olive oil, divided
½ cup Marinara Sauce or store-bought variety
6 ounces (170 g) shredded Mozzarella cheese
½ cup coarsely shredded Parmesan cheese (about 1½ ounces / 43 g)
2 large tomatoes, seeded and chopped (about 1½ cups)
¼ teaspoon kosher salt or ⅛ teaspoon fine salt
¼ cup chopped fresh basil
2 teaspoons wine vinegar

1. Punch down the pizza dough to release as much air as possible. Place the dough in the baking pan and press it out toward the edges. The dough will likely spring back and shrink. Be patient and keep working at it, leaving it alone to relax for a few minutes from time to time. As it stretches, I find it helpful to coat my fingers with 1 tablespoon of olive oil and then poke the dough lightly with my fingertips to keep it from shrinking as much. Don't worry if you can't get it all the way to the pan's edges.
2. Spread the marinara sauce over the dough. You'll be able to see the dough through the sauce in places; you don't want a thick coating. Evenly top the sauce with the Mozzarella cheese.
3. Place the pan on the roast position. Select Roast, set temperature to 425ºF (218ºC), and set time to 12 minutes.
4. After about 8 minutes, remove the pan from the grill. Sprinkle the Parmesan cheese over the pizza. Return the pan to the grill. Alternatively, if you like a crisp crust, use a pizza peel or cake lifter (or even a very large spatula) to slide the pizza off the pan and directly onto the grill rack. Continue cooking.
5. While the pizza cooks, place the tomatoes in a colander or fine-mesh strainer and sprinkle with the salt. Let them drain for a few minutes, then place in a small bowl. Mix in the remaining 1 tablespoon of olive oil, basil, and vinegar.
6. When cooking is complete, the cheese on top will be lightly browned and bubbling and the crust a deep golden brown. Remove the pizza from the baking pan, if you haven't already, and place it on a wire rack to cool for a few minutes (a rack will keep the crust from getting soggy as it cools). Distribute the tomato mixture evenly over the pizza, then transfer to a cutting board to slice and serve.

138.Chickpea and Rice Stuffed Peppers

Prep time: 10 minutes | Cook time: 18 minutes | Serves 4

4 medium red, green, or yellow bell peppers
4 tablespoons extra-virgin olive oil, divided
½ teaspoon kosher salt or ¼ teaspoon fine salt, divided
1 (15-ounce / 425-g) can chickpeas
3 garlic cloves, minced or pressed
½ small onion, finely chopped (about ½ cup)
1½ cups cooked white rice
½ cup diced roasted red peppers
¼ cup chopped parsley
¼ teaspoon freshly ground black pepper
½ teaspoon cumin
¾ cup panko bread crumbs

1. Cut the peppers in half through the stem and remove the seeds and ribs. You can either leave the stem attached or cut it out, as you like. Brush the peppers inside and out with 1 tablespoon of olive oil. Sprinkle the insides with ¼ teaspoon of kosher salt. Place the peppers cut-side up in the baking pan.
2. Pour the beans with their liquid into a large bowl. Using a potato masher, lightly mash the beans. Add the remaining ¼ teaspoon of kosher salt, 1 tablespoon of olive oil, the garlic, onion, rice, roasted red peppers, parsley, black pepper, and cumin. Stir to combine. Spoon the mixture into the bell pepper halves.
3. In a small bowl, stir together the panko and remaining 2 tablespoons of olive oil. Top the peppers with the panko mixture.
4. Place the pan on the roast position. Select Roast, set temperature to 375ºF (191ºC), and set time to 18 minutes.
5. After about 12 minutes, remove the pan from the grill. If the panko is browning unevenly, rotate the pan 180 degrees. Return the pan to the grill and continue cooking.
6. When cooking is complete, the peppers should be slightly wrinkled, and the panko should be deep golden brown.

139. Mushroom and Bean Enchiladas

Prep time: 10 minutes | Cook time: 17 minutes | Serves 4

8 (6-inch) corn tortillas	1 teaspoon chili powder
Cooking oil spray or vegetable oil, for brushing	2 tablespoons salsa
	1½ cups red enchilada sauce
1 (15-ounce / 425-g) can black beans, drained	1 recipe Roasted Mushrooms
¾ cups frozen corn, thawed	8 ounces (227 g) shredded Monterey Jack cheese

1. Spray the tortillas on both sides with cooking oil spray or brush lightly with the oil. Arrange them in the baking pan, overlapping as little as possible.
2. Place the pan on the roast position. Select Roast, set temperature to 325ºF (163ºC), and set time to 5 minutes.
3. While the tortillas warm, place the beans in a medium bowl. Add the corn, chili powder, and salsa and stir to combine. Transfer the mixture to a large sheet of aluminum foil. Fold the foil over the mixture and seal the edges to create a packet. Set aside.
4. After 5 minutes, remove the pan from the grill. Stack the tortillas on a plate and cover with foil.
5. Pour about half of the enchilada sauce on one end of the baking pan. Place a tortilla in the sauce, turning it over to coat it thoroughly. Spoon a couple of tablespoons of mushrooms down the middle of the tortilla and top with a couple tablespoons of cheese. Roll up the tortilla and place it seam-side down on one edge of the pan. Repeat with the remaining tortillas, adding more sauce to the pan as necessary, forming a row of enchiladas from one side of the pan to the other. (Leave room along one side for the beans.) You may not use all the mushrooms, and you should have about ¹/₃ cup of cheese remaining.
6. Spoon most of the remaining sauce over the enchiladas. You don't want them drowning, but they should be nicely coated. Sprinkle the remaining cheese over the enchiladas.
7. Place the packet of beans and corn next to the row of enchiladas.
8. Place the pan on the roast position. Select Roast, set temperature to 350ºF (177ºC), and set time to 12 minutes.
9. When cooking is complete, the cheese will be melted and the sauce will be bubbling. Remove the pan from the grill. Open the beans and corn and stir gently. Adjust the seasoning, adding salt or more salsa as desired.

140. Cheese and Black Bean Tacos

Prep time: 12 minutes | Cook time: 7 minutes | Serves 4

1 (15-ounce / 425-g) can black beans, drained and rinsed	cheese (plain or with jalapeños)
½ cup prepared salsa	8 (6-inch) flour tortillas
1½ teaspoons chili powder	2 tablespoons vegetable or extra-virgin olive oil
2 tablespoons minced onion	Shredded lettuce, for serving
4 ounces (113 g) grated Monterey Jack	

1. Place the beans in a medium bowl, preferably one with a flat bottom. Add the salsa and chili powder. Using a potato masher, coarsely mash the beans and salsa. Add the onion and cheese and stir to combine.
2. Lay out the tortillas on a cutting board and divide the filling among them (2 to 3 tablespoons per tortilla). Fold the tortillas over, pressing lightly to even out the filling. Brush the tacos on one side with half the oil, then place them oiled-side down in the baking pan. Brush the top side with the remaining oil.
3. Place the pan on the air fry position. Select Air Fry, set temperature to 400ºF (204ºC), and set time to 7 minutes.
4. After 4 minutes, remove the pan from the grill. Turn the tacos over. Return the pan to the grill and continue cooking.
5. When cooking is complete, the tacos should be deep golden brown on both sides. Remove the pan from the grill and let cool for a few minutes (the filling will be very hot). Place the tacos on plates and serve with the shredded lettuce, and additional salsa and cheese if desired.

141.Asian-Inspired Broccoli

Prep time: 5 minutes | Cook time: 10 minutes | Serves 2

12 ounces (340 g) broccoli florets
2 tablespoons Asian hot chili oil
1 teaspoon ground Sichuan peppercorns (or black pepper)
2 garlic cloves, finely chopped
1 (2-inch) piece fresh ginger, peeled and finely chopped
Kosher salt and freshly ground black pepper

1. Place the crisper tray on the roast position. Select Roast, set the temperature to 375ºF (191ºC), and set the time to 10 minutes.
2. Toss the broccoli florets with the chili oil, Sichuan peppercorns, garlic, ginger, salt, and pepper in a mixing bowl until thoroughly coated.
3. Transfer the broccoli florets to the crisper tray. Roast for 10 minutes, shaking the crisper tray halfway through, or until the broccoli florets are lightly browned and tender.
4. Remove the broccoli from the crisper tray and serve on a plate.

142.Cashew Stuffed Mushrooms

Prep time: 10 minutes | Cook time: 15 minutes | Serves 6

1 cup basil
½ cup cashew, soaked overnight
½ cup nutritional yeast
1 tablespoon lemon juice
2 cloves garlic
1 tablespoon olive oil
Salt, to taste
1 pound (454 g) baby bella mushroom, stems removed

1. Place the crisper tray on the air fry position. Select Air Fry, set the temperature to 400ºF (204ºC), and set the time to 15 minutes.
2. Prepare the pesto. In a food processor, blend the basil, cashew nuts, nutritional yeast, lemon juice, garlic and olive oil to combine well. Sprinkle with salt, as desired.
3. Turn the mushrooms cap-side down and spread the pesto on the underside of each cap.
4. Transfer to the crisper tray. Air fry for 15 minutes.
5. Serve warm.

143.Creamy Corn Casserole

Prep time: 5 minutes | Cook time: 15 minutes | Serves 4

2 cups frozen yellow corn
1 egg, beaten
3 tablespoons flour
½ cup grated Swiss or Havarti cheese
½ cup light cream
¼ cup milk
Pinch salt
Freshly ground black pepper, to taste
2 tablespoons butter, cut into cubes
Nonstick cooking spray

1. Place the baking pan on the bake position. Select Bake, set the temperature to 320ºF (160ºC), and set the time to 15 minutes.
2. Spritz the baking pan with nonstick cooking spray.
3. Stir together the remaining ingredients except the butter in a medium bowl until well incorporated.
4. Transfer the mixture to the prepared baking pan and scatter with the butter cubes.
5. Bake for 15 minutes, or until the top is golden brown and a toothpick inserted in the center comes out clean.
6. Let the casserole cool for 5 minutes before slicing into wedges and serving.

144.Corn Pakodas

Prep time: 10 minutes | Cook time: 8 minutes | Serves 5

1 cup flour
¼ teaspoon baking soda
¼ teaspoon salt
½ teaspoon curry powder
½ teaspoon red chili powder
¼ teaspoon turmeric powder
¼ cup water
10 cobs baby corn, blanched
Cooking spray

1. Place the crisper tray on the air fry position. Select Air Fry, set the temperature to 425ºF (218ºC), and set the time to 8 minutes.
2. Cover the crisper tray with aluminum foil and spritz with the cooking spray.
3. In a bowl, combine all the ingredients, save for the corn. Stir with a whisk until well combined.
4. Coat the corn in the batter and put inside the crisper tray.
5. Air fry for 8 minutes until a golden brown color is achieved.
6. Serve hot.

145.Lush Ratatouille Casserole

Prep time: 10 minutes | Cook time: 12 minutes | Serves 6

1 small eggplant, peeled and sliced ½-inch thick
1 medium zucchini, sliced ½-inch thick
2 teaspoons kosher salt or 1 teaspoon fine salt, divided
4 tablespoons extra-virgin olive oil, divided
1 small onion, chopped (about 1 cup)
3 garlic cloves, minced or pressed
1 small green bell pepper, cut into ½-inch chunks (about 1 cup)
1 small red bell pepper, cut into ½-inch chunks (about 1 cup)
½ teaspoon dried oregano
¼ teaspoon freshly ground black pepper
1 pint cherry tomatoes
2 tablespoons minced fresh basil
1 cup panko bread crumbs
½ cup grated Parmesan cheese (optional)

1. Salt one side of the eggplant and zucchini slices with ¾ teaspoon of salt. Place the slices salted-side down on a rack placed over a baking sheet. Salt the other sides with another ¾ teaspoon of salt. Let the slices sit for 10 minutes, or until they start to exude water (it will bead up on the surface of the slices and drip down into the baking sheet). Rinse the slices off and blot them dry with a paper towel. Cut the zucchini slices into quarters and the eggplant slices into eighths.
2. Place the zucchini and eggplant in a large bowl and add 2 tablespoons of olive oil, the onion, garlic, bell peppers, oregano, and black pepper. Toss to coat the vegetables with the oil. Place the vegetables in the baking pan.
3. Place the pan on the roast position. Select Roast, set temperature to 375ºF (191ºC), and set time to 12 minutes.
4. While the vegetables are cooking, place the tomatoes and basil into the bowl. Add 1 tablespoon of olive oil and the remaining ½ teaspoon of salt.
5. In a small bowl, mix the panko, remaining 1 tablespoon of olive oil, and Parmesan cheese (if using).
6. After 6 minutes, remove the pan from the grill. Add the tomato mixture to the vegetables in the baking pan and stir to combine. Top with the panko mixture. Return the pan to the grill and continue cooking.
7. When cooking is complete, the vegetables should be tender and the topping golden brown. Remove the pan from the grill and serve.

146.Sriracha Golden Cauliflower

Prep time: 5 minutes | Cook time: 17 minutes | Serves 4

¼ cup vegan butter, melted
¼ cup sriracha sauce
4 cups cauliflower florets
1 cup bread crumbs
1 teaspoon salt

1. Place the crisper tray on the air fry position. Select Air Fry, set the temperature to 375ºF (191ºC), and set the time to 17 minutes.
2. Mix the sriracha and vegan butter in a bowl and pour this mixture over the cauliflower, taking care to cover each floret entirely.
3. In a separate bowl, combine the bread crumbs and salt.
4. Dip the cauliflower florets in the bread crumbs, coating each one well. Transfer to the crisper tray. Air fry for 17 minutes.
5. Serve hot.

147.Cinnamon-Spiced Acorn Squash

Prep time: 5 minutes | Cook time: 15 minutes | Serves 2

1 medium acorn squash, halved crosswise and deseeded
1 teaspoon coconut oil
1 teaspoon light brown sugar
Few dashes of ground cinnamon
Few dashes of ground nutmeg

1. Place the crisper tray on the air fry position. Select Air Fry, set the temperature to 325ºF (163ºC), and set the time to 15 minutes.
2. On a clean work surface, rub the cut sides of the acorn squash with coconut oil. Scatter with the brown sugar, cinnamon, and nutmeg.
3. Put the squash halves in the crisper tray, cut-side up. Air fry for 15 minutes until just tender when pierced in the center with a paring knife.
4. Rest for 5 to 10 minutes and serve warm.

148.Cheese Pepper in Roasted Portobellos

Prep time: 15 minutes | Cook time: 15 minutes | Serves 4

8 portobello mushroom caps, each about 3 inches across
4 tablespoons sherry vinegar or white wine vinegar
1 tablespoon fresh thyme leaves or 1 teaspoon dried
6 garlic cloves, minced or pressed, divided
1 teaspoon Dijon mustard
1 teaspoon kosher salt or ½ teaspoon fine salt, divided
¼ cup plus 3¼
teaspoons extra-virgin olive oil, divided
1 small green bell pepper, thinly sliced
1 small red or yellow bell pepper, thinly sliced
1 small onion, thinly sliced
¼ teaspoon red pepper flakes
Several grinds freshly ground black pepper
4 ounces (113 g) shredded Fontina cheese or other mild melting cheese

1. Rinse off any dirt from the mushroom caps and pat dry.
2. In a small bowl, whisk together the vinegar, thyme, 4 minced garlic cloves, mustard, and ½ teaspoon of kosher salt. Slowly pour in ¼ cup of olive oil, whisking constantly, until an emulsion forms. Alternatively, place the ingredients in a small jar with a tight-fitting lid and shake. Measure out 2 tablespoons and set aside.
3. Place the mushrooms in a resealable plastic bag and add the marinade. Seal the bag, squeezing out as much air as possible. Massage the mushrooms to coat them in the marinade. If you have the time, let marinate about 20 minutes at room temperature, turning the bag over after 10 minutes.
4. In a medium bowl, place the bell peppers, onion, remaining 2 minced garlic cloves, red pepper flakes, remaining ½ teaspoon of salt, and black pepper. Drizzle the remaining 3¼ teaspoons of olive oil over the vegetables and toss to coat.
5. Remove the mushrooms from the marinade and place them gill-side down on one end of the baking pan. Place the bell pepper mixture on the other side of the pan.
6. Place the pan on the roast position. Select Roast, set temperature to 375ºF (191ºC), and set time to 12 minutes.
7. After 7 minutes, remove the pan from the grill. Stir the peppers and turn the mushrooms over. Return the pan to the grill and continue cooking.
8. When cooking is complete, the peppers are tender and browned in places, and the mushrooms have shrunk somewhat. Remove the pan from the grill. Transfer the pepper mixture to a cutting board and coarsely chop.
9. Brush the mushrooms on both sides with the reserved 2 tablespoons marinade. Fill the caps with the pepper mixture. Sprinkle the cheese over the stuffing.
10. Place the pan on the broil position. Select Broil, set temperature to 450ºF (232ºC), and set time to 3 minutes.
11. The mushrooms are done when the cheese is melted and bubbling. Remove the pan and garnish with fresh thyme or parsley, if desired.

149.Charred Green Beans with Sesame Seeds

Prep time: 5 minutes | Cook time: 8 minutes | Serves 4

1 tablespoon reduced-sodium soy sauce or tamari
½ tablespoon Sriracha sauce
4 teaspoons toasted
sesame oil, divided
12 ounces (340 g) trimmed green beans
½ tablespoon toasted sesame seeds

1. Place the crisper tray on the air fry position. Select Air Fry, set the temperature to 375ºF (191ºC), and set the time to 8 minutes.
2. Whisk together the soy sauce, Sriracha sauce, and 1 teaspoon of sesame oil in a small bowl until smooth.
3. Toss the green beans with the remaining sesame oil in a large bowl until evenly coated.
4. Place the green beans in the crisper tray in a single layer. You may need to work in batches to avoid overcrowding.
5. Air fry for 8 minutes until the green beans are lightly charred and tender. Shake the crisper tray halfway through the cooking time.
6. Remove from the crisper tray to a platter. Repeat with the remaining green beans.
7. Pour the prepared sauce over the top of green beans and toss well. Serve sprinkled with the toasted sesame seeds.

150. Asparagus, Pea, and Tortellini Primavera

Prep time: 10 minutes | Cook time: 16 minutes | Serves 4

½ pound (227 g) asparagus, trimmed and cut into 1-inch pieces
8 ounces (227 g) sugar snap peas, trimmed
1 tablespoon extra-virgin olive oil
2 teaspoons kosher salt or 1 teaspoon fine salt, divided
1½ cups water
1 (20-ounce / 567-g) package frozen cheese tortellini
1 cup heavy (whipping) cream
2 garlic cloves, minced
1 cup cherry tomatoes, halved
½ cup grated Parmesan cheese
¼ cup chopped fresh parsley or basil

1. Place the asparagus and peas in a large bowl. Add the olive oil and ½ teaspoon of kosher salt. Toss to coat. Place the vegetables in the baking pan.
2. Place the pan on the bake position. Select Bake, set temperature to 450ºF (232ºC), and set time to 4 minutes.
3. While the vegetables are cooking, dissolve 1 teaspoon of kosher salt in the water. When cooking is complete, remove the pan from the grill and place the tortellini into the pan with the vegetables. Pour the salted water over the tortellini. Return the pan to the grill.
4. Place the pan on the bake position. Select Bake, set temperature to 450ºF (232ºC), and set time to 7 minutes.
5. While the pasta cooks, place the heavy cream in a small bowl. Stir in the garlic and remaining ½ teaspoon of kosher salt.
6. When cooking is complete, remove the pan from the grill and blot off any remaining water with a paper towel. Gently stir the ingredients. Pour the cream over everything and scatter the tomatoes on top.
7. Place the pan on the roast position. Select Roast, set temperature to 375ºF (191ºC), and set time to 5 minutes.
8. After 4 minutes, remove the pan from the grill. The tortellini should be tender and the vegetables just barely crisp; if not, cook for 1 minute more.
9. Remove the pan from the grill. Stir in the Parmesan cheese until it's melted (you might find it easier to transfer the mixture to a bowl to do this). Top with the parsley, and serve.

151. Cheesy Macaroni Balls

Prep time: 10 minutes | Cook time: 10 minutes | Serves 2

2 cups leftover macaroni
1 cup shredded Cheddar cheese
½ cup flour
1 cup bread crumbs
3 large eggs
1 cup milk
½ teaspoon salt
¼ teaspoon black pepper

1. Place the crisper tray on the air fry position. Select Air Fry, set the temperature to 365ºF (185ºC), and set the time to 10 minutes.
2. In a bowl, combine the leftover macaroni and shredded cheese.
3. Pour the flour in a separate bowl. Put the bread crumbs in a third bowl. Finally, in a fourth bowl, mix the eggs and milk with a whisk.
4. With an ice-cream scoop, create balls from the macaroni mixture. Coat them the flour, then in the egg mixture, and lastly in the bread crumbs.
5. Arrange the balls in the crisper tray. Air fry for 10 minutes, giving them an occasional stir. Ensure they crisp up nicely.
6. Serve hot.

152. Simple Pesto Gnocchi

Prep time: 10 minutes | Cook time: 15 minutes | Serves 4

1 (1-pound / 454-g) package gnocchi
1 medium onion, chopped
3 cloves garlic, minced
1 tablespoon extra-virgin olive oil
1 (8-ounce / 227-g) jar pesto
1/3 cup grated Parmesan cheese

1. Place the crisper tray on the air fry position. Select Air Fry, set the temperature to 340ºF (171ºC), and set the time to 15 minutes.
2. In a large bowl combine the onion, garlic, and gnocchi, and drizzle with the olive oil. Mix thoroughly.
3. Transfer the mixture to the crisper tray. Air fry for 15 minutes, stirring occasionally, making sure the gnocchi become light brown and crispy.
4. Add the pesto and Parmesan cheese, and give everything a good stir before serving.

153. Cheesy Broccoli Gratin

Prep time: 5 minutes | Cook time: 12 to 14 minutes | Serves 2

1/3 cup fat-free milk
1 tablespoon all-purpose or gluten-free flour
½ tablespoon olive oil
½ teaspoon ground sage
¼ teaspoon kosher salt
⅛ teaspoon freshly ground black pepper
2 cups roughly chopped broccoli florets
6 tablespoons shredded Cheddar cheese
2 tablespoons panko bread crumbs
1 tablespoon grated Parmesan cheese
Olive oil spray

1. Place the baking pan on the bake position. Select Bake, set the temperature to 330ºF (166ºC), and set the time to 14 minutes.
2. Spritz the baking pan with olive oil spray.
3. Mix the milk, flour, olive oil, sage, salt, and pepper in a medium bowl and whisk to combine. Stir in the broccoli florets, Cheddar cheese, bread crumbs, and Parmesan cheese and toss to coat.
4. Pour the broccoli mixture into the prepared baking pan.
5. Bake for 12 to 14 minutes until the top is golden brown and the broccoli is tender.
6. Serve immediately.

154. Parmesan Asparagus Fries

Prep time: 15 minutes | Cook time: 5 to 7 minutes | Serves 4

2 egg whites
¼ cup water
¼ cup plus 2 tablespoons grated Parmesan cheese, divided
¾ cup panko bread crumbs
¼ teaspoon salt
12 ounces (340 g) fresh asparagus spears, woody ends trimmed
Cooking spray

1. Place the crisper tray on the air fry position. Select Air Fry, set the temperature to 390ºF (199ºC), and set the time to 7 minutes.
2. In a shallow dish, whisk together the egg whites and water until slightly foamy. In a separate shallow dish, thoroughly combine ¼ cup of Parmesan cheese, bread crumbs, and salt.
3. Dip the asparagus in the egg white, then roll in the cheese mixture to coat well.
4. Place the asparagus in the crisper tray in a single layer, leaving space between each spear. You may need to work in batches to avoid overcrowding.
5. Spritz the asparagus with cooking spray. Air fry for 5 to 7 minutes until golden brown and crisp.
6. Repeat with the remaining asparagus spears.
7. Sprinkle with the remaining 2 tablespoons of cheese and serve hot.

155. Stuffed Squash with Tomatoes and Poblano

Prep time: 5 minutes | Cook time: 30 minutes | Serves 4

1 pound (454 g) butternut squash, ends trimmed
2 teaspoons olive oil, divided
6 grape tomatoes, halved
1 poblano pepper, cut into strips
Salt and black pepper, to taste
¼ cup grated Mozzarella cheese

1. Place the crisper tray on the roast position. Select Roast, set the temperature to 350ºF (177ºC), and set the time to 30 minutes.
2. Using a large knife, cut the squash in half lengthwise on a flat work surface. This recipe just needs half of the squash. Scoop out the flesh to make room for the stuffing. Coat the squash half with 1 teaspoon of olive oil.
3. Put the squash half in the crisper tray. Roast for 15 minutes.
4. Meanwhile, thoroughly combine the tomatoes, poblano pepper, remaining 1 teaspoon of olive oil, salt, and pepper in a bowl.
5. Remove the crisper tray and spoon the tomato mixture into the squash. Return to the grill and roast for 12 minutes until the tomatoes are soft.
6. Scatter the Mozzarella cheese on top and continue roasting for about 3 minutes, or until the cheese is melted.
7. Cool for 5 minutes before serving.

156.Kidney Beans Oatmeal in Peppers

Prep time: 15 minutes | Cook time: 6 minutes | Serves 2 to 4

2 large bell peppers, halved lengthwise, deseeded
2 tablespoons cooked kidney beans
2 tablespoons cooked chick peas
2 cups cooked oatmeal

1 teaspoon ground cumin
½ teaspoon paprika
½ teaspoon salt or to taste
¼ teaspoon black pepper powder
¼ cup yogurt

1. Place the crisper tray on the air fry position. Select Air Fry, set the temperature to 355ºF (179ºC), and set the time to 6 minutes.
2. Put the bell peppers, cut-side down, in the crisper tray. Air fry for 2 minutes.
3. Take the peppers out of the grill and let cool.
4. In a bowl, combine the rest of the ingredients.
5. Divide the mixture evenly and use each portion to stuff a pepper.
6. Return the stuffed peppers to the crisper tray. Air fry for 4 minutes.
7. Serve hot.

157.Cheesy Rice and Olives Stuffed Peppers

Prep time: 5 minutes | Cook time: 16 to 17 minutes | Serves 4

4 red bell peppers, tops sliced off
2 cups cooked rice
1 cup crumbled feta cheese
1 onion, chopped
¼ cup sliced kalamata olives

¾ cup tomato sauce
1 tablespoon Greek seasoning
Salt and black pepper, to taste
2 tablespoons chopped fresh dill, for serving

1. Place the baking pan on the bake position. Select Bake, set the temperature to 360ºF (182ºC), and set the time to 15 minutes.
2. Microwave the red bell peppers for 1 to 2 minutes until tender.
3. When ready, transfer the red bell peppers to a plate to cool.
4. Mix together the cooked rice, feta cheese, onion, kalamata olives, tomato sauce, Greek seasoning, salt, and pepper in a medium bowl and stir until well combined.
5. Divide the rice mixture among the red bell peppers and transfer to the greased baking pan.
6. Bake for 15 minutes, or until the rice is heated through and the vegetables are soft.
7. Remove from the crisper tray and serve with the dill sprinkled on top.

158.Prosciutto Mini Mushroom Pizza

Prep time: 10 minutes | Cook time: 5 minutes | Serves 3

3 portobello mushroom caps, cleaned and scooped
3 tablespoons olive oil
Pinch of salt

Pinch of dried Italian seasonings
3 tablespoons tomato sauce
3 tablespoons shredded Mozzarella cheese
12 slices prosciutto

1. Place the crisper tray on the air fry position. Select Air Fry, set the temperature to 330ºF (166ºC), and set the time to 5 minutes.
2. Season both sides of the portobello mushrooms with a drizzle of olive oil, then sprinkle salt and the Italian seasonings on the insides.
3. With a knife, spread the tomato sauce evenly over the mushroom, before adding the Mozzarella on top.
4. Put the portobello in the crisper tray. Air fry for 1 minutes, before taking the crisper tray out of the grill and putting the prosciutto slices on top. air fry for another 4 minutes.
5. Serve warm.

159.Roasted Lemony Broccoli

Prep time: 5 minutes | Cook time: 15 minutes | Serves 6

2 heads broccoli, cut into florets
2 teaspoons extra-virgin olive oil, plus more for coating
1 teaspoon salt
½ teaspoon black pepper
1 clove garlic, minced
½ teaspoon lemon juice

1. Cover the crisper tray with aluminum foil and coat with a light brushing of oil.
2. Place the crisper tray on the roast position. Select Roast, set the temperature to 375ºF (191ºC), and set the time to 15 minutes.
3. In a bowl, combine all ingredients, save for the lemon juice, and transfer to the crisper tray. Roast for 15 minutes.
4. Serve with the lemon juice.

160.Vegetable and Cheese Stuffed Tomatoes

Prep time: 10 minutes | Cook time: 16 to 20 minutes | Serves 4

4 medium beefsteak tomatoes, rinsed
½ cup grated carrot
1 medium onion, chopped
1 garlic clove, minced
2 teaspoons olive oil
2 cups fresh baby spinach
¼ cup crumbled low-sodium feta cheese
½ teaspoon dried basil

1. Place the baking pan on the bake position. Select Bake, set the temperature to 350ºF (177ºC), and set the time to 20 minutes.
2. On your cutting board, cut a thin slice off the top of each tomato. Scoop out a ¼- to ½-inch-thick tomato pulp and place the tomatoes upside down on paper towels to drain. Set aside.
3. Stir together the carrot, onion, garlic, and olive oil in the baking pan. Bake for 4 to 6 minutes, or until the carrot is crisp-tender.
4. Remove the pan from the grill and stir in the spinach, feta cheese, and basil.
5. Spoon ¼ of the vegetable mixture into each tomato and transfer the stuffed tomatoes to the pan.
6. Bake for 12 to 14 minutes, or until the filling is hot and the tomatoes are lightly caramelized.
7. Let the tomatoes cool for 5 minutes and serve.

161.Beef Stuffed Bell Peppers

Prep time: 10 minutes | Cook time: 30 minutes | Serves 4

1 pound (454 g) ground beef
1 tablespoon taco seasoning mix
1 can diced tomatoes and green chilis
4 green bell peppers
1 cup shredded Monterey jack cheese, divided

1. Place the crisper tray on the air fry position. Select Air Fry, set the temperature to 350ºF (177ºC), and set the time to 15 minutes.
2. Set a skillet over a high heat and cook the ground beef for 8 minutes. Make sure it is cooked through and browned all over. Drain the fat.
3. Stir in the taco seasoning mix, and the diced tomatoes and green chilis. Allow the mixture to cook for a further 4 minutes.
4. In the meantime, slice the tops off the green peppers and remove the seeds and membranes.
5. When the meat mixture is fully cooked, spoon equal amounts of it into the peppers and top with the Monterey jack cheese. Then place the peppers into the crisper tray. Air fry for 15 minutes.
6. The peppers are ready when they are soft, and the cheese is bubbling and brown. Serve warm.

162.Cayenne Sesame Nut Mix

Prep time: 10 minutes | Cook time: 2 minutes | Makes 4 cups

1 tablespoon buttery spread, melted	¼ teaspoon freshly ground black pepper
2 teaspoons honey	1 cup cashews
¼ teaspoon cayenne pepper	1 cup almonds
2 teaspoons sesame seeds	1 cup mini pretzels
¼ teaspoon kosher salt	1 cup rice squares cereal
	Cooking spray

1. Place the baking pan on the bake position. Select Bake, set the temperature to 360ºF (182ºC), and set the time to 2 minutes.
2. In a large bowl, combine the buttery spread, honey, cayenne pepper, sesame seeds, kosher salt, and black pepper, then add the cashews, almonds, pretzels, and rice squares, tossing to coat.
3. Spray the baking pan with cooking spray, then pour the mixture into the pan. Bake for 2 minutes.
4. Remove the sesame mix from the grill and allow to cool in the pan on a wire rack for 5 minutes before serving.

163.Bacon-Wrapped Dates

Prep time: 10 minutes | Cook time: 10 to 14 minutes | Serves 6

12 dates, pitted	bacon, cut in half
6 slices high-quality	Cooking spray

1. Place the crisper tray on the bake position. Select Bake, set the temperature to 360ºF (182ºC), and set the time to 7 minutes.
2. Wrap each date with half a bacon slice and secure with a toothpick.
3. Spray the crisper tray with cooking spray, then place 6 bacon-wrapped dates in the crisper tray. Bake for 5 to 7 minutes or until the bacon is crispy. Repeat this process with the remaining dates.
4. Remove the dates and allow to cool on a wire rack for 5 minutes before serving.

164.Caramelized Peaches

Prep time: 10 minutes | Cook time: 10 to 13 minutes | Serves 4

2 tablespoons sugar	4 peaches, cut into wedges
¼ teaspoon ground cinnamon	Cooking spray

1. Lightly spray the crisper tray with cooking spray.
2. Place the crisper tray on the air fry position. Select Air Fry, set the temperature to 350ºF (177ºC), and set the time to 13 minutes.
3. Toss the peaches with the sugar and cinnamon in a medium bowl until evenly coated.
4. Arrange the peaches in the crisper tray in a single layer. Lightly mist the peaches with cooking spray. You may need to work in batches to avoid overcrowding.
5. Air fry for 5 minutes. Flip the peaches and air fry for another 5 to 8 minutes, or until the peaches are caramelized.
6. Repeat with the remaining peaches.
7. Let the peaches cool for 5 minutes and serve warm.

165.Garlicky and Lemony Artichokes

Prep time: 10 minutes | Cook time: 10 minutes | Serves 4

Juice of ½ lemon	Freshly ground black pepper, to taste
½ cup canola oil	2 large artichokes, trimmed and halved
3 garlic cloves, chopped	
Sea salt, to taste	

1. Place the grill plate on the grill position. Select Grill, set the temperature to 450ºF (232ºC), and set the time to 10 minutes.
2. In a medium bowl, combine the lemon juice, oil, and garlic. Season with salt and pepper, then brush the artichoke halves with the lemon-garlic mixture.
3. Place the artichokes on the grill plate, cut side down. Gently press them down to maximize grill marks. Grill for 8 to 10 minutes, occasionally basting generously with the lemon-garlic mixture throughout cooking, until blistered on all sides.

166.Crispy Prosciutto-Wrapped Asparagus

Prep time: 5 minutes | Cook time: 16 to 24 minutes | Serves 6

12 asparagus spears, woody ends trimmed 24 pieces thinly sliced

prosciutto
Cooking spray

1. Place the crisper tray on the air fry position. Select Air Fry, set the temperature to 360ºF (182ºC), and set the time to 4 minutes.
2. Wrap each asparagus spear with 2 slices of prosciutto, then repeat this process with the remaining asparagus and prosciutto.
3. Spray the crisper tray with cooking spray, then place 2 to 3 bundles in the crisper tray. Air fry for 4 minutes. Repeat this process with the remaining asparagus bundles.
4. Remove the bundles and allow to cool on a wire rack for 5 minutes before serving.

167.Cheesy Apple Roll-Ups

Prep time: 5 minutes | Cook time: 4 to 5 minutes | Makes 8 roll-ups

8 slices whole wheat sandwich bread
4 ounces (113 g) Colby Jack cheese, grated

½ small apple, chopped
2 tablespoons butter, melted

1. Place the crisper tray on the air fry position. Select Air Fry, set the temperature to 390ºF (199ºC), and set the time to 5 minutes.
2. Remove the crusts from the bread and flatten the slices with a rolling pin. Don't be gentle. Press hard so that bread will be very thin.
3. Top bread slices with cheese and chopped apple, dividing the ingredients evenly.
4. Roll up each slice tightly and secure each with one or two toothpicks.
5. Brush outside of rolls with melted butter.
6. Place in the crisper tray. Air fry for 4 to 5 minutes, or until outside is crisp and nicely browned.
7. Serve hot.

168.Grilled Carrots with Honey Glazed

Prep time: 10 minutes | Cook time: 10 minutes | Serves 4

6 medium carrots, peeled and cut lengthwise
1 tablespoon canola oil
2 tablespoons

unsalted butter, melted
¼ cup brown sugar, melted
¼ cup honey
⅛ teaspoon sea salt

1. Place the grill plate on the grill position. Select Grill, set the temperature to 450ºF (232ºC), and set the time to 10 minutes.
2. In a large bowl, toss the carrots and oil until well coated.
3. Place carrots on the center of the grill plate. Grill for 5 minutes.
4. Meanwhile, in a small bowl, whisk together the butter, brown sugar, honey, and salt.
5. After 5 minutes, baste the carrots with the glaze. Using tongs, turn the carrots and baste the other side. Grill for another 5 minutes.
6. When cooking is complete, serve immediately.

169.Rosemary Baked Cashews

Prep time: 5 minutes | Cook time: 3 minutes | Makes 2 cups

2 sprigs of fresh rosemary (1 chopped and 1 whole)
1 teaspoon olive oil
1 teaspoon kosher salt

½ teaspoon honey
2 cups roasted and unsalted whole cashews
Cooking spray

1. Place the crisper tray on the bake position. Select Bake, set the temperature to 300ºF (149ºC), and set the time to 3 minutes.
2. In a medium bowl, whisk together the chopped rosemary, olive oil, kosher salt, and honey. Set aside.
3. Spray the crisper tray with cooking spray, then place the cashews and the whole rosemary sprig in the crisper tray. Bake for 3 minutes.
4. Remove the cashews and rosemary from the grill, then discard the rosemary and add the cashews to the olive oil mixture, tossing to coat.
5. Allow to cool for 15 minutes before serving.

170.French Fries

Prep time: 15 minutes | Cook time: 25 minutes | Serves 4

1 pound (454 g) russet or Idaho potatoes, cut in 2-inch	strips 3 tablespoons canola oil

1. Place the potatoes in a large bowl and cover them with cold water. Let soak for 30 minutes. Drain well, then pat with a paper towel until very dry.
2. Place the crisper tray on the air fry position. Select Air Fry, set the temperature to 390ºF (199ºC), and set the time to 25 minutes.
3. Meanwhile, in a large bowl, toss the potatoes with the oil.
4. Add the potatoes to the crisper tray. Air fry for 10 minutes.
5. After 10 minutes, shake the crisper tray well. Place the crisper tray back in the grill to resume cooking.
6. After 10 minutes, check for desired crispness. Continue cooking up to 5 minutes more, if necessary.
7. When cooking is complete, serve immediately with your favorite dipping sauce.

171.Brussels Sprouts and Bacon

Prep time: 10 minutes | Cook time: 12 minutes | Serves 4

1 pound (454 g) Brussels sprouts, trimmed and halved 2 tablespoons extra-virgin olive oil	1 teaspoon sea salt ½ teaspoon freshly ground black pepper 6 slices bacon, chopped

1. Place the crisper tray on the air fry position. Select Air Fry, set the temperature to 390ºF (199ºC), and set the time to 12 minutes.
2. Meanwhile, in a large bowl, toss the Brussels sprouts with the olive oil, salt, pepper, and bacon.
3. Add the Brussels sprouts to the crisper tray. Air fry for 10 minutes.
4. After 6 minutes, shake the crisper tray of Brussels sprouts. Place the crisper tray back in the grill to resume cooking.
5. After 6 minutes, check for desired crispness. Continue cooking up to 2 more minutes, if necessary.

172.Breaded Green Olives

Prep time: 5 minutes | Cook time: 8 minutes | Serves 4

1 (5½-ounce / 156-g) jar pitted green olives ½ cup all-purpose flour Salt and pepper, to	taste ½ cup bread crumbs 1 egg Cooking spray

1. Place the crisper tray on the air fry position. Select Air Fry, set the temperature to 400ºF (204ºC), and set the time to 8 minutes.
2. Remove the olives from the jar and dry thoroughly with paper towels.
3. In a small bowl, combine the flour with salt and pepper to taste. Place the bread crumbs in another small bowl. In a third small bowl, beat the egg.
4. Spritz the crisper tray with cooking spray.
5. Dip the olives in the flour, then the egg, and then the bread crumbs.
6. Place the breaded olives in the crisper tray. It is okay to stack them. Spray the olives with cooking spray. Air fry for 6 minutes. Flip the olives and air fry for an additional 2 minutes, or until brown and crisp.
7. Cool before serving.

173.Balsamic Broccoli

Prep time: 10 minutes | Cook time: 10 minutes | Serves 4

4 tablespoons soy sauce 4 tablespoons balsamic vinegar 2 tablespoons canola oil 2 teaspoons maple	syrup 2 heads broccoli, trimmed into florets Red pepper flakes, for garnish Sesame seeds, for garnish

1. Place the grill plate on the grill position. Select Grill, set the temperature to 450ºF (232ºC), and set the time to 10 minutes.
2. In a large bowl, whisk together the soy sauce, balsamic vinegar, oil, and maple syrup. Add the broccoli and toss to coat evenly.
3. Place the broccoli on the grill plate. Grill for 8 to 10 minutes, until charred on all sides.
4. When cooking is complete, place the broccoli on a large serving platter. Garnish with red pepper flakes and sesame seeds. Serve immediately.

174. Crispy Cod Fingers

Prep time: 5 minutes | Cook time: 12 minutes | Serves 4

2 eggs	Salt and black pepper,
2 tablespoons milk	to taste
2 cups flour	1 cup bread crumbs
1 cup cornmeal	1 pound (454 g) cod
1 teaspoon seafood	fillets, cut into 1-inch
seasoning	strips

1. Place the crisper tray on the air fry position. Select Air Fry, set the temperature to 400ºF (204ºC), and set the time to 12 minutes.
2. Beat the eggs with the milk in a shallow bowl. In another shallow bowl, combine the flour, cornmeal, seafood seasoning, salt, and pepper. On a plate, place the bread crumbs.
3. Dredge the cod strips, one at a time, in the flour mixture, then in the egg mixture, finally in the bread crumb to coat evenly.
4. Arrange the cod strips in the crisper tray. Air fry for 12 minutes until crispy.
5. Transfer the cod strips to a paper towel-lined plate and serve warm.

175. Blistered Lemony Green Beans

Prep time: 5 minutes | Cook time: 10 minutes | Serves 4

1 pound (454 g)	Pinch red pepper
haricots verts or	flakes
green beans, trimmed	Flaky sea salt, to
2 tablespoons	taste
vegetable oil	Freshly ground black
Juice of 1 lemon	pepper, to taste

1. Place the grill plate on the grill position. Select Grill, set the temperature to 450ºF (232ºC), and set the time to 10 minutes.
2. In a medium bowl, toss the green beans in oil until evenly coated.
3. Place the green beans on the grill plate. Grill for 8 to 10 minutes, tossing frequently until blistered on all sides.
4. When cooking is complete, place the green beans on a large serving platter. Squeeze lemon juice over the green beans, top with red pepper flakes, and season with sea salt and black pepper.

176. Grilled Shishito Peppers

Prep time: 5 minutes | Cook time: 10 minutes | Serves 4

3 cups whole shishito	vegetable oil
peppers	Flaky sea salt, for
2 tablespoons	garnish

1. Place the grill plate on the grill position. Select Grill, set the temperature to 450ºF (232ºC), and set the time to 10 minutes.
2. In a medium bowl, toss the peppers in the oil until evenly coated.
3. Place the peppers on the grill plate. Gently press the peppers down to maximize grill marks. Grill for 8 to 10 minutes, until they are blistered on all sides.
4. When cooking is complete, place the peppers in a serving dish and top with the flaky sea salt. Serve immediately.

177. BLT with Grilled Heirloom Tomato

Prep time: 10 minutes | Cook time: 10 minutes | Serves 4

8 slices white bread	Sea salt, to taste
8 tablespoons	Freshly ground black
mayonnaise	pepper, to taste
2 heirloom tomatoes,	8 slices bacon, cooked
sliced ¼-inch thick	8 leaves iceberg
2 tablespoons canola	lettuce
oil	

1. Place the grill plate on the grill position. Select Grill, set the temperature to 450ºF (232ºC), and set the time to 10 minutes.
2. Spread a thin layer of mayonnaise on one side of each piece of bread.
3. Place the bread, mayonnaise-side down, on the grill plate. Grill for 2 to 3 minutes, until crisp.
4. Meanwhile, remove the watery pulp and seeds from the tomato slices. Brush both sides of the tomatoes with the oil and season with salt and pepper.
5. After 2 to 3 minutes, remove the bread and place the tomatoes on the grill. Continue grilling for the remaining 6 to 8 minutes.
6. To assemble, spread a thin layer of mayonnaise on the non-grilled sides of the bread. Layer the tomatoes, bacon, and lettuce on the bread, and top with the remaining slices of bread. Slice each sandwich in half and serve.

178.Roasted Mixed Nuts

Prep time: 5 minutes | Cook time: 20 minutes | Serves 6

2 cups mixed nuts (walnuts, pecans, and almonds)
2 tablespoons egg white
2 tablespoons sugar
1 teaspoon paprika
1 teaspoon ground cinnamon
Cooking spray

1. Spray the crisper tray with cooking spray.
2. Place the crisper tray on the roast position. Select Roast, set the temperature to 300ºF (149ºC), and set the time to 20 minutes.
3. Stir together the mixed nuts, egg white, sugar, paprika, and cinnamon in a small bowl until the nuts are fully coated.
4. Put the nuts in the crisper tray. Roast for 20 minutes. Shake the crisper tray halfway through the cooking time for even cooking.
5. Transfer the nuts to a bowl and serve warm.

179.Bruschetta with Tomato and Basil

Prep time: 5 minutes | Cook time: 6 minutes | Serves 6

4 tomatoes, diced
$^1/_3$ cup shredded fresh basil
¼ cup shredded Parmesan cheese
1 tablespoon balsamic vinegar
1 tablespoon minced garlic
1 teaspoon olive oil
1 teaspoon salt
1 teaspoon freshly ground black pepper
1 loaf French bread, cut into 1-inch-thick slices
Cooking spray

1. Place the crisper tray on the bake position. Select Bake, set the temperature to 250ºF (121ºC), and set the time to 3 minutes.
2. Mix together the tomatoes and basil in a medium bowl. Add the cheese, vinegar, garlic, olive oil, salt, and pepper and stir until well incorporated. Set aside.
3. Spritz the crisper tray with cooking spray. Working in batches, lay the bread slices in the crisper tray in a single layer. Spray the slices with cooking spray.
4. Bake for 3 minutes until golden brown.
5. Remove from the crisper tray to a plate. Repeat with the remaining bread slices.
6. Top each slice with a generous spoonful of the tomato mixture and serve.

180.Spicy Kale Chips

Prep time: 5 minutes | Cook time: 8 to 12 minutes | Serves 4

5 cups kale, large stems removed and chopped
2 teaspoons canola oil
¼ teaspoon smoked
paprika
¼ teaspoon kosher salt
Cooking spray

1. Place the crisper tray on the air fry position. Select Air Fry, set the temperature to 390ºF (199ºC), and set the time to 6 minutes.
2. In a large bowl, toss the kale, canola oil, smoked paprika, and kosher salt.
3. Spray the crisper tray with cooking spray, then place half the kale in the crisper tray. Air fry for 2 to 3 minutes.
4. Shake the crisper tray and air fry for 2 to 3 more minutes, or until crispy. Repeat this process with the remaining kale.
5. Remove the kale and allow to cool on a wire rack for 3 to 5 minutes before serving.

181.Cuban Sandwiches

Prep time: 20 minutes | Cook time: 8 minutes | Makes 4 sandwiches

8 slices ciabatta bread, about ¼-inch thick
Toppings:
6 to 8 ounces (170 to 227 g) thinly sliced leftover roast pork
4 ounces (113 g) thinly sliced deli turkey
Cooking spray
1 tablespoon brown mustard

$^1/_3$ cup bread and butter pickle slices
2 to 3 ounces (57 to 85 g) Pepper Jack cheese slices

1. Place the crisper tray on the air fry position. Select Air Fry, set the temperature to 390ºF (199ºC), and set the time to 8 minutes.
2. On a clean work surface, spray one side of each slice of bread with cooking spray. Spread the other side of each slice of bread evenly with brown mustard.
3. Top 4 of the bread slices with the roast pork, turkey, pickle slices, cheese, and finish with remaining bread slices. Transfer to the crisper tray.
4. Air fry for 8 minutes until golden brown.
5. Cool for 5 minutes and serve warm.

182. Turkey Bacon-Wrapped Dates

Prep time: 10 minutes | Cook time: 5 to 7 minutes | Makes 16 appetizers

16 whole dates, pitted
16 whole almonds
6 to 8 strips turkey bacon, cut in half

Special Equipment:
16 toothpicks, soaked in water for at least 30 minutes

1. Place the crisper tray on the air fry position. Select Air Fry, set the temperature to 390ºF (199ºC), and set the time to 7 minutes.
2. On a flat work surface, stuff each pitted date with a whole almond.
3. Wrap half slice of bacon around each date and secure it with a toothpick.
4. Place the bacon-wrapped dates in the crisper tray. Air fry for 5 to 7 minutes, or until the bacon is cooked to your desired crispiness.
5. Transfer the dates to a paper towel-lined plate to drain. Serve hot.

183. Zucchini and Potato Tots

Prep time: 5 minutes | Cook time: 20 minutes | Serves 4

1 large zucchini, grated
1 medium baked panato, skin removed and mashed
¼ cup shredded
Cheddar cheese
1 large egg, beaten
½ teaspoon kosher salt
Cooking spray

1. Place the baking pan on the air fry position. Select Air Fry, set the temperature to 390ºF (199ºC), and set the time to 10 minutes.
2. Wrap the grated zucchini in a paper towel and squeeze out any excess liquid, then combine the zucchini, baked panato, shredded Cheddar cheese, egg, and kosher salt in a large bowl.
3. Spray the baking pan with cooking spray, then place individual tablespoons of the zucchini mixture in the pan. Air fry for 10 minutes. Repeat this process with the remaining mixture.
4. Remove the tots and allow to cool on a wire rack for 5 minutes before serving.

184. Cajun Zucchini Chips

Prep time: 5 minutes | Cook time: 15 to 16 minutes | Serves 4

2 large zucchinis, cut into ⅛-inch-thick slices
2 teaspoons Cajun seasoning
Cooking spray

1. Spray the crisper tray lightly with cooking spray.
2. Place the crisper tray on the air fry position. Select Air Fry, set the temperature to 370ºF (188ºC), and set the time to 16 minutes.
3. Put the zucchini slices in a medium bowl and spray them generously with cooking spray.
4. Sprinkle the Cajun seasoning over the zucchini and stir to make sure they are evenly coated with oil and seasoning.
5. Place the slices in a single layer in the crisper tray, making sure not to overcrowd. You will need to cook these in several batches.
6. Air fry for 8 minutes. Flip the slices over and air fry for an additional 7 to 8 minutes, or until they are as crisp and brown as you prefer.
7. Serve immediately.

185. Deluxe Cheese Sandwiches

Prep time: 10 minutes | Cook time: 5 to 6 minutes | Serves 4 to 8

8 ounces (227 g) Brie
8 slices oat nut bread
1 large ripe pear, cored and cut into
½-inch-thick slices
2 tablespoons butter, melted

1. Place the baking pan on the bake position. Select Bake, set the temperature to 360ºF (182ºC), and set the time to 6 minutes. .
2. Make the sandwiches: Spread each of 4 slices of bread with ¼ of the Brie. Top the Brie with the pear slices and remaining 4 bread slices.
3. Brush the melted butter lightly on both sides of each sandwich.
4. Arrange the sandwiches in the baking pan. You may need to work in batches to avoid overcrowding.
5. Bake for 5 to 6 minutes until the cheese is melted. Repeat with the remaining sandwiches.
6. Serve warm.

186.Cheesy Summer Squash with Red Onion

Prep time: 15 minutes | Cook time: 15 minutes | Serves 4

½ cup vegetable oil, plus 3 tablespoons
¼ cup white wine vinegar
1 garlic clove, grated
2 summer squash, sliced lengthwise about ¼-inch thick
1 red onion, peeled
and cut into wedges
Sea salt, to taste
Freshly ground black pepper, to taste
1 (8-ounce / 227-g) package crumbled feta cheese
Red pepper flakes, as needed

1. Place the grill plate on the grill position. Select Grill, set the temperature to 450ºF (232ºC), and set the time to 15 minutes.
2. Meanwhile, in a small bowl, whisk together ½ cup oil, vinegar, and garlic, and set aside.
3. In a large bowl, toss the squash and onion with remaining 3 tablespoons of oil until evenly coated. Season with the salt and pepper.
4. Arrange the squash and onions on the grill plate. Grill for 6 minutes.
5. After 6 minutes, flip the squash. Grill for 6 to 9 minutes more.
6. When vegetables are cooked to desired doneness, remove them from the grill. Arrange the vegetables on a large platter and top with the feta cheese. Drizzle the dressing over the top, and sprinkle with the red pepper flakes. Let stand for 15 minutes before serving.

187.Dill Pickles

Prep time: 10 minutes | Cook time: 10 minutes | Serves 4

20 dill pickle slices
¼ cup all-purpose flour
⅛ teaspoon baking powder
3 tablespoons beer or seltzer water
⅛ teaspoon sea salt
2 tablespoons water, plus more if needed
2 tablespoons
cornstarch
1½ cups panko bread crumbs
1 teaspoon paprika
1 teaspoon garlic powder
¼ teaspoon cayenne pepper
2 tablespoons canola oil, divided

1. Pat the pickle slices dry, and place them on a dry plate in the freezer.

2. In a medium bowl, stir together the flour, baking powder, beer, salt, and water. The batter should be the consistency of cake batter. If it is too thick, add more water, 1 teaspoon at a time.
3. Place the cornstarch in a small shallow bowl.
4. In a separate large shallow bowl, combine the bread crumbs, paprika, garlic powder, and cayenne pepper.
5. Remove the pickles from the freezer. Dredge each one in cornstarch. Tap off any excess, then coat in the batter. Lastly, coat evenly with the bread crumb mixture.
6. Place the crisper tray on the air fry position. Select Air Fry, set the temperature to 360ºF (182ºC), and set the time to 10 minutes.
7. Place the breaded pickles in the crisper tray, stacking them if necessary, and gently brush them with 1 tablespoon of oil. Air fry for 5 minutes.
8. After 5 minutes, shake the crisper tray and gently brush the pickles with the remaining 1 tablespoon of oil. Place the crisper tray back in the grill to resume cooking.
9. When cooking is complete, serve immediately.

188.Homemade BBQ Chicken Pizza

Prep time: 5 minutes | Cook time: 8 minutes | Serves 1

1 piece naan bread
¼ cup Barbecue sauce
¼ cup shredded Monterrey Jack cheese
¼ cup shredded Mozzarella cheese
½ chicken herby sausage, sliced
2 tablespoons red onion, thinly sliced
Chopped cilantro or parsley, for garnish
Cooking spray

1. Place the crisper tray on the air fry position. Select Air Fry, set the temperature to 400ºF (204ºC), and set the time to 8 minutes.
2. Spritz the bottom of naan bread with cooking spray, then transfer to the crisper tray.
3. Brush with the Barbecue sauce. Top with the cheeses, sausage, and finish with the red onion.
4. Air fry for 8 minutes until the cheese is melted.
5. Garnish with the chopped cilantro or parsley before slicing to serve.

189.Crispy Spiced Potatoes

Prep time: 10 minutes | Cook time: 20 minutes | Serves 4

2 pounds (907 g) baby red potatoes, quartered
2 tablespoons extra-virgin olive oil
¼ cup dried onion flakes
1 teaspoon dried rosemary
½ teaspoon onion powder
½ teaspoon garlic powder
¼ teaspoon celery powder
¼ teaspoon freshly ground black pepper
½ teaspoon dried parsley
½ teaspoon sea salt

1. Place the crisper tray on the air fry position. Select Air Fry, set the temperature to 390ºF (199ºC), and set the time to 20 minutes.
2. Meanwhile, place all the ingredients in a large bowl and toss until evenly coated.
3. Add the potatoes to the crisper tray. Air fry for 10 minutes.
4. After 10 minutes, shake the crisper tray well. Place the crisper tray back in the grill to resume cooking.
5. After 10 minutes, check for desired crispness. Continue cooking up to 5 minutes more, if necessary.

190.Chile Rellenos Nachos

Prep time: 10 minutes | Cook time: 10 minutes | Serves 6

8 ounces (227 g) tortilla chips
3 cups shredded Monterey Jack cheese
2 (7-ounce / 198-g) cans chopped green chiles, drained
1 (8-ounce / 227-g) can tomato sauce
¼ teaspoon granulated garlic
¼ teaspoon dried oregano
¼ teaspoon freshly ground black pepper
Pinch cinnamon
Pinch cayenne pepper

1. Arrange the tortilla chips close together in a single layer in the baking pan. Sprinkle half of the cheese over the chips. Arrange the green chiles over the cheese as evenly as possible, then cover with the remaining cheese.
2. Place the pan on the roast position. Select Roast, set temperature to 375ºF (191ºC), and set time to 10 minutes.
3. After 5 minutes, rotate the pan 180 degrees and continue cooking.

4. While the nachos are cooking, stir together the tomato sauce, garlic, oregano, pepper, cinnamon, and cayenne in a small bowl.
5. When cooking is complete, the cheese will be melted and starting to crisp around the edges of the pan. Remove the pan from the grill. Drizzle a couple of tablespoons of the sauce over the nachos and serve the rest of the sauce for dipping (you can warm it up, if you like).

191.Buttermilk Marinated Chicken Wings

Prep time: 1 hour 20 minutes | Cook time: 17 to 19 minutes | Serves 4

2 pounds (907 g) chicken wings
Marinade:
1 cup buttermilk
½ teaspoon salt
½ teaspoon black pepper
Coating:
1 cup flour
1 cup panko bread crumbs
2 tablespoons poultry seasoning
2 teaspoons salt
Cooking spray

1. Whisk together all the ingredients for the marinade in a large bowl.
2. Add the chicken wings to the marinade and toss well. Transfer to the refrigerator to marinate for at least an hour.
3. Spritz the crisper tray with cooking spray.
4. Place the crisper tray on the air fry position. Select Air Fry, set the temperature to 360ºF (182ºC), and set the time to 19 minutes.
5. Thoroughly combine all the ingredients for the coating in a shallow bowl.
6. Remove the chicken wings from the marinade and shake off any excess. Roll them in the coating mixture.
7. Place the chicken wings in the crisper tray in a single layer. Mist the wings with cooking spray. You'll need to work in batches to avoid overcrowding.
8. Air fry for 17 to 19 minutes, or until the wings are crisp and golden brown on the outside. Flip the wings halfway through the cooking time.
9. Remove from the crisper tray to a plate and repeat with the remaining wings.
10. Serve hot.

192.Cheesy Crab Toasts

Prep time: 10 minutes | Cook time: 5 minutes | Makes 15 to 18 toasts

1 (6-ounce / 170-g) can flaked crab meat, well drained
3 tablespoons light mayonnaise
¼ cup shredded Parmesan cheese
¼ cup shredded Cheddar cheese

1 teaspoon Worcestershire sauce
½ teaspoon lemon juice
1 loaf artisan bread, French bread, or baguette, cut into ⅜-inch-thick slices

1. Place the crisper tray on the bake position. Select Bake, set the temperature to 360ºF (182ºC), and set the time to 5 minutes.
2. In a large bowl, stir together all the ingredients except the bread slices.
3. On a clean work surface, lay the bread slices. Spread ½ tablespoon of crab mixture onto each slice of bread.
4. Arrange the bread slices in the crisper tray in a single layer. You'll need to work in batches to avoid overcrowding.
5. Bake for 5 minutes until the tops are lightly browned.
6. Transfer to a plate and repeat with the remaining bread slices.
7. Serve warm.

193.Easy Muffuletta Sliders with Olives

Prep time: 10 minutes | Cook time: 5 to 7 minutes | Makes 8 sliders

¼ pound (113 g) thinly sliced deli ham
¼ pound (113 g) thinly sliced pastrami
4 ounces (113 g) low-fat Mozzarella cheese,
Olive Mix:
½ cup sliced green olives with pimentos
¼ cup sliced black olives
¼ cup chopped kalamata olives

grated
8 slider buns, split in half
Cooking spray
1 tablespoon sesame seeds

1 teaspoon red wine vinegar
¼ teaspoon basil
⅛ teaspoon garlic powder

1. Place the crisper tray on the bake position. Select Bake, set the temperature to 360ºF (182ºC), and set the time to 7 minutes.
2. Combine all the ingredients for the olive mix in a small bowl and stir well.

3. Stir together the ham, pastrami, and cheese in a medium bowl and divide the mixture into 8 equal portions.
4. Assemble the sliders: Top each bottom bun with 1 portion of meat and cheese, 2 tablespoons of olive mix, finished by the remaining buns. Lightly spritz the tops with cooking spray. Scatter the sesame seeds on top.
5. Working in batches, arrange the sliders in the crisper tray. Bake for 5 t0 7 minutes until the cheese melts.
6. Transfer to a large plate and repeat with the remaining sliders.
7. Serve immediately.

194.Cheese and Ham Stuffed Baby Bella

Prep time: 15 minutes | Cook time: 12 minutes | Serves 8

4 ounces (113 g) Mozzarella cheese, cut into pieces
½ cup diced ham
2 green onions, chopped
2 tablespoons bread crumbs
½ teaspoon garlic powder

¼ teaspoon ground oregano
¼ teaspoon ground black pepper
1 to 2 teaspoons olive oil
16 fresh Baby Bella mushrooms, stemmed removed

1. Process the cheese, ham, green onions, bread crumbs, garlic powder, oregano, and pepper in a food processor until finely chopped.
2. With the food processor running, slowly drizzle in 1 to 2 teaspoons olive oil until a thick paste has formed. Transfer the mixture to a bowl.
3. Evenly divide the mixture into the mushroom caps and lightly press down the mixture.
4. Place the crisper tray on the roast position. Select Roast, set the temperature to 390ºF (199ºC), and set the time to 12 minutes.
5. Lay the mushrooms in the crisper tray in a single layer. You'll need to work in batches to avoid overcrowding.
6. Roast for 12 minutes until the mushrooms are lightly browned and tender.
7. Remove from the crisper tray to a plate and repeat with the remaining mushrooms.
8. Let the mushrooms cool for 5 minutes and serve warm.

195. Breaded Artichoke Hearts

Prep time: 5 minutes | Cook time: 8 minutes | Serves 14

14 whole artichoke hearts, packed in water
1 egg
½ cup all-purpose flour
⅓ cup panko bread crumbs
1 teaspoon Italian seasoning
Cooking spray

1. Place the crisper tray on the air fry position. Select Air Fry, set the temperature to 380ºF (193ºC), and set the time to 8 minutes.
2. Squeeze excess water from the artichoke hearts and place them on paper towels to dry.
3. In a small bowl, beat the egg. In another small bowl, place the flour. In a third small bowl, combine the bread crumbs and Italian seasoning, and stir.
4. Spritz the crisper tray with cooking spray.
5. Dip the artichoke hearts in the flour, then the egg, and then the bread crumb mixture.
6. Place the breaded artichoke hearts in the crisper tray. Spray them with cooking spray.
7. Air fry for 8 minutes, or until the artichoke hearts have browned and are crisp, flipping once halfway through.
8. Let cool for 5 minutes before serving.

196. Mushroom and Spinach Calzones

Prep time: 15 minutes | Cook time: 26 to 27 minutes | Serves 4

2 tablespoons olive oil
1 onion, chopped
2 garlic cloves, minced
¼ cup chopped mushrooms
1 pound (454 g) spinach, chopped
1 tablespoon Italian seasoning
½ teaspoon oregano
Salt and black pepper, to taste
1½ cups marinara sauce
1 cup ricotta cheese, crumbled
1 (13-ounce / 369-g) pizza crust
Cooking spray

Make the Filling:
1. Heat the olive oil in a pan over medium heat until shimmering.
2. Add the onion, garlic, and mushrooms and sauté for 4 minutes, or until softened.
3. Stir in the spinach and sauté for 2 to 3 minutes, or until the spinach is wilted. Sprinkle with the Italian seasoning, oregano, salt, and pepper and mix well.
4. Add the marinara sauce and cook for about 5 minutes, stirring occasionally, or until the sauce is thickened.
5. Remove the pan from the heat and stir in the ricotta cheese. Set aside.

Make the Calzones:
1. Spritz the crisper tray with cooking spray.
2. Place the crisper tray on the air fry position. Select Air Fry, set the temperature to 375ºF (191ºC), and set the time to 15 minutes.
3. Roll the pizza crust out with a rolling pin on a lightly floured work surface, then cut it into 4 rectangles.
4. Spoon ¼ of the filling into each rectangle and fold in half. Crimp the edges with a fork to seal. Mist them with cooking spray.
5. Place the calzones in the crisper tray. Air fry for 15 minutes, flipping once, or until the calzones are golden brown and crisp.
6. Transfer the calzones to a paper towel-lined plate and serve.

197. Cheesy Steak Fries

Prep time: 5 minutes | Cook time: 20 minutes | Serves 5

1 (28-ounce / 794-g) bag frozen steak fries
Cooking spray
Salt and pepper, to taste
½ cup beef gravy
1 cup shredded Mozzarella cheese
2 scallions, green parts only, chopped

1. Place the crisper tray on the air fry position. Select Air Fry, set the temperature to 400ºF (204ºC), and set the time to 20 minutes.
2. Place the frozen steak fries in the crisper tray. Air fry for 10 minutes. Shake the crisper tray and spritz the fries with cooking spray. Sprinkle with salt and pepper. air fry for an additional 8 minutes.
3. Pour the beef gravy into a medium, microwave-safe bowl. Microwave for 30 seconds, or until the gravy is warm.
4. Sprinkle the fries with the cheese. Air fry for an additional 2 minutes, until the cheese is melted.
5. Transfer the fries to a serving dish. Drizzle the fries with gravy and sprinkle the scallions on top for a green garnish. Serve.

198. Herbed Pita Chips

Prep time: 5 minutes | Cook time: 5 to 6 minutes | Serves 4

¼ teaspoon dried basil	¼ teaspoon ground thyme
¼ teaspoon marjoram	¼ teaspoon salt
¼ teaspoon ground oregano	2 whole 6-inch pitas, whole grain or white
¼ teaspoon garlic powder	Cooking spray

1. Place the crisper tray on the bake position. Select Bake, set the temperature to 330ºF (166ºC), and set the time to 6 minutes.
2. Mix all the seasonings together.
3. Cut each pita half into 4 wedges. Break apart wedges at the fold.
4. Mist one side of pita wedges with oil. Sprinkle with half of seasoning mix.
5. Turn pita wedges over, mist the other side with oil, and sprinkle with remaining seasonings.
6. Place pita wedges in crisper tray. Bake for 2 minutes.
7. Shake the crisper tray and bake for 2 minutes longer. Shake again, and if needed, bake for 1 or 2 more minutes, or until crisp. Watch carefully because at this point they will cook very quickly.
8. Serve hot.

199. Sausage and Mushroom Empanadas

Prep time: 5 minutes | Cook time: 12 minutes | Serves 4

½ pound (227 g) Kielbasa smoked sausage, chopped	¼ teaspoon paprika
4 chopped canned mushrooms	Salt and black pepper, to taste
2 tablespoons chopped onion	½ package puff pastry dough, at room temperature
½ teaspoon ground cumin	1 egg, beaten
	Cooking spray

1. Spritz the crisper tray with cooking spray.
2. Place the crisper tray on the air fry position. Select Air Fry, set the temperature to 360ºF (182ºC), and set the time to 12 minutes.
3. Combine the sausage, mushrooms, onion, cumin, paprika, salt, and pepper in a bowl and stir to mix well.
4. Make the empanadas: Place the puff pastry dough on a lightly floured surface. Cut circles into the dough with a glass. Place 1 tablespoon of the sausage mixture into the center of each pastry circle. Fold each in half and pinch the edges to seal. Using a fork, crimp the edges. Brush them with the beaten egg and mist with cooking spray.
5. Place the empanadas in the crisper tray. Air fry for 12 minutes until golden brown. Flip the empanadas halfway through the cooking time.
6. Allow them to cool for 5 minutes and serve hot.

200. Sweet-and-Spicy Walnuts

Prep time: 5 minutes | Cook time: 15 minutes | Makes 4 cups

1 pound (454 g) walnut halves and pieces	pepper, or to taste
½ cup granulated sugar	3 tablespoons vegetable oil or walnut oil
1 teaspoon cayenne	½ teaspoon fine salt, or to taste

1. Place the nuts in a large bowl and cover with boiling water. Let them steep for a minute or two.
2. While the nuts are steeping, mix the sugar and cayenne together in a small bowl (1 teaspoon of cayenne produces nuts that are spicy but not too hot; use more or less to your taste).
3. Drain the nuts and return them to the bowl. Add the sugar mixture and oil. Stir until the sugar melts and the nuts are coated evenly. Spread the nuts in a single layer in the baking pan.
4. Place the pan on the roast position. Select Roast, set temperature to 325ºF (163ºC), and set time to 15 minutes.
5. After 7 or 8 minutes, remove the pan from the grill. Stir the nuts; they should be browning and fragrant. Return the pan to the grill and continue cooking, but check the nuts frequently. They can go from brown to burned pretty quickly.
6. When cooking is complete, the nuts should be dark golden brown. Remove the pan from the grill. Sprinkle the nuts with the salt and let cool. They can be frozen in an airtight container for up to 1 month.

201.Pears in Prosciutto

Prep time: 12 minutes | Cook time: 6 minutes | Serves 8

2 large ripe Anjou pears	ounces / 57 g)
4 thin slices Parma prosciutto (about 2	2 teaspoons aged balsamic vinegar

1. Peel the pears. Slice into 6 or 8 wedges (depending on the size of the pears) and cut out the core from each wedge.
2. Cut the prosciutto into long strips (one strip per pear wedge). Wrap each pear wedge with a strip of prosciutto. Place the wrapped pears in the baking pan.
3. Place the pan on the broil position. Select Broil, set temperature to 450ºF (232ºC), and set time to 6 minutes.
4. After 2 or 3 minutes, check the pears. The pears should be turned over if the prosciutto is beginning to crisp up and brown. Return the pan to the grill and continue cooking.
5. When cooking is complete, remove the pan from the grill. Serve the pears warm or at room temperature with a drizzle of the balsamic vinegar.

202.Oyster Cracker and Cereal Snack Mix

Prep time: 10 minutes | Cook time: 6 minutes | Makes 6 cups

2 cups oyster crackers	melted
2 cups Chex-style cereal (rice, corn, or wheat, or a combination)	²/₃ cup finely grated Parmesan cheese
1 cup sesame sticks	1½ teaspoon granulated garlic
8 tablespoons unsalted butter,	½ teaspoon kosher salt or ¼ teaspoon fine salt

1. Place the oyster crackers in a large bowl. Add the cereal and sesame sticks. Drizzle with the butter and sprinkle on the cheese, garlic, and salt. Toss to coat. Place the mix in the baking pan in an even layer.
2. Place the pan on the roast position. Select Roast, set temperature to 350ºF (177ºC), and set time to 6 minutes.
3. About halfway through cooking, remove the pan and stir the mixture. Return the pan to the grill and continue cooking.

4. When cooking is complete, the mix should be lightly browned and fragrant. Let cool. The mixture can be stored at room temperature in an airtight container for 3 to 4 days.

203.Mini Tuna Melts

Prep time: 12 minutes | Cook time: 6 minutes | Serves 6

2 (5- to 6-ounce / 142- to 170-g) cans oil-packed tuna, drained	¼ teaspoon celery salt (optional)
1 small stalk celery, chopped	1 tablespoon chopped fresh dill (optional)
1 large scallion, chopped	12 slices cocktail rye bread
¹/₃ cup mayonnaise, or more to taste	2 tablespoons butter, melted
1 tablespoon capers, drained	6 slices sharp Cheddar or Swiss-style cheese (about 3 ounces / 85 g)

1. In a medium bowl, mix together the tuna, celery, scallion, mayonnaise, capers, celery salt, and dill (if using).
2. Brush one side of the bread slices with the butter. Arrange the bread slices in the baking pan, buttered-sides down. Scoop a heaping tablespoon of the tuna mixture on each slice of bread, spreading it out evenly to the edges.
3. Cut the cheese slices to fit the dimensions of the bread and place a cheese slice on each piece.
4. Place the pan on the roast position. Select Roast, set temperature to 375ºF (191ºC), and set time to 6 minutes.
5. After 4 minutes, remove the pan from the grill and check the tuna melts. They usually take at least 5 minutes, but depending on the cheese you're using and the temperature of the tuna salad, it can take anywhere from 4 to 6 minutes. The tuna melts are done when the cheese has melted and the tuna is heated through. If needed, continue cooking.
6. When cooking is complete, remove the pan from the grill. Use a spatula to transfer the tuna melts to a cutting board and slice each one in half diagonally (this will make them easier to eat). Serve warm.

204. Baked Mini Potatoes

Prep time: 15 minutes | Cook time: 20 minutes | Serves 6

12 small red or yellow potatoes, about 2 inches in diameter, depending on size
1 teaspoon kosher salt or ½ teaspoon fine salt, divided
1 tablespoon extra-

virgin olive oil
¼ cup grated sharp Cheddar cheese
¼ cup sour cream
2 tablespoons chopped chives
2 tablespoons grated Parmesan cheese

1. Place the potatoes in a large bowl. Sprinkle with the kosher salt and drizzle with the olive oil. Toss to coat. Place the potatoes in the baking pan. Wipe out the bowl and set aside.
2. Place the pan on the roast position. Select Roast, set temperature to 375ºF (191ºC), and set time to 15 minutes.
3. After 10 minutes, rotate the pan 180 degrees and continue cooking.
4. When cooking is complete, check the potatoes. A sharp knife should pierce the flesh easily; if not, cook for a few more minutes. Remove the pan and let the potatoes cool until you can handle them. Halve the potatoes lengthwise. If needed, cut a small slice from the uncut side for stability. Using a small melon baller or spoon, scoop the flesh into the bowl, leaving a thin shell of skin. Place the potato halves in the baking pan.
5. Mash the scooped-out potatoes until smooth. Add the remaining ½ teaspoon of salt, Cheddar cheese, sour cream, and chives and mix until well combined. Taste and adjust the salt, if needed. Spoon the filling into a pastry bag or heavy plastic bag with one corner snipped off. Pipe the filling into the potato shells, mounding up slightly. Sprinkle with the Parmesan cheese.
6. Place the pan on the roast position. Select Roast, set temperature to 375ºF (191ºC), and set time to 5 minutes.
7. When cooking is complete, the tops should be browning slightly. If necessary, cook for a couple of minutes longer. Remove the pan from the grill and let the potatoes cool slightly before serving.

205. Super Cheesy Pimento Stuffed Mushrooms

Prep time: 15 minutes | Cook time: 12 minutes | Serves 12

24 medium raw white button or cremini mushrooms (about 1½ inches in diameter)
4 ounces (113 g) shredded extra-sharp Cheddar cheese
2 tablespoons grated onion
1 ounce (28 g) chopped jarred pimientos or roasted red pepper (about ¼

cup)
⅛ teaspoon smoked paprika
⅛ teaspoon hot sauce
2 ounces (57 g) cream cheese, at room temperature
2 tablespoons butter, melted, divided
2 tablespoons grated Parmesan cheese
⅓ cup panko bread crumbs

1. Wash the mushrooms and drain. Gently pull out the stems and discard (or save for another use; they make great vegetable stock). If your mushrooms are on the small side, or you feel like some extra work, you can use a small spoon or melon baller to remove some of the gills to form a larger cavity. Set aside.
2. In a medium bowl, combine the Cheddar cheese, onion, pimientos, paprika, hot sauce, and cream cheese. The mixture should be smooth with no large streaks of cream cheese visible.
3. Brush the baking pan with 1 tablespoon of melted butter. Arrange the mushrooms evenly over the pan, hollow-side up.
4. Place the cheese mixture into a large heavy plastic bag and cut off the end. Fill the mushrooms with the cheese mixture.
5. In a small bowl, stir together the Parmesan, panko, and remaining 1 tablespoon of melted butter. Sprinkle a little of the panko mixture over each mushroom (or carefully dip the filled tops of the mushrooms into the mixture to coat).
6. Place the pan on the roast position. Select Roast, set temperature to 350ºF (177ºC), and set time to 18 minutes.
7. After about 9 minutes, rotate the pan 180 degrees and continue cooking.
8. When cooking is complete, let the stuffed mushrooms cool slightly before serving.

206. Sausage Rolls

Prep time: 15 minutes | Cook time: 15 minutes | Serves 12

1 pound (454 g) bulk breakfast sausage	½ teaspoon dried mustard
½ cup finely chopped onion (about ½ medium onion)	1 large egg, beaten lightly
1 garlic clove, minced or pressed	½ cup fresh bread crumbs
½ teaspoon dried sage (optional)	2 sheets (1 package) frozen puff pastry, thawed
¼ teaspoon cayenne pepper	All-purpose flour, for dusting

1. In a medium bowl, break up the sausage. Add the onion, garlic, sage (if using), cayenne, mustard, egg, and bread crumbs. Mix to combine. Divide the sausage mixture in half and tightly wrap each half in plastic wrap. Refrigerate for 5 to 10 minutes.
2. Lay out one of the pastry sheets on a lightly floured cutting board. Using a rolling pin, lightly roll out the pastry to smooth out the dough. Take out one of the sausage packages and form the sausage into a long roll (it's easiest to do this while the sausage is in the plastic wrap). Remove the plastic wrap and place the sausage on top of the puff pastry about 1 inch from one of the long edges. Roll the pastry around the sausage and pinch the edges of the dough together to seal. Repeat with the other pastry sheet and sausage. Slice the logs into lengths about 1½ inches long. (If you have the time, freeze the logs for 10 minutes or so before slicing; it's much easier to slice.) Place the sausage rolls in the baking pan, cut-side down.
3. Place the pan on the roast position. Select Roast, set temperature to 350ºF (177ºC), and set time to 15 minutes.
4. After 7 or 8 minutes, rotate the pan 180 degrees and continue cooking.
5. When cooking is complete, the rolls will be golden brown and sizzling. Remove the pan from the grill and let cool for 5 minutes or so. If you like, serve them with honey mustard for dipping.

207. Cheesy Pepperoni Pizza Bites

Prep time: 12 minutes | Cook time: 16 minutes | Serves 8

½ cup (2 ounces / 57 g) pepperoni, finely chopped	variety
	1 (8-ounce / 227-g) can crescent roll dough
1 cup finely shredded Mozzarella cheese	All-purpose flour, for dusting
¼ cup Marinara Sauce or store-bought	

1. In a small bowl, toss together the pepperoni and cheese. Stir in the marinara sauce. (If you have one, this is a good time to use a food processor. Then you don't have to chop everything so fine; just dump everything in and pulse a few times to mix.)
2. Unroll the dough onto a lightly floured cutting board. Separate it into 4 rectangles. Firmly pinch the perforations together and pat or roll the dough pieces flat.
3. Divide the cheese mixture evenly between the rectangles and spread it out over the dough, leaving a ¼-inch border. Roll a rectangle up tightly, starting with the short end. Pinch the edge down to seal the roll. Repeat with the remaining rolls. If you have time, refrigerate or freeze the rolls for 5 to 10 minutes to firm up. This makes slicing easier.
4. Slice the rolls into 4 or 5 even slices. Place the slices in the baking pan, leaving a few inches between each.
5. Place the pan on the roast position. Select Roast, set temperature to 350ºF (177ºC), and set time to 12 minutes.
6. After 6 minutes, rotate the pan 180 degrees and continue cooking.
7. When cooking is complete, the rolls will be golden brown with crisp edges. Remove the pan from the grill. If you like, serve with additional marinara sauce for dipping.

208.Lemon-Pepper Chicken Wings

Prep time: 5 minutes | Cook time: 24 minutes | Serves 10

2 pounds (907 g) chicken wing flats and drumettes (about 16 to 20 pieces)
1½ teaspoons kosher salt or ¾ teaspoon fine salt

1½ teaspoons baking powder
4½ teaspoons salt-free lemon pepper seasoning

1. Place the wings in a large bowl.
2. In a small bowl, stir together the salt, baking powder, and seasoning mix. Sprinkle the mixture over the wings and toss thoroughly to coat the wings. (This works best with your hands.) If you have time, let the wings sit for 20 to 30 minutes. Place the wings in the baking pan, making sure they don't crowd each other too much.
3. Place the pan on the air fry position. Select Air Fry, set temperature to 375ºF (191ºC), and set time to 24 minutes.
4. After 12 minutes, remove the pan from the grill. Using tongs, turn the wings over. Rotate the pan 180 degrees and return the pan to the grill to continue cooking.
5. When cooking is complete, the wings should be dark golden brown and a bit charred in places. Remove the pan from the grill and let cool for before serving.

209.Jalapeño Poppers

Prep time: 10 minutes | Cook time: 15 minutes | Serves 8

12 large jalapeño peppers (about 3 inches long)
6 ounces (170 g) cream cheese, at room temperature
1 teaspoon chili powder

4 ounces (113 g) shredded Cheddar cheese
2 slices cooked bacon, chopped fine
¼ cup panko bread crumbs
1 tablespoon butter, melted

1. If the jalapeños have stems, cut them off flush with the tops of the chiles. Slice the jalapeños in half lengthwise and scoop out the seeds. For milder poppers, remove the white membranes (the ribs). (You should probably wear latex gloves when you do this, to avoid possible burns. I often forget, and I often regret it.)
2. In a medium bowl, mix the cream cheese, chili powder, and Cheddar cheese. Spoon the cheese mixture into the jalapeño halves and place them in the baking pan. If the jalapeños roll or tip, use a vegetable peeler to scrape away a thin layer of skin on the base so they're more stable.
3. In a small bowl, stir together the bacon, panko, and butter. Top each of the jalapeño halves with the panko mixture.
4. Place the pan on the roast position. Select Roast, set temperature to 375ºF (191ºC), and set time to 15 minutes.
5. After 7 or 8 minutes, rotate the pan 180 degrees and continue cooking until the peppers have softened somewhat, the filling is bubbling, and the panko is browned.
6. When cooking is complete, remove the pan from the grill. Let the poppers cool for a few minutes before serving.

Chapter 6 Poultry

210. Simple Whole Chicken Bake

Prep time: 10 minutes | Cook time: 1 hour | Serves 2 to 4

½ cup melted butter
3 tablespoons garlic, minced
Salt, to taste
1 teaspoon ground black pepper
1 (1-pound / 454-g) whole chicken

1. Place the baking pan on the bake position. Select Bake, set the temperature to 350ºF (177ºC), and set the time to 1 hour.
2. Combine the butter with garlic, salt, and ground black pepper in a small bowl.
3. Brush the butter mixture over the whole chicken, then place the chicken in the baking pan, skin side down.
4. Bake for 1 hour, or until an instant-read thermometer inserted in the thickest part of the chicken registers at least 165ºF (74ºC). Flip the chicken halfway through.
5. Remove the chicken from the grill and allow to cool for 15 minutes before serving.

211. Roasted Cajun Turkey

Prep time: 10 minutes | Cook time: 30 minutes | Serves 4

2 pounds (907 g) turkey thighs, skinless and boneless
1 red onion, sliced
2 bell peppers, sliced
1 habanero pepper, minced
1 carrot, sliced
1 tablespoon Cajun seasoning mix
1 tablespoon fish sauce
2 cups chicken broth
Nonstick cooking spray

1. Place the baking pan on the roast position. Select Roast, set the temperature to 360ºF (182ºC), and set the time to 30 minutes.
2. Spritz the bottom and sides of the pan with nonstick cooking spray.
3. Arrange the turkey thighs in the pan. Add the onion, peppers, and carrot. Sprinkle with Cajun seasoning. Add the fish sauce and chicken broth.
4. Roast for 30 minutes until cooked through. Serve warm.

212. Orange and Honey Glazed Duck with Apples

Prep time: 5 minutes | Cook time: 15 minutes | Serves 2 to 3

1 pound (454 g) duck breasts (2 to 3 breasts)
Kosher salt and pepper, to taste
Juice and zest of 1 orange
¼ cup honey
2 sprigs thyme, plus more for garnish
2 firm tart apples, such as Fuji

1. Place the crisper tray on the roast position. Select Roast, set the temperature to 400ºF (204ºC), and set the time to 13 minutes.
2. Pat the duck breasts dry and, using a sharp knife, make 3 to 4 shallow, diagonal slashes in the skin. Turn the breasts and score the skin on the diagonal in the opposite direction to create a cross-hatch pattern. Season well with salt and pepper.
3. Place the duck breasts skin-side up in the crisper tray. Roast for 8 minutes. Flip and roast for 4 more minutes on the second side.
4. While the duck is roasting, prepare the sauce. Combine the orange juice and zest, honey, and thyme in a small saucepan. Bring to a boil, stirring to dissolve the honey, then reduce the heat and simmer until thickened. Core the apples and cut into quarters. Cut each quarter into 3 or 4 slices depending on the size.
5. After the duck has cooked on both sides, turn it and brush the skin with the orange-honey glaze. Roast for 1 more minute. Remove the duck breasts to a cutting board and allow to rest.
6. Toss the apple slices with the remaining orange-honey sauce in a medium bowl. Arrange the apples in a single layer in the crisper tray. air fry for 10 minutes while the duck breast rests. Slice the duck breasts on the bias and divide them and the apples among 2 or 3 plates.
7. Serve warm, garnished with additional thyme.

213. Herbed Grilled Chicken Thighs

Prep time: 10 minutes | Cook time: 13 minutes | Serves 4

Grated zest of 2 lemons
Juice of 2 lemons
3 sprigs fresh rosemary, leaves finely chopped
3 sprigs fresh sage, leaves finely chopped
2 garlic cloves, minced
¼ teaspoon red pepper flakes
¼ cup canola oil
Sea salt
4 (4- to 7-ounce / 113- to 198-g) boneless chicken thighs

1. In a small bowl, whisk together the lemon zest and juice, rosemary, sage, garlic, red pepper flakes, and oil. Season with salt.
2. Place the chicken and lemon-herb mixture in a large resealable plastic bag or container. Toss to coat evenly. Refrigerate the chicken for at least 30 minutes.
3. Place the grill plate on the grill position. Select Grill, set the temperature to 400ºF (204ºC), and set the time to 13 minutes.
4. Place the chicken on the grill plate. Grill for 10 to 13 minutes.
5. Cooking is complete when the internal temperature of the chicken reaches at least 165ºF (74ºC) on a food thermometer.

214. Lime-Garlic Grilled Chicken

Prep time: 5 minutes | Cook time: 18 minutes | Serves 4

1½ tablespoons extra-virgin olive oil
3 garlic cloves, minced
¼ teaspoon ground cumin
Sea salt, to taste
Freshly ground black pepper, to taste
Grated zest of 1 lime
Juice of 1 lime
4 boneless, skinless chicken breasts

1. In a large shallow bowl, stir together the oil, garlic, cumin, salt, pepper, zest, and lime juice. Add the chicken breasts and coat well. Cover and marinate in the refrigerator for 30 minutes.
2. Place the grill plate on the grill position. Select Grill, set the temperature to 350ºF (177ºC), and set the time to 18 minutes.
3. Place the chicken breasts on the grill plate. Grill for 7 minutes. After 7 minutes, flip the chicken and grill for an additional 7 minutes.

4. Check the chicken for doneness. If needed, grill up to 4 minutes more. Cooking is complete when the internal temperature of the chicken reaches at least 165ºF (74ºC) on a food thermometer.
5. Remove from the grill, and place on a cutting board or platter to rest for 5inutes. Serve.

215. Bacon-Wrapped Turkey

Prep time: 10 minutes | Cook time: 25 minutes | Serves 4

2 (12-ounce / 340-g) turkey tenderloins
1 teaspoon kosher salt or ½ teaspoon fine salt, divided
6 slices bacon (not thick cut)
3 tablespoons balsamic vinegar
2 tablespoons honey
1 tablespoon Dijon mustard
½ teaspoon dried thyme
6 large carrots, peeled and cut into ¼-inch rounds
1 tablespoon extra-virgin olive oil

1. Sprinkle the turkey with ¾ teaspoon of the salt (if your tenderloins are brined, omit this step). Wrap each tenderloin with 3 strips of bacon, securing the bacon with toothpicks if necessary. Place the turkey in the baking pan.
2. In a small bowl, mix together the balsamic vinegar, honey, mustard, and thyme.
3. Place the carrots in a medium bowl and drizzle with the oil. Add 1 tablespoon of the balsamic mixture and ¼ teaspoon of kosher salt and toss to coat. Place these in the pan around the turkey tenderloins. Baste the tenderloins with about one-half of the remaining balsamic mixture.
4. Place the pan on the roast position. Select Roast, set temperature to 375ºF (191ºC), and set time to 25 minutes.
5. After 13 minutes, remove the pan from the grill. Gently stir the carrots. Turn over the tenderloins and baste them with the remaining balsamic mixture. Return the pan to the grill and continue cooking.
6. When cooking is complete, the carrots should be tender and the center of the tenderloins should register 155ºF (68ºC) on a meat thermometer (the temperature will continue to rise). Remove the pan from the grill. Slice the turkey and serve with the carrots.

216. Teriyaki Chicken and Bell Pepper Kebabs

Prep time: 15 minutes | Cook time: 14 minutes | Serves 4

1 pound (454 g) boneless, skinless chicken breasts, cut into 2-inch cubes	2 green bell peppers, seeded and cut into 1-inch cubes
1 cup teriyaki sauce, divided	2 cups fresh pineapple, cut into 1-inch cubes

1. Place the chicken and ½ cup of teriyaki sauce in a large resealable plastic bag or container. Toss to coat evenly. Refrigerate for at least 30 minutes.
2. Place the grill plate on the grill position. Select Grill, set the temperature to 350ºF (177ºC), and set the time to 14 minutes.
3. Assemble the kebabs by threading the chicken onto the wood skewers, alternating with the peppers and pineapple. Ensure the ingredients are pushed almost completely down to the end of the skewers.
4. Place the skewers on the grill plate. Grill for 10 to 14 minutes, occasionally basting the kebabs with the remaining ½ cup of teriyaki sauce while cooking.
5. Cooking is complete when the internal temperature of the chicken reaches 165ºF (74ºC) on a food thermometer.

217. Turkey Stuffed Bell Peppers

Prep time: 20 minutes | Cook time: 15 minutes | Serves 4

½ pound (227 g) lean ground turkey	1 cup mild salsa
4 medium bell peppers	1¼ teaspoons chili powder
1 (15-ounce / 425-g) can black beans, drained and rinsed	1 teaspoon salt
1 cup shredded reduced-fat Cheddar cheese	½ teaspoon ground cumin
1 cup cooked long-grain brown rice	½ teaspoon freshly ground black pepper
	Olive oil spray
	Chopped fresh cilantro, for garnish

1. Place the crisper tray on the air fry position. Select Air Fry, set the temperature to 360ºF (182ºC), and set the time to 15 minutes.
2. In a large skillet over medium-high heat, cook the turkey, breaking it up with a spoon, until browned, about 5 minutes. Drain off any excess fat.
3. Cut about ½ inch off the tops of the peppers and then cut in half lengthwise. Remove and discard the seeds and set the peppers aside.
4. In a large bowl, combine the browned turkey, black beans, Cheddar cheese, rice, salsa, chili powder, salt, cumin, and black pepper. Spoon the mixture into the bell peppers.
5. Lightly spray the crisper tray with olive oil spray.
6. Place the stuffed peppers in the crisper tray. Air fry for 10 to 15 minutes until heated through.
7. Garnish with cilantro and serve.

218. Maple-Teriyaki Chicken Wings

Prep time: 5 minutes | Cook time: 14 minutes | Serves 4

1 cup maple syrup	2 teaspoons onion powder
⅓ cup soy sauce	1 teaspoon freshly ground black pepper
¼ cup teriyaki sauce	2 pounds (907 g) bone-in chicken wings (drumettes and flats)
3 garlic cloves, minced	
2 teaspoons garlic powder	

1. Place the grill plate on the grill position. Select Grill, set the temperature to 350ºF (177ºC), and set the time to 14 minutes.
2. Meanwhile, in a large bowl, whisk together the maple syrup, soy sauce, teriyaki sauce, garlic, garlic powder, onion powder, and black pepper. Add the wings, and use tongs to toss and coat.
3. Place the chicken wings on the grill plate. Grill for 5 minutes. After 5 minutes, flip the wings and grill for an additional 5 minutes.
4. Check the wings for doneness. Cooking is complete when the internal temperature of the meat reaches at least 165ºF (74ºC) on a food thermometer. If needed, grill for up to 4 minutes more.
5. Remove from the grill and serve.

219. Sriracha-Honey Glazed Chicken Thighs

Prep time: 5 minutes | Cook time: 17 minutes | Serves 4

1 cup sriracha
Juice of 2 lemons
¼ cup honey

4 bone-in chicken thighs

1. Place the sriracha, lemon juice, and honey in a large resealable plastic bag or container. Add the chicken thighs and toss to coat evenly. Refrigerate for 30 minutes.
2. Place the grill plate on the grill position. Select Grill, set the temperature to 350ºF (177ºC), and set the time to 14 minutes.
3. Place the chicken thighs onto the grill plate, gently pressing them down to maximize grill marks. Grill for 7 minutes.
4. After 7 minutes, flip the chicken thighs using tongs. Grill for 7 minutes more.
5. Cooking is complete when the internal temperature of the meat reaches at least 165ºF (74ºC) on a food thermometer. If necessary, continue grilling for 2 to 3 minutes more.
6. When cooking is complete, remove the chicken from the grill, and let it rest for 5 minutes before serving.

220. Crispy Dill Pickle Chicken Wings

Prep time: 5 minutes | Cook time: 26 minutes | Serves 4

2 pounds (907 g) bone-in chicken wings (drumettes and flats)
1½ cups dill pickle juice
1½ tablespoons vegetable oil

½ tablespoon dried dill
¾ teaspoon garlic powder
Sea salt, to taste
Freshly ground black pepper, to taste

1. Place the chicken wings in a large shallow bowl. Pour the pickle juice over the top, ensuring all of the wings are coated and as submerged as possible. Cover and refrigerate for 2 hours.
2. Place the crisper tray on the air fry position. Select Air Fry, set the temperature to 390ºF (199ºC), and set the time to 26 minutes.
3. Rinse the brined chicken wings under cool water, then pat them dry with a paper towel. Place in a large bowl.

4. In a small bowl, whisk together the oil, dill, garlic powder, salt, and pepper. Drizzle over the wings and toss to fully coat them.
5. Place the wings in the crisper tray, spreading them out evenly. Air fry for 11 minutes.
6. After 11 minutes, flip the wings with tongs. Air fry for 11 minutes more.
7. Check the wings for doneness. Cooking is complete when the internal temperature of the chicken reaches at least 165ºF (74ºC) on a food thermometer. If neededAir fry for up to 4 more minutes.
8. Remove the wings from the crisper tray and serve immediately.

221. Lemony Chicken and Veggie Kebabs

Prep time: 15 minutes | Cook time: 14 minutes | Serves 4

2 tablespoons plain Greek yogurt
¼ cup extra-virgin olive oil
Juice of 4 lemons
Grated zest of 1 lemon
4 garlic cloves, minced
2 tablespoons dried

oregano
1 teaspoon sea salt
½ teaspoon freshly ground black pepper
1 pound (454 g) boneless, skinless chicken breasts, cut into 2-inch cubes
1 red onion, quartered
1 zucchini, sliced

1. In a large bowl, whisk together the Greek yogurt, oil, lemon juice, zest, garlic, oregano, salt, and pepper until well combined.
2. Place the chicken and half of the marinade into a large resealable plastic bag or container. Move the chicken around to coat evenly. Refrigerate for at least 30 minutes.
3. Place the grill plate on the grill position. Select Grill, set the temperature to 350ºF (177ºC), and set the time to 14 minutes.
4. Assemble the kebabs by threading the chicken on the wood skewers, alternating with the red onion and zucchini. Ensure the ingredients are pushed almost completely down to the end of the skewers.
5. Place the skewers on the grill plate. Grill for 10 to 14 minutes, occasionally basting the kebabs with the remaining marinade while cooking.
6. Cooking is complete when the internal temperature of the chicken reaches 165ºF (74ºC) on a food thermometer.

222. Crispy Chicken Strips

Prep time: 15 minutes | Cook time: 20 minutes | Serves 4

1 tablespoon olive oil
1 pound (454 g) boneless, skinless chicken tenderloins
1 teaspoon salt
½ teaspoon freshly ground black pepper
½ teaspoon paprika
½ teaspoon garlic powder
½ cup whole-wheat seasoned bread crumbs
1 teaspoon dried parsley
Cooking spray

1. Spray the crisper tray lightly with cooking spray.
2. Place the crisper tray on the air fry position. Select Air Fry, set the temperature to 370ºF (188ºC), and set the time to 20 minutes.
3. In a medium bowl, toss the chicken with the salt, pepper, paprika, and garlic powder until evenly coated.
4. Add the olive oil and toss to coat the chicken evenly.
5. In a separate, shallow bowl, mix together the bread crumbs and parsley.
6. Coat each piece of chicken evenly in the bread crumb mixture.
7. Place the chicken in the crisper tray in a single layer and spray it lightly with cooking spray. You may need to cook them in batches.
8. Air fry for 10 minutes. Flip the chicken over, lightly spray it with cooking spray, and air fry for an additional 8 to 10 minutes, until golden brown. Serve.

223. Lemon Parmesan Chicken

Prep time: 10 minutes | Cook time: 20 minutes | Serves 4

1 egg
2 tablespoons lemon juice
2 teaspoons minced garlic
½ teaspoon salt
½ teaspoon freshly ground black pepper
4 boneless, skinless chicken breasts, thin cut
Olive oil spray
½ cup whole-wheat bread crumbs
¼ cup grated Parmesan cheese

1. In a medium bowl, whisk together the egg, lemon juice, garlic, salt, and pepper. Add the chicken breasts, cover, and refrigerate for up to 1 hour.
2. In a shallow bowl, combine the bread crumbs and Parmesan cheese.
3. Spray the crisper tray lightly with olive oil spray.
4. Place the crisper tray on the air fry position. Select Air Fry, set the temperature to 360ºF (182ºC), and set the time to 20 minutes.
5. Remove the chicken breasts from the egg mixture, then dredge them in the bread crumb mixture, and place in the crisper tray in a single layer. Lightly spray the chicken breasts with olive oil spray. You may need to cook the chicken in batches.
6. Air fry for 8 minutes. Flip the chicken over, lightly spray with olive oil spray, and air fry for an additional 7 to 12 minutes, until the chicken reaches an internal temperature of 165ºF (74ºC).
7. Serve warm.

224. Sweet-and-Sour Drumsticks

Prep time: 5 minutes | Cook time: 23 to 25 minutes | Serves 4

6 chicken drumsticks
3 tablespoons lemon juice, divided
3 tablespoons low-sodium soy sauce, divided
1 tablespoon peanut oil
3 tablespoons honey
3 tablespoons brown sugar
2 tablespoons ketchup
¼ cup pineapple juice

1. Place the crisper tray on the bake position. Select Bake, set the temperature to 350ºF (177ºC), and set the time to 18 minutes.
2. Sprinkle the drumsticks with 1 tablespoon of lemon juice and 1 tablespoon of soy sauce. Place in the crisper tray and drizzle with the peanut oil. Toss to coat. Bake for 18 minutes, or until the chicken is almost done.
3. Meanwhile, in a metal bowl, combine the remaining 2 tablespoons of lemon juice, the remaining 2 tablespoons of soy sauce, honey, brown sugar, ketchup, and pineapple juice.
4. Add the cooked chicken to the bowl and stir to coat the chicken well with the sauce.
5. Place the metal bowl in the crisper tray. Bake for 5 to 7 minutes or until the chicken is glazed and registers 165ºF (74ºC) on a meat thermometer. Serve warm.

225. Spicy BBQ Chicken Drumsticks

Prep time: 10 minutes | Cook time: 20 minutes | Serves 4

2 cups barbecue sauce	Sea salt, to taste
Juice of 1 lime	Freshly ground black pepper, to taste
2 tablespoons honey	1 pound (454 g) chicken drumsticks
1 tablespoon hot sauce	

1. In a large bowl, combine the barbecue sauce, lime juice, honey, and hot sauce. Season with salt and pepper. Set aside ½ cup of the sauce. Add the drumsticks to the bowl, and toss until evenly coated.
2. Place the grill plate on the grill position. Select Grill, set the temperature to 350ºF (177ºC), and set the time to 20 minutes.
3. Place the drumsticks on the grill plate. Grill for 18 minutes, basting often during cooking.
4. Cooking is complete when the internal temperature of the meat reaches at least 165ºF (74ºC) on a food thermometer. If necessary, continue grilling for 2 minutes more.

226. Fried Chicken Piccata

Prep time: 5 minutes | Cook time: 22 minutes | Serves 2

2 large eggs	chicken breasts
½ cup all-purpose flour	4 tablespoons unsalted butter
½ teaspoon freshly ground black pepper	Juice of 1 lemon
2 boneless, skinless	1 tablespoon capers, drained

1. Place the crisper tray on the air fry position. Select Air Fry, set the temperature to 375ºF (191ºC), and set the time to 22 minutes.
2. Meanwhile, in a medium shallow bowl, whisk the eggs until they are fully beaten.
3. In a separate medium shallow bowl, combine the flour and black pepper, using a fork to distribute the pepper evenly throughout.
4. Dredge the chicken in the flour to coat it completely, then dip it into the egg, then back in the flour.
5. Place the chicken in the crisper tray. Air fry for 18 minutes.

6. While the chicken is cooking, melt the butter in a skillet over medium heat. Add the lemon juice and capers, and bring to a simmer. Reduce the heat to low, and simmer for 4 minutes.
7. After 18 minutes, check the chicken. Cooking is complete when the internal temperature of the meat reaches at least 165ºF (74ºC) on a food thermometer. If necessary, continue cooking for up to 3 minutes more.
8. Plate the chicken, and drizzle the butter sauce over each serving.

227. Ginger Chicken Thighs

Prep time: 10 minutes | Cook time: 10 minutes | Serves 4

¼ cup julienned peeled fresh ginger	¼ teaspoon kosher salt
2 tablespoons vegetable oil	½ teaspoon cayenne pepper
1 tablespoon honey	Vegetable oil spray
1 tablespoon soy sauce	1 pound (454 g) boneless, skinless chicken thighs, cut crosswise into thirds
1 tablespoon ketchup	
1 teaspoon garam masala	¼ cup chopped fresh cilantro, for garnish
1 teaspoon ground turmeric	

1. In a small bowl, combine the ginger, oil, honey, soy sauce, ketchup, garam masala, turmeric, salt, and cayenne. Whisk until well combined. Place the chicken in a resealable plastic bag and pour the marinade over. Seal the bag and massage to cover all of the chicken with the marinade. Marinate at room temperature for 30 minutes or in the refrigerator for up to 24 hours.
2. Place the crisper tray on the bake position. Select Bake, set the temperature to 350ºF (177ºC), and set the time to 10 minutes.
3. Spray the crisper tray with vegetable oil spray and add the chicken and as much of the marinade and julienned ginger as possible.
4. Bake for 10 minutes. Use a meat thermometer to ensure the chicken has reached an internal temperature of 165ºF (74ºC).
5. To serve, garnish with cilantro.

228. Spiced Breaded Chicken Cutlets

Prep time: 5 minutes | Cook time: 11 minutes | Serves 2

½ pound (227 g) boneless, skinless chicken breasts, horizontally sliced in half, into cutlets
½ tablespoon extra-virgin olive oil
⅛ cup bread crumbs
¼ teaspoon sea salt
¼ teaspoon freshly ground black pepper
¼ teaspoon paprika
¼ teaspoon garlic powder
⅛ teaspoon onion powder

1. Place the crisper tray on the air fry position. Select Air Fry, set the temperature to 375ºF (191ºC), and set the time to 11 minutes.
2. Brush each side of the chicken cutlets with the oil.
3. Combine the bread crumbs, salt, pepper, paprika, garlic powder, and onion powder in a medium shallow bowl. Dredge the chicken cutlets in the bread crumb mixture, turning several times, to ensure the chicken is fully coated.
4. Place the chicken in the crisper tray. Air fry for 9 minutes. Cooking is complete when the internal temperature of the meat reaches at least 165ºF (74ºC) on a food thermometer. If neededAir fry for up to 2 minutes more.
5. Remove the chicken cutlets and serve immediately.

229. Hearty Turkey Burger

Prep time: 5 minutes | Cook time: 13 minutes | Serves 4

1 pound (454 g) ground turkey
½ red onion, minced
1 jalapeño pepper, seeded, stemmed, and minced
3 tablespoons bread crumbs
1½ teaspoons ground cumin
1 teaspoon paprika
½ teaspoon cayenne
pepper
½ teaspoon sea salt
½ teaspoon freshly ground black pepper
4 burger buns, for serving
Lettuce, tomato, and cheese, if desired, for serving
Ketchup and mustard, if desired, for serving

1. Place the grill plate on the grill position. Select Grill, set the temperature to 400ºF (204ºC), and set the time to 13 minutes.

2. Meanwhile, in a large bowl, use your hands to combine the ground turkey, red onion, jalapeño pepper, bread crumbs, cumin, paprika, cayenne pepper, salt, and black pepper. Mix until just combined; be careful not to overwork the burger mixture.
3. Dampen your hands with cool water and form the turkey mixture into four patties.
4. Place the burgers on the grill plate. Grill for 11 minutes.
5. After 11 minutes, check the burgers for doneness. Cooking is complete when the internal temperature reaches at least 165ºF (74ºC) on a food thermometer. If necessary, continue grilling for up to 2 minutes more.
6. Once the burgers are done cooking, place each patty on a bun. Top with your preferred fixings, such as lettuce, tomato, cheese, ketchup, and/or mustard.

230. Turkey Hoisin Burgers

Prep time: 10 minutes | Cook time: 20 minutes | Serves 4

1 pound (454 g) lean ground turkey
¼ cup whole-wheat bread crumbs
¼ cup hoisin sauce
2 tablespoons soy sauce
4 whole-wheat buns
Olive oil spray

1. In a large bowl, mix together the turkey, bread crumbs, hoisin sauce, and soy sauce.
2. Form the mixture into 4 equal patties. Cover with plastic wrap and refrigerate the patties for 30 minutes.
3. Spray the crisper tray lightly with olive oil spray.
4. Place the crisper tray on the air fry position. Select Air Fry, set the temperature to 370ºF (188ºC), and set the time to 20 minutes.
5. Place the patties in the crisper tray in a single layer. Spray the patties lightly with olive oil spray.
6. Air fry for 10 minutes. Flip the patties over, lightly spray with olive oil spray, and air fry for an additional 5 to 10 minutes, until golden brown.
7. Place the patties on buns and top with your choice of low-calorie burger toppings like sliced tomatoes, onions, and cabbage slaw. Serve immediately.

231.Lettuce Chicken Tacos with Peanut Sauce

Prep time: 10 minutes | Cook time: 6 minutes | Serves 4

1 pound (454 g) ground chicken	¼ cup diced onions
2 cloves garlic, minced	¼ teaspoon sea salt
	Cooking spray

Peanut Sauce:

¼ cup creamy peanut butter, at room temperature	juice
2 tablespoons tamari	2 tablespoons grated fresh ginger
1½ teaspoons hot sauce	2 tablespoons chicken broth
2 tablespoons lime	2 teaspoons sugar

For Serving:

2 small heads butter lettuce, leaves separated
Lime slices (optional)

1. Place the baking pan on the bake position. Select Bake, set the temperature to 350ºF (177ºC), and set the time to 5 minutes.
2. Spritz the baking pan with cooking spray.
3. Combine the ground chicken, garlic, and onions in the baking pan, then sprinkle with salt. Use a fork to break the ground chicken and combine them well.
4. Bake for 5 minutes, or until the chicken is lightly browned. Stir them halfway through the cooking time.
5. Meanwhile, combine the ingredients for the sauce in a small bowl. Stir to mix well.
6. Pour the sauce in the pan of chicken, then cook for 1 more minute or until heated through.
7. Unfold the lettuce leaves on a large serving plate, then divide the chicken mixture on the lettuce leaves. Drizzle with lime juice and serve immediately.

232.Lime Chicken with Cilantro

Prep time: 35 minutes | Cook time: 20 minutes | Serves 4

4 (4-ounce / 113-g) boneless, skinless chicken breasts	Chicken seasoning or rub, to taste
½ cup chopped fresh cilantro	Salt and ground black pepper, to taste
Juice of 1 lime	Cooking spray

1. Put the chicken breasts in the large bowl, then add the cilantro, lime juice, chicken seasoning, salt, and black pepper. Toss to coat well.
2. Wrap the bowl in plastic and refrigerate to marinate for at least 30 minutes.
3. Spritz the crisper tray with cooking spray.
4. Place the crisper tray on the air fry position. Select Air Fry, set the temperature to 400ºF (204ºC), and set the time to 10 minutes.
5. Remove the marinated chicken breasts from the bowl and place in the grill. Spritz with cooking spray. You may need to work in batches to avoid overcrowding.
6. Air fry for 10 minutes or until the internal temperature of the chicken reaches at least 165ºF (74ºC). Flip the breasts halfway through.
7. Serve immediately.

233.China Spicy Turkey Thighs

Prep time: 10 minutes | Cook time: 25 minutes | Serves 6

2 pounds (907 g) turkey thighs	1 tablespoon Chinese rice vinegar
1 teaspoon Chinese five-spice powder	1 tablespoon mustard
¼ teaspoon Sichuan pepper	1 tablespoon chili sauce
1 teaspoon pink Himalayan salt	2 tablespoons soy sauce
	Cooking spray

1. Spritz the crisper tray with cooking spray.
2. Place the crisper tray on the air fry position. Select Air Fry, set the temperature to 360ºF (182ºC), and set the time to 22 minutes.
3. Rub the turkey thighs with five-spice powder, Sichuan pepper, and salt on a clean work surface.
4. Put the turkey thighs in the crisper tray and spritz with cooking spray. You may need to work in batches to avoid overcrowding.
5. Air fry for 22 minutes or until well browned. Flip the thighs at least three times during the cooking.
6. Meanwhile, heat the remaining ingredients in a saucepan over medium-high heat. Cook for 3 minutes or until the sauce is thickened and reduces to two thirds.
7. Transfer the thighs onto a plate and baste with sauce before serving.

234. Nutty Chicken Tenders

Prep time: 5 minutes | Cook time: 12 minutes | Serves 4

1 pound (454 g) chicken tenders	½ teaspoon smoked paprika
1 teaspoon kosher salt	¼ cup coarse mustard
1 teaspoon black pepper	2 tablespoons honey
	1 cup finely crushed pecans

1. Place the crisper tray on the bake position. Select Bake, set the temperature to 350ºF (177ºC), and set the time to 12 minutes.
2. Place the chicken in a large bowl. Sprinkle with the salt, pepper, and paprika. Toss until the chicken is coated with the spices. Add the mustard and honey and toss until the chicken is coated.
3. Place the pecans on a plate. Working with one piece of chicken at a time, roll the chicken in the pecans until both sides are coated. Lightly brush off any loose pecans. Place the chicken in the crisper tray.
4. Bake for 12 minutes, or until the chicken is cooked through and the pecans are golden brown.
5. Serve warm.

235. Chicken with Corn and Potatoes

Prep time: 10 minutes | Cook time: 25 minutes | Serves 4

4 bone-in, skin-on chicken thighs	small red potatoes, quartered
2 teaspoons kosher salt or 1 teaspoon fine salt, divided	3 ears corn, shucked and cut into rounds 1- to 1½-inches thick
1 cup Bisquick or similar baking mix	⅓ cup heavy (whipping) cream
½ cup unsalted butter, melted, divided	½ teaspoon freshly ground black pepper
1 pound (454 g)	

1. Sprinkle the chicken on all sides with 1 teaspoon of kosher salt. Place the baking mix in a shallow dish. Brush the thighs on all sides with ¼ cup of butter, then dredge them in the baking mix, coating them all on sides. Place the chicken in the center of the baking pan.
2. Place the potatoes in a large bowl with 2 tablespoons of butter and toss to coat. Place them on one side of the chicken in the pan.
3. Place the corn in a medium bowl and drizzle with the remaining 2 tablespoons of butter. Sprinkle with ¼ teaspoon of kosher salt and toss to coat. Place in the pan on the other side of the chicken.
4. Place the pan on the roast position. Select Roast, set temperature to 375ºF (191ºC), and set time to 25 minutes.
5. After 20 minutes, remove the pan from the grill and transfer the potatoes back to the bowl. Return the pan to grill and continue cooking.
6. As the chicken continues cooking, add the cream, black pepper, and remaining ¾ teaspoon of kosher salt to the potatoes. Lightly mash the potatoes with a potato masher or fork.
7. When cooking is complete, the corn will be tender and the chicken cooked through, reading 165ºF (74ºC) on a meat thermometer. Remove the pan from the grill and serve the chicken with the smashed potatoes and corn on the side.

236. Fried Buffalo Chicken Taquitos

Prep time: 15 minutes | Cook time: 5 to 10 minutes | Serves 6

8 ounces (227 g) fat-free cream cheese, softened	cooked chicken
⅛ cup Buffalo sauce	12 (7-inch) low-carb flour tortillas
2 cups shredded	Olive oil spray

1. Spray the crisper tray lightly with olive oil spray.
2. Place the crisper tray on the air fry position. Select Air Fry, set the temperature to 360ºF (182ºC), and set the time to 10 minutes.
3. In a large bowl, mix together the cream cheese and Buffalo sauce until well combined. Add the chicken and stir until combined.
4. Place the tortillas on a clean workspace. Spoon 2 to 3 tablespoons of the chicken mixture in a thin line down the center of each tortilla. Roll up the tortillas.
5. Place the tortillas in the crisper tray, seam-side down. Spray each tortilla lightly with olive oil spray. You may need to cook the taquitos in batches.
6. Air fry for 5 to 10 minutes until golden brown.
7. Serve hot.

237.Roasted Chicken Tenders with Veggies

Prep time: 10 minutes | Cook time: 18 to 20 minutes | Serves 4

1 pound (454 g) chicken tenders	bread crumbs
1 tablespoon honey	½ teaspoon dried thyme
Pinch salt	1 tablespoon olive oil
Freshly ground black pepper, to taste	2 carrots, sliced
½ cup soft fresh	12 small red potatoes

1. Place the crisper tray on the roast position. Select Roast, set the temperature to 380ºF (193ºC), and set the time to 20 minutes.
2. In a medium bowl, toss the chicken tenders with the honey, salt, and pepper.
3. In a shallow bowl, combine the bread crumbs, thyme, and olive oil, and mix.
4. Coat the tenders in the bread crumbs, pressing firmly onto the meat.
5. Place the carrots and potatoes in the crisper tray and top with the chicken tenders.
6. Roast for 18 to 20 minutes, or until the chicken is cooked to 165ºF (74ºC) and the vegetables are tender, shaking the crisper tray halfway during the cooking time.
7. Serve warm.

238.Dill Chicken Strips

Prep time: 15 minutes | Cook time: 10 minutes | Serves 4

2 whole boneless, skinless chicken breasts, halved lengthwise	1 tablespoon dried dill weed
1 cup Italian dressing	1 tablespoon garlic powder
3 cups finely crushed panato chips	1 large egg, beaten
	Cooking spray

1. In a large resealable bag, combine the chicken and Italian dressing. Seal the bag and refrigerate to marinate at least 1 hour.
2. In a shallow dish, stir together the panato chips, dill, and garlic powder. Place the beaten egg in a second shallow dish.
3. Remove the chicken from the marinade. Roll the chicken pieces in the egg and the panato chip mixture, coating thoroughly.
4. Place the baking pan on the bake position. Select Bake, set the temperature to 325ºF (163ºC), and set the time to 10 minutes.

5. Place the coated chicken in the baking pan and spritz with cooking spray.
6. Bake for 5 minutes. Flip the chicken, spritz it with cooking spray, and bake for 5 minutes more until the outsides are crispy and the insides are no longer pink. Serve immediately.

239.Gnocchi with Chicken and Spinach

Prep time: 10 minutes | Cook time: 13 minutes | Serves 4

1 (1-pound / 454-g) package shelf-stable gnocchi	1 cup heavy (whipping) cream
1¼ cups low-sodium chicken stock	2 tablespoons sun-dried tomato purée
½ teaspoon kosher salt or ¼ teaspoon fine salt	1 garlic clove, minced or smashed
1 pound (454 g) chicken breast, cut into 1-inch chunks	1 cup frozen spinach, thawed and drained
	1 cup grated Parmesan cheese

1. Place the gnocchi in an even layer in the baking pan. Pour the chicken stock over the gnocchi.
2. Place the pan on the bake position. Select Bake, set temperature to 450ºF (232ºC), and set time to 7 minutes.
3. While the gnocchi are cooking, sprinkle the salt over the chicken pieces. In a small bowl, mix together the cream, tomato purée, and garlic.
4. When cooking is complete, blot off any remaining stock, or drain the gnocchi and return it to the pan. Top the gnocchi with the spinach and chicken. Pour the cream mixture over the ingredients in the pan.
5. Place the pan on the roast position. Select Roast, set temperature to 400ºF (204ºC), and set time to 6 minutes.
6. After 4 minutes, remove the pan from the grill and gently stir the ingredients. Return the pan to the grill and continue cooking.
7. When cooking is complete, the gnocchi should be tender and the chicken should be cooked through. Remove the pan from the grill. Stir in the Parmesan cheese until it's melted, and serve.

240. Rosemary Turkey Breast

Prep time: 2 hours 20 minutes | Cook time: 30 minutes | Serves 6

½ teaspoon dried rosemary
2 minced garlic cloves
2 teaspoons salt
1 teaspoon ground black pepper
¼ cup olive oil
2½ pounds (1.1 kg)
turkey breast
¼ cup pure maple syrup
1 tablespoon stone-ground brown mustard
1 tablespoon melted vegan butter

1. Combine the rosemary, garlic, salt, ground black pepper, and olive oil in a large bowl. Stir to mix well.
2. Dunk the turkey breast in the mixture and wrap the bowl in plastic. Refrigerate for 2 hours to marinate.
3. Remove the bowl from the refrigerator and let sit for half an hour before cooking.
4. Spritz the crisper tray with cooking spray.
5. Place the crisper tray on the air fry position. Select Air Fry, set the temperature to 400ºF (204ºC), and set the time to 30 minutes.
6. Remove the turkey from the marinade and place in the crisper tray. Air fry for 20 minutes or until well browned. Flip the breast halfway through.
7. Meanwhile, combine the remaining ingredients in a small bowl. Stir to mix well.
8. Pour half of the butter mixture over the turkey breast in the crisper tray. Air fry for 10 more minutes. Flip the breast and pour the remaining half of butter mixture over halfway through.
9. Transfer the turkey on a plate and slice to serve.

241. Honey Rosemary Chicken

Prep time: 10 minutes | Cook time: 20 minutes | Serves 4

¼ cup balsamic vinegar
¼ cup honey
2 tablespoons olive oil
1 tablespoon dried rosemary leaves
1 teaspoon salt
½ teaspoon freshly
ground black pepper
2 whole boneless, skinless chicken breasts (about 1 pound / 454 g each), halved
Cooking spray

1. In a large resealable bag, combine the vinegar, honey, olive oil, rosemary, salt, and pepper. Add the chicken pieces, seal the bag, and refrigerate to marinate for at least 2 hours.
2. Place the crisper tray on the bake position. Select Bake, set the temperature to 325ºF (163ºC), and set the time to 20 minutes.
3. Line the crisper tray with parchment paper.
4. Remove the chicken from the marinade and place it on the parchment. Spritz with cooking spray.
5. Bake for 10 minutes. Flip the chicken, spritz it with cooking spray, and bake for 10 minutes more until the internal temperature reaches 165ºF (74ºC) and the chicken is no longer pink inside. Let sit for 5 minutes before serving.

242. Blackened Chicken Breasts

Prep time: 10 minutes | Cook time: 20 minutes | Serves 4

1 large egg, beaten
¾ cup Blackened seasoning
2 whole boneless, skinless chicken
breasts (about 1 pound / 454 g each), halved
Cooking spray

1. Line the crisper tray with parchment paper.
2. Place the crisper tray on the air fry position. Select Air Fry, set the temperature to 360ºF (182ºC), and set the time to 20 minutes.
3. Place the beaten egg in one shallow bowl and the Blackened seasoning in another shallow bowl.
4. One at a time, dip the chicken pieces in the beaten egg and the Blackened seasoning, coating thoroughly.
5. Place the chicken pieces on the parchment and spritz with cooking spray.
6. Air fry for 10 minutes. Flip the chicken, spritz it with cooking spray, and air fry for 10 minutes more until the internal temperature reaches 165ºF (74ºC) and the chicken is no longer pink inside.
7. Let sit for 5 minutes before serving.

243. Mayonnaise-Mustard Chicken

Prep time: 10 minutes | Cook time: 15 minutes | Serves 4

6 tablespoons mayonnaise
2 tablespoons coarse-ground mustard
2 teaspoons honey (optional)
2 teaspoons curry powder
1 teaspoon kosher salt
1 teaspoon cayenne pepper
1 pound (454 g) chicken tenders

1. Place the crisper tray on the bake position. Select Bake, set the temperature to 350ºF (177ºC), and set the time to 15 minutes.
2. In a large bowl, whisk together the mayonnaise, mustard, honey (if using), curry powder, salt, and cayenne. Transfer half of the mixture to a serving bowl to serve as a dipping sauce. Add the chicken tenders to the large bowl and toss until well coated.
3. Place the tenders in the crisper tray. Bake for 15 minutes. Use a meat thermometer to ensure the chicken has reached an internal temperature of 165ºF (74ºC).
4. Serve the chicken with the dipping sauce.

244. Sweet and Spicy Turkey Meatballs

Prep time: 15 minutes | Cook time: 15 minutes | Serves 6

1 pound (454 g) lean ground turkey
½ cup whole-wheat panko bread crumbs
1 egg, beaten
1 tablespoon soy sauce
¼ cup plus 1 tablespoon hoisin sauce, divided
2 teaspoons minced garlic
⅛ teaspoon salt
⅛ teaspoon freshly ground black pepper
1 teaspoon sriracha
Olive oil spray

1. Spray the crisper tray lightly with olive oil spray.
2. Place the crisper tray on the air fry position. Select Air Fry, set the temperature to 350ºF (177ºC), and set the time to 15 minutes.
3. In a large bowl, mix together the turkey, panko bread crumbs, egg, soy sauce, 1 tablespoon of hoisin sauce, garlic, salt, and black pepper.
4. Using a tablespoon, form the mixture into 24 meatballs.
5. In a small bowl, combine the remaining ¼ cup of hoisin sauce and sriracha to make a glaze and set aside.
6. Place the meatballs in the crisper tray in a single layer. You may need to cook them in batches.
7. Air fry for 8 minutes. Brush the meatballs generously with the glaze and air fry until cooked through, an additional 4 to 7 minutes.
8. Serve warm.

245. Chicken and Brussels Sprout Curry

Prep time: 10 minutes | Cook time: 20 minutes | Serves 4

1 pound (454 g) boneless, skinless chicken thighs
1 teaspoon kosher salt or ½ teaspoon fine salt, divided
¼ cup unsalted butter, melted
1 tablespoon curry powder
2 medium sweet potatoes, peeled and cut in 1-inch cubes
12 ounces (340 g) Brussels sprouts, halved

1. Salt the chicken thighs with ½ teaspoon of kosher salt. Place them in the center of the baking pan.
2. In a small bowl, stir together the butter and curry powder.
3. Place the sweet potatoes and Brussels sprouts in a large bowl. Drizzle half the curry butter over the vegetables and add the remaining ½ teaspoon of kosher salt. Toss to coat. Transfer the vegetables to the baking pan and arrange in a single layer around the chicken. Brush half of the remaining curry butter over the chicken.
4. Place the pan on the roast position. Select Roast, set temperature to 400ºF (204ºC), and set time to 20 minutes.
5. After 10 minutes, remove the pan from the grill and turn over the chicken thighs. Baste them with the remaining curry butter. Return the pan to the grill and continue cooking.
6. Cooking is complete when the sweet potatoes are tender and the chicken is cooked through and reads 165ºF (74ºC) on a meat thermometer.

246.Spiced Turkey Tenderloin

Prep time: 20 minutes | Cook time: 30 minutes | Serves 4

½ teaspoon paprika	Pinch cayenne pepper
½ teaspoon garlic powder	1½ pounds (680 g) turkey breast tenderloin
½ teaspoon salt	Olive oil spray
½ teaspoon freshly ground black pepper	

1. Spray the crisper tray lightly with olive oil spray.
2. Place the crisper tray on the air fry position. Select Air Fry, set the temperature to 370ºF (188ºC), and set the time to 30 minutes.
3. In a small bowl, combine the paprika, garlic powder, salt, black pepper, and cayenne pepper. Rub the mixture all over the turkey.
4. Place the turkey in the crisper tray and lightly spray with olive oil spray.
5. Air fry for 15 minutes. Flip the turkey over and lightly spray with olive oil spray. air fry until the internal temperature reaches at least 170ºF (77ºC) for an additional 10 to 15 minutes.
6. Let the turkey rest for 10 minutes before slicing and serving.

247.Potato Cheese Crusted Chicken

Prep time: 15 minutes | Cook time: 22 to 25 minutes | Serves 4

¼ cup buttermilk	ground black pepper
1 large egg, beaten	2 whole boneless, skinless chicken breasts (about 1 pound / 454 g each), halved
1 cup instant panato flakes	
¼ cup grated Parmesan cheese	
1 teaspoon salt	Cooking spray
½ teaspoon freshly	

1. Place the crisper tray on the bake position. Select Bake, set the temperature to 325ºF (163ºC), and set the time to 25 minutes.
2. Line the crisper tray with parchment paper.
3. In a shallow bowl, whisk the buttermilk and egg until blended. In another shallow bowl, stir together the panato flakes, cheese, salt, and pepper.
4. One at a time, dip the chicken pieces in the buttermilk mixture and the panato flake mixture, coating thoroughly.

5. Place the coated chicken on the parchment and spritz with cooking spray.
6. Bake for 15 minutes. Flip the chicken, spritz it with cooking spray, and bake for 7 to 10 minutes more until the outside is crispy and the inside is no longer pink. Serve immediately.

248.Pecan-Crusted Turkey Cutlets

Prep time: 10 minutes | Cook time: 10 to 12 minutes | Serves 4

¾ cup panko bread crumbs	¼ cup cornstarch
¼ teaspoon salt	1 egg, beaten
¼ teaspoon pepper	1 pound (454 g) turkey cutlets, ½-inch thick
¼ teaspoon dry mustard	Salt and pepper, to taste
¼ teaspoon poultry seasoning	Cooking spray
½ cup pecans	

1. Place the crisper tray on the air fry position. Select Air Fry, set the temperature to 360ºF (182ºC), and set the time to 12 minutes.
2. Place the panko crumbs, salt, pepper, mustard, and poultry seasoning in a food processor. Process until crumbs are finely crushed. Add pecans and process just until nuts are finely chopped.
3. Place cornstarch in a shallow dish and beaten egg in another. Transfer coating mixture from food processor into a third shallow dish.
4. Sprinkle turkey cutlets with salt and pepper to taste.
5. Dip cutlets in cornstarch and shake off excess, then dip in beaten egg and finally roll in crumbs, pressing to coat well. Spray both sides with cooking spray.
6. Place 2 cutlets in crisper tray in a single layer. Air fry for 10 to 12 minutes. Repeat with the remaining cutlets.
7. Serve warm.

249. Mini Turkey Meatloaves with Carrot

Prep time: 6 minutes | Cook time: 20 to 24 minutes | Serves 4

⅓ cup minced onion
¼ cup grated carrot
2 garlic cloves, minced
2 tablespoons ground almonds
2 teaspoons olive oil
1 teaspoon dried marjoram
1 egg white
¾ pound (340 g) ground turkey breast

1. Place the baking pan on the bake position. Select Bake, set the temperature to 400ºF (204ºC), and set the time to 24 minutes.
2. In a medium bowl, stir together the onion, carrot, garlic, almonds, olive oil, marjoram, and egg white.
3. Add the ground turkey. With your hands, gently but thoroughly mix until combined.
4. Double 16 foil muffin cup liners to make 8 cups. Divide the turkey mixture evenly among the liners. Transfer to the pan.
5. Bake for 20 to 24 minutes, or until the meatloaves reach an internal temperature of 165ºF (74ºC) on a meat thermometer. Serve immediately.

250. Glazed Duck with Cherry Sauce

Prep time: 20 minutes | Cook time: 32 minutes | Serves 12

1 whole duck (about 5 pounds / 2.3 kg in total), split in half, back and rib bones removed, fat trimmed
1 teaspoon olive oil
Salt and freshly ground black pepper, to taste

Cherry Sauce:
1 tablespoon butter
1 shallot, minced
½ cup sherry
1 cup chicken stock
1 teaspoon white wine vinegar
¾ cup cherry
preserves
1 teaspoon fresh thyme leaves
Salt and freshly ground black pepper, to taste

1. Place the crisper tray on the air fry position. Select Air Fry, set the temperature to 400ºF (204ºC), and set the time to 25 minutes.
2. On a clean work surface, rub the duck with olive oil, then sprinkle with salt and ground black pepper to season.
3. Place the duck in the crisper tray, breast side up. Air fry for 25 minutes or until well browned. Flip the duck during the last 10 minutes.
4. Meanwhile, make the cherry sauce: Heat the butter in a nonstick skillet over medium-high heat or until melted.
5. Add the shallot and sauté for 5 minutes or until lightly browned.
6. Add the sherry and simmer for 6 minutes or until it reduces in half.
7. Add the chicken stick, white wine vinegar, and cherry preserves. Stir to combine well. Simmer for 6 more minutes or until thickened.
8. Fold in the thyme leaves and sprinkle with salt and ground black pepper. Stir to mix well.
9. When cooking of the duck is complete, glaze the duck with a quarter of the cherry sauce, then air fry for another 4 minutes.
10. Flip the duck and glaze with another quarter of the cherry sauce. air fry for an additional 3 minutes.
11. Transfer the duck on a large plate and serve with remaining cherry sauce.

251. Easy Asian Turkey Meatballs

Prep time: 10 minutes | Cook time: 11 to 14 minutes | Serves 4

2 tablespoons peanut oil, divided
1 small onion, minced
¼ cup water chestnuts, finely chopped
½ teaspoon ground ginger
2 tablespoons low-sodium soy sauce
¼ cup panko bread crumbs
1 egg, beaten
1 pound (454 g) ground turkey

1. Place the baking pan on the air fry position. Select Air Fry, set the temperature to 400ºF (204ºC), and set the time to 2 minutes.
2. In the baking pan, combine 1 tablespoon of peanut oil and onion. Air fry for 1 to 2 minutes or until crisp and tender. Transfer the onion to a medium bowl.
3. Add the water chestnuts, ground ginger, soy sauce, and bread crumbs to the onion and mix well. Add egg and stir well. Mix in the ground turkey until combined.
4. Form the mixture into 1-inch meatballs. Drizzle the remaining 1 tablespoon of oil over the meatballs. Arrange the meatballs in the pan.
5. Bake for 10 to 12 minutes, or until they are 165ºF (74ºC) on a meat thermometer. Rest for 5 minutes before serving.

252.Italian Chicken Parm Sandwiches

Prep time: 12 minutes | Cook time: 13 minutes | Serves 4

2 (8-ounce / 227-g) boneless, skinless chicken breasts
1 teaspoon kosher salt or ½ teaspoon fine salt, divided
1 cup all-purpose flour
1 teaspoon Italian seasoning or ½ teaspoon each dried oregano and dried basil
2 large eggs
2 tablespoons plain yogurt
2 cups panko bread crumbs
1 ⅓ cups grated Parmesan cheese, divided
2 tablespoons extra-virgin olive oil
4 ciabatta rolls or other sturdy buns, split in half
½ cup marinara sauce
½ cup shredded Mozzarella cheese

1. Lay the chicken breasts on a cutting board and cut each one in half parallel to the board so that you have 4 fairly even, flat fillets. Place a piece of plastic wrap over the chicken pieces and use a rolling pin or small skillet to gently pound them to an even thickness, about ½-inch thick. Season the chicken on both sides with ½ teaspoon of kosher salt.
2. Place the flour on a plate and add the remaining ½ teaspoon of kosher salt and the Italian seasoning. Mix with a fork to distribute evenly. In a wide bowl, whisk together the eggs with the yogurt. In a small bowl combine the panko, 1 cup of Parmesan cheese, and olive oil. Place this in a shallow bowl or plate.
3. Lightly dredge both sides of the chicken pieces in the seasoned flour, and then dip them in the egg wash to coat completely, letting the excess drip off. Finally, dredge the chicken in the bread crumbs. Carefully place the breaded chicken pieces in the crisper tray.
4. Place the crisper tray on the air fry position. Select Air Fry, set temperature to 375ºF (191ºC), and set time to 10 minutes.
5. After 5 minutes, remove the crisper tray from the grill. Carefully turn the chicken over. Return the crisper tray to the grill and continue cooking. When cooking is complete, remove the crisper tray and pan from the grill.
6. Open the rolls in the baking pan, and spread each half with 1 tablespoon of marinara sauce. Place a chicken breast piece on the bottoms of the buns and sprinkle the remaining ⅓ cup of Parmesan cheese over the chicken pieces. Divide the Mozzarella among the top halves of the buns.
7. Place the pan on the broil position. Select Broil, set temperature to 450ºF (232ºC), and set time to 3 minutes.
8. Check the sandwiches after 2 minutes; when cooking is complete, the Mozzarella cheese should be melted and bubbling slightly.
9. Remove the pan from the grill. Close the sandwiches and serve. Add additional marinara sauce if desired.

253.Turkey and Cauliflower Meatloaf

Prep time: 15 minutes | Cook time: 50 minutes | Serves 6

2 pounds (907 g) lean ground turkey
1 ⅓ cups riced cauliflower
2 large eggs, lightly beaten
¼ cup almond flour
⅔ cup chopped yellow or white onion
1 teaspoon ground dried turmeric
1 teaspoon ground cumin
1 teaspoon ground coriander
1 tablespoon minced garlic
1 teaspoon salt
1 teaspoon ground black pepper
Cooking spray

1. Place a loaf pan on the bake position. Select Bake, set the temperature to 350ºF (177ºC), and set the time to 25 minutes.
2. Spritz the loaf pan with cooking spray.
3. Combine all the ingredients in a large bowl. Stir to mix well. Pour half of the mixture in the prepared loaf pan and press with a spatula to coat the bottom evenly. Spritz the mixture with cooking spray.
4. Bake for 25 minutes, or until the meat is well browned and the internal temperature reaches at least 165ºF (74ºC). Repeat with remaining mixture.
5. Remove the loaf pan from the grill and serve immediately.

254. Deep Fried Duck Leg Quarters

Prep time: 5 minutes | Cook time: 45 minutes | Serves 4

4 (½-pound / 227-g) skin-on duck leg quarters
2 medium garlic

cloves, minced
½ teaspoon salt
½ teaspoon ground black pepper

1. Spritz the crisper tray with cooking spray.
2. Place the crisper tray on the air fry position. Select Air Fry, set the temperature to 300ºF (149ºC), and set the time to 45 minutes.
3. On a clean work surface, rub the duck leg quarters with garlic, salt, and black pepper.
4. Arrange the leg quarters in the crisper tray and spritz with cooking spray.
5. Air fry for 30 minutes, then flip the leg quarters and increase the temperature to 375ºF (191ºC). air fry for 15 more minutes or until well browned and crispy.
6. Remove the duck leg quarters from the grill and allow to cool for 10 minutes before serving.

255. Duck Breasts with Marmalade Balsamic Glaze

Prep time: 5 minutes | Cook time: 13 minutes | Serves 4

4 (6-ounce / 170-g) skin-on duck breasts
1 teaspoon salt
¼ cup orange marmalade

1 tablespoon white balsamic vinegar
¾ teaspoon ground black pepper

1. Place the crisper tray on the air fry position. Select Air Fry, set the temperature to 400ºF (204ºC), and set the time to 10 minutes.
2. Cut 10 slits into the skin of the duck breasts, then sprinkle with salt on both sides.
3. Place the breasts in the crisper tray, skin side up. Air fry for 10 minutes.
4. Meanwhile, combine the remaining ingredients in a small bowl. Stir to mix well.
5. When the frying is complete, brush the duck skin with the marmalade mixture. Flip the breast and air fry for 3 more minutes or until the skin is crispy and the breast is well browned.
6. Serve immediately.

256. Southwestern Chicken Skewers

Prep time: 17 minutes | Cook time: 10 minutes | Serves 4

1 pound (454 g) boneless, skinless chicken breast, cut into 1½-inch chunks
1 large onion, cut into large chunks
1 red bell pepper, seeded and cut into 1-inch pieces
1 green bell pepper, seeded and cut into 1-inch pieces
3 tablespoons vegetable oil, divided
2 tablespoons Southwestern Seasoning or store-

bought southwestern or fajita seasoning
2 teaspoons kosher salt or 1 teaspoon fine salt, divided
2 cups corn, fresh or frozen, thawed and drained
¼ teaspoon granulated garlic
1 tablespoon mayonnaise
1 teaspoon freshly squeezed lime juice
3 tablespoons grated Parmesan cheese

Special Equipment:

12 (9- to 12-inch) wooden skewers, soaked in water for at least 30 minutes

1. Place the chicken, onion, and bell peppers in a large bowl. Add 2 tablespoons of oil, the Southwestern Seasoning, and 1½ teaspoons of kosher salt (omit if using a store-bought seasoning mix that includes salt). Toss to coat evenly.
2. Alternate the chicken and vegetables on the skewers, making about 12 skewers (if you use the larger skewers, you'll probably only need 8).
3. Place the corn in a medium bowl, and add the remaining 1 tablespoon of oil. Add the remaining ½ teaspoon of kosher salt and the garlic, and toss to coat. Place the corn in an even layer in the baking pan and place the skewers on top.
4. Place the pan on the roast position. Select Roast, set temperature to 375ºF (191ºC), and set time to 10 minutes.
5. After about 5 minutes, remove the pan from the grill and turn the skewers. Return the pan to the grill and continue cooking.
6. When cooking is complete, remove the pan from the grill. Place the skewers on a platter and cover with aluminum foil to stay warm. Place the corn back into the bowl and add the mayonnaise, lime juice, and Parmesan cheese. Stir to combine.

257. Braised Chicken with Peppers and Polenta

Prep time: 10 minutes | Cook time: 27 minutes | Serves 4

4 bone-in, skin-on chicken thighs (about 1½ pounds / 680 g)
1½ teaspoon kosher salt or ¾ teaspoon fine salt, divided
Cooking oil spray
1 link sweet or hot Italian sausage (about ¼ pound / 113 g), whole
8 ounces (227 g) miniature bell peppers, halved and seeded (or 1 large red bell pepper, thinly sliced)
1 small onion, thinly sliced
2 garlic cloves, minced
1 tablespoon extra-virgin olive oil
4 hot or sweet pickled cherry peppers, seeded and quartered, along with 2 tablespoons pickling liquid from the jar
¼ cup low-sodium chicken stock
4 (1-inch) slices polenta

1. Salt the chicken thighs on both sides with 1 teaspoon of kosher salt. Spray the baking pan with cooking oil spray and place the thighs skin-side down in the pan. Add the sausage.
2. Place the pan on the roast position. Select Roast, set temperature to 375ºF (191ºC), and set time to 27 minutes.
3. While the chicken and sausage cook, place the bell peppers, onion, and garlic in a large bowl. Sprinkle with the remaining ½ teaspoon of kosher salt and add the olive oil. Toss to coat.
4. After 10 minutes, remove the pan from the grill and turn over the chicken thighs and sausage. Add the pepper mixture to the pan. Return the pan to the grill and continue cooking.
5. After another 10 minutes, remove the pan from the grill and add the pickled peppers, pickling liquid, and stock. Stir the pickled peppers into the peppers and onion. Push them to the side and add the polenta slices in a single layer. Return the pan to the grill and continue cooking.
6. When cooking is complete, the peppers and onion should be soft, the polenta warmed through, and the chicken should read 165ºF (74ºC) on a meat thermometer. Remove the pan from the grill. Slice the sausage into thin pieces and stir it into the pepper mixture. Place a slice of polenta on each of four plates and spoon the peppers over. Top with a chicken thigh.

258. Chicken Thighs with Radish Slaw

Prep time: 10 minutes | Cook time: 27 minutes | Serves 4

4 bone-in, skin-on chicken thighs
1½ teaspoon kosher salt or ¾ teaspoon fine salt, divided
1 tablespoon smoked or sweet paprika
½ teaspoon granulated garlic
½ teaspoon dried oregano
¼ teaspoon freshly ground black pepper
Cooking oil spray
3 cups shredded cabbage or coleslaw mix
½ small red or white onion, thinly sliced
4 large radishes, julienned (optional)
3 tablespoons red or white wine vinegar
2 tablespoons extra-virgin olive oil

1. Salt the chicken thighs on both sides with 1 teaspoon of kosher salt. In a small bowl, combine the paprika, garlic, oregano, and black pepper. Sprinkle half this mixture over the skin sides of the thighs. Spray the baking pan with cooking oil spray and place the thighs skin-side down in the pan. Sprinkle the remaining spice mixture over the other sides of the chicken pieces.
2. Place the pan on the roast position. Select Roast, set temperature to 375ºF (191ºC), and set time to 27 minutes.
3. After 10 minutes, remove the pan from the grill and turn over the chicken thighs. Return the pan to the grill and continue cooking.
4. While the chicken cooks, place the cabbage, onion, and radishes (if using) in a large bowl. Sprinkle with the remaining ½ teaspoon of kosher salt, vinegar, and olive oil. Toss to coat.
5. After another 9 to 10 minutes, remove the pan from the grill and place the chicken thighs on a cutting board or plate. Place the cabbage mixture in the pan and toss it with the chicken fat and spices on the bottom of the pan. Spread out the cabbage into an even layer and place the chicken on it, skin-side up. Return the pan to the grill and continue cooking. Roast for another 7 to 8 minutes.
6. When cooking is complete, the cabbage is just becoming tender. Remove the pan from the grill. Taste and adjust the seasoning if necessary. Serve.

259. Thai Sweet-and-Spicy Drumsticks

Prep time: 5 minutes | Cook time: 25 minutes | Serves 4

8 skin-on chicken drumsticks
1 teaspoon kosher salt or ½ teaspoon fine salt, divided
1 pound (454 g) green beans, trimmed

2 garlic cloves, minced
2 tablespoons vegetable oil
⅓ cup Thai sweet chili sauce

1. Salt the drumsticks on all sides with ½ teaspoon of kosher salt. Let sit for a few minutes, then blot dry with a paper towel. Place in the baking pan.
2. Place the pan on the roast position. Select Roast, set temperature to 375°F (191°C), and set time to 25 minutes.
3. While the chicken cooks, place the green beans in a large bowl. Add the remaining ½ teaspoon kosher salt, the garlic, and oil. Toss to coat.
4. After 15 minutes, remove the pan from the grill. Brush the drumsticks with the sweet chili sauce. Place the green beans in the pan. Return the pan to the grill and continue cooking.
5. When cooking is complete, the green beans should be sizzling and browned in spots and the chicken cooked through, reading 165°F (74°C) on a meat thermometer. Serve the chicken with the green beans on the side.

260. Rosemary Turkey Scotch Eggs

Prep time: 15 minutes | Cook time: 12 minutes | Serves 4

1 egg
1 cup panko breadcrumbs
½ teaspoon rosemary
1 pound (454 g) ground turkey

4 hard-boiled eggs, peeled
Salt and ground black pepper, to taste
Cooking spray

1. Spritz the crisper tray with cooking spray.
2. Place the crisper tray on the air fry position. Select Air Fry, set the temperature to 400°F (204°C), and set the time to 12 minutes.
3. Whisk the egg with salt in a bowl. Combine the breadcrumbs with rosemary in a shallow dish.
4. Stir the ground turkey with salt and ground black pepper in a separate large bowl, then divide the ground turkey into four portions.
5. Wrap each hard-boiled egg with a portion of ground turkey. Dredge in the whisked egg, then roll over the breadcrumb mixture.
6. Place the wrapped eggs in the crisper tray and spritz with cooking spray. Air fry for 12 minutes or until golden brown and crunchy. Flip the eggs halfway through.
7. Serve immediately.

261. Chicken and Roasted Tomato Shawarma

Prep time: 10 minutes | Cook time: 18 minutes | Serves 4

1½ pounds (680 g) boneless, skinless chicken thighs
1¼ teaspoon kosher salt or ⅜ teaspoon fine salt, divided
2 tablespoons plus 1 teaspoon extra-virgin olive oil, divided
⅔ cup plus 2 tablespoons plain Greek yogurt, divided

2 tablespoons freshly squeezed lemon juice (about 1 medium lemon)
4 garlic cloves, pressed or minced, divided
1 generous tablespoon Shawarma seasoning
4 pita breads, cut in half
1 pint cherry tomatoes
½ small cucumber
1 tablespoon chopped fresh parsley

1. Sprinkle the chicken thighs on both sides with 1 teaspoon of kosher salt. Place in a resealable plastic bag and set aside while you make the marinade.
2. In a small bowl, mix together 2 tablespoons of olive oil, 2 tablespoons of yogurt, the lemon juice, 3 pressed garlic cloves, and Shawarma Seasoning until thoroughly combined. Pour the marinade over the chicken. Seal the bag, squeezing out as much air as possible. and massage the chicken to coat the it with the sauce. Set aside.
3. Wrap 2 pita breads each in two pieces of aluminum foil and place in the baking pan.
4. Place the pan on the bake position. Select Bake, set temperature to 300ºF (149ºC), and set time to 6 minutes.
5. After 3 minutes, remove the pan from the grill and turn over the foil packets. Return the pan to the grill and continue cooking. When cooking is complete, remove the pan from the grill and place the foil-wrapped pitas on the top of the grill to keep warm.
6. Remove the chicken from the marinade, letting the excess drip off into the bag. Place them in the baking pan. Arrange the tomatoes around the sides of the chicken. Discard the marinade.
7. Place the pan on the broil position. Select Broil, set temperature to 450ºF (232ºC), and set time to 12 minutes.
8. After 6 minutes, remove the pan from the grill and turn over the chicken. Return the pan to the grill and continue cooking.

9. While the chicken cooks, peel and seed the cucumber. Grate or finely chop it. Wrap it in a paper towel to remove as much moisture as possible. Place the cucumber in a small bowl. Add the remaining ⅔ cup of yogurt, ¼ teaspoon kosher salt, 1 teaspoon of olive oil, 1 pressed garlic clove, and parsley. Whisk until combined.
10. When cooking is complete, the chicken should be browned, crisp along its edges, and sizzling. Remove the pan from the grill and place the chicken on a cutting board. Cut each thigh into several pieces. Unwrap the pitas. Spread a tablespoon or two of sauce into a pita half. Add some chicken and add 2 or 3 roasted tomatoes. Serve.

262.Strawberry-Glazed Turkey

Prep time: 15 minutes | Cook time: 37 minutes | Serves 2

2 pounds (907 g) turkey breast
1 tablespoon olive oil

Salt and ground black pepper, to taste
1 cup fresh strawberries

1. Place the crisper tray on the air fry position. Select Air Fry, set the temperature to 375ºF (191ºC), and set the time to 37 minutes.
2. Rub the turkey bread with olive oil on a clean work surface, then sprinkle with salt and ground black pepper.
3. Transfer the turkey in the crisper tray. Air fry for 30 minutes or until the internal temperature of the turkey reaches at least 165ºF (74ºC). flip the turkey breast halfway through.
4. Meanwhile, put the strawberries in a food processor and pulse until smooth.
5. When the cooking of the turkey is complete, spread the puréed strawberries over the turkey. Air fry for 7 more minutes.
6. Serve immediately.

263.Turkey Burgers

Prep time: 10 minutes | Cook time: 25 minutes | Serves 4

2 medium yellow or white onions
1 tablespoon extra-virgin olive oil or vegetable oil
1½ teaspoons kosher salt or ¾ teaspoon fine salt, divided
1¼ pound (567 g) ground turkey

⅓ cup mayonnaise
1 tablespoon Dijon mustard
2 teaspoons Worcestershire sauce
4 slices sharp Cheddar cheese (about 4 ounces / 113 g total)
4 hamburger buns, sliced

1. Trim the onions and cut them in half through the root. Cut one of the halves in half (so you have a quarter). Grate one quarter. Place the grated onion in a large bowl. Thinly slice the remaining onions and place in a medium bowl with the oil and ½ teaspoon of kosher salt. Toss to coat. Place the onions in the baking pan in a single layer.
2. Place the pan on the roast position. Select Roast, set temperature to 350ºF (177ºC), and set time to 10 minutes.
3. While the onions are cooking, add the turkey to the grated onion. Add the remaining 1 teaspoon of kosher salt, mayonnaise, mustard, and Worcestershire sauce. Mix just until combined, being careful not to overwork the turkey. Divide the mixture into 4 patties, each about ¾-inch thick.
4. When cooking is complete, remove the pan from the grill. Move the onions to one side of the pan and place the burgers in the pan. Poke your finger into the center of each burger to make a deep indentation (this helps the burgers cook evenly).
5. Place the pan on the broil position. Select Broil, set temperature to 450ºF (232ºC), and set time to 12 minutes.
6. After 6 minutes, remove the pan. Turn the burgers and stir the onions. (If the onions are getting charred, transfer them to a bowl and cover with foil.) Return the pan to the grill and continue cooking. After about 4 minutes, remove the pan and place the cheese slices on the burgers. Return the pan to the grill and continue cooking for about 1 minute, or until the cheese is melted and the center of the burgers has reached at least 160ºF (71ºC) on a meat thermometer.
7. When cooking is complete, remove the pan from the grill. Loosely cover the burgers with foil.
8. Lay out the buns, cut-side up, on the grill rack. Place the pan on the broil position. Select Broil; set temperature to 450ºF (232ºC), and set time to 3 minutes.
9. Check the buns after 2 minutes; they should be lightly browned.
10. Remove the buns from the grill. Assemble the burgers and add any condiments you like.

264.Mushroom and Beef Meatloaf

Prep time: 10 minutes | Cook time: 25 minutes | Serves 4

1 pound (454 g) ground beef
1 egg, beaten
1 mushrooms, sliced
1 tablespoon thyme
1 small onion, chopped
3 tablespoons bread crumbs
Ground black pepper, to taste

1. Place a loaf pan on the bake position. Select Bake, set the temperature to 400ºF (204ºC), and set the time to 25 minutes.
2. Put all the ingredients into a large bowl and combine entirely.
3. Transfer the meatloaf mixture into the loaf pan.
4. Bake for 25 minutes.
5. Slice up before serving.

265.Pepperoni and Bell Pepper Pockets

Prep time: 5 minutes | Cook time: 8 minutes | Serves 4

4 bread slices, 1-inch thick
Olive oil, for misting
24 slices pepperoni
1 ounce (28 g) roasted red peppers, drained and patted dry
1 ounce (28 g) Pepper Jack cheese, cut into 4 slices

1. Place the crisper tray on the air fry position. Select Air Fry, set the temperature to 360ºF (182ºC), and set the time to 8 minutes.
2. Spray both sides of bread slices with olive oil.
3. Stand slices upright and cut a deep slit in the top to create a pocket (almost to the bottom crust, but not all the way through).
4. Stuff each bread pocket with 6 slices of pepperoni, a large strip of roasted red pepper, and a slice of cheese.
5. Put bread pockets in crisper tray, standing up. Air fry for 8 minutes, until filling is heated through and bread is lightly browned.
6. Serve hot.

266.Fast Lamb Satay

Prep time: 5 minutes | Cook time: 8 minutes | Serves 2

¼ teaspoon cumin
1 teaspoon ginger
½ teaspoons nutmeg
Salt and ground black pepper, to taste
2 boneless lamb steaks
Cooking spray

1. Combine the cumin, ginger, nutmeg, salt and pepper in a bowl.
2. Cube the lamb steaks and massage the spice mixture into each one.
3. Leave to marinate for 10 minutes, then transfer onto metal skewers.
4. Place the crisper tray on the air fry position. Select Air Fry, set the temperature to 400ºF (204ºC), and set the time to 8 minutes.
5. Place the skewers in the crisper tray and spritz with cooking spray. Air fry for 8 minutes.
6. Take care when removing them from the grill and serve.

267.Lamb Ribs with Fresh Mint

Prep time: 5 minutes | Cook time: 18 minutes | Serves 4

2 tablespoons mustard
1 pound (454 g) lamb ribs
1 teaspoon rosemary, chopped
Salt and ground black pepper, to taste
¼ cup mint leaves, chopped
1 cup Greek yogurt

1. Place the crisper tray on the air fry position. Select Air Fry, set the temperature to 350ºF (177ºC), and set the time to 18 minutes.
2. Use a brush to apply the mustard to the lamb ribs, and season with rosemary, salt, and pepper. Transfer to the crisper tray.
3. Air fry for 18 minutes.
4. Meanwhile, combine the mint leaves and yogurt in a bowl.
5. Remove the lamb ribs from the grill when cooked and serve with the mint yogurt.

268. Mozzarella Meatball Sandwiches with Basil

Prep time: 5 minutes | Cook time: 10 minutes | Serves 4

12 frozen meatballs
8 slices Mozzarella cheese
4 sub rolls, halved lengthwise
½ cup marinara sauce, warmed
12 fresh basil leaves

1. Place the crisper tray on the air fry position. Select Air Fry, set the temperature to 350ºF (177ºC), and set the time to 10 minutes.
2. Place the meatballs in the crisper tray. Air fry for 5 minutes.
3. After 5 minutes, shake the crisper tray of meatballs. Place the crisper tray back in the grill to resume cooking.
4. While the meatballs are cooking, place two slices of Mozzarella cheese on each sub roll. Use a spoon to spread the marinara sauce on top of the cheese slices. Press three leaves of basil into the sauce on each roll.
5. When cooking is complete, place three meatballs on each sub roll. Serve immediately.

269. Grilled Fillet Mignon with Pineapple Salsa

Prep time: 15 minutes | Cook time: 8 minutes | Serves 4

4 (6- to 8-ounce / 170- to 227-g) fillet mignon steaks
1 tablespoon canola oil, divided
Sea salt, to taste
Freshly ground black pepper, to taste
½ medium pineapple, cored and diced
1 medium red onion, diced
1 jalapeño pepper, seeded, stemmed, and diced
1 tablespoon freshly squeezed lime juice
¼ cup chopped fresh cilantro leaves
Chili powder
Ground coriander

1. Rub each filet on all sides with ½ tablespoon of the oil, then season with the salt and pepper.
2. Place the grill plate on the grill position. Select Grill, set temperature to 400ºF (204ºC), and set time to 8 minutes.
3. Add the fillets to the grill plate.

4. After 4 minutes, flip the fillets. Continue grilling for an additional 4 minutes, or until the fillets' internal temperature reads 125ºF (52ºC) on a food thermometer. Remove the fillets from the grill; they will continue to cook (called carry-over cooking) to a food-safe temperature even after you've removed them from the grill.
5. Let the fillets rest for a total of 10 minutes; this allows the natural juices to redistribute into the steak.
6. While the fillets rest, in a medium bowl, combine the pineapple, onion, and jalapeño. Stir in the lime juice and cilantro, then season to taste with the chili powder and coriander.
7. Plate the fillets, and pile the salsa on top of each before serving.

270. Asian-Flavored Steak Kebabs

Prep time: 5 minutes | Cook time: 12 minutes | Serves 4

¾ cup soy sauce
5 garlic cloves, minced
3 tablespoons sesame oil
½ cup canola oil
1/3 cup sugar
¼ teaspoon dried ground ginger
2 (10- to 12-ounce / 284- to 340-g) New York strip steaks, cut in 2-inch cubes
1 cup whole white mushrooms
1 red bell pepper, seeded, and cut into 2-inch cubes
1 red onion, cut into 2-inch wedges

1. In a medium bowl, whisk together the soy sauce, garlic, sesame oil, canola oil, sugar, and ginger until well combined. Add the steak and toss to coat. Cover and refrigerate for at least 30 minutes.
2. Place the grill plate on the grill position. Select Grill, set the temperature to 350ºF (177ºC), and set the time to 12 minutes.
3. Assemble the skewers in the following order: steak, mushroom, bell pepper, onion. Ensure the ingredients are pushed almost completely down to the end of the wood skewers.
4. Place the skewers on the grill plate. Grill for 8 minutes without flipping.
5. After 8 minutes, check the steak for desired doneness, grilling up to 4 minutes more if desired.
6. When cooking is complete, serve immediately.

271.Korean BBQ Beef

Prep time: 5 minutes | Cook time: 5 minutes | Serves 4

¹/₃ cup soy sauce	ground black pepper
2 tablespoons sesame oil	1 pound (454 g) rib eye steak, thinly sliced
2½ tablespoons brown sugar	2 scallions, thinly sliced, for garnish
3 garlic cloves, minced	Toasted sesame seeds, for garnish
½ teaspoon freshly	

1. In a small bowl, whisk together the soy sauce, sesame oil, brown sugar, garlic, and black pepper until fully combined.
2. Place the beef into a large shallow bowl, and pour the sauce over the slices. Cover and refrigerate for 1 hour.
3. Place the grill plate on the grill position. Select Grill, set the temperature to 350ºF (177ºC), and set the time to 5 minutes.
4. Place the beef onto the grill plate. Grill for 4 minutes without flipping.
5. After 4 minutes, check the steak for desired doneness, grilling for up to 1 minute more, if desired.
6. When cooking is complete, top with scallions and sesame seeds and serve immediately.

272.Steak and Lettuce Salad

Prep time: 5 minutes | Cook time: 16 minutes | Serves 4 to 6

4 (8-ounce / 227-g) skirt steaks	tomatoes, halved
Sea salt, to taste	¼ cup blue cheese, crumbled
Freshly ground black pepper, to taste	1 cup croutons
6 cups chopped romaine lettuce	2 avocados, peeled and sliced
¾ cup cherry	1 cup blue cheese dressing

1. Place the grill plate on the grill position. Select Grill, set the temperature to 400ºF (204ºC), and set the time to 8 minutes.
2. Season the steaks on both sides with the salt and pepper.
3. Place 2 steaks on the grill plate. Gently press the steaks down to maximize grill marks. Grill for 4 minutes. After 4 minutes, flip the steaks and grill for an additional 4 minutes.
4. Remove the steaks from the grill and transfer to them a cutting board. Tent with aluminum foil.
5. Repeat step 3 with the remaining 2 steaks.
6. While the second set of steaks is cooking, assemble the salad by tossing together the lettuce, tomatoes, blue cheese crumbles, and croutons. Top with the avocado slices.
7. Once the second set of steaks has finished cooking, slice all four of the steaks into thin strips, and place on top of the salad. Drizzle with the blue cheese dressing and serve.

273.Lamb Rack with Pistachio

Prep time: 10 minutes | Cook time: 20 minutes | Serves 2

½ cup finely chopped pistachios	1 tablespoon olive oil
1 teaspoon chopped fresh rosemary	Salt and freshly ground black pepper, to taste
3 tablespoons panko breadcrumbs	1 lamb rack, bones fat trimmed and frenched
2 teaspoons chopped fresh oregano	1 tablespoon Dijon mustard

1. Place the crisper tray on the air fry position. Select Air Fry, set the temperature to 380ºF (193ºC), and set the time to 12 minutes.
2. Put the pistachios, rosemary, breadcrumbs, oregano, olive oil, salt, and black pepper in a food processor. Pulse to combine until smooth.
3. Rub the lamb rack with salt and black pepper on a clean work surface, then place it in the crisper tray.
4. Air fry for 12 minutes or until lightly browned. Flip the lamb halfway through the cooking time.
5. Transfer the lamb to a plate and brush with Dijon mustard on the fat side, then sprinkle with the pistachios mixture over the lamb rack to coat well.
6. Put the lamb rack back to the crisper tray. Air fry for 8 more minutes or until the internal temperature of the rack reaches at least 145ºF (63ºC).
7. Remove the lamb rack from the grill with tongs and allow to cool for 5 minutes before sling to serve.

274. Baby Back Ribs in Gochujang Marinade

Prep time: 10 minutes | Cook time: 22 minutes | Serves 4

¼ cup gochujang paste
¼ cup soy sauce
¼ cup freshly squeezed orange juice
2 tablespoons apple cider vinegar
2 tablespoons sesame oil
6 garlic cloves, minced
1½ tablespoons brown sugar
1 tablespoon grated fresh ginger
1 teaspoon salt
4 (8- to 10-ounce / 227- to 284-g) baby back ribs

1. In a medium bowl, add the gochujang paste, soy sauce, orange juice, vinegar, oil, garlic, sugar, ginger, and salt, and stir to combine.
2. Place the baby back ribs on a baking sheet and coat all sides with the sauce. Cover with aluminum foil and refrigerate for 6 hours.
3. Place the grill plate on the grill position. Select Grill, set the temperature to 350ºF (177ºC), and set the time to 22 minutes.
4. Place the ribs on the grill plate. Grill for 11 minutes. After 11 minutes, flip the ribs and grill for an additional 11 minutes.
5. When cooking is complete, serve immediately.

275. Cheesy Jalapeño Popper Burgers

Prep time: 5 minutes | Cook time: 9 minutes | Serves 4

2 jalapeño peppers, seeded, stemmed, and minced
½ cup shredded Cheddar cheese
4 ounces (113 g) cream cheese, at room temperature
4 slices bacon, cooked and crumbled
2 pounds (907 g) ground beef
½ teaspoon chili powder
¼ teaspoon paprika
¼ teaspoon freshly ground black pepper
4 hamburger buns
4 slices pepper Jack cheese
Lettuce, sliced tomato, and sliced red onion, for topping (optional)

1. Place the grill plate on the grill position. Select Grill, set the temperature to 400ºF (204ºC), and set the time to 9 minutes.
2. In a medium bowl, combine the peppers, Cheddar cheese, cream cheese, and bacon until well combined.
3. Form the ground beef into 8¼-inch-thick patties. Spoon some of the filling mixture onto four of the patties, then place a second patty on top of each to make four burgers. Use your fingers to pinch the edges of the patties together to seal in the filling. Reshape the patties with your hands as needed.
4. Combine the chili powder, paprika, and pepper in a small bowl. Sprinkle the mixture onto both sides of the burgers.
5. Place the burgers on the grill plate. Grill for 4 minutes without flipping. Cooking is complete when the internal temperature of the beef reaches at least 145ºF (63ºC) on a food thermometer. If needed, grill for up to 5 more minutes.
6. Place the burgers on the hamburger buns and top with pepper Jack cheese. Add lettuce, tomato, and red onion, if desired.

276. Spaghetti Squash Lasagna

Prep time: 5 minutes | Cook time: 1 hour 15 minutes | Serves 6

2 large spaghetti squash, cooked (about 2¾ pounds / 1.2 kg)
4 pounds (1.8 kg) ground beef
1 (2½-pound / 1.1-kg) large jar Marinara sauce
25 slices Mozzarella cheese
30 ounces whole-milk ricotta cheese

1. Place the baking pan on the bake position. Select Bake, set the temperature to 375ºF (191ºC), and set the time to 45 minutes.
2. Slice the spaghetti squash and place it face down inside the baking pan. Fill with water until covered.
3. Bake for 45 minutes until skin is soft.
4. Sear the ground beef in a skillet over medium-high heat for 5 minutes or until browned, then add the marinara sauce and heat until warm. Set aside.
5. Scrape the flesh off the cooked squash to resemble strands of spaghetti.
6. Layer the lasagna in a large greased pan in alternating layers of spaghetti squash, beef sauce, Mozzarella, ricotta. Repeat until all the ingredients have been used.
7. Bake for 30 minutes.
8. Serve.

277. Rack of Lamb Chops with Rosemary

Prep time: 5 minutes | Cook time: 14 minutes | Serves 2

3 tablespoons extra-virgin olive oil
1 garlic clove, minced
1 tablespoon fresh rosemary, chopped
½ rack lamb (4 bones)
Sea salt, to taste
Freshly ground black pepper, to taste

1. Combine the oil, garlic, and rosemary in a large bowl. Season the rack of lamb with the salt and pepper, then place the lamb in the bowl, using tongs to turn and coat fully in the oil mixture. Cover and refrigerate for 2 hours.
2. Place the grill plate on the grill position. Select Grill, set the temperature to 400ºF (204ºC), and set the time to 14 minutes.
3. Place the lamb on the grill plate. Grill for 6 minutes. After 6 minutes, flip the lamb and continue grilling for 6 minutes more.
4. Cooking is complete when the internal temperature of the lamb reaches 145ºF (63ºC) on a food thermometer. If needed, grill for up to 2 minutes more.

278. Balsamic London Broil

Prep time: 15 minutes | Cook time: 25 minutes | Serves 8

2 pounds (907 g) London broil
3 large garlic cloves, minced
3 tablespoons balsamic vinegar
3 tablespoons whole-grain mustard
2 tablespoons olive oil
Sea salt and ground black pepper, to taste
½ teaspoons dried hot red pepper flakes

1. Wash and dry the London broil. Score its sides with a knife.
2. Mix the remaining ingredients. Rub this mixture into the broil, coating it well. Allow to marinate for a minimum of 3 hours.
3. Place the crisper tray on the air fry position. Select Air Fry, set the temperature to 400ºF (204ºC), and set the time to 25 minutes.
4. Place the meat in the crisper tray. Air fry for 15 minutes. Turn it over and air fry for an additional 10 minutes before serving.

279. Miso Marinated Steak

Prep time: 5 minutes | Cook time: 12 minutes | Serves 4

¾ pound (340 g) flank steak
1½ tablespoons sake
1 tablespoon brown miso paste
1 teaspoon honey
2 cloves garlic, pressed
1 tablespoon olive oil

1. Put all the ingredients in a Ziploc bag. Shake to cover the steak well with the seasonings and refrigerate for at least 1 hour.
2. Place the crisper tray on the air fry position. Select Air Fry, set the temperature to 400ºF (204ºC), and set the time to 12 minutes.
3. Coat all sides of the steak with cooking spray. Put the steak in the crisper tray.
4. Air fry for 12 minutes, turning the steak twice during the cooking time, then serve immediately.

280. Korean-Style Steak Tips

Prep time: 5 minutes | Cook time: 13 minutes | Serves 4

4 garlic cloves, minced
½ apple, peeled and grated
3 tablespoons sesame oil
3 tablespoons brown sugar
⅓ cup soy sauce
1 teaspoon freshly ground black pepper
Sea salt
1½ pounds (680 g) beef tips

1. In a medium bowl, combine the garlic, apple, sesame oil, sugar, soy sauce, pepper, and salt until well mixed.
2. Place the beef tips in a large shallow bowl and pour the marinade over them. Cover and refrigerate for 30 minutes.
3. Place the grill plate on the grill position. Select Grill, set the temperature to 350ºF (177ºC), and set the time to 13 minutes.
4. Place the steak tips on the grill plate. Grill for 11 minutes.
5. Cooking is complete to medium doneness when the internal temperature of the meat reaches 145ºF (63ºC) on a food thermometer. If desired, grill for up to 2 minutes more.
6. Remove the steak, and set it on a cutting board to rest for 5 minutes. Serve.

281.Cheesy Beef Meatballs

Prep time: 5 minutes | Cook time: 18 minutes | Serves 6

1 pound (454 g) ground beef	garlic
½ cup grated Parmesan cheese	½ cup Mozzarella cheese
1 tablespoon minced	1 teaspoon freshly ground pepper

1. Place the crisper tray on the air fry position. Select Air Fry, set the temperature to 400ºF (204ºC), and set the time to 18 minutes.
2. In a bowl, mix all the ingredients together.
3. Roll the meat mixture into 5 generous meatballs. Transfer to the crisper tray.
4. Air fry for 18 minutes.
5. Serve immediately.

282.Pork Chops in Bourbon

Prep time: 5 minutes | Cook time: 35 minutes | Serves 4

2 cups ketchup	Worcestershire sauce
¾ cup bourbon	½ tablespoon dry mustard powder
¼ cup apple cider vinegar	4 boneless pork chops
¼ cup soy sauce	Sea salt, to taste
1 cup packed brown sugar	Freshly ground black pepper, to taste
3 tablespoons	

1. In a medium saucepan over high heat, combine the ketchup, bourbon, vinegar, soy sauce, sugar, Worcestershire sauce, and mustard powder. Stir to combine and bring to a boil.
2. Reduce the heat to low and simmer, uncovered and stirring occasionally, for 20 minutes. The barbecue sauce will thicken while cooking. Once thickened, remove the pan from the heat and set aside.
3. Place the grill plate on the grill position. Select Grill, set the temperature to 350ºF (177ºC), and set the time to 15 minutes.
4. Place the pork chops on the grill plate. Grill for 8 minutes. After 8 minutes, flip the pork chops and baste the cooked side with the barbecue sauce. Grill for 5 minutes more.
5. Flip the pork chops again, basting both sides with the barbecue sauce. Grill for the final 2 minutes.
6. When cooking is complete, season with salt and pepper and serve immediately.

283.Spiced Flank Steak

Prep time: 10 minutes | Cook time: 8 minutes | Serves 2

1 tablespoon chili powder	1 teaspoon sea salt
1 teaspoon dried oregano	¼ teaspoon freshly ground black pepper
2 teaspoons ground cumin	2 (8-ounce / 227-g) flank steaks

1. Place the grill plate on the grill position. Select Grill, set the temperature to 400ºF (204ºC), and set the time to 8 minutes.
2. In a small bowl, mix together the chili powder, oregano, cumin, salt, and pepper. Use your hands to rub the spice mixture on all sides of the steaks.
3. Place the steaks on the grill plate. Gently press the steaks down to maximize grill marks. Grill for 4 minutes. After 4 minutes, flip the steaks, and grill for 4 minutes more.
4. Remove the steaks from the grill, and transfer them to a cutting board. Let rest for 5 minutes before slicing and serving.

284.Honey-Caramelized Pork Tenderloin

Prep time: 5 minutes | Cook time: 15 to 20 minutes | Serves 4

2 tablespoons honey	powder
1 tablespoon soy sauce	½ teaspoon sea salt
½ teaspoon garlic	1 (1½-pound / 680-g) pork tenderloin

1. Place the grill plate on the grill position. Select Grill, set the temperature to 350ºF (177ºC), and set the time to 20 minutes.
2. Meanwhile, in a small bowl, combine the honey, soy sauce, garlic powder, and salt.
3. Place the pork tenderloin on the grill plate. Baste all sides with the honey glaze. Grill for 8 minutes. After 8 minutes, flip the pork tenderloin and baste with any remaining glaze. Grill for 7 minutes more.
4. Cooking is complete when the internal temperature of the pork reaches 145ºF (63ºC) on a food thermometer. If needed, grill for up to 5 minutes more.
5. Remove the pork, and set it on a cutting board to rest for 5 minutes. Slice and serve.

285.Citrus Pork Loin Roast

Prep time: 10 minutes | Cook time: 45 minutes | Serves 8

1 tablespoon lime juice	1 teaspoon dried lemongrass
1 tablespoon orange marmalade	2 pound (907 g) boneless pork loin roast
1 teaspoon coarse brown mustard	Salt and ground black pepper, to taste
1 teaspoon curry powder	Cooking spray

1. Place the crisper tray on the air fry position. Select Air Fry, set the temperature to 360ºF (182ºC), and set the time to 45 minutes.
2. Mix the lime juice, marmalade, mustard, curry powder, and lemongrass.
3. Rub mixture all over the surface of the pork loin. Season with salt and pepper.
4. Spray the crisper tray with cooking spray and place pork roast diagonally in the crisper tray.
5. Air fry for 45 minutes, until the internal temperature reaches at least 145ºF (63ºC).
6. Wrap roast in foil and let rest for 10 minutes before slicing.
7. Serve immediately.

286.Potato and Prosciutto Salad

Prep time: 10 minutes | Cook time: 7 minutes | Serves 8

Salad:

4 pounds (1.8 kg) potatoes, boiled and cubed	diced
	2 cups shredded Cheddar cheese
15 slices prosciutto,	

Dressing:

15 ounces (425 g) sour cream	1 teaspoon salt
2 tablespoons mayonnaise	1 teaspoon black pepper
	1 teaspoon dried basil

1. Place the baking pan on the air fry position. Select Air Fry, set the temperature to 350ºF (177ºC), and set the time to 7 minutes.
2. Put the potatoes, prosciutto, and Cheddar in the baking pan. Air fry for 7 minutes.
3. In a separate bowl, mix the sour cream, mayonnaise, salt, pepper, and basil using a whisk.
4. Coat the salad with the dressing and serve.

287.Barbecue Pork Ribs

Prep time: 5 minutes | Cook time: 30 minutes | Serves 4

1 tablespoon barbecue dry rub	cider vinegar
1 teaspoon mustard	1 teaspoon sesame oil
1 tablespoon apple	1 pound (454 g) pork ribs, chopped

1. Combine the dry rub, mustard, apple cider vinegar, and sesame oil, then coat the ribs with this mixture. Refrigerate the ribs for 20 minutes.
2. Place the crisper tray on the air fry position. Select Air Fry, set the temperature to 360ºF (182ºC), and set the time to 30 minutes.
3. When the ribs are ready, place them in the crisper tray. Air fry for 15 minutes. Flip them and air fry on the other side for a further 15 minutes.
4. Serve immediately.

288.Swedish Beef Meatballs

Prep time: 10 minutes | Cook time: 12 minutes | Serves 8

1 pound (454 g) ground beef	½ teaspoons garlic salt
1 egg, beaten	Pepper and salt, to taste
2 carrots, shredded	
2 bread slices, crumbled	1 cup tomato sauce
1 small onion, minced	2 cups pasta sauce

1. Place the crisper tray on the air fry position. Select Air Fry, set the temperature to 400ºF (204ºC), and set the time to 7 minutes.
2. In a bowl, combine the ground beef, egg, carrots, crumbled bread, onion, garlic salt, pepper and salt.
3. Divide the mixture into equal amounts and shape each one into a small meatball.
4. Put them in the crisper tray. Air fry for 7 minutes.
5. Transfer the meatballs to a dish and top with the tomato sauce and pasta sauce.
6. Set the dish into the pan and allow to air fry at 320ºF (160ºC) for 5 more minutes. Serve hot.

289.Easy Beef Schnitzel

Prep time: 5 minutes | Cook time: 12 minutes | Serves 1

½ cup friendly bread crumbs
2 tablespoons olive oil
Pepper and salt, to taste
1 egg, beaten
1 thin beef schnitzel

1. Place the crisper tray on the air fry position. Select Air Fry, set the temperature to 350ºF (177ºC), and set the time to 12 minutes.
2. In a shallow dish, combine the bread crumbs, oil, pepper, and salt.
3. In a second shallow dish, place the beaten egg.
4. Dredge the schnitzel in the egg before rolling it in the bread crumbs.
5. Put the coated schnitzel in the crisper tray. Air fry for 12 minutes. Flip the schnitzel halfway through.
6. Serve immediately.

290.Vietnamese Pork Chops

Prep time: 15 minutes | Cook time: 12 minutes | Serves 2

1 tablespoon chopped shallot
1 tablespoon chopped garlic
1 tablespoon fish sauce
3 tablespoons lemongrass
1 teaspoon soy sauce
1 tablespoon brown sugar
1 tablespoon olive oil
1 teaspoon ground black pepper
2 pork chops

1. Combine shallot, garlic, fish sauce, lemongrass, soy sauce, brown sugar, olive oil, and pepper in a bowl. Stir to mix well.
2. Put the pork chops in the bowl. Toss to coat well. Place the bowl in the refrigerator to marinate for 2 hours.
3. Place the crisper tray on the air fry position. Select Air Fry, set the temperature to 400ºF (204ºC), and set the time to 12 minutes.
4. Remove the pork chops from the bowl and discard the marinade. Transfer the chops into the crisper tray.
5. Air fry for 12 minutes or until lightly browned. Flip the pork chops halfway through the cooking time.
6. Remove the pork chops from the crisper tray and serve hot.

291.Smoked Beef

Prep time: 10 minutes | Cook time: 45 minutes | Serves 8

2 pounds (907 g) roast beef, at room temperature
2 tablespoons extra-virgin olive oil
1 teaspoon sea salt flakes
1 teaspoon ground black pepper
1 teaspoon smoked paprika
Few dashes of liquid smoke
2 jalapeño peppers, thinly sliced

1. Place the baking pan on the roast position. Select Roast, set the temperature to 330ºF (166ºC), and set the time to 45 minutes.
2. With kitchen towels, pat the beef dry.
3. Massage the extra-virgin olive oil, salt, black pepper, and paprika into the meat. Cover with liquid smoke.
4. Put the beef in the pan. Roast for 30 minutes. Flip the roast over and allow to roast for another 15 minutes.
5. When cooked through, serve topped with sliced jalapeños.

292.Teriyaki Pork and Mushroom Rolls

Prep time: 10 minutes | Cook time: 8 minutes | Serves 6

4 tablespoons brown sugar
4 tablespoons mirin
4 tablespoons soy sauce
1 teaspoon almond flour
2-inch ginger, chopped
6 (4-ounce / 113-g) pork belly slices
6 ounces (170 g) Enoki mushrooms

1. Mix the brown sugar, mirin, soy sauce, almond flour, and ginger together until brown sugar dissolves.
2. Take pork belly slices and wrap around a bundle of mushrooms. Brush each roll with teriyaki sauce. Chill for half an hour.
3. Place the crisper tray on the air fry position. Select Air Fry, set the temperature to 350ºF (177ºC), and set the time to 8 minutes.
4. Add marinated pork rolls to the crisper tray.
5. Air fry for 8 minutes. Flip the rolls halfway through.
6. Serve immediately.

293. Beef and Vegetable Cubes

Prep time: 15 minutes | Cook time: 17 minutes | Serves 4

2 tablespoons olive oil
1 tablespoon apple cider vinegar
1 teaspoon fine sea salt
½ teaspoons ground black pepper
1 teaspoon shallot powder
¾ teaspoon smoked cayenne pepper
½ teaspoons garlic powder
¼ teaspoon ground cumin
1 pound (454 g) top round steak, cut into cubes
4 ounces (113 g) broccoli, cut into florets
4 ounces (113 g) mushrooms, sliced
1 teaspoon dried basil
1 teaspoon celery seeds

1. Massage the olive oil, vinegar, salt, black pepper, shallot powder, cayenne pepper, garlic powder, and cumin into the cubed steak, ensuring to coat each piece evenly.
2. Allow to marinate for a minimum of 3 hours.
3. Place the crisper tray on the air fry position. Select Air Fry, set the temperature to 365ºF (185ºC), and set the time to 12 minutes.
4. Put the beef cubes in the crisper tray. Air fry for 12 minutes.
5. When the steak is cooked through, place it in a bowl.
6. Wipe the grease from the crisper tray and pour in the vegetables. Season them with basil and celery seeds.
7. Increase the temperature of the grill to 400ºF (204ºC) and air fry for 5 to 6 minutes. When the vegetables are hot, serve them with the steak.

294. Char Siew

Prep time: 10 minutes | Cook time: 20 minutes | Serves 4 to 6

1 strip of pork shoulder butt with a good amount of fat marbling
Olive oil, for brushing the pan
Marinade:
1 teaspoon sesame oil
4 tablespoons raw honey
1 teaspoon low-sodium dark soy sauce
1 teaspoon light soy sauce
1 tablespoon rose wine
2 tablespoons Hoisin sauce

1. Combine all the marinade ingredients together in a Ziploc bag. Put pork in bag, making sure all sections of pork strip are engulfed in the marinade. Chill for 3 to 24 hours.
2. Take out the strip 30 minutes before planning to roast.
3. Place the baking pan on the roast position. Select Roast, set the temperature to 350ºF (177ºC), and set the time to 20 minutes.
4. Put foil on the pan and brush with olive oil. Put marinated pork strip onto prepared pan.
5. Roast for 20 minutes.
6. Glaze with marinade every 5 to 10 minutes.
7. Remove strip and leave to cool a few minutes before slicing.
8. Serve immediately.

295. Tonkatsu

Prep time: 5 minutes | Cook time: 10 minutes per batch | Serves 4

²/₃ cup all-purpose flour
2 large egg whites
1 cup panko breadcrumbs
4 (4-ounce / 113-g) center-cut boneless pork loin chops (about ½ inch thick)
Cooking spray

1. Spritz the crisper tray with cooking spray.
2. Place the crisper tray on the air fry position. Select Air Fry, set the temperature to 375ºF (191ºC), and set the time to 10 minutes.
3. Pour the flour in a bowl. Whisk the egg whites in a separate bowl. Spread the breadcrumbs on a large plate.
4. Dredge the pork loin chops in the flour first, press to coat well, then shake the excess off and dunk the chops in the eggs whites, and then roll the chops over the breadcrumbs. Shake the excess off.
5. Arrange the pork chops in batches in a single layer in the crisper tray and spritz with cooking spray.
6. Air fry for 10 minutes or until the pork chops are lightly browned and crunchy. Flip the chops halfway through. Repeat with remaining chops.
7. Serve immediately.

296. Bacon-Wrapped Sausage with Tomato Relish

Prep time: 1 hour 15 minutes | Cook time: 32 minutes | Serves 4

8 pork sausages
Relish:
8 large tomatoes, chopped
1 small onion, peeled
1 clove garlic, peeled
1 tablespoon white wine vinegar
3 tablespoons

8 bacon strips

chopped parsley
1 teaspoon smoked paprika
2 tablespoons sugar
Salt and ground black pepper, to taste

1. Purée the tomatoes, onion, and garlic in a food processor until well mixed and smooth.
2. Pour the purée in a saucepan and drizzle with white wine vinegar. Sprinkle with salt and ground black pepper. Simmer over medium heat for 10 minutes.
3. Add the parsley, paprika, and sugar to the saucepan and cook for 10 more minutes or until it has a thick consistency. Keep stirring during the cooking. Refrigerate for an hour to chill.
4. Place the crisper tray on the air fry position. Select Air Fry, set the temperature to 350ºF (177ºC), and set the time to 12 minutes.
5. Wrap the sausage with bacon strips and secure with toothpicks, then place them in the crisper tray.
6. Air fry for 12 minutes or until the bacon is crispy and browned. Flip the bacon-wrapped sausage halfway through.
7. Transfer the bacon-wrapped sausage on a plate and baste with the relish or just serve with the relish alongside.

297. Apple-Glazed Pork

Prep time: 15 minutes | Cook time: 19 minutes | Serves 4

1 sliced apple
1 small onion, sliced
2 tablespoons apple cider vinegar, divided
½ teaspoon thyme
½ teaspoon rosemary
¼ teaspoon brown sugar

3 tablespoons olive oil, divided
¼ teaspoon smoked paprika
4 pork chops
Salt and ground black pepper, to taste

1. Place the baking pan on the bake position. Select Bake, set the temperature to 350ºF (177ºC), and set the time to 4 minutes.
2. Combine the apple slices, onion, 1 tablespoon of vinegar, thyme, rosemary, brown sugar, and 2 tablespoons of olive oil in the baking pan. Stir to mix well.
3. Bake for 4 minutes.
4. Meanwhile, combine the remaining vinegar and olive oil, and paprika in a large bowl. Sprinkle with salt and ground black pepper. Stir to mix well. Dredge the pork in the mixture and toss to coat well.
5. Remove the baking pan from the grill and put in the pork. Air fry for 10 minutes to lightly brown the pork. Flip the pork chops halfway through.
6. Remove the pork from the grill and baste with baked apple mixture on both sides. Put the pork back to the grill and air fry for an additional 5 minutes. Flip halfway through.
7. Serve immediately.

298. Golden Wasabi Spam

Prep time: 5 minutes | Cook time: 12 minutes | Serves 3

²/₃ cup all-purpose flour
2 large eggs
1½ tablespoons wasabi paste

2 cups panko breadcrumbs
6 ½-inch-thick spam slices
Cooking spray

1. Spritz the crisper tray with cooking spray.
2. Place the crisper tray on the air fry position. Select Air Fry, set the temperature to 400ºF (204ºC), and set the time to 12 minutes.
3. Pour the flour in a shallow plate. Whisk the eggs with wasabi in a large bowl. Pour the panko in a separate shallow plate.
4. Dredge the spam slices in the flour first, then dunk in the egg mixture, and then roll the spam over the panko to coat well. Shake the excess off.
5. Arrange the spam slices in a single layer in the crisper tray and spritz with cooking spray.
6. Air fry for 12 minutes or until the spam slices are golden and crispy. Flip the spam slices halfway through.
7. Serve immediately.

299.Citrus Carnitas

Prep time: 1 hour 10 minutes | Cook time: 25 minutes | Serves 6

2½ pounds (1.1 kg) boneless country-style pork ribs, cut into 2-inch pieces
3 tablespoons olive brine
1 tablespoon minced fresh oregano leaves
1/3 cup orange juice
1 teaspoon ground cumin
1 tablespoon minced garlic
1 teaspoon salt
1 teaspoon ground black pepper
Cooking spray

1. Combine all the ingredients in a large bowl. Toss to coat the pork ribs well. Wrap the bowl in plastic and refrigerate for at least an hour to marinate.
2. Spritz the crisper tray with cooking spray.
3. Place the crisper tray on the air fry position. Select Air Fry, set the temperature to 400ºF (204ºC), and set the time to 25 minutes.
4. Arrange the marinated pork ribs in a single layer in the crisper tray and spritz with cooking spray.
5. Air fry for 25 minutes or until well browned. Flip the ribs halfway through.
6. Serve immediately.

300.Classic Walliser Schnitzel

Prep time: 5 minutes | Cook time: 14 minutes | Serves 2

½ cup pork rinds
½ tablespoon fresh parsley
½ teaspoon fennel seed
½ teaspoon mustard
1/3 tablespoon cider vinegar
1 teaspoon garlic salt
1/3 teaspoon ground black pepper
2 eggs
2 pork schnitzel, halved
Cooking spray

1. Spritz the crisper tray with cooking spray.
2. Place the crisper tray on the air fry position. Select Air Fry, set the temperature to 350ºF (177ºC), and set the time to 14 minutes.
3. Put the pork rinds, parsley, fennel seeds, and mustard in a food processor. Pour in the vinegar and sprinkle with salt and ground black pepper. Pulse until well combined and smooth.
4. Pour the pork rind mixture in a large bowl. Whisk the eggs in a separate bowl.
5. Dunk the pork schnitzel in the whisked eggs, then dunk in the pork rind mixture to coat well. Shake the excess off.
6. Arrange the schnitzel in the crisper tray and spritz with cooking spray. Air fry for 14 minutes or until golden and crispy. Flip the schnitzel halfway through.
7. Serve immediately.

301.Pork, Pepper, and Pineapple Kebabs

Prep time: 10 minutes | Cook time: 12 minutes | Serves 4

¼ teaspoon kosher salt or 1/8 teaspoon fine salt
1 medium pork tenderloin (about 1 pound / 454 g), cut into 1½-inch chunks
1 red bell pepper, seeded and cut into 1-inch pieces
1 green bell pepper, seeded and cut into 1-inch pieces
2 cups fresh pineapple chunks
¾ cup teriyaki sauce

Special Equipment:
12 (9- to 12-inch) wooden skewers soaked in water for about 30 minutes

1. Sprinkle the salt over the pork cubes.
2. Alternate the pork, bell peppers, and pineapple on the skewers, making about 12 skewers (if you use the larger skewers, you'll probably only need 8). Liberally brush the skewers with about half of the teriyaki sauce. Transfer to the baking pan.
3. Place the pan on the roast position. Select Roast, set temperature to 375ºF (191ºC), and set time to 10 minutes.
4. After about 5 minutes, remove the pan from the grill. Turn over the skewers and brush with the remaining teriyaki sauce. Return the pan to the grill and continue cooking.
5. When cooking is complete, the vegetables should be tender and browned in spots, and the pork browned and cooked through. Remove the pan from the grill and serve.

302.Lechon Kawali

Prep time: 10 minutes | Cook time: 30 minutes | Serves 4

1 pound (454 g) pork belly, cut into three thick chunks	1 teaspoon kosher salt
6 garlic cloves	1 teaspoon ground black pepper
2 bay leaves	3 cups water
2 tablespoons soy sauce	Cooking spray

1. Put all the ingredients in a pressure cooker, then put the lid on and cook on high for 15 minutes.
2. Natural release the pressure and release any remaining pressure, transfer the tender pork belly on a clean work surface. Allow to cool under room temperature until you can handle.
3. Generously spritz the crisper tray with cooking spray.
4. Place the crisper tray on the air fry position. Select Air Fry, set the temperature to 400ºF (204ºC), and set the time to 15 minutes.
5. Cut each chunk into two slices, then put the pork slices in the crisper tray.
6. Air fry for 15 minutes or until the pork fat is crispy. Spritz the pork with more cooking spray, if necessary.
7. Serve immediately.

303.Grapes with Italian Sausages and Polenta

Prep time: 10 minutes | Cook time: 20 minutes | Serves 6

2 pounds (907 g) seedless red grapes	Freshly ground black pepper
3 shallots, sliced	6 links (about 1½ pounds / 680 g) hot or sweet Italian sausage
2 teaspoons fresh thyme or 1 teaspoon dried thyme	
2 tablespoons extra-virgin olive oil	3 tablespoons sherry vinegar or balsamic vinegar
½ teaspoon kosher salt or ¼ teaspoon fine salt	6 (1-inch-thick) slices polenta

1. Place the grapes in a large bowl. Add the shallots, thyme, olive oil, salt, and pepper. Gently toss. Place the grapes in the baking pan. Arrange the sausage links evenly in the pan.

2. Place the pan on the roast position. Select Roast, set temperature to 375ºF (191ºC), and set time to 20 minutes.
3. After 10 minutes, remove the pan. Turn over the sausages and sprinkle the vinegar over the sausages and grapes. Gently toss the grapes and move them to one side of the pan. Place the polenta slices in the pan. Return the pan to the grill and continue cooking.
4. When cooking is complete, the grapes should be very soft and the sausages browned.

304.Spicy Pork Chops with Carrots and Mushrooms

Prep time: 10 minutes | Cook time: 15 to 18 minutes | Serves 4

2 carrots, cut into sticks	1 teaspoon dried oregano
1 cup mushrooms, sliced	1 teaspoon dried thyme
2 garlic cloves, minced	1 teaspoon cayenne pepper
2 tablespoons olive oil	Salt and ground black pepper, to taste
1 pound (454 g) boneless pork chops	Cooking spray

1. Spritz the crisper tray with cooking spray.
2. Place the crisper tray on the air fry position. Select Air Fry, set the temperature to 360ºF (182ºC), and set the time to 18 minutes.
3. In a mixing bowl, toss together the carrots, mushrooms, garlic, olive oil and salt until well combined.
4. Add the pork chops to a different bowl and season with oregano, thyme, cayenne pepper, salt and black pepper.
5. Lower the vegetable mixture in the prepared crisper tray. Place the seasoned pork chops on top. Air fry for 15 to 18 minutes, or until the pork is well browned and the vegetables are tender, flipping the pork and shaking the crisper tray once halfway through.
6. Transfer the pork chops to the serving dishes and let cool for 5 minutes. Serve warm with vegetable on the side.

305.Crispy Pork Tenderloin

Prep time: 5 minutes | Cook time: 10 minutes | Serves 6

2 large egg whites
1½ tablespoons Dijon mustard
2 cups crushed pretzel crumbs

1½ pounds (680 g) pork tenderloin, cut into ¼-pound (113-g) sections
Cooking spray

1. Spritz the crisper tray with cooking spray.
2. Place the crisper tray on the air fry position. Select Air Fry, set the temperature to 350ºF (177ºC), and set the time to 10 minutes.
3. Whisk the egg whites with Dijon mustard in a bowl until bubbly. Pour the pretzel crumbs in a separate bowl.
4. Dredge the pork tenderloin in the egg white mixture and press to coat. Shake the excess off and roll the tenderloin over the pretzel crumbs.
5. Arrange the well-coated pork tenderloin in batches in a single layer in the crisper tray and spritz with cooking spray.
6. Air fry for 10 minutes or until the pork is golden brown and crispy. Flip the pork halfway through. Repeat with remaining pork sections.
7. Serve immediately.

306.Homemade Teriyaki Pork Ribs

Prep time: 5 minutes | Cook time: 30 minutes | Serves 4

¼ cup soy sauce
¼ cup honey
1 teaspoon garlic powder
1 teaspoon ground

dried ginger
4 (8-ounce / 227-g) boneless country-style pork ribs
Cooking spray

1. Spritz the crisper tray with cooking spray.
2. Place the crisper tray on the air fry position. Select Air Fry, set the temperature to 350ºF (177ºC), and set the time to 30 minutes.
3. Make the teriyaki sauce: combine the soy sauce, honey, garlic powder, and ginger in a bowl. Stir to mix well.
4. Brush the ribs with half of the teriyaki sauce, then arrange the ribs in the crisper tray. Spritz with cooking spray. You may need to work in batches to avoid overcrowding.

5. Air fry for 30 minutes or until the internal temperature of the ribs reaches at least 145ºF (63ºC). Brush the ribs with remaining teriyaki sauce and flip halfway through.
6. Serve immediately.

307.Crispy Broccoli with Steak

Prep time: 10 minutes | Cook time: 15 minutes | Serves 4

12 ounces (340 g) broccoli florets (about 4 cups)
1 pound (454 g) sirloin or flat iron steak, cut into thin strips
½ teaspoon kosher salt or ¼ teaspoon

fine salt
¾ cup Asian Sauce
1 teaspoon sriracha or chile-garlic sauce
3 tablespoons freshly squeezed orange juice
1 teaspoon cornstarch
1 medium onion, thinly sliced

1. Place a large piece of aluminum foil in the baking pan. Place the broccoli on top and sprinkle with 3 tablespoons of water. Seal the broccoli in the foil in a single layer.
2. Place the pan on the roast position. Select Roast, set temperature to 375ºF (191ºC), and set time to 6 minutes.
3. While the broccoli steams, sprinkle the steak with the salt. In a small bowl, whisk together the Asian-Style Sauce, sriracha, orange juice, and cornstarch. Place the onion and beef in a large bowl.
4. When cooking is complete, remove the pan from the grill. Open the packet of broccoli and use tongs to transfer the broccoli to the bowl with the beef and onion, discarding the foil and remaining water. Pour the sauce over the beef and vegetables and toss to coat. Place the mixture in the baking pan.
5. Place the pan on the roast position. Select Roast, set temperature to 375ºF (191ºC), and set time to 9 minutes.
6. After about 4 minutes, remove the pan from the grill and gently toss the ingredients. Return the pan to grill and continue cooking.
7. When cooking is complete, the sauce should be thickened, the vegetables tender, and the beef barely pink in the center. Serve plain or with steamed rice.

308.Sausage Ratatouille

Prep time: 10 minutes | Cook time: 25 minutes | Serves 4

4 pork sausages
Ratatouille:

2 zucchinis, sliced
1 eggplant, sliced
15 ounces (425 g)
tomatoes, sliced
1 red bell pepper,
sliced
1 medium red onion,
sliced
1 cup canned butter

beans, drained
1 tablespoon balsamic
vinegar
2 garlic cloves,
minced
1 red chili, chopped
2 tablespoons fresh
thyme, chopped
2 tablespoons olive oil

1. Place the crisper tray on the air fry position. Select Air Fry, set the temperature to 390ºF (199ºC), and set the time to 10 minutes.
2. Place the sausages in the crisper tray. Air fry for 10 minutes or until the sausage is lightly browned. Flip the sausages halfway through.
3. Meanwhile, make the ratatouille: arrange the vegetable slices on the the baking pan alternatively, then add the remaining ingredients on top.
4. Transfer the sausage to a plate. Bake for 15 minutes or until the vegetables are tender.
5. Serve the ratatouille with the sausage on top.

309.Simple Pork Meatballs with Red Chili

Prep time: 5 minutes | Cook time: 15 minutes | Serves 4

1 pound (454 g)
ground pork
2 cloves garlic, finely
minced
1 cup scallions, finely
chopped
1½ tablespoons
Worcestershire sauce
½ teaspoon freshly

grated ginger root
1 teaspoon turmeric
powder
1 tablespoon oyster
sauce
1 small sliced red
chili, for garnish
Cooking spray

1. Spritz the crisper tray with cooking spray.
2. Place the crisper tray on the air fry position. Select Air Fry, set the temperature to 350ºF (177ºC), and set the time to 15 minutes.

3. Combine all the ingredients, except for the red chili in a large bowl. Toss to mix well.
4. Shape the mixture into equally sized balls, then arrange them in the crisper tray and spritz with cooking spray.
5. Air fry for 15 minutes or until the balls are lightly browned. Flip the balls halfway through.
6. Serve the pork meatballs with red chili on top.

310.Smoky Paprika Pork and Vegetable Kabobs

Prep time: 25 minutes | Cook time: 15 minutes | Serves 4

1 pound (454 g) pork
tenderloin, cubed
1 teaspoon smoked
paprika
Salt and ground black
pepper, to taste
1 green bell pepper,

cut into chunks
1 zucchini, cut into
chunks
1 red onion, sliced
1 tablespoon oregano
Cooking spray

Special Equipment:
Small bamboo skewers, soaked in water for 20 minutes to keep them from burning while cooking

1. Spritz the crisper tray with cooking spray.
2. Place the crisper tray on the air fry position. Select Air Fry, set the temperature to 350ºF (177ºC), and set the time to 15 minutes.
3. Add the pork to a bowl and season with the smoked paprika, salt and black pepper. Thread the seasoned pork cubes and vegetables alternately onto the soaked skewers.
4. Arrange the skewers in the prepared crisper tray and spray with cooking spray.
5. Air fry for 15 minutes, or until the pork is well browned and the vegetables are tender, flipping once halfway through.
6. Transfer the skewers to the serving dishes and sprinkle with oregano. Serve hot.

311.Spicy Pork with Candy Onions

Prep time: 10 minutes | Cook time: 52 minutes | Serves 4

2 teaspoons sesame oil	Sea salt and ground black pepper, to taste
1 teaspoon dried sage, crushed	2 pounds (907 g) pork leg roast, scored
1 teaspoon cayenne pepper	½ pound (227 g) candy onions, sliced
1 rosemary sprig, chopped	4 cloves garlic, finely chopped
1 thyme sprig, chopped	2 chili peppers, minced

1. Place the baking pan on the air fry position. Select Air Fry, set the temperature to 400ºF (204ºC), and set the time to 52 minutes.
2. In a mixing bowl, combine the sesame oil, sage, cayenne pepper, rosemary, thyme, salt and black pepper until well mixed. In another bowl, place the pork leg and brush with the seasoning mixture.
3. Place the seasoned pork leg in the baking pan. Air fry for 40 minutes, or until lightly browned, flipping halfway through. Add the candy onions, garlic and chili peppers to the pan and air fry for another 12 minutes.
4. Transfer the pork leg to a plate. Let cool for 5 minutes and slice. Spread the juices left in the pan over the pork and serve warm with the candy onions.

312.Pork Sausage with Cauliflower Mash

Prep time: 5 minutes | Cook time: 27 minutes | Serves 6

1 pound (454 g) cauliflower, chopped	1 teaspoon cumin powder
6 pork sausages, chopped	½ teaspoon tarragon
½ onion, sliced	½ teaspoon sea salt
3 eggs, beaten	½ teaspoon ground black pepper
⅓ cup Colby cheese	Cooking spray

1. Place the baking pan on the bake position. Select Bake, set the temperature to 365ºF (185ºC), and set the time to 27 minutes.
2. Spritz the baking pan with cooking spray.
3. In a saucepan over medium heat, boil the cauliflower until tender. Place the boiled cauliflower in a food processor and pulse until puréed. Transfer to a large bowl and combine with remaining ingredients until well blended.
4. Pour the cauliflower and sausage mixture into the baking pan. Bake for 27 minutes, or until lightly browned.
5. Divide the mixture among six serving dishes and serve warm.

313.Steak and Bell Pepper Fajitas

Prep time: 10 minutes | Cook time: 15 minutes | Serves 4

8 (6-inch) flour or corn tortillas
1 pound (454 g) top sirloin steak, sliced ¼-inch thick
1 red bell pepper, seeded and sliced ½-inch thick
1 green bell pepper, seeded and sliced ½-inch thick
1 jalapeño, seeded and sliced thin
1 medium onion, sliced ½-inch thick
2 tablespoons vegetable oil
2 tablespoons Mexican seasoning
1 teaspoon kosher salt or ½ teaspoon fine salt
Salsa
1 small avocado, sliced

1. Place a large sheet of aluminum foil in the baking pan. Place the tortillas on the foil in two stacks and wrap in the foil.
2. Place the pan on the roast position. Select Roast, set temperature to 325ºF (163ºC), and set time to 6 minutes.
3. After 3 minutes, remove the pan from the grill and flip the packet of tortillas over. Return the pan to the grill and continue cooking.
4. While the tortillas warm, place the steak, bell peppers, jalapeño, and onion in a large bowl and drizzle the oil over. Sprinkle with the Mexican seasoning and salt, and toss to coat.
5. When cooking is complete, remove the pan from the grill and place the packet of tortillas on top of the grill to keep warm. Place the beef and peppers mixture in the baking pan, spreading out into a single layer as much as possible.
6. Place the pan on the roast position. Select Roast, set temperature to 375ºF (191ºC), and set time to 9 minutes.
7. After about 5 minutes, remove the pan from the grill and stir the ingredients. Return the pan to the grill and continue cooking.
8. When cooking is complete, the vegetables will be soft and browned in places, and the beef will be browned on the outside and barely pink inside. Remove the pan from the grill. Unwrap the tortillas and spoon the fajita mixture into the tortillas. Serve with salsa and avocado slices.

314.Pork and Water Chestnut Lettuce Cups

Prep time: 10 minutes | Cook time: 12 minutes | Serves 4

1 medium pork tenderloin (about 1 pound / 454 g), silver skin and external fat trimmed
⅔ cup Asian Sauce, divided
1 teaspoon cornstarch
1 medium jalapeño, seeded and minced
1 can diced water chestnuts
½ large (or 1 very small) red bell pepper, seeded and chopped
2 scallions, chopped, white and green parts separated
1 head butter lettuce or Boston lettuce
½ cup roasted, chopped almonds or peanuts (optional)
¼ cup coarsely chopped cilantro (optional)

1. Cut the tenderloin into ¼-inch slices and place them in the baking pan. Baste with about 3 tablespoons of Asian-Style Sauce. Stir the cornstarch into the remaining sauce and set aside.
2. Place the pan on the roast position. Select Roast, set temperature to 375ºF (191ºC), and set time to 12 minutes.
3. After 5 minutes, remove the pan from the grill. Place the pork slices on a cutting board. Place the jalapeño, water chestnuts, red pepper, and the white parts of the scallions in the baking pan and pour the remaining sauce over. Stir to coat the vegetables with the sauce. Return the pan to the grill and continue cooking.
4. While the vegetables cook, chop the pork into small pieces. Separate the lettuce leaves, discarding any tough outer leaves and setting aside the small inner leaves for another use. You'll want 12 to 18 leaves, depending on size and your appetites.
5. After 5 minutes, remove the pan from the grill. Add the pork to the vegetables, stirring to combine. Return the pan to the grill and continue cooking for the remaining 2 minutes, until the pork is warmed back up and the sauce has reduced slightly.
6. When cooking is complete, remove the pan from the grill. Place the pork and vegetables in a medium serving bowl and stir in half the green parts of the scallions. To serve, spoon some of the pork and vegetables into each of the lettuce leaves. Top with the remaining scallion greens and garnish with the nuts and cilantro (if using).

315. Scratch Meatball Hoagies

Prep time: 15 minutes | Cook time: 24 minutes | Serves 4

1 large egg	Parmesan cheese, divided
¼ cup whole milk	1 teaspoon kosher salt or ½ teaspoon fine salt
24 saltines, crushed but not pulverized	
1 pound (454 g) ground chuck	4 hoagie or sub rolls, split
1 pound (454 g) Italian sausage, casings removed	1 cup marinara sauce
4 tablespoons grated	¾ cup shredded Mozzarella cheese

1. In a large bowl, whisk the egg into the milk, then stir in the crackers. Let sit for 5 minutes to hydrate.
2. With your hands, break the ground chuck and sausage into the milk mixture, alternating beef and sausage. When you've added half of the meat, sprinkle 2 tablespoons of the grated Parmesan and the salt over it, then continue breaking up the meat until it's all in the bowl. Gently mix everything together. Try not to overwork the meat, but get it all combined.
3. Form the mixture into balls about the size of a golf ball. You should get about 24 meatballs. Flatten the balls slightly to prevent them from rolling, then arrange them in the baking pan, about 2 inches apart.
4. Place the pan on the roast position. Select Roast, set temperature to 400ºF (204ºC), and set time to 20 minutes.
5. After 10 minutes, remove the pan from the grill and turn over the meatballs. Return the pan to the grill and continue cooking.
6. When cooking is complete, remove the pan from the grill. Place the meatballs on a rack. Wipe off the baking pan (it doesn't have to be completely clean; you just want to remove the fat from the meatballs. If you can't help yourself, you can wash it.)
7. Open the rolls, cut-side up, in the baking pan. Place 3 to 4 meatballs on the base of each roll, and top each sandwich with ¼ cup of marinara sauce. Divide the Mozzarella among the top halves of the buns and sprinkle the remaining 2 tablespoons of Parmesan cheese over the Mozzarella.
8. Place the pan on the broil position. Select Broil, set temperature to 450ºF (232ºC), and set time to 4 minutes.
9. Check the sandwiches after 2 minutes; the Mozzarella cheese should be melted and bubbling slightly.
10. When cooking is complete, remove the pan from the grill. Close the sandwiches and serve.

316. Asparagus and Prosciutto Tart

Prep time: 10 minutes | Cook time: 25 minutes | Serves 4

1 sheet (½ package) frozen puff pastry, thawed	trimmed
All-purpose flour, for dusting	8 ounces (227 g) thinly sliced prosciutto, sliced into ribbons about ½-inch wide
½ cup grated Parmesan cheese	
1 pound (454 g) (or more) asparagus,	2 teaspoons aged balsamic vinegar

1. Unwrap and unfold the puff pastry on a lightly floured cutting board. Using a rolling pin, roll it very lightly, just to press the folds together. Place it in the baking pan.
2. Roll about ½ inch of the pastry edges up to form a ridge around the perimeter. Crimp the corners together so you have a solid rim around the pastry. Prick the bottom of the pastry all over with a fork (this will keep it flat as it bakes). Sprinkle the cheese over the bottom of the pastry.
3. Trim the asparagus spears so they fit within the border of the pastry shell. Arrange them on top of the cheese in a single layer. You can point all the spears the same way, but I think it looks best to alternate, with 4 or 5 spears pointing one way, then the next few pointing the opposite direction. Arrange the prosciutto over the top more or less evenly.
4. Place the pan on the bake position. Select Bake, set temperature to 375ºF (191ºC), and set time to 25 minutes.
5. After about 15 minutes, check the tart, rotating the pan if the crust is not browning evenly. Continue cooking.
6. When cooking is complete, the pastry should be golden brown, and the edges of the prosciutto pieces browned. Remove the pan from the grill. Let the tart cool for a few minutes before slicing. Just before serving, drizzle the balsamic vinegar over the tart.

317. Tandoori Lamb Chops with Red Potatoes

Prep time: 10 minutes | Cook time: 20 minutes | Serves 4

8 (½-inch thick) lamb loin chops (about 2 pounds / 907 g)
2 teaspoons kosher salt or 1 teaspoon fine salt, divided
¾ cup plain whole milk yogurt
1 tablespoon freshly grated ginger (1- or 2-inch piece) or 1 teaspoon ground ginger
2 garlic cloves, minced or smashed
1 teaspoon smoked paprika
½ teaspoon cayenne pepper
1 teaspoon curry powder
12 ounces (340 g) small red potatoes, quartered
Cooking oil spray

1. Salt the lamb chops on both sides with 1 teaspoon of kosher salt and let sit while you prepare the marinade.
2. In a large bowl, whisk together the yogurt, ginger, garlic, paprika, cayenne pepper, curry powder, and remaining 1 teaspoon of kosher salt. Pour all but 2 tablespoons of the marinade into a resealable plastic bag, leaving those 2 tablespoons in the bowl. Place the lamb chops in the bag. Squeeze out as much air as possible and squish the bag around to coat the chops with the marinade. Set aside.
3. Add the potatoes to the bowl with the remaining marinade and toss to coat. Spray the baking pan with cooking oil spray. Place the potatoes in the pan.
4. Place the pan on the roast position. Select Roast, set temperature to 375ºF (191ºC), and set time to 10 minutes.
5. When cooking is complete, remove the pan from the grill. Remove the chops from the marinade, draining off all but a thin coat (and discarding the marinade and plastic bag), and place them in the baking pan.
6. Place the pan on the broil position. Select Broil, set temperature to 450ºF (232ºC), and set time to 10 minutes.
7. After 5 minutes, remove the pan from the grill and turn over the chops and potatoes. Return the pan to the grill and continue cooking.
8. When cooking is complete, the lamb should read 145ºF (63ºC) for medium rare on a meat thermometer; continue cooking for an additional few minutes if you want it more well done. Remove the pan from the grill and serve.

318. Braised Pork with Butternut Squash

Prep time: 15 minutes | Cook time: 13 minutes | Serves 4

4 boneless pork loin chops, ¾- to 1-inch thick
1 teaspoon kosher salt or ½ teaspoon fine salt, divided
2 tablespoons Dijon mustard
2 tablespoons brown sugar
1 pound (454 g) butternut squash, cut into 1-inch cubes
1 large Gala or Braeburn apple, peeled and cut into 12 to 16 wedges
1 medium onion, thinly sliced
½ teaspoon dried thyme
¼ teaspoon freshly ground black pepper
1 tablespoon unsalted butter, melted
½ cup low-sodium chicken stock

1. Sprinkle the pork chops on both sides with ½ teaspoon of kosher salt. In a small bowl, whisk together the mustard and brown sugar. Baste about half of the mixture on one side of the pork chops. Place the chops, basted-side up, in the baking pan.
2. Place the squash in a large bowl. Add the apple, onion, thyme, remaining ½ teaspoon of kosher salt, pepper, and butter and toss to coat. Arrange the squash-fruit mixture around the chops in the pan. Pour the chicken stock over the mixture, avoiding the chops.
3. Place the pan on the roast position. Select Roast, set temperature to 350ºF (177ºC), and set time to 13 minutes.
4. After about 7 minutes, remove the pan from the grill. Gently toss the squash mixture and turn over the chops. Baste the chops with the remaining mustard mixture. Return the pan to the grill and continue cooking.
5. When cooking is complete, the pork chops should register at least 145ºF (63ºC) in the center on a meat thermometer, and the squash and apples should be tender. If necessary, continue cooking for up to 3 minutes more.
6. Remove the pan from the grill. Spoon the squash and apples onto four plates, and place a pork chop on top. If you like, sprinkle with a little fresh thyme or parsley.

319.Mushroom and Italian Sausage Calzones

Prep time: 10 minutes | Cook time: 24 minutes | Serves 4

2 links Italian sausages (about ½ pound / 227 g)
1 pound (454 g) store-bought pizza dough or frozen bread dough, thawed
3 tablespoons extra-virgin olive oil, divided

¼ cup marinara sauce
½ cup Roasted Mushrooms
1 cup shredded Mozzarella cheese or Mozzarella blend

1. Place the sausages in the baking pan.
2. Place the pan on the roast position. Select Roast, set temperature to 375ºF (191ºC), and set time to 12 minutes.
3. After 6 minutes, remove the pan from the grill and turn over the sausages. Return the pan to the grill and continue cooking.
4. While the sausages cook, divide the pizza dough into 4 equal pieces. One at a time, place a piece of dough onto a square of parchment paper 9 inches in diameter. Brush the dough on both sides with ¾ teaspoon of olive oil, then top the dough with another piece of parchment. Press the dough into a 7-inch circle. Remove the top piece of parchment and set aside. Repeat with the remaining pieces of dough.
5. When cooking is complete, remove the pan from the grill. Place the sausages on a cutting board. Let them cool for several minutes, then slice into ¼-inch rounds and cut each round into 4 pieces. (Don't worry if the very center of the sausage isn't cooked; it will cook again inside the calzones.)
6. One at a time, spread a tablespoon of marinara sauce over half of a dough circle, leaving a ½-inch border at the edges. Cover with a quarter of the sausage pieces and add a quarter of the mushrooms. Sprinkle with ¼ cup of cheese. Pull the other side of the dough over the filling and pinch the edges together to seal. Transfer from the parchment to the baking pan. Repeat with the other rounds of dough, sauce, sausage, mushrooms, and cheese.
7. Brush the tops of the calzones with 1 tablespoon of olive oil.
8. Place the pan on the roast position. Select Roast, set temperature to 450ºF (232ºC), and set time to 12 minutes.
9. After 6 minutes, remove the pan from the grill. The calzones should be golden brown. Turn over the calzones and brush the tops with the remaining 1 tablespoon of olive oil. Return the pan to the grill and continue cooking.
10. When cooking is complete, the crust should be a deep golden brown on both sides. Remove the pan from the grill. The center will be molten; let cool for several minutes before serving.

320.Roasted Cod with Sesame Seeds

Prep time: 5 minutes | Cook time: 7 to 9 minutes | Makes 1 fillet

1 tablespoon reduced-sodium soy sauce
2 teaspoons honey
Cooking spray
6 ounces (170 g) fresh cod fillet
1 teaspoon sesame seeds

1. Place the crisper tray on the roast position. Select Roast, set the temperature to 360ºF (182ºC), and set the time to 10 minutes.
2. In a small bowl, combine the soy sauce and honey.
3. Spray the crisper tray with cooking spray, then place the cod in the crisper tray, brush with the soy mixture, and sprinkle sesame seeds on top.
4. Roast for 7 to 9 minutes, or until opaque.
5. Remove the fish and allow to cool on a wire rack for 5 minutes before serving.

321.Garlic Scallops

Prep time: 10 minutes | Cook time: 10 to 15 minutes | Serves 4

2 teaspoons olive oil
1 packet dry zesty Italian dressing mix
1 teaspoon minced garlic
16 ounces (454 g) small scallops, patted dry
Cooking spray

1. Place the crisper tray on the air fry position. Select Air Fry, set the temperature to 400ºF (204ºC), and set the time to 15 minutes.
2. Spray the crisper tray lightly with cooking spray.
3. In a large zip-top plastic bag, combine the olive oil, Italian dressing mix, and garlic.
4. Add the scallops, seal the zip-top bag, and coat the scallops in the seasoning mixture.
5. Place the scallops in the crisper tray and lightly spray with cooking spray.
6. Air fry for 5 minutes, shake the crisper tray, and air fry for 5 to 10 more minutes, or until the scallops reach an internal temperature of 120ºF (49ºC).
7. Serve immediately.

322.Baked Flounder Fillets

Prep time: 8 minutes | Cook time: 12 minutes | Serves 2

2 flounder fillets, patted dry
1 egg
½ teaspoon Worcestershire sauce
¼ cup almond flour
¼ cup coconut flour
½ teaspoon coarse sea salt
½ teaspoon lemon pepper
¼ teaspoon chili powder
Cooking spray

1. Place the crisper tray on the bake position. Select Bake, set the temperature to 390ºF (199ºC), and set the time to 12 minutes.
2. Spritz the crisper tray with cooking spray.
3. In a shallow bowl, beat together the egg with Worcestershire sauce until well incorporated.
4. In another bowl, thoroughly combine the almond flour, coconut flour, sea salt, lemon pepper, and chili powder.
5. Dredge the fillets in the egg mixture, shaking off any excess, then roll in the flour mixture to coat well.
6. Place the fillets in the crisper tray. Bake for 7 minutes. Flip the fillets and spray with cooking spray. Continue cooking for 5 minutes, or until the fish is flaky.
7. Serve warm.

323.Paprika Shrimp

Prep time: 5 minutes | Cook time: 10 minutes | Serves 4

1 pound (454 g) tiger shrimp
2 tablespoons olive oil
½ tablespoon old bay seasoning
¼ tablespoon smoked paprika
¼ teaspoon cayenne pepper
A pinch of sea salt

1. Place the crisper tray on the air fry position. Select Air Fry, set the temperature to 380ºF (193ºC), and set the time to 10 minutes.
2. Toss all the ingredients in a large bowl until the shrimp are evenly coated.
3. Arrange the shrimp in the crisper tray. Air fry for 10 minutes, shaking the crisper tray halfway through, or until the shrimp are pink and cooked through.
4. Serve hot.

324. Garlic Shrimp with Parsley

Prep time: 10 minutes | Cook time: 5 minutes | Serves 4

18 shrimp, shelled and deveined
2 garlic cloves, peeled and minced
2 tablespoons extra-virgin olive oil
2 tablespoons freshly squeezed lemon juice
½ cup fresh parsley, coarsely chopped
1 teaspoon onion powder
1 teaspoon lemon-pepper seasoning
½ teaspoon hot paprika
½ teaspoon salt
¼ teaspoon cumin powder

1. Toss all the ingredients in a mixing bowl until the shrimp are well coated.
2. Cover and allow to marinate in the refrigerator for 30 minutes.
3. Place the crisper tray on the air fry position. Select Air Fry, set the temperature to 400ºF (204ºC), and set the time to 5 minutes.
4. Arrange the shrimp in the crisper tray. Air fry for 5 minutes, or until the shrimp are pink on the outside and opaque in the center.
5. Remove from the crisper tray and serve warm.

325. Honey Salmon and Asparagus Platter

Prep time: 10 minutes | Cook time: 15 minutes | Serves 4

4 (6-ounce / 170-g) salmon fillets, with or without skin
1 teaspoon kosher salt or ½ teaspoon fine salt, divided
1 tablespoon honey
2 teaspoons Dijon mustard
2 tablespoons unsalted butter, melted, or extra-virgin olive oil for dairy-free
2 pounds (907 g) asparagus, trimmed
Lemon wedges, for serving

1. Sprinkle the salmon on both sides with ½ teaspoon of kosher salt.
2. In a small bowl, whisk together the honey, mustard, and 1 tablespoon of butter.
3. Place the asparagus in the baking pan. Drizzle with the remaining 1 tablespoon of butter and sprinkle with the remaining ½ teaspoon of salt. Toss to coat. Move the asparagus to the outside of the baking pan.
4. Pat the salmon dry with a paper towel. Place the fillets in the baking pan (skin-side down if using skin-on fillets). Brush with the honey mustard sauce.
5. Place the pan on the roast position. Select Roast, set temperature to 375ºF (191ºC), and set time to 15 minutes.
6. After 7 to 8 minutes, remove the pan from the grill and toss the asparagus. Return the pan to the grill and continue cooking.
7. When cooking is complete, remove the pan from the grill. Place the salmon and asparagus on plate. Squeeze a little lemon juice over the fish and vegetables, and serve.

326. Southwest Shrimp and Cabbage Tacos

Prep time: 15 minutes | Cook time: 10 minutes | Serves 4

4 corn tortillas
Nonstick cooking spray
1 pound (454 g) fresh jumbo shrimp
Juice of ½ lemon
1 teaspoon chili powder
1 teaspoon ground cumin
1 teaspoon Southwestern seasoning
¼ teaspoon cayenne pepper
2 cups shredded green cabbage
1 avocado, peeled and sliced

1. Place the grill plate on the grill position. Select Grill, set the temperature to 450ºF (232ºC), and set the time to 10 minutes.
2. Spray both sides of the tortillas with cooking spray, and in a large bowl, toss the shrimp with the lemon juice, chili powder, cumin, Southwestern seasoning, and cayenne pepper, until evenly coated. Let marinate while grilling the tortillas in the next step.
3. Place 1 tortilla on the grill plate. Grill for 1 minute. After 1 minute, remove the tortilla; set aside. Repeat with the remaining 3 tortillas.
4. After removing the final tortilla, carefully place the shrimp on the grill plate. Grill for 5 minutes. (There is no need to flip the shrimp during grilling.)
5. Remove the shrimp from the grill, arrange on the grilled tortillas, and top with cabbage and avocado. Feel free to include other toppings, such as cotija cheese, cilantro, and lime wedges.

327. Garlicky Shrimp Caesar Salad

Prep time: 10 minutes | Cook time: 5 minutes | Serves 4

1 pound (454 g) fresh jumbo shrimp
Juice of ½ lemon
3 garlic cloves, minced
Sea salt, to taste
Freshly ground black pepper, to taste
2 heads romaine lettuce, chopped
¾ cup Caesar dressing
½ cup grated Parmesan cheese

1. Place the grill plate on the grill position. Select Grill, set the temperature to 450ºF (232ºC), and set the time to 5 minutes.
2. In a large bowl, toss the shrimp with the lemon juice, garlic, salt, and pepper. Let marinate for 10 minutes.
3. Place the shrimp on the grill plate. Grill for 5 minutes. (There is no need to flip the shrimp during grilling.)
4. While the shrimp grills, toss the romaine lettuce with the Caesar dressing, then divide evenly among four plates or bowls.
5. When cooking is complete, use tongs to remove the shrimp from the grill and place on top of each salad. Sprinkle with the Parmesan cheese and serve.

328. Grilled Swordfish Steaks

Prep time: 5 minutes | Cook time: 8 minutes | Serves 4

1 tablespoon freshly squeezed lemon juice
1 tablespoon extra-virgin olive oil
Sea salt, to taste
Freshly ground black pepper, to taste
4 (8-ounce / 227-g) fresh swordfish steaks, about 1-inch thick
4 tablespoons unsalted butter
1 lemon, sliced crosswise into 8 slices
2 tablespoons capers, drained

1. In a large shallow bowl, whisk together the lemon juice and oil. Season the swordfish steaks with salt and pepper on each side, and place them in the oil mixture. Turn to coat both sides. Refrigerate for 15 minutes.
2. Place the grill plate on the grill position. Select Grill, set the temperature to 450ºF (232ºC), and set the time to 8 minutes.
3. Place the swordfish on the grill plate. Grill for 9 minutes. (There is no need to flip the swordfish during cooking.)
4. While the swordfish grills, melt the butter in a small saucepan over medium heat. Stir and grill for about 3 minutes, until the butter has slightly browned. Add the lemon slices and capers to the pan, and grill for 1 minute. Turn off the heat.
5. Remove the swordfish from the grill and transfer it to a cutting board. Slice the fish into thick strips, transfer to serving platter, pour the caper sauce over the top, and serve immediately.

329. Spiced Crab Cakes

Prep time: 10 minutes | Cook time: 10 minutes | Serves 4

1 egg
½ cup mayonnaise, plus 3 tablespoons
Juice of ½ lemon
1 tablespoon minced scallions (green parts only)
1 teaspoon Old Bay seasoning
8 ounces (227 g) lump crab meat
$^1/_3$ cup bread crumbs
Nonstick cooking spray
½ teaspoon cayenne pepper
¼ teaspoon paprika
¼ teaspoon garlic powder
¼ teaspoon chili powder
¼ teaspoon onion powder
¼ teaspoon freshly ground black pepper
⅛ teaspoon ground nutmeg

1. Place the crisper tray on the air fry position. Select Air Fry, set the temperature to 375ºF (191ºC), and set the time to 10 minutes.
2. In a medium bowl, whisk together the egg, 3 tablespoons of mayonnaise, lemon juice, scallions, and Old Bay seasoning. Gently stir in the crab meat, making sure not to break up the meat into small pieces. Add the bread crumbs, and gradually mix them in. Form the mixture into four patties.
3. Place the crab cakes in the crisper tray and coat them with the cooking spray. Air fry for 10 minutes.
4. While the crab cakes are cooking, in a small bowl, mix the remaining ½ cup of mayonnaise, cayenne pepper, paprika, garlic powder, chili powder, onion powder, black pepper, and nutmeg until fully combined.
5. When cooking is complete, serve the crab cakes with the Cajun aioli spooned on top.

330. Grilled Salmon in Lemony Sriracha Glaze

Prep time: 10 minutes | Cook time: 8 minutes | Serves 4

1 cup sriracha
Juice of 2 lemons
¼ cup honey
4 (6-ounce / 170-g)

skinless salmon fillets
Chives, chopped, for garnish

1. Place the sriracha, lemon juice, and honey in a large resealable plastic bag or container. Add the salmon fillets and coat evenly. Refrigerate for 30 minutes.
2. Place the grill plate on the grill position. Select Grill, set the temperature to 450ºF (232ºC), and set the time to 8 minutes.
3. Place the fillets on the grill plate, gently pressing them down to maximize grill marks. Grill for 6 minutes. (There is no need to flip the fish during cooking.)
4. After 6 minutes, check the fillets for doneness; the internal temperature should read at least 140ºF (60ºC) on a food thermometer. If necessary, continue cooking up to 2 minutes more.
5. When cooking is complete, remove the fillets from the grill. Plate, and garnish with the chives.

331. Crispy Cod Sandwich

Prep time: 10 minutes | Cook time: 15 minutes | Serves 4

2 large eggs
10 ounces (284 g) beer (an ale, IPA, or any type you have on hand will work)
1½ teaspoons hot sauce
1½ cups cornstarch
1½ cups all-purpose flour
1 teaspoon sea salt

1 teaspoon freshly ground black pepper
4 (5- or 6-ounce / 142- or 170-g) fresh cod fillets
Nonstick cooking spray
4 soft rolls, sliced
Tartar sauce
Lettuce leaves
Lemon wedges

1. Place the crisper tray on the air fry position. Select Air Fry, set the temperature to 375ºF (191ºC), and set the time to 15 minutes.
2. Whisk together the eggs, beer, and hot sauce in a large shallow bowl. In a separate large bowl, whisk together the cornstarch, flour, salt, and pepper.
3. One at a time, coat the cod fillets in the egg mixture, then dredge them in the flour mixture and coat on all sides. Repeat with the remaining cod fillets.
4. Spray the crisper tray with the cooking spray. Place the fish fillets in the crisper tray and coat them with the cooking spray. Air fry for 15 minutes.
5. After 15 minutes, check the fish for desired crispiness. Remove from the crisper tray.
6. Assemble the sandwiches by spreading tartar sauce on one half of each of the sliced rolls. Add one fish fillet and lettuce leaves, and serve with lemon wedges.

332. Miso-Glazed Cod with Bok Choy

Prep time: 5 minutes | Cook time: 17 minutes | Serves 4

4 (6-ounce / 170-g) cod fillets
¼ cup miso
3 tablespoons brown sugar
1 teaspoon sesame oil, divided
1 tablespoon white

wine or mirin
2 tablespoons soy sauce
¼ teaspoon red pepper flakes
1 pound (454 g) baby bok choy, halved lengthwise

1. Place the cod, miso, brown sugar, ¾ teaspoon of sesame oil, and white wine in a large resealable plastic bag or container. Move the fillets around to coat evenly with the marinade. Refrigerate for 30 minutes.
2. Place the grill plate on the grill position. Select Grill, set the temperature to 450ºF (232ºC), and set the time to 8 minutes.
3. Place the fillets on the grill plate. Gently press them down to maximize grill marks. Grill for 8 minutes. (There is no need to flip the fish during grilling.)
4. While the cod grills, in a small bowl, whisk together the remaining ¼ teaspoon of sesame oil, soy sauce, and red pepper flakes. Brush the bok choy halves with the soy sauce mixture on all sides.
5. Remove the cod from the grill and set aside on a cutting board to rest. Tent with aluminum foil to keep warm.
6. Place the bok choy on the grill plate, cut-side down. Grill for 9 minutes. (There is no need to flip the bok choy during grilling.)
7. Remove the bok choy from the grill, plate with the cod, and serve.

333. Tuna and Cucumber Salad

Prep time: 10 minutes | Cook time: 6 minutes | Serves 4

2 tablespoons rice wine vinegar
¼ teaspoon sea salt, plus additional for seasoning
½ teaspoon freshly ground black pepper, plus additional for seasoning
6 tablespoons extra-virgin olive oil
1½ pounds (680 g) ahi tuna, cut into four strips
2 tablespoons sesame oil
1 (10-ounce / 284-g) bag baby greens
½ English cucumber, sliced

1. Place the grill plate on the grill position. Select Grill, set the temperature to 450ºF (232ºC), and set the time to 6 minutes.
2. Meanwhile, in a small bowl, whisk together the rice vinegar, ¼ teaspoon of salt, and ½ teaspoon of pepper. Slowly pour in the oil while whisking, until the vinaigrette is fully combined.
3. Season the tuna with salt and pepper, and drizzle with the sesame oil.
4. Place the tuna strips on the grill plate. Grill for 4 to 6 minutes. (There is no need to flip during cooking.)
5. While the tuna cooks, divide the baby greens and cucumber slices evenly among four plates or bowls.
6. When cooking is complete, top each salad with one tuna strip. Drizzle the vinaigrette over the top, and serve immediately.

334. Lime-Honey Salmon with Mango Salsa

Prep time: 10 minutes | Cook time: 8 minutes | Serves 4

2 tablespoons unsalted butter, melted
⅓ cup honey
1 tablespoon soy sauce
Juice of 3 limes, divided
Grated zest of ½ lime
3 garlic cloves, minced and divided
4 (6-ounce / 170-g) skinless salmon fillets
1 mango, peeled and diced
1 avocado, peeled and diced
½ tomato, diced
½ red onion, diced
1 jalapeño pepper, seeded, stemmed, and diced
1 tablespoon extra-virgin olive oil
Sea salt, to taste
Freshly ground black pepper, to taste

1. Place the butter, honey, soy sauce, juice of 2 limes, lime zest, and 2 minced garlic cloves in a large resealable plastic bag or container. Add the salmon fillets and coat evenly with the marinade. Refrigerate for 30 minutes.
2. While the salmon is marinating, in a large bowl, combine the mango, avocado, tomato, onion, remaining minced garlic clove, jalapeño, remaining juice of 1 lime, oil, salt, and pepper. Cover and refrigerate.
3. Place the grill plate on the grill position. Select Grill, set the temperature to 450ºF (232ºC), and set the time to 8 minutes.
4. Place the fillets on the grill plate, gently pressing them down to maximize grill marks. Grill for 6 minutes. (There is no need to flip the fish during grilling.)
5. After 6 minutes, check the fillets for doneness; the internal temperature should read at least 140ºF (60ºC) on a food thermometer. If necessary, continue cooking up to 2 minutes more.
6. When cooking is complete, top the fillets with salsa and serve immediately.

335. Blackened Shrimp Tacos

Prep time: 10 minutes | Cook time: 10 to 15 minutes | Serves 4

12 ounces (340 g) medium shrimp, deveined, with tails off
1 teaspoon olive oil
1 to 2 teaspoons Blackened seasoning
8 corn tortillas, warmed
1 (14-ounce / 397-g) bag coleslaw mix
2 limes, cut in half
Cooking spray

1. Place the crisper tray on the air fry position. Select Air Fry, set the temperature to 400ºF (204ºC), and set the time to 15 minutes.
2. Spray the crisper tray lightly with cooking spray.
3. Dry the shrimp with a paper towel to remove excess water.
4. In a medium bowl, toss the shrimp with olive oil and Blackened seasoning.
5. Place the shrimp in the crisper tray. Air fry for 5 minutes. Shake the crisper tray, lightly spray with cooking spray, and cook until the shrimp are cooked through and starting to brown, 5 to 10 more minutes.
6. Fill each tortilla with the coleslaw mix and top with the blackened shrimp. Squeeze fresh lime juice over top and serve.

336.Crispy Catfish Strips

Prep time: 5 minutes | Cook time: 16 to 18 minutes | Serves 4

1 cup buttermilk
5 catfish fillets, cut into 1½-inch strips
Cooking spray
1 cup cornmeal
1 tablespoon Creole, Cajun, or Old Bay seasoning

1. Pour the buttermilk into a shallow baking pan. Place the catfish in the dish and refrigerate for at least 1 hour to help remove any fishy taste.
2. Place the crisper tray on the air fry position. Select Air Fry, set the temperature to 400ºF (204ºC), and set the time to 18 minutes.
3. Spray the crisper tray lightly with cooking spray.
4. In a shallow bowl, combine cornmeal and Creole seasoning.
5. Shake any excess buttermilk off the catfish. Place each strip in the cornmeal mixture and coat completely. Press the cornmeal into the catfish gently to help it stick.
6. Place the strips in the crisper tray in a single layer. Lightly spray the catfish with cooking spray. You may need to cook the catfish in more than one batch.
7. Air fry for 8 minutes. Turn the catfish strips over and lightly spray with cooking spray. air fry until golden brown and crispy, for 8 to 10 more minutes.
8. Serve warm.

337.Lime-Chili Shrimp Bowl

Prep time: 10 minutes | Cook time: 10 to 15 minutes | Serves 4

2 teaspoons lime juice
1 teaspoon olive oil
1 teaspoon honey
1 teaspoon minced garlic
1 teaspoon chili powder
Salt, to taste
12 ounces (340 g) medium shrimp, peeled and deveined
2 cups cooked brown rice
1 (15-ounce / 425-g) can seasoned black beans, warmed
1 large avocado, chopped
1 cup sliced cherry tomatoes
Cooking spray

1. Place the crisper tray on the air fry position. Select Air Fry, set the temperature to 400ºF (204ºC), and set the time to 15 minutes.
2. Spray the crisper tray lightly with cooking spray.
3. In a medium bowl, mix together the lime juice, olive oil, honey, garlic, chili powder, and salt to make a marinade.
4. Add the shrimp and toss to coat evenly in the marinade.
5. Place the shrimp in the crisper tray. Air fry for 5 minutes. Shake the crisper tray and air fry until the shrimp are cooked through and starting to brown, an additional 5 to 10 minutes.
6. To assemble the bowls, spoon ¼ of the rice, black beans, avocado, and cherry tomatoes into each of four bowls. Top with the shrimp and serve.

338.Cajun-Style Salmon Burgers

Prep time: 10 minutes | Cook time: 10 to 15 minutes | Serves 4

4 (5-ounce / 142-g) cans pink salmon in water, any skin and bones removed, drained
2 eggs, beaten
1 cup whole-wheat bread crumbs
4 tablespoons light mayonnaise
2 teaspoons Cajun seasoning
2 teaspoons dry mustard
4 whole-wheat buns
Cooking spray

1. In a medium bowl, mix the salmon, egg, bread crumbs, mayonnaise, Cajun seasoning, and dry mustard. Cover with plastic wrap and refrigerate for 30 minutes.
2. Place the crisper tray on the air fry position. Select Air Fry, set the temperature to 360ºF (182ºC), and set the time to 15 minutes.
3. Spray the crisper tray lightly with cooking spray.
4. Shape the mixture into four ½-inch-thick patties about the same size as the buns.
5. Place the salmon patties in the crisper tray in a single layer and lightly spray the tops with cooking spray. You may need to cook them in batches.
6. Air fry for 6 to 8 minutes. Turn the patties over and lightly spray with cooking spray. air fry until crispy on the outside, for 4 to 7 more minutes.
7. Serve on whole-wheat buns.

339.Spicy Orange Shrimp

Prep time: 20 minutes | Cook time: 10 to 15 minutes | Serves 4

⅓ cup orange juice
3 teaspoons minced garlic
1 teaspoon Old Bay seasoning
¼ to ½ teaspoon

cayenne pepper
1 pound (454 g) medium shrimp, peeled and deveined, with tails off
Cooking spray

1. In a medium bowl, combine the orange juice, garlic, Old Bay seasoning, and cayenne pepper.
2. Dry the shrimp with paper towels to remove excess water.
3. Add the shrimp to the marinade and stir to evenly coat. Cover with plastic wrap and place in the refrigerator for 30 minutes so the shrimp can soak up the marinade.
4. Place the crisper tray on the air fry position. Select Air Fry, set the temperature to 400ºF (204ºC), and set the time to 15 minutes.
5. Spray the crisper tray lightly with cooking spray.
6. Place the shrimp into the crisper tray. Air fry for 5 minutes. Shake the crisper tray and lightly spray with olive oil. air fry until the shrimp are opaque and crisp, 5 to 10 more minutes.
7. Serve immediately.

340.Coconut Breaded Shrimp

Prep time: 15 minutes | Cook time: 15 minutes | Serves 4

½ cup all-purpose flour
2 teaspoons freshly ground black pepper
½ teaspoon sea salt
2 large eggs
¾ cup unsweetened coconut flakes

¼ cup panko bread crumbs
24 peeled, deveined shrimp
Nonstick cooking spray
Sweet chili sauce, for serving

1. Place the crisper tray on the air fry position. Select Air Fry, set the temperature to 400ºF (204ºC), and set the time to 8 minutes.
2. In a medium shallow bowl, mix together the flour, black pepper, and salt. In a second medium shallow bowl, whisk the eggs. In a third, combine the coconut flakes and bread crumbs.

3. Dredge each shrimp in the flour mixture, then in the egg. Press each shrimp into the coconut mixture on both sides, leaving the tail uncoated.
4. Place half of the shrimp into the crisper tray and coat them with the cooking spray. Air fry for 7 minutes.
5. Remove the cooked shrimp and add the remaining uncooked shrimp to the crisper tray. Spray them with the cooking spray and air fry for 7 minutes.
6. Serve with sweet chili sauce.

341.Mediterranean Salmon and Veg Dish

Prep time: 10 minutes | Cook time: 15 minutes | Serves 4

4 (6-ounce / 170-g) salmon fillets, with or without skin
1 teaspoon kosher salt or ½ teaspoon fine salt, divided
2 pints cherry or grape tomatoes, halved if large, divided

3 tablespoons extra-virgin olive oil, divided
1 small red bell pepper, seeded and chopped
2 garlic cloves, minced
2 tablespoons chopped fresh basil, divided

1. Sprinkle the salmon on both sides with ½ teaspoon of kosher salt.
2. Place about half of the tomatoes in a large bowl, reserving the remainder. Add the remaining ½ teaspoon of kosher salt, 2 tablespoons of olive oil, the bell pepper, garlic, and 1 tablespoon of basil. Toss to coat the vegetables with the oil. Place the vegetables in the baking pan.
3. Pat the salmon dry with a paper towel. Place the fillets in the pan (skin-side down). Brush them with the remaining 1 tablespoon of olive oil.
4. Place the pan on the roast position. Select Roast, set temperature to 375ºF (191ºC), and set time to 15 minutes.
5. After 7 minutes, remove the pan from the grill and add the remaining tomatoes. Return the pan to the grill and continue cooking for about 6 minutes.
6. When cooking is complete, the fish will flake apart with a fork. If the fish is not done, return the pan to the grill for another minute or so. Remove the pan from the grill. Before serving, sprinkle the remaining 1 tablespoon of basil over the dish.

342.Crispy Fish Sticks

Prep time: 10 minutes | Cook time: 10 minutes | Serves 4

1 pound (454 g) cod fillets	1 tablespoon dried parsley
¼ cup all-purpose flour	1 teaspoon paprika
1 large egg	½ teaspoon freshly ground black pepper
1 teaspoon Dijon mustard	Nonstick cooking spray
½ cup bread crumbs	

1. Place the crisper tray on the air fry position. Select Air Fry, set the temperature to 390ºF (199ºC), and set the time to 10 minutes.
2. Cut the fish fillets into ¾- to 1-inch-wide strips.
3. Place the flour on a plate. In a medium shallow bowl, whisk together the egg and Dijon mustard. In a separate medium shallow bowl, combine the bread crumbs, dried parsley, paprika, and black pepper.
4. One at a time, dredge the cod strips in the flour, shaking off any excess, then coat them in the egg mixture. Finally, dredge them in the bread crumb mixture, and coat on all sides.
5. Spray the crisper tray with the cooking spray. Place the cod fillet strips in the crisper tray, and coat them with the cooking spray. Air fry for 10 minutes.
6. Remove the fish sticks from the crisper tray and serve.

343.Simple Salmon Patty Bites

Prep time: 15 minutes | Cook time: 10 to 15 minutes | Serves 4

4 (5-ounce / 142-g) cans pink salmon, skinless, boneless in water, drained	minced red bell pepper
2 eggs, beaten	2 tablespoons parsley flakes
1 cup whole-wheat panko bread crumbs	2 teaspoons Old Bay seasoning
4 tablespoons finely	Cooking spray

1. Place the crisper tray on the air fry position. Select Air Fry, set the temperature to 360ºF (182ºC), and set the time to 15 minutes.
2. Spray the crisper tray lightly with cooking spray.
3. In a medium bowl, mix the salmon, eggs, panko bread crumbs, red bell pepper, parsley flakes, and Old Bay seasoning.
4. Using a small cookie scoop, form the mixture into 20 balls.
5. Place the salmon bites in the crisper tray in a single layer and spray lightly with cooking spray. You may need to cook them in batches.
6. Air fry for 10 to 15 minutes until crispy, shaking the crisper tray a couple of times for even cooking.
7. Serve immediately.

344.Scallops with Mushrooms and Snow Peas

Prep time: 10 minutes | Cook time: 8 minutes | Serves 4

1 pound (454 g) sea scallops	snow peas, trimmed
3 tablespoons hoisin sauce	3 teaspoons vegetable oil, divided
½ cup toasted sesame seeds	1 teaspoon sesame oil
6 ounces (170 g)	1 teaspoon soy sauce
	1 cup Roasted Mushrooms

1. With a basting brush, coat the flat sides of the scallops with the hoisin sauce. Place the sesame seeds in a flat dish. Place the coated sides of the scallops in the seeds, pressing them into the scallops to adhere. Repeat with the other sides of the scallops, so both flat sides are coated with hoisin sauce and sesame seeds.
2. In a medium bowl, toss the snow peas with 1 teaspoon of vegetable oil, the sesame oil, and soy sauce.
3. Brush the baking pan with the remaining 2 teaspoons of vegetable oil. Place the scallops in the center of the pan. Arrange the snow peas in a single layer around the scallops.
4. Place the pan on the roast position. Select Roast, set temperature to 375ºF (191ºC), and set time to 8 minutes.
5. After 5 minutes, remove the pan from the grill. Using a small spatula, carefully turn the scallops over. Add the mushrooms to the peas and stir to combine. Return the pan to the grill and continue cooking.
6. When cooking is complete, the peas should be sizzling and the scallops just cooked through. Remove the pan from the grill and serve.

345.Lemony Shrimp and Zucchini

Prep time: 15 minutes | Cook time: 7 to 8 minutes | Serves 4

1¼ pounds (567 g) extra-large raw shrimp, peeled and deveined
2 medium zucchinis (about 8 ounces / 227 g each), halved lengthwise and cut into ½-inch-thick slices
1½ tablespoons olive oil
½ teaspoon garlic salt
1½ teaspoons dried oregano
⅛ teaspoon crushed red pepper flakes (optional)
Juice of ½ lemon
1 tablespoon chopped fresh mint
1 tablespoon chopped fresh dill

1. Place the crisper tray on the air fry position. Select Air Fry, set the temperature to 350ºF (177ºC), and set the time to 8 minutes.
2. In a large bowl, combine the shrimp, zucchini, oil, garlic salt, oregano, and pepper flakes (if using) and toss to coat.
3. Working in batches, arrange a single layer of the shrimp and zucchini in the crisper tray. Air fry for 7 to 8 minutes, shaking the crisper tray halfway, until the zucchini is golden and the shrimp are cooked through.
4. Transfer to a serving dish and tent with foil while you air fry the remaining shrimp and zucchini.
5. Top with the lemon juice, mint, and dill and serve.

346.Spanish Garlic Shrimp

Prep time: 10 minutes | Cook time: 10 to 15 minutes | Serves 4

2 teaspoons minced garlic
2 teaspoons lemon juice
2 teaspoons olive oil
½ to 1 teaspoon
crushed red pepper
12 ounces (340 g) medium shrimp, deveined, with tails on
Cooking spray

1. In a medium bowl, mix together the garlic, lemon juice, olive oil, and crushed red pepper to make a marinade.
2. Add the shrimp and toss to coat in the marinade. Cover with plastic wrap and place the bowl in the refrigerator for 30 minutes.
3. Spray the crisper tray lightly with cooking spray.
4. Place the crisper tray on the air fry position. Select Air Fry, set the temperature to 400ºF (204ºC), and set the time to 15 minutes.
5. Place the shrimp in the crisper tray. Air fry for 5 minutes. Shake the crisper tray and air fry until the shrimp are cooked through and nicely browned, for an additional 5 to 10 minutes. Cool for 5 minutes before serving.

347.Blackened Salmon

Prep time: 10 minutes | Cook time: 5 to 7 minutes | Serves 4

Salmon:

1 tablespoon sweet paprika
½ teaspoon cayenne pepper
1 teaspoon garlic powder
1 teaspoon dried oregano
1 teaspoon dried
thyme
¾ teaspoon kosher salt
⅛ teaspoon freshly ground black pepper
Cooking spray
4 (6 ounces / 170 g each) wild salmon fillets

Cucumber-Avocado Salsa:

2 tablespoons chopped red onion
1½ tablespoons fresh lemon juice
1 teaspoon extra-virgin olive oil
¼ teaspoon plus ⅛
teaspoon kosher salt
Freshly ground black pepper, to taste
4 Persian cucumbers, diced
6 ounces (170 g) Hass avocado, diced

1. For the salmon: In a small bowl, combine the paprika, cayenne, garlic powder, oregano, thyme, salt, and black pepper. Spray both sides of the fish with oil and rub all over. Coat the fish all over with the spices.
2. For the cucumber-avocado salsa: In a medium bowl, combine the red onion, lemon juice, olive oil, salt, and pepper. Let stand for 5 minutes, then add the cucumbers and avocado.
3. Place the crisper tray on the air fry position. Select Air Fry, set the temperature to 400ºF (204ºC), and set the time to 7 minutes.
4. Working in batches, arrange the salmon fillets skin side down in the crisper tray. Air fry for 5 to 7 minutes, or until the fish flakes easily with a fork, depending on the thickness of the fish.
5. Serve topped with the salsa.

348.Vegetable and Fish Tacos

Prep time: 10 minutes | Cook time: 9 to 12 minutes | Serves 4

1 pound (454 g) white fish fillets
2 teaspoons olive oil
3 tablespoons freshly squeezed lemon juice, divided
1½ cups chopped red cabbage
1 large carrot, grated
½ cup low-sodium salsa
⅓ cup low-fat Greek yogurt
4 soft low-sodium whole-wheat tortillas

1. Place the crisper tray on the air fry position. Select Air Fry, set the temperature to 400ºF (204ºC), and set the time to 12 minutes.
2. Brush the fish with the olive oil and sprinkle with 1 tablespoon of lemon juice. Air fry for 9 to 12 minutes, or until the fish just flakes when tested with a fork.
3. Meanwhile, in a medium bowl, stir together the remaining 2 tablespoons of lemon juice, the red cabbage, carrot, salsa, and yogurt.
4. When the fish is cooked, remove it from the crisper tray and break it up into large pieces.
5. Offer the fish, tortillas, and the cabbage mixture, and let each person assemble a taco.
6. Serve immediately.

349.Crispy Crab and Fish Cakes

Prep time: 20 minutes | Cook time: 10 to 12 minutes | Serves 4

8 ounces (227 g) imitation crab meat
4 ounces (113 g) leftover cooked fish (such as cod, pollock, or haddock)
2 tablespoons minced celery
2 tablespoons minced green onion
2 tablespoons light mayonnaise
1 tablespoon plus 2 teaspoons Worcestershire sauce
¾ cup crushed saltine cracker crumbs
2 teaspoons dried parsley flakes
1 teaspoon prepared yellow mustard
½ teaspoon garlic powder
½ teaspoon dried dill weed, crushed
½ teaspoon Old Bay seasoning
½ cup panko bread crumbs
Cooking spray

1. Place the crisper tray on the bake position. Select Bake, set the temperature to 390ºF (199ºC), and set the time to 12 minutes.
2. Pulse the crab meat and fish in a food processor until finely chopped.
3. Transfer the meat mixture to a large bowl, along with the celery, green onion, mayo, Worcestershire sauce, cracker crumbs, parsley flakes, mustard, garlic powder, dill weed, and Old Bay seasoning. Stir to mix well.
4. Scoop out the meat mixture and form into 8 equal-sized patties with your hands.
5. Place the panko bread crumbs on a plate. Roll the patties in the bread crumbs until they are evenly coated on both sides. Spritz the patties with cooking spray.
6. Put the patties in the crisper tray. Bake for 10 to 12 minutes, flipping them halfway through, or until they are golden brown and cooked through.
7. Divide the patties among four plates and serve.

350.Green Curry Shrimp

Prep time: 15 minutes | Cook time: 5 minutes | Serves 4

1 to 2 tablespoons Thai green curry paste
2 tablespoons coconut oil, melted
1 tablespoon half-and-half or coconut milk
1 teaspoon fish sauce
1 teaspoon soy sauce
1 teaspoon minced
fresh ginger
1 clove garlic, minced
1 pound (454 g) jumbo raw shrimp, peeled and deveined
¼ cup chopped fresh Thai basil or sweet basil
¼ cup chopped fresh cilantro

1. In the baking pan, combine the curry paste, coconut oil, half-and-half, fish sauce, soy sauce, ginger, and garlic. Whisk until well combined.
2. Add the shrimp and toss until well coated. Marinate at room temperature for 15 to 30 minutes.
3. Place the crisper tray on the air fry position. Select Air Fry, set the temperature to 400ºF (204ºC), and set the time to 5 minutes.
4. Air fry for 5 minutes, stirring halfway through the cooking time.
5. Transfer the shrimp to a serving bowl or platter. Garnish with the basil and cilantro. Serve immediately.

351. Goat Cheese Shrimp

Prep time: 15 minutes | Cook time: 7 to 8 minutes | Serves 2

1 pound (454 g) shrimp, deveined
1½ tablespoons olive oil
1½ tablespoons balsamic vinegar
1 tablespoon coconut aminos
½ tablespoon fresh parsley, roughly chopped
Sea salt flakes, to taste
1 teaspoon Dijon mustard
½ teaspoon smoked cayenne pepper
½ teaspoon garlic powder
Salt and ground black peppercorns, to taste
1 cup shredded goat cheese

1. Place the crisper tray on the air fry position. Select Air Fry, set the temperature to 385ºF (196ºC), and set the time to 8 minutes.
2. Except for the cheese, stir together all the ingredients in a large bowl until the shrimp are evenly coated.
3. Arrange the shrimp in the crisper tray. Air fry for 7 to 8 minutes, shaking the crisper tray halfway through, or until the shrimp are pink and cooked through.
4. Serve the shrimp with the shredded goat cheese sprinkled on top.

352. Air-Fried Scallops

Prep time: 10 minutes | Cook time: 12 minutes | Serves 2

¹/₃ cup shallots, chopped
1½ tablespoons olive oil
1½ tablespoons coconut aminos
1 tablespoon Mediterranean seasoning mix
½ tablespoon balsamic vinegar
½ teaspoon ginger, grated
1 clove garlic, chopped
1 pound (454 g) scallops, cleaned
Cooking spray
Belgian endive, for garnish

1. Place all the ingredients except the scallops and Belgian endive in a small skillet over medium heat and stir to combine. Let this mixture simmer for about 2 minutes.
2. Remove the mixture from the skillet to a large bowl and set aside to cool.
3. Add the scallops, coating them all over, then transfer to the refrigerator to marinate for at least 2 hours.
4. Place the crisper tray on the air fry position. Select Air Fry, set the temperature to 345ºF (174ºC), and set the time to 10 minutes.
5. Arrange the scallops in the crisper tray in a single layer and spray with cooking spray.
6. Air fry for 10 minutes, flipping the scallops halfway through, or until the scallops are tender and opaque.
7. Serve garnished with the Belgian endive.

353. Tilapia Meunière

Prep time: 10 minutes | Cook time: 20 minutes | Serves 4

10 ounces (283 g) Yukon Gold potatoes, sliced ¼-inch thick
5 tablespoons unsalted butter, melted, divided
1 teaspoon kosher salt or ½ teaspoon fine salt, divided
4 (8-ounce / 227-g) tilapia fillets
½ pound (227 g) green beans, trimmed
Juice of 1 lemon
2 tablespoons chopped fresh parsley

1. Place the potatoes in a large bowl. Drizzle with 2 tablespoons of butter and ¼ teaspoon of kosher salt. Place in the baking pan.
2. Place the pan on the roast position. Select Roast, set temperature to 375ºF (191ºC), and set time to 20 minutes.
3. While the potatoes cook, salt the fish fillets on both sides with ½ teaspoon of kosher salt. Place the green beans in the potato bowl and toss with the remaining ¼ teaspoon of kosher salt and 1 tablespoon of butter.
4. After 10 minutes, remove the pan from the grill and move the potatoes to one side. Place the fish fillets in the center of the pan and add the green beans on the other side. Drizzle the fish with 2 tablespoons of butter. Return the pan to the grill and continue cooking.
5. When cooking is complete, the fish should flake apart with a fork. The beans should be tender and starting to crisp. Remove the pan from the grill. To serve, drizzle the lemon juice over the fish, and sprinkle the parsley over the fish and vegetables.

354.Fired Shrimp with Mayonnaise Sauce

Prep time: 5 minutes | Cook time: 7 minutes | Serves 4

Shrimp:

12 jumbo shrimp	cracked mixed
½ teaspoon garlic salt	peppercorns
¼ teaspoon freshly	

Sauce:

4 tablespoons	mustard
mayonnaise	1 teaspoon chipanle
1 teaspoon grated	powder
lemon rind	½ teaspoon cumin
1 teaspoon Dijon	powder

1. Place the crisper tray on the air fry position. Select Air Fry, set the temperature to 395ºF (202ºC), and set the time to 7 minutes.
2. In a medium bowl, season the shrimp with garlic salt and cracked mixed peppercorns.
3. Place the shrimp in the crisper tray. Air fry for 5 minutes. Flip the shrimp and cook for another 2 minutes until they are pink and no longer opaque.
4. Meanwhile, stir together all the ingredients for the sauce in a small bowl until well mixed.
5. Remove the shrimp from the crisper tray and serve alongside the sauce.

355.Roasted Tuna Salade Niçoise

Prep time: 10 minutes | Cook time: 15 minutes | Serves 4

10 ounces (283 g)	mustard
small red potatoes,	Freshly ground black
quartered	pepper
8 tablespoons extra-	1 (9-ounce / 255-g)
virgin olive oil, divided	bag spring greens,
1 teaspoon kosher	washed and dried if
salt or ½ teaspoon	necessary
fine salt, divided	2 (5-ounce / 142-g)
½ pound (227 g)	cans oil-packed tuna,
green beans, trimmed	drained
1 pint cherry	2 hard-cooked eggs,
tomatoes	peeled and quartered
3 tablespoons red or	$^1/_3$ cup Nicoise or
white wine vinegar	kalamata olives,
1 teaspoon Dijon	pitted

1. Place the potatoes in a large bowl. Drizzle with 1 tablespoon of olive oil and ¼

teaspoon of kosher salt. Place in the baking pan.
2. Place the pan on the roast position. Select Roast, set temperature to 375ºF (191ºC), and set time to 15 minutes.
3. While the potatoes are cooking, place the green beans and cherry tomatoes in the bowl and toss with 1 tablespoon of oil and ¼ teaspoon of kosher salt.
4. After 10 minutes, remove the pan from the grill. Add the green beans and tomatoes to the pan. Return the pan to the grill and continue cooking.
5. While the vegetables cook, make the vinaigrette: In a small jar or bowl, shake or whisk together the remaining 6 tablespoons of olive oil, vinegar, mustard, the remaining ½ teaspoon of kosher salt, and a few grinds of black pepper.
6. When cooking is complete, remove the pan from the grill. Let the vegetables cool for a few minutes.
7. Arrange the greens on a platter and spoon the tuna into the middle of the greens. Surround the tuna with the potatoes, green beans, tomatoes, and egg quarters. Drizzle with the vinaigrette and scatter the olives on top.

356.Piri-Piri King Prawn

Prep time: 10 minutes | Cook time: 8 minutes | Serves 2

12 king prawns,	1 teaspoon garlic
rinsed	paste
1 tablespoon coconut	1 teaspoon curry
oil	powder
Salt and ground black	½ teaspoon piri piri
pepper, to taste	powder
1 teaspoon onion	½ teaspoon cumin
powder	powder

1. Place the crisper tray on the air fry position. Select Air Fry, set the temperature to 360ºF (182ºC), and set the time to 8 minutes.
2. Combine all the ingredients in a large bowl and toss until the prawns are completely coated.
3. Place the prawns in the crisper tray. Air fry for 8 minutes, shaking the crisper tray halfway through, or until the prawns turn pink.
4. Serve hot.

357. Crispy Cod Cakes with Salad Greens

Prep time: 15 minutes | Cook time: 12 minutes | Serves 4

1 pound (454 g) cod fillets, cut into chunks
1/3 cup packed fresh basil leaves
3 cloves garlic, crushed
½ teaspoon smoked paprika
¼ teaspoon salt
¼ teaspoon pepper
1 large egg, beaten
1 cup panko bread crumbs
Cooking spray
Salad greens, for serving

1. In a food processor, pulse cod, basil, garlic, smoked paprika, salt, and pepper until cod is finely chopped, stirring occasionally. Form into 8 patties, about 2 inches in diameter. Dip each first into the egg, then into the panko, patting to adhere. Spray with oil on one side.
2. Place the crisper tray on the air fry position. Select Air Fry, set the temperature to 400ºF (204ºC), and set the time to 12 minutes.
3. Working in batches, place half the cakes in the crisper tray, oil-side down; spray with oil. Air fry for 12 minutes, until golden brown and cooked through.
4. Serve cod cakes with salad greens.

358. Roasted Shrimp with Potatoes and Kielbasa

Prep time: 10 minutes | Cook time: 15 minutes | Serves 4

1 pound (454 g) small red potatoes
2 ears corn, shucked and cut into rounds 1 to 1½ inches thick
½ cup unsalted butter, melted
2 tablespoons Old Bay or similar seasoning
1 (12- to 13-ounce / 340- to 369-g) package kielbasa or other smoked sausages
3 garlic cloves, minced or pressed
1 pound (454 g) medium (21–25 or 25–30 count) shrimp, peeled and deveined

1. If the potatoes are 2 inches or smaller in diameter, cut them in half. If larger, cut in quarters. Place in a large bowl and add the corn pieces.
2. In a small bowl, mix together the butter and Old Bay seasoning. Drizzle half the butter mixture over the potatoes and corn

and toss to coat. Place the vegetables in the baking pan, reserving the bowl.
3. Place the pan on the roast position. Select Roast, set temperature to 350ºF (177ºC), and set time to 15 minutes.
4. While the vegetables cook, cut the sausages into 2-inch lengths, then cut each piece in half lengthwise. Stir the garlic into the remaining butter mixture. Place the shrimp and sausage pieces in the vegetable bowl.
5. After 10 minutes, remove the pan from the grill. Place the vegetables in the bowl. Pour the garlic butter over and toss to coat. Place the vegetables, sausage, and shrimp in the pan.
6. Return the pan to the grill and continue cooking. After 5 minutes, check the shrimp. They should be pink and opaque. If they are not quite cooked through, return pan to the grill for 1 minute more.
7. When cooking is complete, remove the pan from the grill and serve.

359. Herbed Scallops with Vegetables

Prep time: 15 minutes | Cook time: 8 to 11 minutes | Serves 4

1 cup frozen peas
1 cup green beans
1 cup frozen chopped broccoli
2 teaspoons olive oil
½ teaspoon dried oregano
½ teaspoon dried basil
12 ounces (340 g) sea scallops, rinsed and patted dry

1. Place the crisper tray on the air fry position. Select Air Fry, set the temperature to 400ºF (204ºC), and set the time to 6 minutes.
2. Put the peas, green beans, and broccoli in a large bowl. Drizzle with the olive oil and toss to coat well. Transfer the vegetables to the crisper tray. Air fry for 4 to 6 minutes, or until they are fork-tender.
3. Remove the vegetables from the crisper tray to a serving bowl. Scatter with the oregano and basil and set aside.
4. Place the scallops in the crisper tray. Air fry for 4 to 5 minutes, or until the scallops are firm and just opaque in the center.
5. Transfer the cooked scallops to the bowl of vegetables and toss well. Serve warm.

360.Garlic-Lemon Tilapia

Prep time: 5 minutes | Cook time: 10 to 15 minutes | Serves 4

1 tablespoon lemon juice
1 tablespoon olive oil
1 teaspoon minced garlic

½ teaspoon chili powder
4 (6-ounce / 170-g) tilapia fillets

1. Place the crisper tray on the air fry position. Select Air Fry, set the temperature to 380ºF (193ºC), and set the time to 15 minutes.
2. Line the crisper tray with parchment paper.
3. In a large, shallow bowl, mix together the lemon juice, olive oil, garlic, and chili powder to make a marinade. Place the tilapia fillets in the bowl and coat evenly.
4. Place the fillets in the crisper tray in a single layer, leaving space between each fillet. You may need to cook in more than one batch.
5. Air fry for 10 to 15 minutes until the fish is cooked and flakes easily with a fork.
6. Serve hot.

361.Caesar Shrimp Salad

Prep time: 10 minutes | Cook time: 13 minutes | Serves 4

½ baguette, cut into 1-inch cubes (about 2½ cups)
4 tablespoons extra-virgin olive oil, divided
¼ teaspoon kosher salt or ⅛ teaspoon fine salt
¼ teaspoon granulated garlic
2 romaine lettuce hearts

¾ cup Caesar Dressing or store-bought variety, divided
1 pound (454 g) medium (21–25 or 25–30 count) shrimp, peeled and deveined
2 ounces (57 g) Parmesan cheese, coarsely grated or shaved (about ⅔ cup)

1. For the croutons, place the bread cubes in a medium bowl. Drizzle with 3 tablespoons of olive oil and sprinkle with the salt and granulated garlic. Toss to coat the bread cubes. Place in the crisper tray in a single layer.
2. Place the crisper tray on the air fry position. Select Air Fry, set temperature to 400ºF (204ºC), and set time to 4 minutes.
3. After about 2 minutes, remove the crisper tray and toss the croutons, reinsert the crisper tray in the grill, and continue cooking. When cooking is complete, the croutons will be crisp and golden brown. Remove the crisper tray from the grill and set aside.
4. While the croutons cook, halve the romaine hearts lengthwise (through the root). Trim the end of the root off, but leave enough to keep the halves intact. Brush the cut side of the lettuce with 2 tablespoons of Caesar Dressing.
5. Place the shrimp in a large bowl and toss with the ¼ cup of Caesar Dressing. Set aside.
6. Brush the baking pan with the remaining 1 tablespoon of olive oil. Place the romaine halves cut-side down in the pan. Brush the tops with another 2 tablespoons of Caesar Dressing.
7. Place the pan on the roast position. Select Roast, set temperature to 375ºF (191ºC), and set time to 10 minutes.
8. After 5 minutes, remove the pan and turn over the romaine halves. Spoon the shrimp around the lettuce. Return the pan to the grill and continue cooking.
9. When cooking is complete, the shrimp should be pink and opaque. If they are not quite cooked through, return pan to the grill for 1 minute more.
10. To serve, place a romaine half on each of four plates. Divide the shrimp among the plates and garnish with croutons and Parmesan cheese.

362.Coconut Chili Fish Curry

Prep time: 10 minutes | Cook time: 20 to 22 minutes | Serves 4

2 tablespoons sunflower oil, divided
1 pound (454 g) fish, chopped
1 ripe tomato, pureéd
2 red chilies, chopped
1 shallot, minced
1 garlic clove, minced

1 cup coconut milk
1 tablespoon coriander powder
1 teaspoon red curry paste
½ teaspoon fenugreek seeds
Salt and white pepper, to taste

1. Place the crisper tray on the air fry position. Select Air Fry, set the temperature to 380ºF (193ºC), and set the time to 10 minutes.
2. Coat the crisper tray with 1 tablespoon of sunflower oil.
3. Place the fish in the crisper tray. Air fry for 10 minutes. Flip the fish halfway through the cooking time.
4. When done, transfer the cooked fish to the baking pan greased with the remaining 1 tablespoon of sunflower oil. Stir in the remaining ingredients and return to the grill.
5. Reduce the temperature to 350ºF (177ºC) and air fry for another 10 to 12 minutes until heated through.
6. Cool for 5 to 8 minutes before serving.

363.Double-Cheese Clam Pizza

Prep time: 15 minutes | Cook time: 12 minutes | Serves 4

¼ cup extra-virgin olive oil, plus a little extra for forming the crust
2 large garlic cloves, chopped
¼ teaspoon red pepper flakes
1 pound (454 g) store-bought pizza dough
½ cup shredded Mozzarella cheese (4 ounces /

113 g)
2 (6.5-ounce / 184-g) cans chopped clams, drained
¼ cup grated Parmesan cheese
½ cup coarsely chopped fresh parsley
2 teaspoons chopped fresh oregano (optional)

1. In a small bowl, whisk together the olive oil with the garlic and red pepper flakes. Let it sit while you work on the dough.
2. Punch down the pizza dough to release as much air as possible. Place the dough in the baking pan and press it out toward the edges. The dough will likely spring back and shrink. Be patient and keep working at it, leaving it to relax for a few minutes from time to time. As it stretches, I find it helpful to coat my fingers with some olive oil and then poke the dough lightly with my fingertips to keep it from shrinking as much. Don't worry if you can't get it all the way to the edges of the pan.
3. Brush half of the garlic oil over the dough. Evenly distribute the Mozzarella cheese over the dough.
4. Place the pan on the roast position. Select Roast, set temperature to 425ºF (218ºC), and set time to 12 minutes.
5. After about 8 minutes, remove the pan from the grill. Scatter the clams over the pizza and sprinkle the Parmesan cheese on top. Return the pan to the grill and continue cooking for another 4 to 6 minutes. If you like a crisp crust, you can use a pizza peel or cake lifter (or even a very large spatula) to slide the pizza off the pan and directly onto the rack.
6. When cooking is complete, the cheese on top is lightly browned and bubbling and the crust is deep golden brown. Remove the pan from the grill (if you haven't already). Place the pizza on a wire rack to cool for a few minutes (a rack will keep the crust from getting soggy as it cools). Sprinkle the parsley and oregano (if using) over the pizza and drizzle with the remaining garlic oil. Slice and serve.

364.Crab Ratatouille with Eggplant and Tomatoes

Prep time: 15 minutes | Cook time: 11 to 14 minutes | Serves 4

1½ cups peeled and cubed eggplant
2 large tomatoes, chopped
1 red bell pepper, chopped
1 onion, chopped
1 tablespoon olive oil

½ teaspoon dried basil
½ teaspoon dried thyme
Pinch salt
Freshly ground black pepper, to taste
1½ cups cooked crab meat

1. Place the baking pan on the roast position. Select Roast, set the temperature to 400ºF (204ºC). and set the time to 15 minutes.
2. In the pan, stir together the eggplant, tomatoes, bell pepper, onion, olive oil, basil and thyme. Season with salt and pepper.
3. Roast for 9 minutes.
4. Add the crab meat and stir well and roast for another 2 to 5 minutes, or until the vegetables are softened and the ratatouille is bubbling.
5. Serve warm.

365.Cajun-Style Fish Tacos

Prep time: 5 minutes | Cook time: 10 to 15 minutes | Serves 6

2 teaspoons avocado oil
1 tablespoon Cajun seasoning
4 tilapia fillets

1 (14-ounce / 397-g) package coleslaw mix
12 corn tortillas
2 limes, cut into wedges

1. Place the crisper tray on the air fry position. Select Air Fry, set the temperature to 380ºF (193ºC), and set the time to 15 minutes.
2. Line the crisper tray with parchment paper.
3. In a medium, shallow bowl, mix the avocado oil and the Cajun seasoning to make a marinade. Add the tilapia fillets and coat evenly.
4. Place the fillets in the crisper tray in a single layer, leaving room between each fillet. You may need to cook in batches.
5. Air fry for 10 to 15 minutes until the fish is cooked and easily flakes with a fork.
6. Assemble the tacos by placing some of the coleslaw mix in each tortilla. Add ¹/₃ of a tilapia fillet to each tortilla. Squeeze some lime juice over the top of each taco and serve.

366.Breaded Scallops

Prep time: 5 minutes | Cook time: 6 to 8 minutes | Serves 4

1 egg
3 tablespoons flour
1 cup bread crumbs

1 pound (454 g) fresh scallops
2 tablespoons olive oil
Salt and black pepper, to taste

1. Place the crisper tray on the air fry position. Select Air Fry, set the temperature to 360ºF (182ºC), and set the time to 8 minutes.
2. In a bowl, lightly beat the egg. Place the flour and bread crumbs into separate shallow dishes.
3. Dredge the scallops in the flour and shake off any excess. Dip the flour-coated scallops in the beaten egg and roll in the bread crumbs.
4. Brush the scallops generously with olive oil and season with salt and pepper, to taste.
5. Arrange the scallops in the crisper tray. Air fry for 6 to 8 minutes, or until the scallops are firm and reach an internal temperature of just 145ºF (63ºC) on a meat thermometer. Shake the crisper tray halfway through the cooking time.
6. Let the scallops cool for 5 minutes and serve.

367. Teriyaki Salmon

Prep time: 15 minutes | Cook time: 15 minutes | Serves 4

¾ cup teriyaki sauce
4 (6-ounce / 170-g) skinless salmon fillets
4 heads baby bok choy, root ends trimmed off and cut in half lengthwise through the root
1 tablespoon vegetable oil
1 teaspoon sesame oil
1 tablespoon toasted sesame seeds

1. Set aside ¼ cup of Teriyaki Sauce and pour the rest into a resealable plastic bag. Place the salmon in the bag and seal, squeezing as much air out as possible. Let the salmon marinate for at least 10 minutes (longer if you have the time).
2. Place the bok choy halves in the baking pan. Drizzle the vegetable and sesame oils over the vegetables and toss to coat. Drizzle about a tablespoon of the reserved Teriyaki Sauce over the bok choy, then push them to the sides of the pan.
3. Place the salmon fillets in the middle of the baking pan.
4. Place the pan on the roast position. Select Roast, set temperature to 375ºF (191ºC), and set time to 15 minutes.
5. When cooking is complete, remove the pan from the grill. Brush the salmon with the remaining Teriyaki Sauce. Garnish with the sesame seeds. Serve with steamed rice, if desired.

368. Bacon-Wrapped Scallops

Prep time: 5 minutes | Cook time: 10 minutes | Serves 4

8 slices bacon, cut in half
16 sea scallops, patted dry
Cooking spray
Salt and freshly ground black pepper, to taste
16 toothpicks, soaked in water for at least 30 minutes

1. Place the crisper tray on the air fry position. Select Air Fry, set the temperature to 370ºF (188ºC), and set the time to 10 minutes.
2. On a clean work surface, wrap half of a slice of bacon around each scallop and secure with a toothpick.
3. Lay the bacon-wrapped scallops in the crisper tray in a single layer. You may need to work in batches to avoid overcrowding.
4. Spritz the scallops with cooking spray and sprinkle the salt and pepper to season.
5. Air fry for 10 minutes, flipping the scallops halfway through, or until the bacon is cooked through and the scallops are firm.
6. Remove the scallops from the crisper tray to a plate and repeat with the remaining scallops. Serve warm.

369.Breaded Calamari with Lemon

Prep time: 5 minutes | Cook time: 12 minutes | Serves 4

2 large eggs
2 garlic cloves, minced
½ cup cornstarch
1 cup bread crumbs

1 pound (454 g) calamari rings
Cooking spray
1 lemon, sliced

1. In a small bowl, whisk the eggs with minced garlic. Place the cornstarch and bread crumbs into separate shallow dishes.
2. Dredge the calamari rings in the cornstarch, then dip in the egg mixture, shaking off any excess, finally roll them in the bread crumbs to coat well. Let the calamari rings sit for 10 minutes in the refrigerator.
3. Place the crisper tray on the air fry position. Select Air Fry, set the temperature to 390°F (199°C), and set the time to 12 minutes.
4. Spritz the crisper tray with cooking spray.
5. Put the calamari rings in the crisper tray. Air fry for 12 minutes until cooked through. Shake the crisper tray halfway through the cooking time.
6. Serve the calamari rings with the lemon slices sprinkled on top.

370.Easy Shrimp and Vegetable Paella

Prep time: 5 minutes | Cook time: 14 to 17 minutes | Serves 4

1 (10-ounce / 284-g) package frozen cooked rice, thawed
1 (6-ounce / 170-g) jar artichoke hearts, drained and chopped
¼ cup vegetable broth

½ teaspoon dried thyme
½ teaspoon turmeric
1 cup frozen cooked small shrimp
½ cup frozen baby peas
1 tomato, diced

1. Place the baking pan on the bake position. Select Bake, set the temperature to 340°F (171°C), and set the time to 17 minutes.
2. Mix together the cooked rice, chopped artichoke hearts, vegetable broth, thyme, and turmeric in the baking pan and stir to combine.
3. Bake for 9 minutes, or until the rice is heated through.
4. Remove the pan from the grill and fold in the shrimp, baby peas, and diced tomato and mix well.
5. Return to the grill and continue baking for 5 to 8 minutes, or until the shrimp are done and the paella is bubbling.
6. Cool for 5 minutes before serving.

Chapter 9 Desserts

371.Cinnamon Candied Apples

Prep time: 15 minutes | Cook time: 12 minutes | Serves 4

1 cup packed light brown sugar
2 teaspoons ground cinnamon

2 medium Granny Smith apples, peeled and diced

1. Place the baking pan on the bake position. Select Bake, set the temperature to 350ºF (177ºC), and set the time to 12 minutes.
2. Thoroughly combine the brown sugar and cinnamon in a medium bowl.
3. Add the apples to the bowl and stir until well coated. Transfer the apples to the baking pan.
4. Bake for 9 minutes. Stir the apples once and bake for an additional 3 minutes until softened.
5. Serve warm.

372.Pound Cake with Mixed Berries

Prep time: 10 minutes | Cook time: 8 minutes | Serves 6

3 tablespoons unsalted butter, at room temperature
6 slices pound cake, sliced about 1-inch thick
1 cup fresh

raspberries
1 cup fresh blueberries
3 tablespoons sugar
½ tablespoon fresh mint, minced

1. Place the grill plate on the grill position. Select Grill, set the temperature to 450ºF (232ºC), and set the time to 8 minutes.
2. Evenly spread the butter on both sides of each slice of pound cake.
3. Place the pound cake on the grill plate. Grill for 2 minutes.
4. After 2 minutes, flip the pound cake and grill for 2 minutes more, until golden brown. Repeat steps 3 and 4 for all of the pound cake slices.
5. While the pound cake grills, in a medium mixing bowl, combine the raspberries, blueberries, sugar, and mint.
6. When cooking is complete, plate the cake slices and serve topped with the berry mixture.

373.Fudge Pie

Prep time: 15 minutes | Cook time: 25 to 30 minutes | Serves 8

1½ cups sugar
½ cup self-rising flour
1/3 cup unsweetened cocoa powder
3 large eggs, beaten
12 tablespoons (1½ sticks) butter, melted

1½ teaspoons vanilla extract
1 (9-inch) unbaked pie crust
¼ cup confectioners' sugar (optional)

1. Place the baking pan on the bake position. Select Bake, set the temperature to 350ºF (177ºC), and set the time to 30 minutes.
2. Thoroughly combine the sugar, flour, and cocoa powder in a medium bowl. Add the beaten eggs and butter and whisk to combine. Stir in the vanilla.
3. Pour the prepared filling into the pie crust and transfer to the pan.
4. Bake for 25 to 30 minutes until just set.
5. Allow the pie to cool for 5 minutes. Sprinkle with the confectioners' sugar, if desired. Serve warm.

374.Lemony Blackberry Crisp

Prep time: 5 minutes | Cook time: 20 minutes | Serves 1

2 tablespoons lemon juice
1/3 cup powdered erythritol

¼ teaspoon xantham gum
2 cup blackberries
1 cup crunchy granola

1. Place the baking pan on the bake position. Select Bake, set the temperature to 350ºF (177ºC), and set the time to 15 minutes.
2. In a bowl, combine the lemon juice, erythritol, xantham gum, and blackberries. Transfer to the baking pan and cover with aluminum foil.
3. Bake for 12 minutes.
4. Take care when removing the pan from the grill. Give the blackberries a stir and top with the granola.
5. Return the pan to the grill and bake at 320ºF (160ºC) for an additional 3 minutes. Serve once the granola has turned brown and enjoy.

375. Grilled Peaches with Bourbon Butter Sauce

Prep time: 10 minutes | Cook time: 12 minutes | Serves 4

4 tablespoons salted butter
¼ cup bourbon
½ cup brown sugar
4 ripe peaches, halved and pitted
¼ cup candied pecans

1. Place the grill plate on the grill position. Select Grill, set the temperature to 450ºF (232ºC), and set the time to 12 minutes.
2. In a saucepan over medium heat, melt the butter for about 5 minutes. Once the butter is browned, remove the pan from the heat and carefully add the bourbon.
3. Return the saucepan to medium-high heat and add the brown sugar. Bring to a boil and let the sugar dissolve for 5 minutes, stirring occasionally.
4. Pour the bourbon butter sauce into a medium shallow bowl and arrange the peaches cut-side down to coat in the sauce.
5. Place the fruit on the grill plate in a single layer (you may need to do this in multiple batches). Gently press the fruit down to maximize grill marks. Grill for 10 to 12 minutes without flipping. If working in batches, repeat this step for all the peaches.
6. When cooking is complete, remove the peaches and top each with the pecans. Drizzle with the remaining bourbon butter sauce and serve immediately.

376. Rum Grilled Pineapple Sundaes

Prep time: 15 minutes | Cook time: 8 minutes | Serves 6

½ cup dark rum
½ cup packed brown sugar
1 teaspoon ground cinnamon, plus more for garnish
1 pineapple, cored and sliced
Vanilla ice cream, for serving

1. In a large shallow bowl or storage container, combine the rum, sugar, and cinnamon. Add the pineapple slices and arrange them in a single layer. Coat with the mixture, then let soak for at least 5 minutes per side.
2. Place the grill plate on the grill position. Select Grill, set the temperature to 450ºF (232ºC), and set the time to 8 minutes.
3. Strain the extra rum sauce from the pineapple.
4. Place the fruit on the grill plate in a single layer (you may need to do this in multiple batches). Gently press the fruit down to maximize grill marks. Grill for about 6 to 8 minutes without flipping. If working in batches, remove the pineapple, and repeat this step for the remaining pineapple slices.
5. When cooking is complete, remove, and top each pineapple ring with a scoop of ice cream. Sprinkle with cinnamon and serve immediately.

377. Ultimate Skillet Brownies

Prep time: 15 minutes | Cook time: 40 minutes | Serves 6

½ cup all-purpose flour
¼ cup unsweetened cocoa powder
¾ teaspoon sea salt
2 large eggs
1 tablespoon water
½ cup granulated sugar
½ cup dark brown sugar
1 tablespoon vanilla extract
8 ounces (227 g) semisweet chocolate chips, melted
¾ cup unsalted butter, melted
Nonstick cooking spray

1. In a medium bowl, whisk together the flour, cocoa powder, and salt.
2. In a large bowl, whisk together the eggs, water, sugar, brown sugar, and vanilla until smooth.
3. In a microwave-safe bowl, melt the chocolate in the microwave. In a separate microwave-safe bowl, melt the butter.
4. In a separate medium bowl, stir together the chocolate and butter until evenly combined. Whisk into the egg mixture. Then slowly add the dry ingredients, stirring just until incorporated.
5. Place the baking pan on the bake position. Select Bake, set the temperature to 350ºF (177ºC), and set the time to 40 minutes.
6. Lightly grease the baking pan with cooking spray. Pour the batter into the pan, spreading evenly.
7. Bake for 40 minutes.
8. After 40 minutes, check that baking is complete. A wooden toothpick inserted into the center of the brownies should come out clean.

378.Curry Peaches, Pears, and Plums

Prep time: 5 minutes | Cook time: 5 minutes | Serves 6 to 8

2 peaches	butter
2 firm pears	1 tablespoon honey
2 plums	2 to 3 teaspoons
2 tablespoons melted	curry powder

1. Place the crisper tray on the bake position. Select Bake, set the temperature to 325ºF (163ºC), and set the time to 8 minutes.
2. Cut the peaches in half, remove the pits, and cut each half in half again. Cut the pears in half, core them, and remove the stem. Cut each half in half again. Do the same with the plums.
3. Spread a large sheet of heavy-duty foil on the work surface. Arrange the fruit on the foil and drizzle with the butter and honey. Sprinkle with the curry powder.
4. Wrap the fruit in the foil, making sure to leave some air space in the packet.
5. Put the foil package in the crisper tray. Bake for 5 to 8 minutes, shaking the crisper tray once during the cooking time, until the fruit is soft.
6. Serve immediately.

379.Apple, Peach, and Cranberry Crisp

Prep time: 10 minutes | Cook time: 12 minutes | Serves 8

1 apple, peeled and chopped	2 tablespoons honey
2 peaches, peeled and chopped	¹/₃ cup brown sugar
	¼ cup flour
¹/₃ cup dried cranberries	½ cup oatmeal
	3 tablespoons softened butter

1. Place the baking pan on the bake position. Select Bake, set the temperature to 370ºF (188ºC), and set the time to 12 minutes.
2. In the baking pan, combine the apple, peaches, cranberries, and honey, and mix well.
3. In a medium bowl, combine the brown sugar, flour, oatmeal, and butter, and mix until crumbly. Sprinkle this mixture over the fruit in the pan.
4. Bake for 10 to 12 minutes or until the fruit is bubbly and the topping is golden brown. Serve warm.

380.Marshmallow Banana Boat

Prep time: 10 minutes | Cook time: 6 minutes | Serves 4

4 ripe bananas	½ cup chocolate chips
1 cup mini marshmallows	½ cup peanut butter chips

1. Place the grill plate on the grill position. Select Grill, set the temperature to 350ºF (177ºC), and set the time to 6 minutes.
2. Slice each banana lengthwise while still in its peel, making sure not to cut all the way through. Using both hands, pull the banana peel open like you would a book, revealing the banana inside. Divide the marshmallows, chocolate chips, and peanut butter chips among the bananas, stuffing them inside the skin.
3. Place the stuffed banana on the grill plate. Grill for 4 to 6 minutes, until the chocolate is melted and the marshmallows are toasted.

381.Chocolate and Coconut Cake

Prep time: 5 minutes | Cook time: 15 minutes | Serves 6

½ cup unsweetened chocolate, chopped	2 eggs, whisked
½ stick butter, at room temperature	½ teaspoon vanilla extract
1 tablespoon liquid stevia	A pinch of fine sea salt
1½ cups coconut flour	Cooking spray

1. Place the chocolate, butter, and stevia in a microwave-safe bowl. Microwave for about 30 seconds until melted.
2. Let the chocolate mixture cool for 5 to 10 minutes.
3. Add the remaining ingredients to the bowl of chocolate mixture and whisk to incorporate.
4. Place the baking pan on the bake position. Select Bake, set the temperature to 330ºF (166ºC), and set the time to 15 minutes.
5. Lightly spray the baking pan with cooking spray.
6. Scrape the chocolate mixture into the prepared baking pan.
7. Bake for 15 minutes, or until the top springs back lightly when gently pressed with your fingers.
8. Let the cake cool for 5 minutes and serve.

382.Orange Cake

Prep time: 10 minutes | Cook time: 23 minutes | Serves 8

Nonstick baking spray with flour
1¼ cups all-purpose flour
⅓ cup yellow cornmeal
¾ cup white sugar
1 teaspoon baking soda
¼ cup safflower oil
1¼ cups orange juice, divided
1 teaspoon vanilla
¼ cup powdered sugar

1. Place the baking pan on the bake position. Select Bake, set the temperature to 350ºF (177ºC), and set the time to 23 minutes.
2. Spray the baking pan with nonstick spray and set aside.
3. In a medium bowl, combine the flour, cornmeal, sugar, baking soda, safflower oil, 1 cup of the orange juice, and vanilla, and mix well.
4. Pour the batter into the baking pan. Bake for 23 minutes or until a toothpick inserted in the center of the cake comes out clean.
5. Remove the cake from the grill and place on a cooling rack. Using a toothpick, make about 20 holes in the cake.
6. In a small bowl, combine remaining ¼ cup of orange juice and the powdered sugar and stir well. Drizzle this mixture over the hot cake slowly so the cake absorbs it.
7. Cool completely, then cut into wedges to serve.

383.Graham Cracker Cheesecake

Prep time: 10 minutes | Cook time: 20 minutes | Serves 8

1 cup graham cracker crumbs
3 tablespoons softened butter
1½ (8-ounce / 227-g) packages cream cheese, softened
⅓ cup sugar
2 eggs
1 tablespoon flour
1 teaspoon vanilla
¼ cup chocolate syrup

1. For the crust, combine the graham cracker crumbs and butter in a small bowl and mix well. Press into the bottom of the baking pan and put in the freezer to set.
2. For the filling, combine the cream cheese and sugar in a medium bowl and mix well. Beat in the eggs, one at a time. Add the flour and vanilla.

3. Place the baking pan on the bake position. Select Bake, set the temperature to 450ºF (232ºC), and set the time to 20 minutes.
4. Remove ⅔ cup of the filling to a small bowl and stir in the chocolate syrup until combined.
5. Pour the vanilla filling into the pan with the crust. Drop the chocolate filling over the vanilla filling by the spoonful. With a clean butter knife, stir the fillings in a zigzag pattern to marbleize them.
6. Bake for 20 minutes or until the cheesecake is just set.
7. Cool on a wire rack for 1 hour, then chill in the refrigerator until the cheesecake is firm.
8. Serve immediately.

384.Strawberry Pizza

Prep time: 10 minutes | Cook time: 6 minutes | Serves 4

2 tablespoons all-purpose flour, plus more as needed
½ store-bought pizza dough (about 8 ounces / 227 g)
1 tablespoon canola
oil
1 cup sliced fresh strawberries
1 tablespoon sugar
½ cup chocolate-hazelnut spread

1. Place the grill plate on the grill position. Select Grill, set the temperature to 450ºF (232ºC), and set the time to 6 minutes.
2. Dust a clean work surface with the flour. Place the dough on the floured surface, and roll it out to a 9-inch round of even thickness. Dust your rolling pin and work surface with additional flour, as needed, to ensure the dough does not stick.
3. Brush the surface of the rolled-out dough evenly with half the oil. Flip the dough over, and brush with the remaining oil. Poke the dough with a fork 5 or 6 times across its surface to prevent air pockets from forming during cooking.
4. Place the dough on the grill plate. Grill for 3 minutes.
5. After 3 minutes, flip the dough. Continue grilling for the remaining 3 minutes.
6. Meanwhile, in a medium mixing bowl, combine the strawberries and sugar.
7. Transfer the pizza to a cutting board and let cool. Top with the chocolate-hazelnut spread and strawberries. Cut into pieces and serve.

385. Simple Corn Biscuits

Prep time: 15 minutes | Cook time: 15 minutes | Serves 6

1½ cups all-purpose flour, plus additional for dusting
½ cup yellow cornmeal
2½ teaspoons baking powder

½ teaspoon sea salt
1/3 cup vegetable shortening
2/3 cup buttermilk
Nonstick cooking spray

1. In a large bowl, combine the flour, cornmeal, baking powder, and salt.
2. Add the shortening, and cut it into the flour mixture, until well combined and the dough resembles a coarse meal. Add the buttermilk and stir together just until moistened.
3. Place the crisper tray on the air fry position. Select Air Fry, set the temperature to 350ºF (177ºC), and set the time to 15 minutes.
4. Dust a clean work surface with flour. Knead the mixture on the floured surface until a cohesive dough forms. Roll out the dough to an even thickness, then cut into biscuits with a 2-inch biscuit cutter.
5. Coat the crisper tray with cooking spray. Place 6 to 8 biscuits in the crisper tray, well spaced, and spray each with cooking spray. Air fry for 12 to 15 minutes, until golden brown.
6. Gently remove the biscuits from the crisper tray, and place them on a wire rack to cool. Repeat with the remaining dough.

386. Oatmeal and Carrot Cookie Cups

Prep time: 10 minutes | Cook time: 8 minutes | Makes 16 cups

3 tablespoons unsalted butter, at room temperature
¼ cup packed brown sugar
1 tablespoon honey
1 egg white
½ teaspoon vanilla extract

1/3 cup finely grated carrot
½ cup quick-cooking oatmeal
1/3 cup whole-wheat pastry flour
½ teaspoon baking soda
¼ cup dried cherries

1. Place the baking pan on the bake position. Select Bake, set the temperature to 350ºF (177ºC), and set the time to 8 minutes.
2. In a medium bowl, beat the butter, brown sugar, and honey until well combined.
3. Add the egg white, vanilla, and carrot. Beat to combine.
4. Stir in the oatmeal, pastry flour, and baking soda.
5. Stir in the dried cherries.
6. Double up 32 mini muffin foil cups to make 16 cups. Fill each with about 4 teaspoons of dough. Place the cookie cups directly in the pan.
7. Bake for 8 minutes, 8 at a time, or until light golden brown and just set. Serve warm.

387. Coffee Chocolate Cake

Prep time: 5 minutes | Cook time: 30 minutes | Serves 8

Dry Ingredients:

1½ cups almond flour
½ cup coconut meal
2/3 cup Swerve

1 teaspoon baking powder
¼ teaspoon salt

Wet Ingredients:

1 egg
1 stick butter, melted

½ cup hot strongly brewed coffee

Topping:

½ cup confectioner's Swerve
¼ cup coconut flour
3 tablespoons coconut oil

1 teaspoon ground cinnamon
½ teaspoon ground cardamom

1. Place the baking pan on the bake position. Select Bake, set the temperature to 330ºF (166ºC), and set the time to 30 minutes.
2. In a medium bowl, combine the almond flour, coconut meal, Swerve, baking powder, and salt.
3. In a large bowl, whisk the egg, melted butter, and coffee until smooth.
4. Add the dry mixture to the wet and stir until well incorporated. Transfer the batter to the greased baking pan.
5. Stir together all the ingredients for the topping in a small bowl. Spread the topping over the batter and smooth the top with a spatula.
6. Bake for 30 minutes, or until the cake springs back when gently pressed with your fingers.
7. Rest for 10 minutes before serving.

388. Chocolate Coconut Brownies

Prep time: 15 minutes | Cook time: 15 minutes | Serves 8

½ cup coconut oil
2 ounces (57 g) dark chocolate
1 cup sugar
2½ tablespoons water
4 whisked eggs
¼ teaspoon ground cinnamon
½ teaspoons ground anise star
¼ teaspoon coconut extract
½ teaspoons vanilla extract
1 tablespoon honey
½ cup flour
½ cup desiccated coconut
Sugar, for dusting

1. Place the baking pan on the bake position. Select Bake, set the temperature to 355ºF (179ºC), and set the time to 15 minutes.
2. Melt the coconut oil and dark chocolate in the microwave.
3. Combine with the sugar, water, eggs, cinnamon, anise, coconut extract, vanilla, and honey in a large bowl.
4. Stir in the flour and desiccated coconut. Incorporate everything well.
5. Lightly grease the baking pan with butter. Transfer the mixture to the pan.
6. Bake for 15 minutes.
7. Remove from the grill and allow to cool slightly.
8. Take care when taking it out of the baking pan. Slice it into squares.
9. Dust with sugar before serving.

389. Rich Chocolate Cookie

Prep time: 10 minutes | Cook time: 9 minutes | Serves 4

Nonstick baking spray with flour
3 tablespoons softened butter
¹/₃ cup plus 1 tablespoon brown sugar
1 egg yolk
½ cup flour
2 tablespoons ground white chocolate
¼ teaspoon baking soda
½ teaspoon vanilla
¾ cup chocolate chips

1. Place the baking pan on the bake position. Select Bake, set the temperature to 350ºF (177ºC), and set the time to 9 minutes.
2. In a medium bowl, beat the butter and brown sugar together until fluffy. Stir in the egg yolk.
3. Add the flour, white chocolate, baking soda, and vanilla, and mix well. Stir in the chocolate chips.
4. Line the baking pan with parchment paper. Spray the parchment paper with nonstick baking spray with flour.
5. Spread the batter into the prepared pan, leaving a ½-inch border on all sides.
6. Bake for 9 minutes or until the cookie is light brown and just barely set.
7. Remove the pan from the grill and let cool for 10 minutes. Remove the cookie from the pan, remove the parchment paper, and let cool on a wire rack.
8. Serve immediately.

390. Chocolate and Peanut Butter Lava Cupcakes

Prep time: 10 minutes | Cook time: 10 to 13 minutes | Serves 8

Nonstick baking spray with flour
1¹/₃ cups chocolate cake mix
1 egg
1 egg yolk
¼ cup safflower oil
¼ cup hot water
¹/₃ cup sour cream
3 tablespoons peanut butter
1 tablespoon powdered sugar

1. Place the baking pan on the bake position. Select Bake, set the temperature to 350ºF (177ºC), and set the time to 13 minutes.
2. Double up 16 foil muffin cups to make 8 cups. Spray each lightly with nonstick spray; set aside.
3. In a medium bowl, combine the cake mix, egg, egg yolk, safflower oil, water, and sour cream, and beat until combined.
4. In a small bowl, combine the peanut butter and powdered sugar and mix well. Form this mixture into 8 balls.
5. Spoon about ¼ cup of the chocolate batter into each muffin cup and top with a peanut butter ball. Spoon remaining batter on top of the peanut butter balls to cover them.
6. Arrange the cups in the pan, leaving some space between each. Bake for 10 to 13 minutes or until the tops look dry and set.
7. Let the cupcakes cool for about 10 minutes, then serve warm.

391.Black Forest Pies

Prep time: 10 minutes | Cook time: 15 minutes | Serves 6

3 tablespoons milk or dark chocolate chips
2 tablespoons thick, hot fudge sauce
2 tablespoons chopped dried cherries
1 (10-by-15-inch) sheet frozen puff pastry, thawed
1 egg white, beaten
2 tablespoons sugar
½ teaspoon cinnamon

1. Place the crisper tray on the bake position. Select Bake, set the temperature to 350ºF (177ºC), and set the time to 15 minutes.
2. In a small bowl, combine the chocolate chips, fudge sauce, and dried cherries.
3. Roll out the puff pastry on a floured surface. Cut into 6 squares with a sharp knife.
4. Divide the chocolate chip mixture into the center of each puff pastry square. Fold the squares in half to make triangles. Firmly press the edges with the tines of a fork to seal.
5. Brush the triangles on all sides sparingly with the beaten egg white. Sprinkle the tops with sugar and cinnamon.
6. Put in the crisper tray. Bake for 15 minutes or until the triangles are golden brown. The filling will be hot, so cool for at least 20 minutes before serving.

392.Churros with Chocolate-Yogurt Sauce

Prep time: 15 minutes | Cook time: 30 minutes | Serves 8

1 cup water
1 stick unsalted butter, cut into 8 pieces
½ cup sugar, plus 1 tablespoon
1 cup all-purpose flour
1 teaspoon vanilla
extract
3 large eggs
2 teaspoons ground cinnamon
Nonstick cooking spray
4 ounces (113 g) dark chocolate, chopped
¼ cup Greek yogurt

1. In a medium saucepan over medium-high heat, combine the water, butter, and the 1 tablespoon of sugar. Bring to a simmer. Add the flour, stirring it in quickly. Continue to cook, stirring constantly, until the mixture is thick, about 3 minutes. Transfer to a large bowl.

2. Using a spoon, beat the flour mixture for about 1 minute, until cooled slightly. Stir in the vanilla, then the eggs, one at a time.
3. Transfer the dough to a plastic bag or a piping bag. Let the dough rest for 1 hour at room temperature.
4. Place the crisper tray on the air fry position. Select Air Fry, set the temperature to 375ºF (191ºC), and set the time to 30 minutes.
5. Meanwhile, in a medium shallow bowl, combine the cinnamon and remaining ½ cup of sugar.
6. Spray the crisper tray with the nonstick cooking spray. Take the plastic bag with your dough and cut off one corner. Pipe the batter directly into the crisper tray, making 6 (3-inch-long) churros, placed at least ½ inch apart. Air fry for 10 minutes.
7. Meanwhile, in a small microwave-safe mixing bowl, melt the chocolate in the microwave, stirring it after every 30 seconds, until completely melted and smooth. Add the yogurt and whisk until smooth.
8. After 10 minutes, carefully transfer the churros to the sugar mixture and toss to coat evenly. Repeat piping and air frying with the remaining batter, adding time as needed.
9. Serve the churros with the warm chocolate dipping sauce.

393.Banana and Walnut Cake

Prep time: 10 minutes | Cook time: 25 minutes | Serves 6

1 pound (454 g) bananas, mashed
8 ounces (227 g) flour
6 ounces (170 g) sugar
3.5 ounces (99 g)
walnuts, chopped
2.5 ounces (71 g) butter, melted
2 eggs, lightly beaten
¼ teaspoon baking soda

1. Place the baking pan on the bake position. Select Bake, set the temperature to 355ºF (179ºC), and set the time to 10 minutes.
2. In a bowl, combine the sugar, butter, egg, flour, and baking soda with a whisk. Stir in the bananas and walnuts.
3. Transfer the mixture to the greased baking pan. Bake for 10 minutes.
4. Reduce the temperature to 330ºF (166ºC) and bake for another 15 minutes. Serve hot.

394.Fresh Blueberry Cobbler

Prep time: 15 minutes | Cook time: 30 minutes | Serves 6

4 cups fresh blueberries
1 teaspoon grated lemon zest
1 cup sugar, plus 2 tablespoons
1 cup all-purpose flour, plus 2 tablespoons
Juice of 1 lemon
2 teaspoons baking powder
¼ teaspoon salt
6 tablespoons unsalted butter
¾ cup whole milk
⅛ teaspoon ground cinnamon

1. In a medium bowl, combine the blueberries, lemon zest, 2 tablespoons of sugar, 2 tablespoons of flour, and lemon juice.
2. In a medium bowl, combine the remaining 1 cup of flour and 1 cup of sugar, baking powder, and salt. Cut the butter into the flour mixture until it forms an even crumb texture. Stir in the milk until a dough forms.
3. Place the baking pan on the bake position. Select Bake, set the temperature to 350ºF (177ºC), and set the time to 30 minutes.
4. Meanwhile, pour the blueberry mixture into the baking pan, spreading it evenly across the pan. Gently pour the batter over the blueberry mixture, then sprinkle the cinnamon over the top.
5. Bake for 30 minutes, until lightly golden.
6. When cooking is complete, serve warm.

395.Pumpkin Pudding

Prep time: 10 minutes | Cook time: 15 minutes | Serves 4

3 cups pumpkin purée
3 tablespoons honey
1 tablespoon ginger
1 tablespoon cinnamon
1 teaspoon clove
1 teaspoon nutmeg
1 cup full-fat cream
2 eggs
1 cup sugar

1. Place the baking pan on the bake position. Select Bake, set the temperature to 390ºF (199ºC), and set the time to 15 minutes.
2. In a bowl, stir all the ingredients together to combine.
3. Scrape the mixture into the greased baking pan. Bake for 15 minutes.
4. Serve warm.

396.Sugar-Glazed Biscuit Bites

Prep time: 15 minutes | Cook time: 12 minutes | Serves 8

⅔ cup all-purpose flour, plus additional for dusting
⅔ cup whole-wheat flour
2 tablespoons granulated sugar
1 teaspoon baking powder
¼ teaspoon ground cinnamon
¼ teaspoon sea salt
4 tablespoons salted butter, cold and cut into small pieces
⅓ cup whole milk
Nonstick cooking spray
2 cups powdered sugar
3 tablespoons water

1. In a large bowl, combine the all-purpose flour, whole-wheat flour, sugar, baking powder, cinnamon, and salt. Add the cold butter pieces, and cut them into the flour mixture using a pastry cutter or a fork, until well-combined and the mixture resembles a course meal. Add the milk to the mixture, and stir together until the dough comes together into a ball.
2. Place the crisper tray on the air fry position. Select Air Fry, set the temperature to 350ºF (177ºC), and set the time to 12 minutes.
3. Dust a clean work surface with the all-purpose flour. Place the dough on the floured surface, and knead until the dough is smooth and forms a cohesive ball, about 30 seconds. Cut the dough into 16 equal pieces. Gently roll each piece into a smooth ball.
4. Coat the crisper tray well with cooking spray. Place 8 biscuit bites in the crisper tray, leaving room between each, and spray each with cooking spray. Air fry for 10 to 12 minutes, until golden brown.
5. Meanwhile, in a medium mixing bowl, whisk together the powdered sugar and water until it forms a smooth glaze.
6. Gently remove the bites from the crisper tray, and place them on a wire rack covered with aluminum foil. Repeat step 4 with the remaining biscuit bites.
7. Spoon half the glaze over the bites and let cool 5 minutes, then spoon over the remaining glaze.

397. Pineapple and Chocolate Cake

Prep time: 10 minutes | Cook time: 35 to 40 minutes | Serves 4

2 cups flour
4 ounces (113 g) butter, melted
¼ cup sugar
½ pound (227 g) pineapple, chopped
½ cup pineapple juice
1 ounce (28 g) dark chocolate, grated
1 large egg
2 tablespoons skimmed milk

1. Grease a cake tin with a little oil or butter.
2. Place the cake tin on the bake position. Select Bake, set the temperature to 370ºF (188ºC), and set the time to 40 minutes.
3. In a bowl, combine the butter and flour to create a crumbly consistency.
4. Add the sugar, chopped pineapple, juice, and grated dark chocolate and mix well.
5. In a separate bowl, combine the egg and milk. Add this mixture to the flour mixture and stir well until a soft dough forms.
6. Pour the mixture into the cake tin and transfer to the grill.
7. Bake for 35 to 40 minutes.
8. Serve immediately.

398. Ultimate Coconut Chocolate Cake

Prep time: 5 minutes | Cook time: 15 minutes | Serves 10

1¼ cups unsweetened bakers' chocolate
1 stick butter
1 teaspoon liquid stevia
¹/₃ cup shredded coconut
2 tablespoons coconut milk
2 eggs, beaten
Cooking spray

1. Place the baking pan on the bake position. Select Bake, set the temperature to 330ºF (166ºC), and set the time to 15 minutes.
2. Lightly spritz the baking pan with cooking spray.
3. Place the chocolate, butter, and stevia in a microwave-safe bowl. Microwave for about 30 seconds until melted. Let the chocolate mixture cool to room temperature.
4. Add the remaining ingredients to the chocolate mixture and stir until well incorporated. Pour the batter into the prepared baking pan.
5. Bake for 15 minutes, or until a toothpick inserted in the center comes out clean.
6. Remove from the pan and allow to cool for about 10 minutes before serving.

399. Chocolate Molten Cake

Prep time: 5 minutes | Cook time: 10 minutes | Serves 4

3.5 ounces (99 g) butter, melted
3½ tablespoons sugar
3.5 ounces (99 g) chocolate, melted
1½ tablespoons flour
2 eggs

1. Place the baking pan on the bake position. Select Bake, set the temperature to 375ºF (191ºC), and set the time to 10 minutes.
2. Grease four ramekins with a little butter.
3. Rigorously combine the eggs, butter, and sugar before stirring in the melted chocolate.
4. Slowly fold in the flour.
5. Spoon an equal amount of the mixture into each ramekin.
6. Put them in the pan. Bake for 10 minutes.
7. Put the ramekins upside-down on plates and let the cakes fall out. Serve hot.

400. Orange Coconut Cake

Prep time: 5 minutes | Cook time: 17 minutes | Serves 6

1 stick butter, melted
¾ cup granulated Swerve
2 eggs, beaten
¾ cup coconut flour
¼ teaspoon salt
¹/₃ teaspoon grated nutmeg
¹/₃ cup coconut milk
1¼ cups almond flour
½ teaspoon baking powder
2 tablespoons unsweetened orange jam
Cooking spray

1. Place the baking pan on the bake position. Select Bake, set the temperature to 355ºF (179ºC), and set the time to 17 minutes.
2. Coat the baking pan with cooking spray. Set aside.
3. In a large mixing bowl, whisk together the melted butter and granulated Swerve until fluffy.
4. Mix in the beaten eggs and whisk again until smooth. Stir in the coconut flour, salt, and nutmeg and gradually pour in the coconut milk. Add the remaining ingredients and stir until well incorporated.
5. Scrape the batter into the baking pan.
6. Bake for 17 minutes until the top of the cake springs back when gently pressed with your fingers.
7. Remove from the grill to a wire rack to cool. Serve chilled.

401.Pear and Apple Crisp

Prep time: 10 minutes | Cook time: 20 minutes | Serves 6

½ pound (227 g) apples, cored and chopped
½ pound (227 g) pears, cored and chopped
1 cup flour
1 cup sugar
1 tablespoon butter
1 teaspoon ground cinnamon
¼ teaspoon ground cloves
1 teaspoon vanilla extract
¼ cup chopped walnuts
Whipped cream, for serving

1. Place the baking pan on the bake position. Select Bake, set the temperature to 340ºF (171ºC), and set the time to 20 minutes.
2. Lightly grease the baking pan and place the apples and pears inside.
3. Combine the rest of the ingredients, minus the walnuts and the whipped cream, until a coarse, crumbly texture is achieved.
4. Pour the mixture over the fruits and spread it evenly. Top with the chopped walnuts.
5. Bake for 20 minutes or until the top turns golden brown.
6. Serve at room temperature with whipped cream.

402.Chocolate S'mores

Prep time: 5 minutes | Cook time: 3 minutes | Serves 12

12 whole cinnamon graham crackers
2 (1.55-ounce / 44-g) chocolate bars, broken into 12 pieces
12 marshmallows

1. Place the crisper tray on the bake position. Select Bake, set the temperature to 350ºF (177ºC), and set the time to 3 minutes.
2. Halve each graham cracker into 2 squares.
3. Put 6 graham cracker squares in the crisper tray. Do not stack. Put a piece of chocolate into each. Bake for 2 minutes.
4. Open the grill and add a marshmallow onto each piece of melted chocolate. Bake for 1 additional minute.
5. Remove the cooked s'mores from the grill, then repeat steps 2 and 3 for the remaining 6 s'mores.
6. Top with the remaining graham cracker squares and serve.

403.Lemon Ricotta Cake

Prep time: 5 minutes | Cook time: 25 minutes | Serves 6

17.5 ounces (496 g) ricotta cheese
5.4 ounces (153 g) sugar
3 eggs, beaten
3 tablespoons flour
1 lemon, juiced and zested
2 teaspoons vanilla extract

1. Place the baking pan on the bake position. Select Bake, set the temperature to 320ºF (160ºC), and set the time to 25 minutes.
2. In a large mixing bowl, stir together all the ingredients until the mixture reaches a creamy consistency.
3. Pour the mixture into the baking pan.
4. Bake for 25 minutes until a toothpick inserted in the center comes out clean.
5. Allow to cool for 10 minutes on a wire rack before serving.

404.Chocolate Pecan Pie

Prep time: 20 minutes | Cook time: 25 minutes | Serves 8

1 (9-inch) unbaked pie crust
Filling:
2 large eggs
⅓ cup butter, melted
1 cup sugar
½ cup all-purpose flour
1 cup milk chocolate chips
1½ cups coarsely chopped pecans
2 tablespoons bourbon

1. Place the baking pan on the bake position. Select Bake, set the temperature to 350ºF (177ºC), and set the time to 25 minutes.
2. Whisk the eggs and melted butter in a large bowl until creamy.
3. Add the sugar and flour and stir to incorporate. Mix in the milk chocolate chips, pecans, and bourbon and stir until well combined.
4. Use a fork to prick holes in the bottom and sides of the pie crust. Pour the prepared filling into the pie crust. Place the pie crust in the pan.
5. Bake for 25 minutes until a toothpick inserted in the center comes out clean.
6. Allow the pie cool for 10 minutes in the crisper tray before serving.

405.Orange and Anise Cake

Prep time: 5 minutes | Cook time: 20 minutes | Serves 6

1 stick butter, at room temperature	unbleached almond flour
5 tablespoons liquid monk fruit	1 teaspoon baking soda
2 eggs plus 1 egg yolk, beaten	½ teaspoon baking powder
⅓ cup hazelnuts, roughly chopped	½ teaspoon ground cinnamon
3 tablespoons sugar-free orange marmalade	½ teaspoon ground allspice
6 ounces (170 g)	½ ground anise seed
	Cooking spray

1. Place the baking pan on the bake position. Select Bake, set the temperature to 310ºF (154ºC), and set the time to 20 minutes.
2. Lightly spritz the baking pan with cooking spray.
3. In a mixing bowl, whisk the butter and liquid monk fruit until the mixture is pale and smooth. Mix in the beaten eggs, hazelnuts, and marmalade and whisk again until well incorporated.
4. Add the almond flour, baking soda, baking powder, cinnamon, allspice, anise seed and stir to mix well.
5. Scrape the batter into the prepared baking pan. Bake for 20 minutes, or until the top of the cake springs back when gently pressed with your fingers.
6. Transfer to a wire rack and let the cake cool to room temperature. Serve immediately.

406.Classic Pound Cake

Prep time: 5 minutes | Cook time: 30 minutes | Serves 8

1 stick butter, at room temperature	powder
1 cup Swerve	¼ teaspoon salt
4 eggs	1 teaspoon vanilla essence
1½ cups coconut flour	A pinch of ground star anise
½ cup buttermilk	A pinch of freshly grated nutmeg
½ teaspoon baking soda	Cooking spray
½ teaspoon baking	

1. Place the baking pan on the bake position. Select Bake, set the temperature to 320ºF (160ºC), and set the time to 30 minutes.

2. Spray the baking pan with cooking spray.
3. With an electric mixer or hand mixer, beat the butter and Swerve until creamy. One at a time, mix in the eggs and whisk until fluffy. Add the remaining ingredients and stir to combine.
4. Transfer the batter to the prepared baking pan. Bake for 30 minutes until the center of the cake is springy. Rotate the pan halfway through the cooking time.
5. Allow the cake to cool in the pan for 10 minutes before removing and serving.

407.Oatmeal and Chocolate Bars

Prep time: 10 minutes | Cook time: 20 minutes | Makes 4 dozen (1-by-1½-inch) bars

1 cup unsalted butter, at room temperature	1½ cups all-purpose flour
1 cup dark brown sugar	1 teaspoon baking soda
½ cup granulated sugar	1 teaspoon baking powder
2 large eggs	2 cups old-fashioned rolled oats
1 tablespoon vanilla extract	2 cups chocolate chips
Pinch salt	

1. In a large mixing bowl or stand mixer, beat together the butter, brown sugar, and granulated sugar until creamy and light in color.
2. Add the eggs one at a time, mixing after each addition. Add the vanilla and salt and mix to combine.
3. In a separate bowl, combine the flour, baking soda, baking powder, and oats. Add to the butter mixture and mix until combined. By hand, stir in the chocolate chips. (If you have a stand mixer, you can do this with the machine, but hand mixers usually aren't strong enough to handle these ingredients.)
4. Spread the dough into the baking pan in an even layer. It will fill the entire pan.
5. Place the pan on the bake position. Select Bake, set temperature to 350ºF (177ºC), and set time to 20 minutes.
6. After 15 minutes, check the cookie, rotating the pan if the crust is not browning evenly. Continue cooking for a total of 18 to 20 minutes or until golden brown. Remove the pan from the grill and let cool completely before cutting.

408. Easy Blackberry Cobbler

Prep time: 15 minutes | Cook time: 25 to 30 minutes | Serves 6

3 cups fresh or frozen blackberries	extract
1¾ cups sugar, divided	8 tablespoons (1 stick) butter, melted
1 teaspoon vanilla	1 cup self-rising flour
	Cooking spray

1. Place the baking pan on the bake position. Select Bake, set the temperature to 350ºF (177ºC), and set the time to 30 minutes.
2. Spritz the baking pan with cooking spray.
3. Mix the blackberries, 1 cup of sugar, and vanilla in a medium bowl and stir to combine.
4. Stir together the melted butter, remaining sugar, and flour in a separate medium bowl.
5. Spread the blackberry mixture evenly in the prepared pan and top with the butter mixture.
6. Bake for 20 to 25 minutes. Check for doneness and bake for another 5 minutes, if needed.
7. Remove from the grill and place on a wire rack to cool to room temperature. Serve immediately.

409. Black and White Brownies

Prep time: 10 minutes | Cook time: 20 minutes | Makes 1 dozen brownies

1 egg	¹⁄₃ cup all-purpose flour
¼ cup brown sugar	¼ cup cocoa powder
2 tablespoons white sugar	¼ cup white chocolate chips
2 tablespoons safflower oil	Nonstick cooking spray
1 teaspoon vanilla	

1. Place the baking pan on the bake position. Select Bake, set the temperature to 340ºF (171ºC), and set the time to 20 minutes.
2. Spritz the baking pan with nonstick cooking spray.
3. Whisk together the egg, brown sugar, and white sugar in a medium bowl. Mix in the safflower oil and vanilla and stir to combine.
4. Add the flour and cocoa powder and stir just until incorporated. Fold in the white chocolate chips.
5. Scrape the batter into the prepared baking pan.
6. Bake for 20 minutes, or until the brownie springs back when touched lightly with your fingers.
7. Transfer to a wire rack and let cool for 30 minutes before slicing to serve.

410. Blueberry and Peach Galette

Prep time: 10 minutes | Cook time: 20 minutes | Serves 6

2 large peaches or nectarines, peeled and cut into ½-inch slices (about 2 cups)	purpose flour
	¼ teaspoon ground allspice or cinnamon
1 pint blueberries, rinsed and picked through (about 2 cups)	½ teaspoon grated lemon zest (optional)
	Pinch kosher or fine salt
¹⁄₃ cup plus 2 tablespoons granulated sugar, divided	1 (9-inch) refrigerated piecrust (or use homemade)
2 tablespoons unbleached all-	2 teaspoons unsalted butter, cut into pea-size pieces
	1 large egg, beaten

1. In a medium bowl, gently mix the peaches and blueberries with ¹⁄₃ cup of sugar, flour, allspice, lemon zest (if using), and salt.
2. In the baking pan, unroll the crust, patching any tears if necessary. Arrange the fruit in the center of the crust, leaving about 1½ inches of space around the edges. Distribute the butter pieces over the fruit. Fold the outside edge of the crust over the outer circle of the fruit, making pleats as necessary. Brush the crust with the egg. Sprinkle the remaining 2 tablespoons of sugar over the crust and fruit.
3. Place the pan on the bake position. Select Bake, set temperature to 350ºF (177ºC), and set time to 20 minutes.
4. After about 15 minutes, check the galette, rotating the pan if the crust is not browning evenly. The galette is done when the crust is deep golden brown and the fruit is bubbling.
5. Remove the pan from the grill and let cool for 10 minutes, then cut into wedges and serve warm.

411. Peanut Butter-Chocolate Bread Pudding

Prep time: 10 minutes | Cook time: 10 to 12 minutes | Serves 8

1 egg
1 egg yolk
¾ cup chocolate milk
3 tablespoons brown sugar
3 tablespoons peanut butter

2 tablespoons cocoa powder
1 teaspoon vanilla
5 slices firm white bread, cubed
Nonstick cooking spray

1. Place the baking pan on the bake position. Select Bake, set the temperature to 330ºF (166ºC), and set the time to 12 minutes.
2. Spritz the baking pan with nonstick cooking spray.
3. Whisk together the egg, egg yolk, chocolate milk, brown sugar, peanut butter, cocoa powder, and vanilla until well combined.
4. Fold in the bread cubes and stir to mix well. Allow the bread soak for 10 minutes.
5. When ready, transfer the egg mixture to the prepared baking pan.
6. Bake for 10 to 12 minutes, or until the pudding is just firm to the touch.
7. Serve at room temperature.

412. Pear Tart

Prep time: 15 minutes | Cook time: 25 minutes | Serves 8

Juice of 1 lemon
3 medium or 2 large ripe or almost ripe pears
1 sheet (½ package) frozen puff pastry, thawed

All-purpose flour, for dusting
4 tablespoons caramel sauce, divided

1. In a large bowl, mix the lemon juice with about 1 quart of water.
2. Peel the pears and remove the stems. Cut them in half through the stem end. Use a melon baller to remove the seeds and cut out the blossom end. Remove any tough fibers between the stem end and the center. As you work, place the pear halves in the acidulated water.
3. Unwrap and unfold the puff pastry on a lightly floured cutting board. Using a rolling pin, roll it very lightly, just to press the folds together. Transfer it to the baking pan.
4. Roll about ½ inch of the pastry edges up to form a ridge around the perimeter. Crimp the corners together so you have a solid rim around the pastry to hold in the liquid as the tart cooks. Brush the bottom of the pastry with 2 tablespoons of caramel sauce. (If the sauce is cold, it may be very stiff. You can microwave it for a few seconds, or set the jar in a bowl of very hot water for a few minutes to make it easier to brush).
5. Remove the pear halves from the water and blot them dry with paper towels. Place one of the halves on the board cut-side down and cut ¼-inch-thick slices radially (think of cutting really thin wedges, rather than slicing straight up and down). Repeat with the remaining halves. Arrange the pear slices over the pastry. You can get as fancy as you like, but I find that three rows of slices fills the tart, looks good, and isn't difficult to achieve. Drizzle the remaining 2 tablespoons of caramel sauce over the pears.
6. Place the pan on the bake position. Select Bake, set temperature to 350ºF (177ºC), and set time to 25 minutes.
7. After 15 minutes, check the tart, rotating the pan if the crust is not browning evenly. Continue cooking.
8. When cooking is complete, the pastry will be golden brown, the pears soft, and the caramel bubbling. Remove the pan from the grill and let the tart cool for about 10 minutes. The tart can be served warm or at room temperature. If there is a lot of liquid floating around the pears, you can blot it off with paper towels, which will keep the crust crisper and won't diminish the flavor.

413.Chia Pudding

Prep time: 5 minutes | Cook time: 4 minutes | Serves 2

1 cup chia seeds
1 cup unsweetened coconut milk
1 teaspoon liquid stevia

1 tablespoon coconut oil
1 teaspoon butter, melted

1. Place the baking pan on the bake position. Select Bake, set the temperature to 360ºF (182ºC), and set the time to 4 minutes.
2. Mix together the chia seeds, coconut milk, and stevia in a large bowl. Add the coconut oil and melted butter and stir until well blended.
3. Divide the mixture evenly between the ramekins, filling only about ²/₃ of the way. Transfer to the pan.
4. Bake for 4 minutes.
5. Allow to cool for 5 minutes and serve warm.

414.Pistachio and Walnut Baklava

Prep time: 10 minutes | Cook time: 16 minutes | Serves 10

1 cup shelled raw pistachios
1 cup walnut pieces
½ cup unsalted butter, melted
3 tablespoons granulated sugar

¼ cup plus 2 tablespoons honey, divided
1 teaspoon ground cinnamon
2 (1.9-ounce / 54-g) packages frozen miniature phyllo tart shells

1. Place the pistachios and walnuts in the crisper tray in an even layer.
2. Place the crisper tray on the air fry position. Select Air Fry, set temperature to 350ºF (177ºC), and set time to 4 minutes.
3. After 2 minutes, remove the crisper tray and stir the nuts. Return the crisper tray to the grill and continue cooking until the nuts are golden brown and fragrant, 1 to 2 minutes more.
4. While the nuts are toasting, place the butter into a medium bowl. Add the sugar, ¼ cup of honey, and cinnamon. Stir to combine.
5. When the nuts are toasted, remove the crisper tray from the grill and place them on a cutting board and let cool for a couple of minutes. Finely chop the nuts—not so that they're pulverized, but so no large chunks remain. If you have a food processor, a few pulses of the blade should do it. If you have an old-fashioned nut chopper, this is a great time to pull it out. Add the chopped nuts, with all the "nut dust," to the sugar mixture and stir to combine.
6. Place the phyllo cups in the baking pan, which will be cool by now. Evenly fill the phyllo cups with the nut mixture, mounding it up. (You'll think you have too much filling, but you won't; trust me.) As you work, stir the nuts in the bowl frequently so that the syrup is even distributed throughout the filling.
7. Place the pan on the bake position. Select Bake, set temperature to 350ºF (177ºC), and set time to 12 minutes.
8. After about 8 minutes, check the cups, and rotate the pan if the they are not browning evenly. Continue cooking until the cups are dark golden brown and the syrup is bubbling (it might ooze out; don't worry about that).
9. As soon as you remove the baklava from the grill, drizzle each cup with about ⅛ teaspoon or so of the remaining honey over the top. Let cool completely before serving.

415.Blackberry Chocolate Cake

Prep time: 10 minutes | Cook time: 22 minutes | Serves 8

½ cup butter, at room temperature
2 ounces (57 g) Swerve
4 eggs
1 cup almond flour
1 teaspoon baking soda

$\frac{1}{3}$ teaspoon baking powder
½ cup cocoa powder
1 teaspoon orange zest
$\frac{1}{3}$ cup fresh blackberries

1. Place the baking pan on the bake position. Select Bake, set the temperature to 335ºF (168ºC), and set the time to 22 minutes.
2. With an electric mixer or hand mixer, beat the butter and Swerve until creamy.
3. One at a time, mix in the eggs and beat again until fluffy.
4. Add the almond flour, baking soda, baking powder, cocoa powder, orange zest and mix well. Add the butter mixture to the almond flour mixture and stir until well blended. Fold in the blackberries.
5. Scrape the batter to the baking pan. Bake for 22 minutes. Check the cake for doneness: If a toothpick inserted into the center of the cake comes out clean, it's done.
6. Allow the cake cool on a wire rack to room temperature. Serve immediately.

416.Shortbread

Prep time: 10 minutes | Cook time: 36 to 40 minutes | Makes 4 dozen cookies

1 cup granulated sugar
1 tablespoon grated lemon zest
1 pound (454 g) unsalted butter, at room temperature

¼ teaspoon fine salt
4 cups all-purpose flour
$\frac{1}{3}$ cup cornstarch
Cooking oil spray

1. In a stand mixer fitted with the paddle attachment, beat the sugar and lemon zest on medium speed for a minute or two, then let sit for about 5 minutes. (If you don't have a stand mixer, use a hand mixer.) Add the butter and salt, and beat until well blended and fluffy.
2. In a large bowl, whisk together the flour and cornstarch. Gradually add the dry ingredients to the butter mixture and mix just until combined. (If you're using a hand mixer, you may have to finish mixing by hand; the dough is quite stiff.)
3. Spray the baking pan with cooking oil spray and fit in a piece of parchment paper. Press the dough into the pan until very even and smooth.
4. Place the pan on the bake position. Select Bake, set temperature to 325ºF (163ºC), and set time to 36 minutes.
5. After 20 minutes, check the shortbread, rotating the pan if it is not browning evenly. Continue for 16 minutes more, or until light golden brown. This will yield shortbread bars that are crumbly and just slightly soft. For crisper shortbread, cook for an additional 3 to 4 minutes, then turn the grill off and let the shortbread stay in the grill for a few more minutes until it's a few shades darker.
6. When cooking is complete, remove the pan from the grill. These bars are easiest to cut when they're slightly warm. Let cool. If you like, dust the bars with confectioners' sugar or granulated sugar.

Chapter 10 Holiday Specials

417.Kale Salad Sushi Rolls with Sriracha Mayonnaise

Prep time: 10 minutes | Cook time: 10 minutes | Serves 12

Kale Salad:

1½ cups chopped kale
1 tablespoon sesame seeds
¾ teaspoon soy sauce
¾ teaspoon toasted sesame oil
½ teaspoon rice vinegar
¼ teaspoon ginger
⅛ teaspoon garlic powder

Sushi Rolls:

3 sheets sushi nori
1 batch cauliflower rice
½ avocado, sliced
Sriracha Mayonnaise:
¼ cup Sriracha sauce
¼ cup vegan mayonnaise

Coating:

½ cup panko breadcrumbs

1. Place the crisper tray on the air fry position. Select Air Fry, set the temperature to 390ºF (199ºC), and set the time to 10 minutes.
2. In a medium bowl, toss all the ingredients for the salad together until well coated and set aside.
3. Place a sheet of nori on a clean work surface and spread the cauliflower rice in an even layer on the nori. Scoop 2 to 3 tablespoon of kale salad on the rice and spread over. Place 1 or 2 avocado slices on top. Roll up the sushi, pressing gently to get a nice, tight roll. Repeat to make the remaining 2 rolls.
4. In a bowl, stir together the Sriracha sauce and mayonnaise until smooth. Add breadcrumbs to a separate bowl.
5. Dredge the sushi rolls in Sriracha Mayonnaise, then roll in breadcrumbs till well coated.
6. Place the coated sushi rolls in the crisper tray. Air fry for 10 minutes, or until golden brown and crispy. Flip the sushi rolls gently halfway through to ensure even cooking..
7. Transfer to a platter and rest for 5 minutes before slicing each roll into 8 pieces. Serve warm.

418.Milky Pecan Tart

Prep time: 2hours 25 minutes | Cook time: 30 minutes | Serves 8

Tart Crust:

¼ cup firmly packed brown sugar
⅓ cup butter, softened
1 cup all-purpose flour
¼ teaspoon kosher salt

Filling:

¼ cup whole milk
4 tablespoons butter, diced
½ cup packed brown sugar
¼ cup pure maple
syrup
1½ cups finely chopped pecans
¼ teaspoon pure vanilla extract
¼ teaspoon sea salt

1. Place the baking pan on the bake position. Select Bake, set the temperature to 350ºF (177ºC), and set the time to 25 minutes.
2. Line the baking pan with aluminum foil, then spritz the pan with cooking spray.
3. Stir the brown sugar and butter in a bowl with a hand mixer until puffed, then add the flour and salt and stir until crumbled.
4. Pour the mixture in the prepared baking pan and tilt the pan to coat the bottom evenly.
5. Bake for 13 minutes or until the crust is golden brown.
6. Meanwhile, pour the milk, butter, sugar, and maple syrup in a saucepan. Stir to mix well. Bring to a simmer, then cook for 1 more minute. Stir constantly.
7. Turn off the heat and mix the pecans and vanilla into the filling mixture.
8. Pour the filling mixture over the golden crust and spread with a spatula to coat the crust evenly.
9. Bake in the grill for an additional 12 minutes or until the filling mixture is set and frothy.
10. Remove the baking pan from the grill and sprinkle with salt. Allow to sit for 10 minutes or until cooled.
11. Transfer the pan to the refrigerator to chill for at least 2 hours, then remove the aluminum foil and slice to serve.

419.Golden Nuggets

Prep time: 15 minutes | Cook time: 4 minutes per batch | Makes 20 nuggets

1 cup all-purpose flour, plus more for dusting
1 teaspoon baking powder
½ teaspoon butter, at room temperature, plus more for brushing
¼ teaspoon salt
¼ cup water
⅛ teaspoon onion powder
¼ teaspoon garlic powder
⅛ teaspoon seasoning salt
Cooking spray

1. Place the crisper tray on the air fry position. Select Air Fry, set the temperature to 370ºF (188ºC), and set the time to 4 minutes.
2. Line the crisper tray with parchment paper.
3. Mix the flour, baking powder, butter, and salt in a large bowl. Stir to mix well. Gradually whisk in the water until a sanity dough forms.
4. Put the dough on a lightly floured work surface, then roll it out into a ½-inch thick rectangle with a rolling pin.
5. Cut the dough into about twenty 1- or 2-inch squares, then arrange the squares in a single layer in the crisper tray. Spritz with cooking spray. You need to work in batches to avoid overcrowding.
6. Combine onion powder, garlic powder, and seasoning salt in a small bowl. Stir to mix well, then sprinkle the squares with the powder mixture.
7. Air fry for 4 minutes or until golden brown. Flip the squares halfway through the cooking time.
8. Remove the golden nuggets from the grill and brush with more butter immediately. Serve warm.

420.Hasselback Potatoes

Prep time: 5 minutes | Cook time: 50 minutes | Serves 4

4 russet potatoes, peeled
Salt and freshly ground black pepper,
to taste
¼ cup grated Parmesan cheese
Cooking spray

1. Place the crisper tray on the air fry position. Select Air Fry, set the temperature to 400ºF (204ºC), and set the time to 50 minutes.
2. Spray the crisper tray lightly with cooking spray.
3. Make thin parallel cuts into each panato, ⅛-inch to ¼-inch apart, stopping at about ½ of the way through. The panato needs to stay intact along the bottom.
4. Spray the potatoes with cooking spray and use the hands or a silicone brush to completely coat the potatoes lightly in oil.
5. Put the potatoes, sliced side up, in the crisper tray in a single layer. Leave a little room between each panato. Sprinkle the potatoes lightly with salt and black pepper.
6. Air fry for 20 minutes. Reposition the potatoes and spritz lightly with cooking spray again. air fry until the potatoes are fork-tender and crispy and browned, for another 20 to 30 minutes.
7. Sprinkle the potatoes with Parmesan cheese and serve.

421.Jewish Blintzes

Prep time: 5 minutes | Cook time: 10 minutes | Makes 8 blintzes

2 (7½-ounce / 213-g) packages farmer cheese, mashed
¼ cup cream cheese
¼ teaspoon vanilla extract
¼ cup granulated white sugar
8 egg roll wrappers
4 tablespoons butter, melted

1. Place the crisper tray on the air fry position. Select Air Fry, set the temperature to 375ºF (191ºC), and set the time to 10 minutes.
2. Combine the farmer cheese, cream cheese, vanilla extract, and sugar in a bowl. Stir to mix well.
3. Unfold the egg roll wrappers on a clean work surface, spread ¼ cup of the filling at the edge of each wrapper and leave a ½-inch edge uncovering.
4. Wet the edges of the wrappers with water and fold the uncovered edge over the filling. Fold the left and right sides in the center, then tuck the edge under the filling and fold to wrap the filling.
5. Brush the wrappers with melted butter, then arrange the wrappers in a single layer in the crisper tray, seam side down. Leave a little space between each two wrappers. Work in batches to avoid overcrowding.
6. Air fry for 10 minutes or until golden brown.
7. Serve immediately.

422. Teriyaki Shrimp Skewers

Prep time: 10 minutes | Cook time: 6 minutes | Makes 12 skewered shrimp

1½ tablespoons mirin
1½ teaspoons ginger juice
1½ tablespoons soy sauce
12 large shrimp (about 20 shrimps per pound), peeled and deveined
1 large egg
¾ cup panko breadcrumbs
Cooking spray

1. Combine the mirin, ginger juice, and soy sauce in a large bowl. Stir to mix well.
2. Dunk the shrimp in the bowl of mirin mixture, then wrap the bowl in plastic and refrigerate for 1 hour to marinate.
3. Place the crisper tray on the air fry position. Select Air Fry, set the temperature to 400ºF (204ºC), and set the time to 6 minutes.
4. Spritz the crisper tray with cooking spray.
5. Run twelve 4-inch skewers through each shrimp.
6. Whisk the egg in the bowl of marinade to combine well. Pour the breadcrumbs on a plate.
7. Dredge the shrimp skewers in the egg mixture, then shake the excess off and roll over the breadcrumbs to coat well.
8. Arrange the shrimp skewers in the crisper tray and spritz with cooking spray. You need to work in batches to avoid overcrowding.
9. Air fry for 6 minutes or until the shrimp are opaque and firm. Flip the shrimp skewers halfway through.
10. Serve immediately.

423. Pão de Queijo

Prep time: 37 minutes | Cook time: 24 minutes | Makes 12 balls

2 tablespoons butter, plus more for greasing
½ cup milk
1½ cups tapioca flour
½ teaspoon salt
1 large egg
²/₃ cup finely grated aged Asiago cheese

1. Put the butter in a saucepan and pour in the milk, heat over medium heat until the liquid boils. Keep stirring.
2. Turn off the heat and mix in the tapioca flour and salt to form a soft dough. Transfer the dough in a large bowl, then wrap the bowl in plastic and let sit for 15 minutes.
3. Break the egg in the bowl of dough and whisk with a hand mixer for 2 minutes or until a sanity dough forms. Fold the cheese in the dough. Cover the bowl in plastic again and let sit for 10 more minutes.
4. Place a cake pan on the bake position. Select Bake, set the temperature to 375ºF (191ºC), and set the time to 12 minutes.
5. Grease the cake pan with butter.
6. Scoop 2 tablespoons of the dough into the cake pan. Repeat with the remaining dough to make dough 12 balls. Keep a little distance between each two balls. You may need to work in batches to avoid overcrowding.
7. Bake for 12 minutes or until the balls are golden brown and fluffy. Flip the balls halfway through the cooking time.
8. Remove the balls from the grill and allow to cool for 5 minutes before serving.

424. Spicy Black Olives

Prep time: 10 minutes | Cook time: 5 minutes | Serves 4

12 ounces (340 g) pitted black extra-large olives
¼ cup all-purpose flour
1 cup panko bread crumbs
2 teaspoons dried thyme
1 teaspoon red pepper flakes
1 teaspoon smoked paprika
1 egg beaten with 1 tablespoon water
Vegetable oil for spraying

1. Place the crisper tray on the air fry position. Select Air Fry, set the temperature to 400ºF (204ºC), and set the time to 5 minutes.
2. Drain the olives and place them on a paper towel–lined plate to dry.
3. Put the flour on a plate. Combine the panko, thyme, red pepper flakes, and paprika on a separate plate. Dip an olive in the flour, shaking off any excess, then coat with egg mixture. Dredge the olive in the panko mixture, pressing to make the crumbs adhere, and place the breaded olive on a platter. Repeat with the remaining olives.
4. Spray the olives with oil and place them in a single layer in the crisper tray. Work in batches if necessary so as not to overcrowd the crisper tray.
5. Air fry for 5 minutes until the breading is browned and crispy. Serve warm

425.Pigs in a Blanket

Prep time: 10 minutes | Cook time: 8 minutes per batch | Makes 16 rolls

1 can refrigerated crescent roll dough
1 small package mini smoked sausages, patted dry

2 tablespoons melted butter
2 teaspoons sesame seeds
1 teaspoon onion powder

1. Place the baking pan on the bake position. Select Bake, set the temperature to 330ºF (166ºC), and set the time to 8 minutes.
2. Place the crescent roll dough on a clean work surface and separate into 8 pieces. Cut each piece in half and you will have 16 triangles.
3. Make the pigs in the blanket: Arrange each sausage on each dough triangle, then roll the sausages up.
4. Brush the pigs with melted butter and place half of the pigs in the blanket in the baking pan. Sprinkle with sesame seeds and onion powder.
5. Bake for 8 minutes or until the pigs are fluffy and golden brown. Flip the pigs halfway through.
6. Serve immediately.

426.Shrimp with Sriracha and Worcestershire Sauce

Prep time: 15 minutes | Cook time: 10 minutes per batch | Serves 4

1 tablespoon Sriracha sauce
1 teaspoon Worcestershire sauce
2 tablespoons sweet chili sauce
¾ cup mayonnaise
1 egg, beaten

1 cup panko breadcrumbs
1 pound (454 g) raw shrimp, shelled and deveined, rinsed and drained
Lime wedges, for serving
Cooking spray

1. Place the crisper tray on the air fry position. Select Air Fry, set the temperature to 360ºF (182ºC), and set the time to 10 minutes.
2. Spritz the crisper tray with cooking spray.
3. Combine the Sriracha sauce, Worcestershire sauce, chili sauce, and mayo in a bowl. Stir to mix well. Reserve $^1/_3$ cup of the mixture as the dipping sauce.
4. Combine the remaining sauce mixture with the beaten egg. Stir to mix well. Put the panko in a separate bowl.
5. Dredge the shrimp in the sauce mixture first, then into the panko. Roll the shrimp to coat well. Shake the excess off.
6. Place the shrimp in the crisper tray, then spritz with cooking spray. You may need to work in batches to avoid overcrowding.
7. Air fry for 10 minutes or until opaque. Flip the shrimp halfway through the cooking time.
8. Remove the shrimp from the grill and serve with reserve sauce mixture and squeeze the lime wedges over.

427.Simple Butter Cake

Prep time: 25 minutes | Cook time: 20 minutes | Serves 8

1 cup all-purpose flour
1¼ teaspoons baking powder
¼ teaspoon salt
½ cup plus 1½ tablespoons granulated white sugar
9½ tablespoons butter, at room temperature

2 large eggs
1 large egg yolk
2½ tablespoons milk
1 teaspoon vanilla extract
Cooking spray

1. Place a cake pan on the bake position. Select Bake, set the temperature to 325ºF (163ºC), and set the time to 20 minutes.
2. Spritz the cake pan with cooking spray.
3. Combine the flour, baking powder, and salt in a large bowl. Stir to mix well.
4. Whip the sugar and butter in a separate bowl with a hand mixer on medium speed for 3 minutes.
5. Whip the eggs, egg yolk, milk, and vanilla extract into the sugar and butter mix with a hand mixer.
6. Pour in the flour mixture and whip with hand mixer until sanity and smooth.
7. Scrape the batter into the cake pan and level the batter with a spatula.
8. Bake for 20 minutes or until a toothpick inserted in the center comes out clean. Check the doneness during the last 5 minutes of the baking.
9. Invert the cake on a cooling rack and allow to cool for 15 minutes before slicing to serve.

428.Bourbon Monkey Bread

Prep time: 15 minutes | Cook time: 25 minutes | Serves 6 to 8

1 (16.3-ounce / 462-g) can store-bought refrigerated biscuit dough
¼ cup packed light brown sugar
1 teaspoon ground cinnamon
½ teaspoon freshly grated nutmeg
½ teaspoon ground ginger
½ teaspoon kosher salt
¼ teaspoon ground allspice
⅛ teaspoon ground cloves
4 tablespoons (½ stick) unsalted butter, melted
½ cup powdered sugar
2 teaspoons bourbon
2 tablespoons chopped candied cherries
2 tablespoons chopped pecans

1. Place a cake pan on the bake position. Select Bake, set the temperature to 310ºF (154ºC), and set the time to 25 minutes.
2. Open the can and separate the biscuits, then cut each into quarters. Toss the biscuit quarters in a large bowl with the brown sugar, cinnamon, nutmeg, ginger, salt, allspice, and cloves until evenly coated.
3. Transfer the dough pieces and any sugar left in the bowl to the cake pan and drizzle evenly with the melted butter.
4. Bake for 25 minutes until the monkey bread is golden brown and cooked through in the middle. Transfer the pan to a wire rack and let cool completely. Unmold from the pan.
5. In a small bowl, whisk the powdered sugar and the bourbon into a smooth glaze. Drizzle the glaze over the cooled monkey bread and, while the glaze is still wet, sprinkle with the cherries and pecans to serve.

429.Garlicky Olive Stromboli

Prep time: 25 minutes | Cook time: 25 minutes | Serves 8

4 large cloves garlic, unpeeled
3 tablespoons grated Parmesan cheese
½ cup packed fresh basil leaves
½ cup marinated, pitted green and black olives
¼ teaspoon crushed red pepper
½ pound (227 g) pizza dough, at room temperature
4 ounces (113 g) sliced provolone cheese (about 8 slices)
Cooking spray

1. Place the crisper tray on the air fry position. Select Air Fry, set the temperature to 370ºF (188ºC), and set the time to 10 minutes.
2. Spritz the crisper tray with cooking spray.
3. Put the unpeeled garlic in the crisper tray.
4. Air fry for 10 minutes or until the garlic is softened completely. Remove them from the grill and allow to cool until you can handle.

5. Peel the garlic and place into a food processor with 2 tablespoons of Parmesan, basil, olives, and crushed red pepper. Pulse to mix well. Set aside.
6. Arrange the pizza dough on a clean work surface, then roll it out with a rolling pin into a rectangle. Cut the rectangle in half.
7. Sprinkle half of the garlic mixture over each rectangle half, and leave ½-inch edges uncover. Top them with the provolone cheese.
8. Brush one long side of each rectangle half with water, then roll them up. Spritz the crisper tray with cooking spray. Transfer the rolls to the crisper tray. Spritz with cooking spray and scatter with remaining Parmesan.
9. Air fry for 15 minutes or until golden brown. Flip the rolls halfway through.
10. Remove the rolls from the grill and allow to cool for a few minutes before serving.

430.Hearty Honey Yeast Rolls

Prep time: 10 minutes | Cook time: 20 minutes | Makes 8 rolls

¼ cup whole milk, heated to 115ºF (46ºC) in the microwave
½ teaspoon active dry yeast
1 tablespoon honey
2/3 cup all-purpose flour, plus more for dusting

½ teaspoon kosher salt
2 tablespoons unsalted butter, at room temperature, plus more for greasing
Flaky sea salt, to taste

1. In a large bowl, whisk together the milk, yeast, and honey and let stand until foamy, about 10 minutes.
2. Stir in the flour and salt until just combined. Stir in the butter until absorbed. Scrape the dough onto a lightly floured work surface and knead until smooth, about 6 minutes. Transfer the dough to a lightly greased bowl, cover loosely with a sheet of plastic wrap or a kitchen towel, and let sit until nearly doubled in size, about 1 hour.
3. Uncover the dough, lightly press it down to expel the bubbles, then portion it into 8 equal pieces. Prep the work surface by wiping it clean with a damp paper towel (if there is flour on the work surface, it will prevent the dough from sticking lightly to the surface, which helps it form a ball). Roll each piece into a ball by cupping the palm of the hand around the dough against the work surface and moving the heel of the hand in a circular motion while using the thumb to contain the dough and tighten it into a perfectly round ball. Once all the balls are formed, nestle them side by side in the crisper tray.
4. Cover the rolls loosely with a kitchen towel or a sheet of plastic wrap and let sit until lightly risen and puffed, 20 to 30 minutes.
5. Place the crisper tray on the air fry position. Select Air Fry, set the temperature to 270ºF (132ºC), and set the time to 12 minutes.
6. Uncover the rolls and gently brush with more butter, being careful not to press the rolls too hard. Air fry for 12 minutes until the rolls are light golden brown and fluffy.
7. Remove the rolls from the grill and brush liberally with more butter, if you like, and sprinkle each roll with a pinch of sea salt. Serve warm.

431. Supplì al Telefono (Risotto Croquettes)

Prep time: 1 hour 40 minutes | Cook time: 1 hour | Serves 6

Risotto Croquettes:

4 tablespoons unsalted butter
1 small yellow onion, minced
1 cup Arborio rice
3½ cups chicken stock
½ cup dry white wine
3 eggs
Zest of 1 lemon
½ cup grated Parmesan cheese

2 ounces (57 g) fresh Mozzarella cheese
¼ cup peas
2 tablespoons water
½ cup all-purpose flour
1½ cups panko breadcrumbs
Kosher salt and ground black pepper, to taste
Cooking spray

Tomato Sauce:

2 tablespoons extra-virgin olive oil
4 cloves garlic, minced
¼ teaspoon red pepper flakes

1 (28-ounce / 794-g) can crushed tomatoes
2 teaspoons granulated sugar
Kosher salt and ground black pepper, to taste

1. Melt the butter in a pan over medium heat, then add the onion and salt to taste. Sauté for 5 minutes or until the onion in translucent.
2. Add the rice and stir to coat well. Cook for 3 minutes or until the rice is lightly browned. Pour in the chicken stock and wine.
3. Bring to a boil. Then cook for 20 minutes or until the rice is tender and liquid is almost absorbed.
4. Make the risotto: When the rice is cooked, break the egg into the pan. Add the lemon zest and Parmesan cheese. Sprinkle with salt and ground black pepper. Stir to mix well.
5. Pour the risotto in the baking pan, then level with a spatula to spread the risotto evenly. Wrap the baking pan in plastic and refrigerate for1 hour.
6. Meanwhile, heat the olive oil in a saucepan over medium heat until shimmering.
7. Add the garlic and sprinkle with red pepper flakes. Sauté for a minute or until fragrant.
8. Add the crushed tomatoes and sprinkle with sugar. Stir to mix well. Bring to a boil. Reduce the heat to low and simmer for 15 minutes or until lightly thickened. Sprinkle with salt and pepper to taste. Set aside until ready to serve.
9. Remove the risotto from the refrigerator. Scoop the risotto into twelve 2-inch balls, then flatten the balls with your hands.
10. Arrange a about ½-inch piece of Mozzarella and 5 peas in the center of each flattened ball, then wrap them back into balls.
11. Transfer the balls in the baking pan lined with parchment paper, then refrigerate for 15 minutes or until firm.
12. Place the crisper tray on the bake position. Select Bake, set the temperature to 400ºF (204ºC), and set the time to 10 minutes.
13. Whisk the remaining 2 eggs with 2 tablespoons of water in a bowl. Pour the flour in a second bowl and pour the panko in a third bowl.
14. Dredge the risotto balls in the bowl of flour first, then into the eggs, and then into the panko. Shake the excess off.
15. Transfer the balls to the crisper tray and spritz with cooking spray. You may need to work in batches to avoid overcrowding.
16. Bake for 10 minutes or until golden brown. Flip the balls halfway through.
17. Serve the risotto balls with the tomato sauce.

Chapter 11 Fast and Easy Everyday Favorites

432.Crispy Brussels Sprouts

Prep time: 5 minutes | Cook time: 20 minutes | Serves 4

¼ teaspoon salt
⅛ teaspoon ground black pepper
1 tablespoon extra-virgin olive oil

1 pound (454 g) Brussels sprouts, trimmed and halved
Lemon wedges, for garnish

1. Place the crisper tray on the air fry position. Select Air Fry, set the temperature to 350ºF (177ºC), and set the time to 20 minutes.
2. Combine the salt, black pepper, and olive oil in a large bowl. Stir to mix well.
3. Add the Brussels sprouts to the bowl of mixture and toss to coat well.
4. Arrange the Brussels sprouts in the crisper tray. Air fry for 20 minutes or until lightly browned and wilted. Shake the crisper tray two times during the cooking.
5. Transfer the cooked Brussels sprouts to a large plate and squeeze the lemon wedges on top to serve.

433.Baked Cheese Sandwich

Prep time: 5 minutes | Cook time: 8 minutes | Serves 2

2 tablespoons mayonnaise
4 thick slices sourdough bread

4 thick slices Brie cheese
8 slices hot capicola

1. Place the crisper tray on the bake position. Select Bake, set the temperature to 350ºF (177ºC), and set the time to 8 minutes.
2. Spread the mayonnaise on one side of each slice of bread. Place 2 slices of bread in the crisper tray, mayonnaise-side down.
3. Place the slices of Brie and capicola on the bread and cover with the remaining two slices of bread, mayonnaise-side up.
4. Bake for 8 minutes, or until the cheese has melted.
5. Serve immediately.

434.Simple Baked Green Beans

Prep time: 5 minutes | Cook time: 10 minutes | Makes 2 cups

½ teaspoon lemon pepper
2 teaspoons granulated garlic
½ teaspoon salt

1 tablespoon olive oil
2 cups fresh green beans, trimmed and snapped in half

1. Place the crisper tray on the bake position. Select Bake, set the temperature to 370ºF (188ºC), and set the time to 10 minutes.
2. Combine the lemon pepper, garlic, salt, and olive oil in a bowl. Stir to mix well.
3. Add the green beans to the bowl of mixture and toss to coat well.
4. Arrange the green beans in the crisper tray. Bake for 10 minutes or until tender and crispy. Shake the crisper tray halfway through to make sure the green beans are cooked evenly.
5. Serve immediately.

435.Cheesy Chile Toast

Prep time: 5 minutes | Cook time: 5 minutes | Serves 1

2 tablespoons grated Parmesan cheese
2 tablespoons grated Mozzarella cheese
2 teaspoons salted butter, at room temperature

10 to 15 thin slices serrano chile or jalapeño
2 slices sourdough bread
½ teaspoon black pepper

1. Place the crisper tray on the bake position. Select Bake, set the temperature to 325ºF (163ºC), and set the time to 5 minutes.
2. In a small bowl, stir together the Parmesan, Mozzarella, butter, and chiles.
3. Spread half the mixture onto one side of each slice of bread. Sprinkle with the pepper. Place the slices, cheese-side up, in the crisper tray.
4. Bake for 5 minutes, or until the cheese has melted and started to brown slightly.
5. Serve immediately.

436.Hot Wings

Prep time: 5 minutes | Cook time: 30 minutes | Makes 16 wings

16 chicken wings
3 tablespoons hot

sauce
Cooking spray

1. Place the crisper tray on the air fry position. Select Air Fry, set the temperature to 360ºF (182ºC), and set the time to 15 minutes.
2. Spritz the crisper tray with cooking spray.
3. Arrange the chicken wings in the crisper tray. You need to work in batches to avoid overcrowding.
4. Air fry for 15 minutes or until well browned. Shake the crisper tray at lease three times during the cooking.
5. Transfer the wings on a plate and serve with hot sauce.

437.Indian-Style Sweet Potato Fries

Prep time: 5 minutes | Cook time: 8 minutes | Makes 20 fries

Seasoning Mixture:

¾ teaspoon ground coriander
½ teaspoon garam masala
½ teaspoon garlic

powder
½ teaspoon ground cumin
¼ teaspoon ground cayenne pepper

Fries:

2 large sweet potatoes, peeled
2 teaspoons olive oil

1. Place the crisper tray on the air fry position. Select Air Fry, set the temperature to 400ºF (204ºC), and set the time to 8 minutes.
2. In a small bowl, combine the coriander, garam masala, garlic powder, cumin, and cayenne pepper.
3. Slice the sweet potatoes into ¼-inch-thick fries.
4. In a large bowl, toss the sliced sweet potatoes with the olive oil and the seasoning mixture.
5. Transfer the seasoned sweet potatoes to the crisper tray. Air fry for 8 minutes, until crispy.
6. Serve warm.

438.Bacon-Wrapped Jalapeño Poppers

Prep time: 5 minutes | Cook time: 12 minutes | Serves 6

6 large jalapeños
4 ounces (113 g) ⅓-less-fat cream cheese
¼ cup shredded reduced-fat sharp

Cheddar cheese
2 scallions, green tops only, sliced
6 slices center-cut bacon, halved

1. Place the crisper tray on the bake position. Select Bake, set the temperature to 325ºF (163ºC), and set the time to 12 minutes.
2. Wearing rubber gloves, halve the jalapeños lengthwise to make 12 pieces. Scoop out the seeds and membranes and discard.
3. In a medium bowl, combine the cream cheese, Cheddar, and scallions. Using a small spoon or spatula, fill the jalapeños with the cream cheese filling. Wrap a bacon strip around each pepper and secure with a toothpick.
4. Working in batches, place the stuffed peppers in a single layer in the crisper tray. Bake for 12 minutes, until the peppers are tender, the bacon is browned and crisp, and the cheese is melted.
5. Serve warm.

439.Easy Devils on Horseback

Prep time: 5 minutes | Cook time: 7 minutes | Serves 12

24 petite pitted prunes (4½ ounces / 128 g)
¼ cup crumbled blue

cheese, divided
8 slices center-cut bacon, cut crosswise into thirds

1. Place the crisper tray on the air fry position. Select Air Fry, set the temperature to 400ºF (204ºC), and set the time to 7 minutes.
2. Halve the prunes lengthwise, but don't cut them all the way through. Place ½ teaspoon of cheese in the center of each prune. Wrap a piece of bacon around each prune and secure the bacon with a toothpick.
3. Working in batches, arrange a single layer of the prunes in the crisper tray. Air fry for about 7 minutes, flipping halfway, until the bacon is cooked through and crisp.
4. Let cool slightly and serve warm.

440. Classic Mexican Street Corn

Prep time: 5 minutes | Cook time: 7 minutes | Serves 4

4 medium ears corn, husked
Cooking spray
2 tablespoons mayonnaise
1 tablespoon fresh lime juice
½ teaspoon ancho
chile powder
¼ teaspoon kosher salt
2 ounces (57 g) crumbled Cotija or feta cheese
2 tablespoons chopped fresh cilantro

1. Place the crisper tray on the air fry position. Select Air Fry, set the temperature to 375ºF (191ºC), and set the time to 7 minutes.
2. Spritz the corn with cooking spray. Working in batches, arrange the ears of corn in the crisper tray in a single layer. Air fry for about 7 minutes, flipping halfway, until the kernels are tender when pierced with a paring knife. When cool enough to handle, cut the corn kernels off the cob.
3. In a large bowl, mix together mayonnaise, lime juice, ancho powder, and salt. Add the corn kernels and mix to combine. Transfer to a serving dish and top with the Cotija and cilantro. Serve immediately.

441. Herb-Roasted Veggies

Prep time: 10 minutes | Cook time: 14 to 18 minutes | Serves 4

1 red bell pepper, sliced
1 (8-ounce / 227-g) package sliced mushrooms
1 cup green beans, cut into 2-inch pieces
⅓ cup diced red
onion
3 garlic cloves, sliced
1 teaspoon olive oil
½ teaspoon dried basil
½ teaspoon dried tarragon

1. Place the crisper tray on the roast position. Select Roast, set the temperature to 350ºF (177ºC), and set the time to 18 minutes.
2. In a medium bowl, mix the red bell pepper, mushrooms, green beans, red onion, and garlic. Drizzle with the olive oil. Toss to coat.
3. Add the herbs and toss again.
4. Place the vegetables in the crisper tray. Roast for 14 to 18 minutes, or until tender. Serve immediately.

442. Scalloped Veggie Mix

Prep time: 10 minutes | Cook time: 15 minutes | Serves 4

1 Yukon Gold panato, thinly sliced
1 small sweet panato, peeled and thinly sliced
1 medium carrot, thinly sliced
¼ cup minced onion
3 garlic cloves, minced
¾ cup 2 percent milk
2 tablespoons cornstarch
½ teaspoon dried thyme

1. Place the baking pan on the bake position. Select Bake, set the temperature to 380ºF (193ºC), and set the time to 15 minutes.
2. In the baking pan, layer the panato, sweet panato, carrot, onion, and garlic.
3. In a small bowl, whisk the milk, cornstarch, and thyme until blended. Pour the milk mixture evenly over the vegetables in the pan.
4. Bake for 15 minutes. Check the casserole—it should be golden brown on top, and the vegetables should be tender.
5. Serve immediately.

443. Peppery Brown Rice Fritters

Prep time: 10 minutes | Cook time: 8 to 10 minutes | Serves 4

1 (10-ounce / 284-g) bag frozen cooked brown rice, thawed
1 egg
3 tablespoons brown rice flour
⅓ cup finely grated carrots
⅓ cup minced red bell pepper
2 tablespoons minced fresh basil
3 tablespoons grated Parmesan cheese
2 teaspoons olive oil

1. Place the crisper tray on the air fry position. Select Air Fry, set the temperature to 380ºF (193ºC), and set the time to 10 minutes.
2. In a small bowl, combine the thawed rice, egg, and flour and mix to blend.
3. Stir in the carrots, bell pepper, basil, and Parmesan cheese.
4. Form the mixture into 8 fritters and drizzle with the olive oil.
5. Put the fritters carefully into the crisper tray. Air fry for 8 to 10 minutes, or until the fritters are golden brown and cooked through.
6. Serve immediately.

444.Indian Masala Omelet

Prep time: 10 minutes | Cook time: 12 minutes | Serves 2

4 large eggs
½ cup diced onion
½ cup diced tomato
¼ cup chopped fresh cilantro
1 jalapeño, deseeded and finely chopped
½ teaspoon ground
turmeric
½ teaspoon kosher salt
½ teaspoon cayenne pepper
Olive oil, for greasing the pan

1. Placea 3-cup Bundt pan on the bake position. Select Bake, set the temperature to 250ºF (121ºC), and set the time to 12 minutes.
2. Generously grease the Bundt pan.
3. In a large bowl, beat the eggs. Stir in the onion, tomato, cilantro, jalapeño, turmeric, salt, and cayenne.
4. Pour the egg mixture into the prepared pan. Bake for 12 minutes, or until the eggs are cooked through. Carefully unmold and cut the omelet into four pieces.
5. Serve immediately.

445.Garlicky Baked Cherry Tomatoes

Prep time: 5 minutes | Cook time: 4 to 6 minutes | Serves 2

2 cups cherry tomatoes
1 clove garlic, thinly sliced
1 teaspoon olive oil
⅛ teaspoon kosher
salt
1 tablespoon freshly chopped basil, for topping
Cooking spray

1. Place the baking pan on the bake position. Select Bake, set the temperature to 360ºF (182ºC), and set the time to 6 minutes.
2. Spritz the baking pan with cooking spray and set aside.
3. In a large bowl, toss together the cherry tomatoes, sliced garlic, olive oil, and kosher salt. Spread the mixture in an even layer in the prepared pan.
4. Bake for 4 to 6 minutes, or until the tomatoes become soft and wilted.
5. Transfer to a bowl and rest for 5 minutes. Top with the chopped basil and serve warm.

446.Simple Sweet Potato Soufflé

Prep time: 10 minutes | Cook time: 30 minutes | Serves 4

1 sweet panato, baked and mashed
2 tablespoons unsalted butter, divided
1 large egg, separated
¼ cup whole milk
½ teaspoon kosher salt

1. Place the baking pan on the bake position. Select Bake, set the temperature to 330ºF (166ºC), and set the time to 15 minutes.
2. In a medium bowl, combine the sweet panato, 1 tablespoon of melted butter, egg yolk, milk, and salt. Set aside.
3. In a separate medium bowl, whisk the egg white until stiff peaks form.
4. Using a spatula, gently fold the egg white into the sweet panato mixture.
5. Coat the inside of four 3-inch ramekins with the remaining 1 tablespoon of butter, then fill each ramekin halfway full. Place 2 ramekins in the pan.
6. Bake for 15 minutes. Repeat this process with the remaining ramekins.
7. Remove the ramekins from the grill and allow to cool on a wire rack for 10 minutes before serving

447.Sweet and Sour Peanuts

Prep time: 5 minutes | Cook time: 5 minutes | Serves 9

3 cups shelled raw peanuts
1 tablespoon hot red pepper sauce
3 tablespoons granulated white sugar

1. Place the crisper tray on the air fry position. Select Air Fry, set the temperature to 400ºF (204ºC), and set the time to 5 minutes.
2. Put the peanuts in a large bowl, then drizzle with hot red pepper sauce and sprinkle with sugar. Toss to coat well.
3. Pour the peanuts in the crisper tray. Air fry for 5 minutes or until the peanuts are crispy and browned. Shake the crisper tray halfway through.
4. Serve immediately.

448. Roasted Carrot Chips

Prep time: 5 minutes | Cook time: 15 minutes | Makes 3 cups

3 large carrots, peeled and sliced into long and thick chips diagonally
1 tablespoon granulated garlic
1 teaspoon salt
¼ teaspoon ground black pepper
1 tablespoon olive oil
1 tablespoon finely chopped fresh parsley

1. Place the baking pan on the roast position. Select Roast, set the temperature to 360ºF (182ºC), and set the time to 15 minutes.
2. Toss the carrots with garlic, salt, ground black pepper, and olive oil in a large bowl to coat well.
3. Place the carrots in the pan. Roast for 15 minutes or until the carrot chips are soft. Shake the crisper tray halfway through.
4. Serve the carrot chips with parsley on top.

449. Southwest Corn and Bell Pepper Roast

Prep time: 10 minutes | Cook time: 10 minutes | Serves 4

For the Corn:

1½ cups thawed frozen corn kernels
1 cup mixed diced bell peppers
1 jalapeño, diced
1 cup diced yellow onion
½ teaspoon ancho chile powder
1 tablespoon fresh lemon juice
1 teaspoon ground cumin
½ teaspoon kosher salt
Cooking spray

For Serving:

¼ cup feta cheese
¼ cup chopped fresh cilantro
1 tablespoon fresh lemon juice

1. Place the crisper tray on the air fry position. Select Air Fry, set the temperature to 375ºF (191ºC), and set the time to 10 minutes.
2. Spritz the crisper tray with cooking spray.
3. Combine the ingredients for the corn in a large bowl. Stir to mix well.
4. Pout the mixture into the crisper tray. Air fry for 10 minutes or until the corn and bell peppers are soft. Shake the crisper tray halfway through the cooking time.
5. Transfer them onto a large plate, then spread with feta cheese and cilantro. Drizzle with lemon juice and serve.

450. Spicy Old Bay Shrimp

Prep time: 7 minutes | Cook time: 10 minutes | Makes 2 cups

½ teaspoon Old Bay Seasoning
1 teaspoon ground cayenne pepper
½ teaspoon paprika
1 tablespoon olive oil
⅛ teaspoon salt
½ pound (227 g) shrimps, peeled and deveined
Juice of half a lemon

1. Place the crisper tray on the air fry position. Select Air Fry, set the temperature to 390ºF (199ºC), and set the time to 10 minutes.
2. Combine the Old Bay Seasoning, cayenne pepper, paprika, olive oil, and salt in a large bowl, then add the shrimps and toss to coat well.
3. Put the shrimps in the crisper tray. Air fry for 10 minutes or until opaque. Flip the shrimps halfway through.
4. Serve the shrimps with lemon juice on top.

451. Lemony and Garlicky Asparagus

Prep time: 5 minutes | Cook time: 10 minutes | Makes 10 spears

10 spears asparagus (about ½ pound / 227 g in total), snap the ends off
1 tablespoon lemon juice
2 teaspoons minced garlic
½ teaspoon salt
¼ teaspoon ground black pepper
Cooking spray

1. Place the crisper tray on the air fry position. Select Air Fry, set the temperature to 400ºF (204ºC), and set the time to 10 minutes.
2. Line the crisper tray with parchment paper.
3. Put the asparagus spears in a large bowl. Drizzle with lemon juice and sprinkle with minced garlic, salt, and ground black pepper. Toss to coat well.
4. Transfer the asparagus in the crisper tray and spritz with cooking spray. Air fry for 10 minutes or until wilted and soft. Flip the asparagus halfway through.
5. Serve immediately.

452.South Carolina Shrimp and Corn Bake

Prep time: 10 minutes | Cook time: 18 minutes | Serves 2

1 ear corn, husk and silk removed, cut into 2-inch rounds
8 ounces (227 g) red potatoes, unpeeled, cut into 1-inch pieces
2 teaspoons Old Bay Seasoning, divided
2 teaspoons vegetable oil, divided
¼ teaspoon ground black pepper
8 ounces (227 g) large shrimps (about 12 shrimps), deveined
6 ounces (170 g) andouille or chorizo sausage, cut into 1-inch pieces
2 garlic cloves, minced
1 tablespoon chopped fresh parsley

1. Place the baking pan on the bake position. Select Bake, set the temperature to 400ºF (204ºC), and set the time to 12 minutes.
2. Put the corn rounds and potatoes in a large bowl. Sprinkle with 1 teaspoon of Old Bay seasoning and drizzle with vegetable oil. Toss to coat well.
3. Transfer the corn rounds and potatoes to the baking pan.
4. Bake for 12 minutes or until soft and browned. Flip halfway through the cooking time.
5. Meanwhile, cut slits into the shrimps but be careful not to cut them through. Combine the shrimps, sausage, remaining Old Bay seasoning, and remaining vegetable oil in the large bowl. Toss to coat well.
6. When the baking of the potatoes and corn rounds is complete, add the shrimps and sausage and bake for 6 more minutes or until the shrimps are opaque. Flip halfway through the cooking time.
7. When the baking is finished, serve them on a plate and spread with parsley before serving.

453.Beet Salad with Lemon Vinaigrette

Prep time: 10 minutes | Cook time: 12 to 15 minutes | Serves 4

6 medium red and golden beets, peeled and sliced
1 teaspoon olive oil
¼ teaspoon kosher salt
Vinaigrette:
2 teaspoons olive oil
2 tablespoons chopped fresh chives
½ cup crumbled feta cheese
8 cups mixed greens
Cooking spray

Juice of 1 lemon

1. Place the crisper tray on the air fry position. Select Air Fry, set the temperature to 360ºF (182ºC), and set the time to 15 minutes.
2. In a large bowl, toss the beets, olive oil, and kosher salt.
3. Spray the crisper tray with cooking spray, then place the beets in the crisper tray. Air fry for 12 to 15 minutes or until tender.
4. While the beets cook, make the vinaigrette in a large bowl by whisking together the olive oil, lemon juice, and chives.
5. Remove the beets from the grill, toss in the vinaigrette, and allow to cool for 5 minutes. Add the feta and serve on top of the mixed greens.

454.Golden Salmon and Carrot Croquettes

Prep time: 15 minutes | Cook time: 10 minutes | Serves 6

2 egg whites
1 cup almond flour
1 cup panko breadcrumbs
1 pound (454 g) chopped salmon fillet
2/3 cup grated carrots

2 tablespoons minced garlic cloves
½ cup chopped onion
2 tablespoons chopped chives
Cooking spray

1. Place the crisper tray on the air fry position. Select Air Fry, set the temperature to 350ºF (177ºC), and set the time to 10 minutes.
2. Spritz the crisper tray with cooking spray.
3. Whisk the egg whites in a bowl. Put the flour in a second bowl. Pour the breadcrumbs in a third bowl. Set aside.
4. Combine the salmon, carrots, garlic, onion, and chives in a large bowl. Stir to mix well.
5. Form the mixture into balls with your hands. Dredge the balls into the flour, then egg, and then breadcrumbs to coat well.
6. Arrange the salmon balls in the crisper tray and spritz with cooking spray.
7. Air fry for 10 minutes or until crispy and browned. Shake the crisper tray halfway through.
8. Serve immediately.

455.Parsnip Fries with Garlic-Yogurt Dip

Prep time: 10 minutes | Cook time: 10 minutes | Serves 4

3 medium parsnips, peeled, cut into sticks
¼ teaspoon kosher salt
1 teaspoon olive oil
Dip:
¼ cup plain Greek yogurt
⅛ teaspoon garlic powder
1 tablespoon sour cream

1 garlic clove, unpeeled
Cooking spray

¼ teaspoon kosher salt
Freshly ground black pepper, to taste

1. Place the crisper tray on the air fry position. Select Air Fry, set the temperature to 360ºF (182ºC), and set the time to 10 minutes.
2. Spritz the crisper tray with cooking spray.
3. Put the parsnip sticks in a large bowl, then sprinkle with salt and drizzle with olive oil.
4. Transfer the parsnip into the crisper tray and add the garlic.
5. Air fry for 5 minutes, then remove the garlic from the grill and shake the crisper tray. air fry for 5 more minutes or until the parsnip sticks are crisp.
6. Meanwhile, peel the garlic and crush it. Combine the crushed garlic with the ingredients for the dip. Stir to mix well.
7. When the frying is complete, remove the parsnip fries from the grill and serve with the dipping sauce.

Chapter 12 Casseroles, Frittatas, and Quiches

456. Easy Mac and Cheese

Prep time: 10 minutes | Cook time: 10 minutes | Serves 2

1 cup cooked macaroni
1 cup grated Cheddar cheese
½ cup warm milk
Salt and ground black pepper, to taste
1 tablespoon grated Parmesan cheese

1. Place the baking pan on the bake position. Select Bake, set the temperature to 350ºF (177ºC), and set the time to 10 minutes.
2. In the baking pan, mix all the ingredients, except for Parmesan.
3. Bake for 10 minutes.
4. Add the Parmesan cheese on top and serve.

457. Western Prosciutto Casserole

Prep time: 5 minutes | Cook time: 10 minutes | Serves 2

1 cup day-old whole grain bread, cubed
3 large eggs, beaten
2 tablespoons water
⅛ teaspoon kosher salt
1 ounce (28 g) prosciutto, roughly chopped
1 ounce (28 g) Pepper Jack cheese, roughly chopped
1 tablespoon chopped fresh chives
Nonstick cooking spray

1. Place the baking pan on the bake position. Select Bake, set the temperature to 360ºF (182ºC), and set the time to 10 minutes.
2. Spray the baking pan with nonstick cooking spray, then place the bread cubes in the pan.
3. In a medium bowl, stir together the beaten eggs and water, then stir in the kosher salt, prosciutto, cheese, and chives. Pour the egg mixture over the bread cubes.
4. Bake for 10 minutes, or until the eggs are set and the top is golden brown.
5. Serve warm.

458. Mini Quiche Cups

Prep time: 15 minutes | Cook time: 16 minutes | Makes 10 quiche cups

4 ounces (113 g) ground pork sausage
3 eggs
¾ cup milk
Cooking spray
4 ounces (113 g) sharp Cheddar cheese, grated

Special Equipment:
20 foil muffin cups

1. Place the crisper tray on the air fry position. Select Air Fry, set the temperature to 390ºF (199ºC), and set the time to 6 minutes.
2. Spritz the crisper tray with cooking spray.
3. Divide sausage into 3 portions and shape each into a thin patty.
4. Put patties in the crisper tray. Air fry for 6 minutes.
5. While sausage is cooking, prepare the egg mixture. Combine the eggs and milk in a large bowl and whisk until well blended. Set aside.
6. When sausage has cooked fully, remove patties from the crisper tray, drain well, and use a fork to crumble the meat into small pieces.
7. Double the foil cups into 10 sets. Remove paper liners from the top muffin cups and spray the foil cups lightly with cooking spray.
8. Divide crumbled sausage among the 10 muffin cup sets.
9. Top each with grated cheese, divided evenly among the cups.
10. Put 5 cups in the crisper tray.
11. Pour egg mixture into each cup, filling until each cup is at least ⅔ full.
12. Bake for 8 minutes. Check for doneness. A knife inserted into the center shouldn't have any raw egg on it when removed.
13. Repeat steps 8 through 11 for the remaining quiches.
14. Serve warm.

459.Shrimp Green Casserole

Prep time: 15 minutes | Cook time: 22 minutes | Serves 4

1 pound (454 g) shrimp, cleaned and deveined
2 cups cauliflower, cut into florets
2 green bell pepper, sliced
1 shallot, sliced
2 tablespoons sesame oil
1 cup tomato paste
Cooking spray

1. Place the baking pan on the bake position. Select Bake, set the temperature to 360ºF (182ºC), and set the time to 22 minutes.
2. Spritz the baking pan with cooking spray.
3. Arrange the shrimp and vegetables in the baking pan. Then, drizzle the sesame oil over the vegetables. Pour the tomato paste over the vegetables.
4. Bake for 10 minutes. Stir with a large spoon and bake for a further 12 minutes.
5. Serve warm.

460.Ritzy Vegetable Frittata

Prep time: 15 minutes | Cook time: 21 minutes | Serves 2

4 eggs
¼ cup milk
Sea salt and ground black pepper, to taste
1 zucchini, sliced
½ bunch asparagus, sliced
½ cup mushrooms, sliced
½ cup spinach, shredded
½ cup red onion, sliced
½ tablespoon olive oil
5 tablespoons feta cheese, crumbled
4 tablespoons Cheddar cheese, grated
¼ bunch chives, minced

1. In a bowl, mix the eggs, milk, salt and pepper.
2. Over a medium heat, sauté the vegetables for 6 minutes with the olive oil in a nonstick pan.
3. Put some parchment paper in the base of the baking pan. Pour in the vegetables, followed by the egg mixture. Top with the feta and grated Cheddar.
4. Place the baking pan on the bake position. Select Bake, set the temperature to 320ºF (160ºC), and set the time to 15 minutes.
5. Bake for 15 minutes. Remove the frittata from the grill and leave to cool for 5 minutes.
6. Top with the minced chives and serve.

461.Greek Frittata

Prep time: 7 minutes | Cook time: 8 minutes | Serves 2

1 cup chopped mushrooms
2 cups spinach, chopped
4 eggs, lightly beaten
3 ounces (85 g) feta cheese, crumbled
2 tablespoons heavy cream
A handful of fresh parsley, chopped
Salt and ground black pepper, to taste
Cooking spray

1. Place the baking pan on the bake position. Select Bake, set the temperature to 350ºF (177ºC), and set the time to 8 minutes.
2. Spritz the baking pan with cooking spray.
3. Whisk together all the ingredients in a large bowl. Stir to mix well.
4. Pour the mixture in the prepared baking pan.
5. Bake for 8 minutes or until the eggs are set.
6. Serve immediately.

462.Mediterranean Quiche

Prep time: 10 minutes | Cook time: 30 minutes | Serves 4

4 eggs
¼ cup chopped Kalamata olives
½ cup chopped tomatoes
¼ cup chopped onion
½ cup milk
1 cup crumbled feta
cheese
½ tablespoon chopped oregano
½ tablespoon chopped basil
Salt and ground black pepper, to taste
Cooking spray

1. Place the baking pan on the bake position. Select Bake, set the temperature to 340ºF (171ºC), and set the time to 30 minutes.
2. Spritz the baking pan with cooking spray.
3. Whisk the eggs with remaining ingredients in a large bowl. Stir to mix well.
4. Pour the mixture into the prepared baking pan.
5. Bake for 30 minutes or until the eggs are set and a toothpick inserted in the center comes out clean. Check the doneness of the quiche during the last 10 minutes of baking.
6. Serve immediately.

463.Herbed Cheddar Frittata

Prep time: 10 minutes | Cook time: 20 minutes | Serves 4

½ cup shredded Cheddar cheese	2 tablespoons chopped fresh parsley
½ cup half-and-half	½ teaspoon kosher salt
4 large eggs	½ teaspoon ground black pepper
2 tablespoons chopped scallion greens	Cooking spray

1. Place the baking pan on the bake position. Select Bake, set the temperature to 300ºF (149ºC), and set the time to 20 minutes.
2. Spritz the baking pan with cooking spray.
3. Whisk together all the ingredients in a large bowl, then pour the mixture into the prepared baking pan.
4. Bake for 20 minutes or until set.
5. Serve immediately.

464.Taco Beef and Chile Casserole

Prep time: 10 minutes | Cook time: 15 minutes | Serves 4

1 pound (454 g) 85% lean ground beef	2 large eggs
1 tablespoon taco seasoning	1 cup shredded Mexican cheese blend
1 (7-ounce / 198-g) can diced mild green chiles	2 tablespoons all-purpose flour
½ cup milk	½ teaspoon kosher salt
	Cooking spray

1. Place the baking pan on the bake position. Select Bake, set the temperature to 350ºF (177ºC), and set the time to 15 minutes.
2. Spritz the baking pan with cooking spray.
3. Toss the ground beef with taco seasoning in a large bowl to mix well. Pour the seasoned ground beef in the prepared baking pan.
4. Combing the remaining ingredients in a medium bowl. Whisk to mix well, then pour the mixture over the ground beef.
5. Bake for 15 minutes or until a toothpick inserted in the center comes out clean.
6. Remove the casserole from the grill and allow to cool for 5 minutes, then slice to serve.

465.Goat Cheese and Asparagus Frittata

Prep time: 5 minutes | Cook time: 25 minutes | Serves 2 to 4

1 cup asparagus spears, cut into 1-inch pieces	2 ounces (57 g) goat cheese, crumbled
1 teaspoon vegetable oil	1 tablespoon minced chives, optional
1 tablespoon milk	Kosher salt and pepper, to taste
6 eggs, beaten	

1. Place a cake pan on the bake position. Select Bake, set the temperature to 400ºF (204ºC), and set the time to 5 minutes.
2. Add the asparagus spears to a small bowl and drizzle with the vegetable oil. Toss until well coated and transfer to the cake pan.
3. Bake for 5 minutes, or until the asparagus become tender and slightly wilted. Remove then pan from the grill.
4. Stir together the milk and eggs in a medium bowl. Pour the mixture over the asparagus in the pan. Sprinkle with the goat cheese and the chives (if using) over the eggs. Season with a pinch of salt and pepper.
5. Place the pan back to the grill and bake at 320ºF (160ºC) for 20 minutes or until the top is lightly golden and the eggs are set.
6. Transfer to a serving dish. Slice and serve.

466.Shrimp Spinach Frittata

Prep time: 6 minutes | Cook time: 14 minutes | Serves 4

4 whole eggs	½ cup rice, cooked
1 teaspoon dried basil	½ cup Monterey Jack cheese, grated
½ cup shrimp, cooked and chopped	Salt, to taste
½ cup baby spinach	Cooking spray

1. Place the baking pan on the bake position. Select Bake, set the temperature to 360ºF (182ºC), and set the time to 14 minutes.
2. Spritz the baking pan with cooking spray.
3. Whisk the eggs with basil and salt in a large bowl until bubbly, then mix in the shrimp, spinach, rice, and cheese.
4. Pour the mixture into the baking pan.
5. Bake for 14 minutes or until the eggs are set and the frittata is golden brown.
6. Slice to serve.

467. Sumptuous Beef and Bean Chili Casserole

Prep time: 15 minutes | Cook time: 31 minutes | Serves 4

1 tablespoon olive oil
½ cup finely chopped bell pepper
½ cup chopped celery
1 onion, chopped
2 garlic cloves, minced
1 pound (454 g) ground beef
1 can diced tomatoes
½ teaspoon parsley
½ tablespoon chili powder
1 teaspoon chopped cilantro
1½ cups vegetable broth
1 (8-ounce / 227-g) can cannellini beans
Salt and ground black pepper, to taste

1. Place the baking pan on the bake position. Select Bake, set the temperature to 350ºF (177ºC), and set the time to 10 minutes.
2. Heat the olive oil in a nonstick skillet over medium heat until shimmering.
3. Add the bell pepper, celery, onion, and garlic to the skillet and sauté for 5 minutes or until the onion is translucent.
4. Add the ground beef and sauté for an additional 6 minutes or until lightly browned.
5. Mix in the tomatoes, parsley, chili powder, cilantro and vegetable broth, then cook for 10 more minutes. Stir constantly.
6. Pour them in the baking pan, then mix in the beans and sprinkle with salt and ground black pepper.
7. Bake for 10 minutes or until the vegetables are tender and the beef is well browned.
8. Remove the baking pan from the grill and serve immediately.

468. Chicken Divan

Prep time: 5 minutes | Cook time: 24 minutes | Serves 4

4 chicken breasts
Salt and ground black pepper, to taste
1 head broccoli, cut into florets
½ cup cream of
mushroom soup
1 cup shredded Cheddar cheese
½ cup croutons
Cooking spray

1. Place the crisper tray on the air fry position. Select Air Fry, set the temperature to 390ºF (199ºC), and set the time to 14 minutes.
2. Spritz the crisper tray with cooking spray.
3. Put the chicken breasts in the crisper tray and sprinkle with salt and ground black pepper.
4. Air fry for 14 minutes or until well browned and tender. Flip the breasts halfway through the cooking time.
5. Remove the breasts from the grill and allow to cool for a few minutes on a plate, then cut the breasts into bite-size pieces.
6. Combine the chicken, broccoli, mushroom soup, and Cheddar cheese in a large bowl. Stir to mix well.
7. Spritz the baking pan with cooking spray. Pour the chicken mixture into the pan. Spread the croutons over the mixture.
8. Bake for 10 minutes or until the croutons are lightly browned and the mixture is set.
9. Remove the baking pan from the grill and serve immediately.

469. Creamy Pork Gratin

Prep time: 15 minutes | Cook time: 21 minutes | Serves 4

2 tablespoons olive oil
2 pounds (907 g) pork tenderloin, cut into serving-size pieces
1 teaspoon dried marjoram
¼ teaspoon chili powder
1 teaspoon coarse sea
salt
½ teaspoon freshly ground black pepper
1 cup Ricotta cheese
1½ cups chicken broth
1 tablespoon mustard
Cooking spray

1. Place the baking pan on the bake position. Select Bake, set the temperature to 350ºF (177ºC), and set the time to 15 minutes.
2. Spritz the baking pan with cooking spray.
3. Heat the olive oil in a nonstick skillet over medium-high heat until shimmering.
4. Add the pork and sauté for 6 minutes or until lightly browned.
5. Transfer the pork to the prepared baking pan and sprinkle with marjoram, chili powder, salt, and ground black pepper.
6. Combine the remaining ingredients in a large bowl. Stir to mix well. Pour the mixture over the pork in the pan.
7. Bake for 15 minutes or until frothy and the cheese melts. Stir the mixture halfway through.
8. Serve immediately.

470.Chorizo, Corn, and Potato Frittata

Prep time: 8 minutes | Cook time: 12 minutes | Serves 4

2 tablespoons olive oil
1 chorizo, sliced
4 eggs
½ cup corn

1 large panato, boiled and cubed
1 tablespoon chopped parsley
½ cup feta cheese, crumbled
Salt and ground black pepper, to taste

1. Place the baking pan on the bake position. Select Bake, set the temperature to 330ºF (166ºC), and set the time to 8 minutes.
2. Heat the olive oil in a nonstick skillet over medium heat until shimmering.
3. Add the chorizo and cook for 4 minutes or until golden brown.
4. Whisk the eggs in a bowl, then sprinkle with salt and ground black pepper.
5. Mix the remaining ingredients in the egg mixture, then pour the chorizo and its fat into the baking pan. Pour in the egg mixture.
6. Bake for 8 minutes or until the eggs are set.
7. Serve immediately.

471.Sumptuous Vegetable Frittata

Prep time: 15 minutes | Cook time: 20 minutes | Serves 2

4 eggs
$^1/_3$ cup milk
2 teaspoons olive oil
1 large zucchini, sliced
2 asparagus, sliced thinly
$^1/_3$ cup sliced mushrooms

1 cup baby spinach
1 small red onion, sliced
$^1/_3$ cup crumbled feta cheese
$^1/_3$ cup grated Cheddar cheese
¼ cup chopped chives
Salt and ground black pepper, to taste

1. Place the baking pan on the bake position. Select Bake, set the temperature to 380ºF (193ºC), and set the time to 15 minutes.
2. Line the baking pan with parchment paper.
3. Whisk together the eggs, milk, salt, and ground black pepper in a large bowl. Set aside.
4. Heat the olive oil in a nonstick skillet over medium heat until shimmering.
5. Add the zucchini, asparagus, mushrooms, spinach, and onion to the skillet and sauté for 5 minutes or until tender.
6. Pour the sautéed vegetables into the prepared baking pan, then spread the egg mixture over and scatter with cheeses.
7. Bake for 15 minutes or until the eggs are set the edges are lightly browned.
8. Remove the frittata from the grill and sprinkle with chives before serving.

472.Broccoli, Carrot, and Tomato Quiche

Prep time: 6 minutes | Cook time: 14 minutes | Serves 4

4 eggs
1 teaspoon dried thyme
1 cup whole milk
1 steamed carrots, diced
2 cups steamed broccoli florets
2 medium tomatoes, diced

¼ cup crumbled feta cheese
1 cup grated Cheddar cheese
1 teaspoon chopped parsley
Salt and ground black pepper, to taste
Cooking spray

1. Place the baking pan on the bake position. Select Bake, set the temperature to 350ºF (177ºC), and set the time to 14 minutes.
2. Spritz the baking pan with cooking spray.
3. Whisk together the eggs, thyme, salt, and ground black pepper in a bowl and fold in the milk while mixing.

4. Put the carrots, broccoli, and tomatoes in the prepared baking pan, then spread with feta cheese and ½ cup Cheddar cheese. Pour the egg mixture over, then scatter with remaining Cheddar on top.
5. Bake for 14 minutes or until the eggs are set and the quiche is puffed.
6. Remove the quiche from the grill and top with chopped parsley, then slice to serve.

473.Keto Cheese Quiche

Prep time: 20 minutes | Cook time: 1 hour | Serves 8

Crust:

1¼ cups blanched almond flour
1 large egg, beaten
Filling:
4 ounces (113 g) cream cheese
1 cup shredded Swiss cheese
1/3 cup minced leeks
4 large eggs, beaten
½ cup chicken broth

1¼ cups grated Parmesan cheese
¼ teaspoon fine sea salt

1/8 teaspoon cayenne pepper
¾ teaspoon fine sea salt
1 tablespoon unsalted butter, melted
Chopped green onions, for garnish
Cooking spray

1. Place a pie pan on the bake position. Select Bake, set the temperature to 325ºF (163ºC), and set the time to 27 minutes.
2. Spritz the pie pan with cooking spray.
3. Combine the flour, egg, Parmesan, and salt in a large bowl. Stir to mix until a satiny and firm dough forms.
4. Arrange the dough between two grease parchment papers, then roll the dough into a $^1/_{16}$-inch thick circle.
5. Make the crust: Transfer the dough into the prepared pie pan and press to coat the bottom.
6. Bake for 12 minutes or until the edges of the crust are lightly browned.
7. Meanwhile, combine the ingredient for the filling, except for the green onions in a large bowl.
8. Pour the filling over the cooked crust and cover the edges of the crust with aluminum foil. Bake for 15 more minutes, then reduce the heat to 300ºF (149ºC) and bake for another 30 minutes or until a toothpick inserted in the center comes out clean.
9. Remove the pie pan from the grill and allow to cool for 10 minutes before serving.

474.Smoked Trout and Crème Fraiche Frittata

Prep time: 8 minutes | Cook time: 17 minutes | Serves 4

2 tablespoons olive oil
1 onion, sliced
1 egg, beaten
½ tablespoon horseradish sauce

6 tablespoons crème fraiche
1 cup diced smoked trout
2 tablespoons chopped fresh dill
Cooking spray

1. Place the baking pan on the bake position. Select Bake, set the temperature to 350ºF (177ºC), and set the time to 14 minutes.
2. Spritz the baking pan with cooking spray.
3. Heat the olive oil in a nonstick skillet over medium heat until shimmering.
4. Add the onion and sauté for 3 minutes or until translucent.
5. Combine the egg, horseradish sauce, and crème fraiche in a large bowl. Stir to mix well, then mix in the sautéed onion, smoked trout, and dill.
6. Pour the mixture in the prepared baking pan. Bake for 14 minutes or until the egg is set and the edges are lightly browned.
7. Serve immediately.

475.Mutton Roast with Barbecue Dip

Prep time: 15 minutes | Cook time: 4½ hours | Serves 8 to 10

1 mutton roast (shoulder or leg), 5 pounds (2.3 kg)

Barbecue Dip:

1 cup water
¼ cup Worcestershire sauce
¼ cup apple cider vinegar
1 tablespoon freshly ground black pepper
1 tablespoon packed brown sugar
1 tablespoon freshly squeezed lemon juice
1 tablespoon salt
½ teaspoon ground allspice

Baste:

1 cup apple cider vinegar
½ cup Worcestershire sauce
¼ cup freshly
squeezed lemon juice
2 tablespoons freshly ground black pepper
1 tablespoon salt

1. To make the barbecue dip: Combine the dip ingredients in a jar. Cover with a lid and refrigerate, shaking periodically. Warm the dip in the microwave just before serving.
2. To make the baste: Combine the baste ingredients in a small bowl and set aside.
3. Using kitchen twine, tie the mutton roast into a uniform shape. Run a long sword skewer through the center of the roast lengthwise to create a pilot hole. Run the rotisserie spit through the hole and secure with the forks. Balance as necessary.
4. Select Grill, set the temperature to 375ºF (190ºC), and set the time to 4½ hours.
5. Place the roast in the grill and set a drip tray underneath. Apply the baste mixture every 30 minutes, until the roast reaches an internal temperature of 185ºF (85ºC). The roast will shrink during cooking, so adjust the forks when appropriate.
6. Remove from the heat, carefully remove the rotisserie forks and slide the spit out, and then set the roast on a large cutting board. Tent the roast with aluminum foil and let the meat rest for 20 minutes.
7. Shred or carve the mutton into small pieces. Serve with the warmed barbecue dip on the side.

476.Pulled Pork with Paprika

Prep time: 10 minutes | Cook time: 6 hours | Serves 10

1 pork butt, 5 to 6 pounds (2.3 to 2.7 kg)
Rub:

2 tablespoons paprika
2 tablespoons packed brown sugar
1 tablespoon kosher salt
1 tablespoon mild chili powder
1 teaspoon freshly ground black pepper
1 teaspoon celery salt
½ teaspoon cayenne
½ teaspoon garlic powder

1. Run a long sword skewer through the center of the roast lengthwise to create a pilot hole. Run the rotisserie spit through the hole and secure with the forks. Balance as necessary.
2. To make the rub: Combine the rub ingredients in a small bowl and apply evenly all over the roast. Let sit at room temperature for 15 minutes.
3. Select Grill, set the temperature to 350ºF (180ºC), and set the time to 6 hours.
4. Place the roast in the grill with a drip tray underneath. Roast until the internal temperature reaches 185ºF (85ºC). The roast will shrink during cooking, so adjust the forks when appropriate.
5. Remove from the heat, carefully remove the rotisserie forks and slide the spit out, and then set the pork on a large cutting board. Tent the roast with aluminum foil and let the meat rest for 20 minutes. Remove the foil and let stand for an additional 10 minutes.
6. Using two forks, check to see how easily the meat shreds. Some parts will do this more easily than others. Be sure to use heat-resistant gloves to break the roast apart. Begin shredding each large chunk one at a time. Add pieces to a large bowl and either add the barbecue sauce directly to the shredded meat or serve on the side. Keep the bowl covered as you're working on each section. This will help keep the meat warm. Serve by itself or with your favorite sides or in sandwiches.

477. Tri-Tip Roast with Ketchup Sauce

Prep time: 15 minutes | Cook time: 1 hour 30 minutes | Serves 8

2 tri-tip roasts, 2 pounds (907 g) each
Sauce:

¾ cup ketchup	cider vinegar
¾ cup Dr Pepper	¼ teaspoon freshly
¼ cup packed brown	ground black pepper
sugar	⅛ teaspoon salt
2 teaspoons apple	

Rub:

1 tablespoon kosher	1½ teaspoons mild
salt	chili powder
1½ teaspoons freshly	½ teaspoon garlic
ground black pepper	powder
1½ teaspoons paprika	

1. Place one tri-tip on top of the other with the small ends on opposite sides. Fold in these ends and tie the roasts with kitchen twine, creating one single, uniform roast. Run a long sword skewer through the center of the roast lengthwise to create a pilot hole. Run the rotisserie spit through the hole and secure with the forks. Balance as necessary.
2. To make the sauce: Combine the sauce ingredients in a small saucepan and simmer over medium heat for 5 to 6 minutes, stirring often. Watch for burning and lower the heat if necessary. Remove from the heat and let sit for 15 to 30 minutes before using.
3. To make the rub: Combine the rub ingredients in a small bowl and evenly apply all over the roast.
4. Select Grill, set the temperature to 400ºF (205ºC), and set the time to 85 minutes.
5. Place the roast in the grill and set a drip tray underneath. During the last 30 minutes of cooking time, begin basting with the sauce. Do this 6 to 8 times, until the roast is well coated with the barbecue sauce and the internal temperature reaches 140ºF (60ºC). The roast will shrink during the cooking process, so adjust the forks when appropriate.
6. Remove the roast from the grill, carefully remove the rotisserie forks and slide the spit out, and then place the roast on a large cutting board. Cover the meat with aluminum foil and let rest for 12 to 15 minutes. Cut off the twine. Separate the roasts, slice against the grain, and serve.

478. Rosemary Prime Rib Roast in Red Wine

Prep time: 10 minutes | Cook time: 2 hours | Serves 8 to 10

1 boneless prime rib roast, 4 to 5 pounds (1.8 to 2.3 kg)
Rub:

3 to 3½ tablespoons	2 or 3 cloves garlic,
kosher salt	minced
1 tablespoon finely	2 teaspoons freshly
chopped fresh	ground black pepper
rosemary	

Baste:

1 cup Cabernet	1½ teaspoons soy
Sauvignon	sauce
½ cup low-sodium	1½ teaspoons
beef broth	Worcestershire sauce

1. To make the rub: Combine the rub ingredients in a small bowl and mix well. Use the salt to grind the garlic and rosemary together.
2. Run a long sword skewer through the center of the roast lengthwise to create a pilot hole. Run the rotisserie spit through the hole and secure with the forks. Balance as necessary.
3. Apply the rub to the roast. Cover with plastic wrap and set in a safe place at room temperature for 30 minutes (rotisserie spit and all).
4. To make the baste: Combine the baste ingredients in a small bowl and store in the refrigerator until ready to use. It will separate, so stir occasionally. Warm the baste for 30 seconds to 1 minute in the microwave before applying to the roast.
5. Select Grill, set the temperature to 400ºF (205ºC), and set the time to 2 hours.
6. Place the roast in the grill and set a drip tray underneath. Baste intermittently during the last half of the cooking time, until it reaches the desired doneness: 125ºF (52ºC) for rare, 135ºF (57ºC) for medium rare, 145ºF (63ºC) for medium, 155ºF (68ºC) for medium well, or 165ºF (74ºC) for well done. The roast will shrink during cooking, so adjust the forks when appropriate.
7. Carefully remove the rotisserie forks and slide the spit out, and then set the roast on a large cutting board. Tent the roast with aluminum foil and let the meat rest for 15 to 20 minutes. Slice and serve.

479.Prime Rib Roast with Garlic Rub

Prep time: 5 minutes | Cook time: 2 hours | Serves 8 to 10

1 4-bone prime rib roast (8 to 10 pounds / 3.6 to 4.5 kg)
Rub:

3½ tablespoons kosher salt	1½ tablespoons olive oil
3 or 4 cloves garlic, minced	1 tablespoon coarsely ground black pepper

1. Trim off any straggling pieces of meat or fat from the roast. If the fat cap is too thick, cut it down to between ¼ to ½ inch in thickness depending on how you like your prime rib. Run a long sword skewer through the center of the roast lengthwise to create a pilot hole. Run the rotisserie spit through the hole and secure with the forks. Balance as necessary. This is a large roast and it is important that it be well balanced.
2. To make the rub: Combine the rub ingredients in a small bowl and apply evenly to the roast. Concentrate the rub on the rounded end and not the cut sides, though it should still get some. The rub will then be on the edges of the slices once the roast has been carved.
3. Select Grill, set the temperature to 400ºF (205ºC), and set the time to 2 hours.
4. Place the roast in the grill and set a drip tray underneath. Roast until it is near the desired doneness: 125ºF (52ºC) for rare, 135ºF (57ºC) for medium rare, 145ºF (63ºC) for medium, 155ºF (68ºC) for medium well, or 165ºF (74ºC) for well done. The roast will shrink during cooking, so adjust the forks when appropriate.
5. Carefully remove the rotisserie forks and slide the spit out, and then place the roast on a large cutting board. Tent the roast with aluminum foil and let the meat rest for 15 to 20 minutes. The roast temperature will continue to rise an additional 5ºF during the rest phase. Cut away the bones first by passing a knife against the bones and cutting through (save the bones for later). Cut the meat into slices $1/3$ to ½ inch thick.

480.Prime Rib Roast with Grainy Mustard

Prep time: 10 minutes | Cook time: 2 hours | Serves 8 to 10

1 4-bone prime rib roast (8 to 10 pounds / 3.6 to 4.5 kg)
Rub:

½ cup grainy mustard	chopped fresh marjoram
¼ cup olive oil	1 tablespoon chopped fresh thyme
1 large shallot, finely chopped	1 tablespoon coarsely ground black pepper
3 tablespoons kosher salt	
1½ tablespoons	

1. Trim off any straggling pieces of meat or fat from the roast. If the fat cap is too thick, cut it down to between ¼ to ½ inch in thickness depending on how you like your prime rib.
2. To make the rub: Combine the rub ingredients in a small bowl and coat the roast thoroughly with it. Loosely cover with plastic wrap and let the roast sit at room temperature for 30 minutes.
3. Run a long sword skewer through the center of the roast lengthwise to create a pilot hole. Run the rotisserie spit through the hole and secure with the forks. Balance as necessary.
4. Select Grill, set the temperature to 400ºF (205ºC), and set the time to 2 hours.
5. Place the roast in the grill and set a drip tray underneath. Roast until it is near the desired doneness: 125ºF (52ºC) for rare, 135ºF (57ºC) for medium rare, 145ºF (63ºC) for medium, 155ºF (68ºC) for medium well, or 165ºF (74ºC) for well done. The roast will shrink during cooking, so adjust the forks when appropriate. Remove the roast when it is 5ºF to 10ºF below the desired doneness. It will continue to cook during the resting phase.
6. Carefully remove the rotisserie forks and slide the spit out, and then place the roast on a large cutting board. Tent the roast with aluminum foil and a kitchen towel and let the meat rest for 15 to 20 minutes. Cut away the bones first by passing a knife against the bones and cutting through (save the bones for later). Cut the meat into thin slices.

481.Ham with Honey-Orange Glaze

Prep time: 10 minutes | Cook time: 45 minutes | Serves 12 to 14

1 ham, bone in and unsliced, 7 to 8 pounds (3.2 to 3.6 kg)
1 cup packed brown sugar
Glaze:

1½ cups orange juice	⅛ teaspoon ground allspice
½ cup honey	⅛ teaspoon ground cloves
2 tablespoons packed brown sugar	
¼ teaspoon ground cinnamon	⅛ teaspoon white pepper
⅛ teaspoon ground nutmeg	2 tablespoons unsalted butter

1. To make the glaze: Combine the orange juice, honey, brown sugar, and spices in a saucepan and bring almost to a boil over medium-high heat. Decrease the heat to medium and simmer for 10 minutes, stirring often. The mixture should be a little runnier than real maple syrup. Remove from the heat and add the butter, stirring until melted. Let the mixture cool.
2. Run a long sword skewer through the center of the ham lengthwise to create a pilot hole. There is a bone in the middle of this ham, but generally it is just to one side. The skewer should easily go through, but feel for the bone before you start so you will know how to navigate around it. Run the rotisserie spit through the hole and secure with the forks. Balance the ham on the spit as well as possible.
3. Select Grill, set the temperature to 375ºF (190ºC), and set the time to 45 minutes.
4. Place the ham in the grill and set a drip tray underneath, if there is room. The ham should not take too long to heat up. Look for an internal temperature around 130ºF (54ºC). The surface should be hot.
5. Baste the ham with the glaze after 20 minutes in the grill. Repeat the process every 5 minutes and about 3 more times.
6. During the last 5 to 10 minutes of cooking time, the ham should be hot as well as sticky from the glaze. Increase the temperature to 400ºF (205ºC) and sprinkle the brown sugar evenly on the surface of the ham in small amounts until it is completely coated. Continue to cook until the sugar starts to bubble. Move quickly, as sugar tends to burn.
7. Once the sugar is bubbling rapidly, remove the ham from the heat and place on a large cutting board. Remove the rotisserie forks and slide the spit out, loosely cover the ham with aluminum foil, and let it rest for 5 minutes. Carve into thin slices and serve warm.

482.Bourbon Ham with Apple Butter

Prep time: 5 minutes | Cook time: 50 minutes | Serves 10 to 12

1 ham, unsliced, 5 to 6 pounds (2.3 to 2.7 kg)
Baste:

⅓ cup apple butter	mustard
¼ cup packed brown sugar	¼ teaspoon ground ginger
2 tablespoons bourbon	¼ teaspoon white pepper
1½ teaspoons Dijon	

1. Run a long sword skewer through the center of the ham lengthwise to create a pilot hole. Run the rotisserie spit through the hole and secure with the forks. Balance as necessary and secure tightly. Place the ham in the grill and cook for 50 to 60 minutes. If there is room, set a drip tray underneath.
2. To make the baste: Combine all the baste ingredients in a small saucepan and simmer over medium heat for 2 minutes, stirring often. Remove from the heat and let sit for 5 to 10 minutes before using.
3. Select Grill, set the temperature to 400ºF (205ºC), and set the time to 45 minutes.
4. Place the ham in the grill and set a drip tray underneath, if there is room. During the last 20 minutes of the cooking time, begin basting the ham with the apple butter-bourbon mixture. Make at least 4 or 5 passes with the baste to coat evenly. Focus the coating on the outside of the ham and not on the cut side. The ham should not take too long to heat up. Look for an internal temperature around 130ºF (54ºC). The surface should be hot.
5. Remove from the heat, carefully remove the rotisserie forks and slide the spit out, and then set the ham on a large cutting board. Tent the ham with aluminum foil and let the meat rest for 10 minutes. Carve and serve immediately.

483. Baby Back Ribs with Ketchup Sauce

Prep time: 15 minutes | Cook time: 2½ hours | Serves 4 to 6

2 racks baby back ribs
Sauce:

1 tablespoon vegetable oil	¼ cup red wine vinegar
1 cup finely chopped sweet onion	¼ cup packed brown sugar
2 cloves garlic, minced	2 tablespoons yellow mustard
1½ cups ketchup	⅛ teaspoon salt

Rub:

1 tablespoon paprika	ground black pepper
2 teaspoons salt	½ teaspoon cayenne
2 teaspoons freshly	

1. To make the sauce: Heat the oil in a medium-size saucepan over medium heat. Add the onions and sauté for 5 minutes. Add the garlic and sauté for 15 seconds. Add the remaining sauce ingredients and simmer for 4 to 5 minutes, stirring often. Remove from the heat and let cool for 15 to 30 minutes before using.
2. To make the rub: Combine the rub ingredients in a small bowl and set aside.
3. Place the ribs on a cutting board and pat dry with paper towels. Cut away any excess fat from the ribs. Remove the membrane from the back of the ribs by using a blunt knife to work the membrane away from the bone in one corner. Grab hold of the membrane with a paper towel for a good grip and gently peel away. With a little practice, this becomes an easy process. Apply the rub all over the ribs' surface, focusing more on the meat side than the bone side.
4. Place one rack of ribs bone-side up on a large cutting board. Place the other rack of ribs bone-side down on top. Position to match up the racks of ribs as evenly as possible. With kitchen twine, tie the racks together between ever other bone, end to end. The whole bundle should be secure and tight. Run the rotisserie spit between the racks and secure tightly with the rotisserie forks. There will be a little movement in the middle, which is fine. As the ribs cook it may be necessary to tighten the forks to keep them secure. Make sure the forks pass through the meat of each rack on each end.
5. Select Grill, set the temperature to 375ºF (190ºC), and set the time to 2½ hours.
6. Place the racks in the grill and set a drip tray underneath. Roast until the internal temperature reaches 185ºF (85ºC). Test the temperature in several locations. Baste the ribs evenly with barbecue sauce during the last 45 minutes of cooking time.
7. Remove from the heat, carefully remove the rotisserie forks and slide the spit out, and then set the ribs on a large cutting board. Tent the ribs with aluminum foil and let the meat rest for 5 to 10 minutes.
8. Cut away the twine and cut the racks into individual ribs. Serve.

484. Dijon Chicken with Herbes De Provence

Prep time: 5 minutes | Cook time: 1 hour | Serves 4

1 (4-pound / 1.8-kg) chicken
Mustard Paste:

¼ cup Dijon mustard	de Provence
1 tablespoon kosher salt	1 teaspoon freshly ground black pepper
1 tablespoon Herbes	

1. Mix the mustard paste ingredients in a small bowl. Rub the chicken with the mustard paste, inside and out. Gently work your fingers under the skin on the breast, then rub some of the paste directly onto the breast meat. Refrigerate for at least two hours, preferably overnight.
2. One hour before cooking, remove the chicken from the refrigerator. Fold the wingtips under the wings and truss the chicken. Skewer the chicken on the rotisserie spit, securing it with the rotisserie forks. Let the chicken rest at room temperature.
3. Select Grill, set the temperature to 450ºF (235ºC), and set the time to 1 hour. Set a drip tray in the middle of the grill.
4. Put the spit in the grill and make sure the drip tray is centered beneath the chicken. Cook until the chicken reaches 160ºF (70ºC) in the thickest part of the breast.
5. Remove the chicken from the rotisserie spit and remove the twine trussing the chicken. Be careful - the spit and forks are blazing hot. Let the chicken rest for 15 minutes, then carve and serve.

485. Prime Rib Roast with Whiskey Baste

Prep time: 10 minutes | Cook time: 2 hours | Serves 8 to 10

1 4-bone prime rib roast (8 to 10 pounds / 3.6 to 4.5 kg)

Rub:

¼ cup coarse salt
1 small shallot, finely chopped
2 cloves garlic, minced
2 tablespoons olive oil
1 tablespoon coarsely ground black pepper
Zest of 1 large lemon
1 teaspoon paprika
1 teaspoon sugar

Baste:

$^1/_3$ cup whiskey
¼ cup water
Juice of 1 lemon
⅛ teaspoon salt

1. Trim off any straggling pieces of meat or fat from the roast. If the fat cap is too thick, cut it down to between ¼ to ½ inch in thickness depending on how you like your prime rib.
2. Run a long sword skewer through the center of the roast lengthwise to create a pilot hole. Run the rotisserie spit through the hole and secure with the forks. Balance as necessary.
3. To make the rub: Combine the rub ingredients in a small bowl to form an even paste. Use additional olive oil if necessary to get it to a thick but workable consistency. Apply evenly to the roast, focusing on the outer shell of the roast.
4. To make the baste: Combine the baste ingredients in a small bowl and set aside for 15 to 30 minutes to come to room temperature.
5. Select Grill, set the temperature to 400ºF (205ºC), and set the time to 2 hours.
6. Place the roast in the grill and set a drip tray underneath.
7. During the last hour of cooking time, begin basting. Apply the baste gently so as not to wash away the seasonings on the outside of the roast. Do this 6 to 8 times, until the roast is well coated with the baste. Roast until it is near the desired doneness: 125ºF (52ºC) for rare, 135ºF (57ºC) for medium rare, 145ºF (63ºC) for medium, 155ºF (68ºC) for medium well, or 165ºF (74ºC) for well done. The roast will shrink during cooking, so adjust the forks when appropriate.
8. Carefully remove the rotisserie forks and slide the spit out, and then set the roast on a large cutting board. Tent the roast with aluminum foil and let the meat rest for 15 to 20 minutes. Cut away the bones first by passing a knife against the bones and cutting through (save the bones for later). Cut the meat into thin slices.

486. Chicken with Teriyaki Sauce

Prep time: 5 minutes | Cook time: 1 hour 10 minutes | Serves 4

1 (4-pound / 1.8-kg) chicken
1 tablespoon kosher salt

Teriyaki Sauce:

¼ cup soy sauce
¼ cup mirin (Japanese sweet rice wine)
¼ cup honey (or sugar)
¼ inch slice of ginger, smashed

1. Season the chicken with the salt, inside and out. Gently work your fingers under the skin on the breast, then rub some of the salt directly onto the breast meat. Fold the wingtips under the wings and truss the chicken. Skewer the chicken on the rotisserie spit, securing it with the rotisserie forks. Let the chicken rest at room temperature.
2. Select Grill, set the temperature to 450ºF (235ºC), and set the time to 1 hour. Set a drip tray in the middle of the grill.
3. Combine the soy sauce, mirin, honey, and ginger in a saucepan. Bring to a boil over medium-high heat, stirring often, then decrease the heat to low and simmer for 10 minutes, until the liquid is reduced by half.
4. Put the spit in the grill and make sure the drip tray is centered beneath the chicken. Cook until the chicken reaches 160ºF (70ºC) in the thickest part of the breast. During the last 15 minutes of cooking, brush the chicken with the teriyaki sauce every five minutes.
5. Remove the chicken from the rotisserie spit and transfer to a platter. Be careful - the spit and forks are blazing hot. Remove the trussing twine, then brush the chicken one last time with the teriyaki sauce. Let the chicken rest for 15 minutes, then carve and serve, passing any remaining teriyaki sauce at the table.

487.Pork Loin with Apple Cider Brine

Prep time: 10 minutes | Cook time: 50 minutes | Serves 4

2 (2-pound / 907-g) boneless pork loin roasts
Apple Cider Brine:

2 quarts apple cider   ½ cup table salt
1 quart water
Dried Fruit Stuffing:

2 cups mixed dried   1 teaspoon fresh
fruit, chopped (apples,   ground black pepper
apricots, cranberries   ½ teaspoon dried
and raisins)   ginger

1. Combine the brine ingredients in a large container and stir until the salt and sugar dissolve. Roll cut the pork roasts to open them up like a book. Set a roast with the fat cap facing down. Make a cut the length of the roast, one third of the way from the bottom, which goes almost all the way to the other side of the roast but not through. Open the roast up like a book along that cut, then make another cut halfway up the opened part of the roast, almost all the way to the other side, and open up the roast again. Submerge the pork roasts in the brine. Store in the refrigerator for one to four hours.
2. One hour before cooking, remove the pork from the brine and pat dry with paper towels. Open up the pork with the cut side facing up, and sprinkle evenly with the chopped fruit, ginger, and pepper. Carefully roll the pork back into a cylinder, then truss each roast at the edges to hold the cylinder shape. Truss the roasts together with the fat caps facing out, then skewer on the rotisserie spit, running the spit between the roasts and securing them with the rotisserie forks. Let the pork rest at room temperature.
3. Select Grill, set the temperature to 450ºF (235ºC), and set the time to 50 minutes. Set a drip tray in the middle of the grill.
4. Put the spit in the grill and make sure the drip tray is centered beneath the pork roast. Cook the pork until it reaches 135ºF (57ºC) in its thickest part.
5. Remove the pork from the rotisserie spit and remove the twine trussing the roast. Be careful - the spit and forks are blazing hot. Let the pork rest for 15 minutes, then slice into ½ inch thick rounds and serve.

488.Lamb Leg with Tapenade Stuffing

Prep time: 10 minutes | Cook time: 45 minutes | Serves 3

1 (2½-pound / 1.1-kg) boneless leg of lamb
1 tablespoon kosher salt
Tapenade:

1 clove garlic, peeled   ground black pepper
2 basil leaves   1 anchovy fillet,
1 cup pitted Kalamata   rinsed (optional)
olives, rinsed   2 tablespoons
1 teaspoon capers   grapeseed oil or
Juice of ½ lemon   vegetable oil
½ teaspoon fresh

1. Season the leg of lamb with the salt, then refrigerate for at least two hours, preferably overnight.
2. Drop the garlic clove into a running food processor and process until completely minced. Turn the processor off, add the basil, and process with one second pulses until finely minced. Add the olives, capers, lemon juice, pepper, and anchovy. Process with one second pulses until finely minced, scraping down the sides of the bowl if necessary. Turn the processor on and slowly pour the oil through the feed tube into the running processor. Once all the oil is added the tapenade should be a thick paste. Use immediately, or store in the refrigerator for up to a week.
3. One hour before cooking, remove the lamb from the refrigerator. Right before heating the grill, spread the tapenade over the cut side of the lamb, fold the roast back into its original shape, and truss it. (You're going to lose a little of the tapenade as you truss the roast; that's OK.) Skewer the lamb on the rotisserie spit, securing it with the rotisserie forks. Let the lamb rest at room temperature until the grill is ready.
4. Select Grill, set the temperature to 450ºF (235ºC), and set the time to 45 minutes. Set a drip tray in the middle of the grill.
5. Put the spit in the grill and make sure the drip tray is centered beneath the lamb. Cook the lamb until it reaches 130ºF (54ºC) in its thickest part for medium. (Cook to 115ºF (46ºC) for rare, 120ºF (49ºC) for medium-rare.)
6. Remove the lamb from the rotisserie spit and remove the twine trussing the roast. Be careful - the spit and forks are blazing hot. Let the lamb rest for 15 minutes, then carve and serve.

489. Tri-Tip with Chimichurri Sauce

Prep time: 20 minutes | Cook time: 1 hour 20 minutes | Serves 10 to 12

2 tri-tip roasts, 4 to 5 pounds (1.8 to 2.3 kg) each

Chimichurri Sauce:

½ cup packed fresh flat-leaf parsley, chopped
⅓ cup packed fresh cilantro leaves, chopped
3 or 4 cloves garlic
1 small shallot, chopped
2 tablespoons white vinegar
¼ teaspoon salt
¼ teaspoon freshly ground black pepper
¼ teaspoon red pepper flakes (optional)
½ cup olive oil

Rub:

1½ tablespoons kosher salt
2 teaspoons freshly ground black pepper
1 teaspoon onion powder
½ teaspoon cayenne

1. To make the chimichurri sauce: Prepare the sauce 1 to 2 hours before the meat will be finished cooking. Place all the sauce ingredients, except the oil, into a food processor. Pulse a few times. Slowly pour in the oil while pulsing 10 or so more times. You do not want to purée the chimichurri, but all the ingredients should be finely chopped and well combined with the oil. Remove the sauce from the food processor, transfer to a bowl, and set aside until ready to eat.
2. Place one tri-tip on top of the other with the small ends on opposite sides. Fold in these ends and tie the roasts with kitchen twine, creating one single, uniform roast. Run a long sword skewer through the center of the roast lengthwise to create a pilot hole. Run the rotisserie spit through the hole and secure with the forks. Balance as necessary.
3. To make the rub: Combine the rub ingredients in a small bowl and apply evenly all over the meat.
4. Select Grill, set the temperature to 400ºF (205ºC), and set the time to 80 minutes.
5. Place the roast in the grill and set a drip tray underneath. Roast until near the desired doneness. The roast will shrink during the cooking process, so adjust the forks when appropriate.

6. Carefully remove the rotisserie forks and slide the spit out, and then place the roast on a large cutting board. Cover the meat with aluminum foil and let rest for 15 minutes. Cut off the twine. Separate the roasts, slice against the grain ⅓ to ½ inch thick and serve with the chimichurri sauce.

490. Lamb Leg with Brown Sugar Rub

Prep time: 10 minutes | Cook time: 1 hour 20 minutes | Serves 6 to 8

1 boneless leg of lamb (partial bone-in is fine), 4 to 5 pounds (1.8 to 2.3 kg)

Rub:

¼ cup packed brown sugar
1 tablespoon coarse salt
2 teaspoons smoked paprika
1½ to 2 teaspoons spicy chili powder or cayenne
2 teaspoons onion powder
1 teaspoon garlic powder
1 teaspoon freshly ground black pepper
½ teaspoon ground cloves
⅛ teaspoon ground cinnamon

1. Trim off the excess fat and any loose hanging pieces from the lamb. With kitchen twine, tie the roast into a uniform and solid roast. It will take four to five ties to hold it together properly. Run a long sword skewer through the center of the roast lengthwise to create a pilot hole. Run the rotisserie spit through the hole and secure with the forks. Balance as necessary.
2. To make the rub: Combine the rub ingredients in a small bowl and apply evenly to the lamb. Make sure you get as much of the rub on the meat as possible.
3. Select Grill, set the temperature to 375ºF (190ºC), and set the time to 80 minutes.
4. Place the lamb in the grill and set a drip tray underneath. Roast until the lamb reaches an internal temperature of 140ºF (60ºC) for medium or 150ºF (66ºC) for medium well. The lamb will shrink during cooking, so adjust the forks when appropriate.
5. Remove from the heat, carefully remove the rotisserie forks and slide the spit out, and then set the lamb on a large cutting board. Tent the roast with aluminum foil and let the meat rest for 10 to 12 minutes. Cut off the twine and carve. Serve.

491.Chicken with Brown Sugar Brine

Prep time: 5 minutes | Cook time: 1 hour | Serves 4

1 (4-pound / 1.8-kg) chicken
Brine:

2 quarts cold water
½ cup table salt (or 1 cup kosher salt)
¼ cup brown sugar
½ head of garlic (6 to 8 cloves), skin on, crushed
3 bay leaves, crumbled
1 tablespoon peppercorns, crushed or coarsely ground

1. Combine the brine ingredients in large container, and stir until the salt and sugar dissolve. Submerge the chicken in the brine. Store in the refrigerator for at least one hour, preferably four hours, no longer than eight hours.
2. Remove the chicken from the brine and pat dry with paper towels, picking off any pieces of bay leaves or garlic that stick to the chicken. Fold the wingtips underneath the wings, then truss the chicken. Skewer the chicken on the rotisserie spit, securing it with the rotisserie forks. Let the chicken rest at room temperature.
3. Select Grill, set the temperature to 450ºF (235ºC), and set the time to 1 hour. Set a drip tray in the middle of the grill.
4. Put the spit in the grill and make sure the drip tray is centered beneath the chicken. Cook until the chicken reaches 160ºF (70ºC) in the thickest part of the breast.
5. Remove the chicken from the rotisserie spit and remove the twine trussing the chicken. Be careful - the spit and forks are blazing hot. Let the chicken rest for 15 minutes, then carve and serve.

492.Sirloin Roast with Porcini Baste

Prep time: 20 minutes | Cook time: 2 hours | Serves 8

1 top sirloin roast, 4 to 4½ pounds (1.8 to 2.0 kg)
Wet Rub:

½ cup dried porcini mushrooms
¼ cup olive oil
4 teaspoons salt
1 tablespoon chopped fresh thyme
2 cloves garlic, minced
1 teaspoon onion powder
1 teaspoon chili powder
1 teaspoon coarsely ground black pepper

Baste:

½ cup dried porcini mushrooms
1 or 2 cups boiling water
½ cup red wine (Cabernet Sauvignon recommended)
1 tablespoon wet rub mixture
1 teaspoon Worcestershire sauce

1. For the wet rub: Chop the mushrooms into small pieces. Place in a clean spice or coffee grinder and grind to a fine powder. Transfer to a bowl and add the remaining rub ingredients. Remove 1 tablespoon (6 g) of the mixture and set aside.
2. If the sirloin roast is loose or uneven, tie it with kitchen twine to hold it to a consistent and even shape. Run a long sword skewer through the center of the roast lengthwise to create a pilot hole. Run the rotisserie spit through the hole and secure with the forks. Balance as necessary. Apply the wet rub evenly to the meat.
3. Select Grill, set the temperature to 400ºF (205ºC), and set the time to 2 hours.
4. Place the roast in the grill and set a drip tray underneath. Roast until it reaches the desired doneness: 125ºF (52ºC) for rare, 135ºF (57ºC) for medium rare, 145ºF (63ºC) for medium, 155ºF (68ºC) for medium well, or 165ºF (74ºC) for well done. Adjust the forks when appropriate.
5. While the roast cooks, make the baste: Add the dried porcini mushrooms to 1 cup boiling water, or 2 cups boiling water if you would like to use the porcini broth for the gravy. Steep the mushrooms for 30 minutes, covered. Strain the broth and reserve the porcinis (for the gravy) and broth separately. Divide the broth into two equal portions, one for the baste and one for the gravy. Combine 1 cup broth with remaining baste ingredients. Let sit for 15 to 30 minutes to come to room temperature before using. Begin basting the roast during the last half of the cooking time and repeat every 10 to 12 minutes until the roast is ready.
6. Carefully remove the rotisserie forks and slide the spit out. Tent the roast with aluminum foil and let the meat rest for 20 minutes. Cut into ¼-inch slices and serve.

493.Lamb Leg with Feta Stuffing

Prep time: 5 minutes | Cook time: 45 minutes | Serves 3

1 (2½-pound / 1.1-kg) boneless leg of lamb roast
2 teaspoons kosher salt
Feta Stuffing:

2 ounces crumbled feta cheese
1 teaspoon minced fresh rosemary
1 teaspoon minced fresh thyme
Zest of ½ lemon

1. Season the leg of lamb with the salt, then refrigerate for at least two hours, preferably overnight.
2. One hour before cooking, remove the lamb from the refrigerator. Just before heating the grill, mix the stuffing ingredients. Open up the lamb like a book, then spread the stuffing over the cut side of the lamb. Fold the roast back into its original shape. Truss the lamb, then skewer it on the rotisserie spit, securing it with the rotisserie forks. (You're going to lose a little of the stuffing when you tie down the trussing twine; that's OK.) Let the lamb rest at room temperature until the grill is ready.
3. Select Grill, set the temperature to 450ºF (235ºC), and set the time to 45 minutes. Set a drip tray in the middle of the grill.
4. Put the spit in the grill and make sure the drip tray is centered beneath the lamb. Cook the lamb until it reaches 130ºF (54ºC) in its thickest part for medium. (Cook to 115ºF (46ºC) for rare, 120ºF (49ºC) for medium-rare.)
5. Remove the lamb from the rotisserie spit and remove the twine trussing the roast. Be careful - the spit and forks are blazing hot. Let the lamb rest for 15 minutes, then carve and serve.

494.Port-Marinated Chuck Roast

Prep time: 15 minutes | Cook time: 1 hour | Serves 8

1 chuck roast, 4 to 4½ pounds (1.8 to 2.0 kg)
1¼ teaspoons salt
½ teaspoon freshly ground black pepper
Marinade:

1 tablespoon olive oil
1 shallot, finely chopped
2 or 3 cloves garlic, minced
1½ cups tawny port
¼ cup beef broth
1½ tablespoons balsamic vinegar
1 teaspoon Worcestershire sauce
1 teaspoon chopped fresh thyme
¼ teaspoon salt
¼ teaspoon freshly ground black pepper

1. To make the marinade: Heat the olive oil in a saucepan over medium-low heat and cook the shallot for 3 minutes until translucent. Add the garlic and cook for 30 seconds. Increase the heat to medium-high and add the port. Stir thoroughly and cook for 1 minute. Add the remaining ingredients and simmer the sauce for 5 minutes, stirring occasionally. Remove from the heat and let cool for 10 to 15 minutes. Divide the mixture into two even portions, reserving one half for the baste and one for the marinade. Store in the refrigerator until ready to cook, then bring to room temperature before using.
2. Trim away excess fat from the outer edges of the chuck roast. Place the roast in a resealable plastic bag. Add half of the port mixture to the bag, making sure that all of the meat is well covered. Seal the bag and place in the refrigerator for 6 to 8 hours.
3. Remove the roast from the bag, discarding the marinade, and place on a large cutting board or platter. With kitchen twine, tie the roast into a round and uniform shape, pulling tightly. Start in the center and work toward the ends until it is tied into a solid round roast. This will take four or five ties. Run a long sword skewer through the center of the roast lengthwise to create a pilot hole. Run the rotisserie spit through the hole and secure with the forks. Balance as necessary. Season the roast with the salt and pepper.
4. Select Grill, set the temperature to 400ºF (205ºC), and set the time to 1 hour.
5. Place the roast in the grill and set a drip tray underneath. Roast until it reaches the desired doneness: 125ºF (52ºC) for rare, 135ºF (57ºC) for medium rare, 145ºF (63ºC) for medium, 155ºF (68ºC) for medium well, or 165ºF (74ºC) for well done. Baste halfway through the cooking time, and repeat the process at least 3 times until the roast is done.
6. Remove from the heat, carefully remove the rotisserie forks and slide the spit out, and then set the roast on a large cutting board. Tent the roast with aluminum foil and let the meat rest for 15 to 20 minutes. Cut off the twine. Slice into ¼-inch slices and serve.

495. Lamb Shoulder with Mustard Herb Paste

Prep time: 5 minutes | Cook time: 2 hours | Serves 4

1 (4-pound / 1.8-kg) boneless lamb shoulder roast

Mustard Herb Paste:

¼ cup whole grain mustard

1 tablespoon kosher salt

1 tablespoon minced fresh thyme

1 teaspoon minced fresh oregano

1 teaspoon minced fresh rosemary

1 teaspoon fresh ground black pepper

1. Mix the paste ingredients in a small bowl. Open up the lamb like a book, then rub all over with the paste, working it into any natural seams in the meat. Refrigerate for at least two hours, preferably overnight.
2. One hour before cooking, remove the lamb from the refrigerator. Fold the lamb into its original shape, truss the lamb, and skewer it on the rotisserie spit, securing it with the rotisserie forks. Let the lamb rest at room temperature until the grill is ready.
3. Select Grill, set the temperature to 375ºF (190ºC), and set the time to 2 hours. Set a drip tray in the middle of the grill.
4. Put the spit in the grill and make sure the drip tray is centered beneath the lamb shoulder. Cook the lamb until it reaches 190ºF (88ºC) in its thickest part.
5. Remove the lamb shoulder from the rotisserie spit and remove the twine trussing the roast. Be careful - the spit and forks are blazing hot. Let the lamb rest for 15 minutes, then carve and serve.

496. Spareribs with Ketchup-Garlic Sauce

Prep time: 15 minutes | Cook time: 3½ hours | Serves 4 to 6

2 racks spareribs

Sauce:

1 tablespoon olive oil

2 cloves garlic, minced

1 cup ketchup

¾ cup water

1/3 cup packed brown sugar

1 tablespoon paprika

2 teaspoons mild chili powder

¼ teaspoon cayenne

Rub:

1/3 cup packed brown sugar

2 tablespoons paprika

2 teaspoons salt

2 teaspoons mild chili powder

1 teaspoon onion powder

½ teaspoon garlic powder

¼ teaspoon cayenne

1. To make the sauce: Heat the oil in a medium-size saucepan over medium heat and sauté the garlic for 15 seconds, until aromatic. Add the remaining sauce ingredients and simmer for 5 minutes, stirring often. Remove from the heat and let cool to room temperature before using.
2. To make the rub: Combine the rub ingredients in a small bowl and set aside.
3. Place the ribs on a cutting board and pat dry with paper towels. Cut away any excess fat from the ribs. Remove the membrane from the back of the ribs by using a blunt knife to work the membrane away from the bone in one corner. Grab hold of the membrane with a paper towel for a good grip and gently peel away. With a little practice, this becomes an easy process.
4. Lay the rib racks meat-side down. Apply a small portion of the rub, just enough to season, to the bone side of the racks. Lay one rack on top of the other, bone side to bone side, to form an even shape. Tie the two racks together with kitchen twine between every other bone. The ribs should be held tightly together. Run the rotisserie spit between the racks and secure with the forks. The fork tines should run through the meat as best as possible. The ribs will move a little as the rotisserie turns. They should not flop around, however. Secure to prevent this. Apply the remaining rub evenly over the outer surface of the ribs. A general rule with rubs is that what sticks is the amount needed.
5. Select Grill, set the temperature to 375ºF (190ºC), and set the time to 3½ hours.
6. Place the ribs in the grill and set a drip tray underneath. Roast until the ribs reach an internal temperature of 185ºF (85ºC). Test the temperature in several locations. Baste the ribs several times with the sauce during the last hour of cooking to build up a sticky surface.
7. Remove from the heat, carefully remove the rotisserie forks and slide the spit out, and then set the ribs on a large cutting board. Tent the ribs with aluminum foil and let the meat rest for 5 to 10 minutes. Cut away the twine and cut the racks into individual ribs. Serve.

497.Chipotle Chuck Roast with Garlic

Prep time: 10 minutes | Cook time: 2½ hours | Serves 6 to 8

1 chuck roast, 3½ to 4 pounds (1.5 to 1.8 kg)
Marinade:

1 (7-ounce / 198-g) can chipotle peppers in adobo	1 tablespoon ground cumin
1 cup diced onion	2 tablespoons water
½ cup beef or vegetable broth	1 tablespoon white vinegar
3 cloves garlic, cut into fourths	1 tablespoon salt
	2 teaspoons dried oregano

1. To make the marinade: Place the marinade ingredients in a food processor and pulse 8 to 10 times. Everything should be very finely chopped and combined. Reserve 1 cup of the mixture to use as a baste and refrigerate until ready to cook, then bring to room temperature before using.
2. Trim away any loose or excess pieces of fat from the roast. Place in a large glass dish or large resealable plastic bag. Pour the marinade over the meat, making sure all sides are well covered. Seal the bag or cover the dish with plastic wrap and place in the refrigerator for 12 to 24 hours.
3. Remove the roast from the bag, discarding the marinade. Lay the roast out on a large cutting board. With kitchen twine, tie the roast into a round and uniform shape, pulling tightly. Start in the center and work toward the ends until it is tied into a solid round roast. This will take four or five ties. Run a long sword skewer through the center of the roast lengthwise to create a pilot hole. Run the rotisserie spit through the hole and secure with the forks. Balance as necessary.
4. Select Grill, set the temperature to 400ºF (205ºC), and set the time to 2½ hours.
5. Place the roast in the grill and set a drip tray underneath. Roast until the meat reaches an internal temperature of about 160ºF (70ºC). Baste with the reserved marinade during the last 30 to 40 minutes of cooking. This roast is intentionally overcooked so that it can be shredded easily. It will be tender and juicy.

6. Remove from the heat, carefully remove the rotisserie forks and slide the spit out, and then set the roast on a large cutting board. Tent the roast with aluminum foil and let the meat rest for 20 minutes. Cut off the twine. Shred into small pieces or carve into thin slices and serve with warmed tortillas, Spanish rice, beans, and fresh salsa.

498.Bacon-Wrapped Sirloin Roast

Prep time: 5 minutes | Cook time: 45 minutes | Serves 4

1 (4-pound / 1.8-kg) sirloin roast	salt
1 tablespoon kosher	4 slices bacon

1. Season the roast with the salt, then refrigerate for at least two hours, preferably overnight.
2. One hour before cooking, remove the roast from the refrigerator. Cut the butcher's twine and lay the strings on a platter, spaced where you want to tie the roast. Put two slices of bacon on top of the string, with a gap between them. Put the sirloin on top of the bacon, then lay the last two pieces of bacon on top of the roast. Tie the twine to truss the roast and the bacon. Trim off any loose ends of bacon so they don't burn in the grill. Skewer the roast on the rotisserie spit, securing it with the rotisserie forks. Let the beef rest at room temperature until the grill is ready.
3. Select Grill, set the temperature to 450ºF (235ºC), and set the time to 45 minutes. Set a drip tray in the middle of the grill.
4. Put the spit in the grill and make sure the drip tray is centered beneath the sirloin roast. Cook the beef until it reaches 120ºF (49ºC) in its thickest part for medium-rare. (Cook to 115ºF (46ºC) for rare, 130ºF (54ºC) for medium.)
5. Remove the sirloin roast from the rotisserie spit and remove the twine trussing the roast, leaving as much bacon behind as possible. Be careful - the spit and forks are blazing hot. Let the beef rest for 15 minutes, then carve into thin slices and serve.

499.Barbecued Whole Chicken

Prep time: 15 minutes | Cook time: 1 hour 10 minutes | Serves 4 to 6

1 whole chicken, 3 to 4 pounds (1.4 to 1.8 kg)
1 medium-size onion, peeled but whole (for cavity)

Barbecue Sauce:

¾ cup ketchup
²/₃ cup cherry cola
¼ cup apple cider vinegar
2 tablespoons packed brown sugar
1 tablespoon molasses
¼ teaspoon salt
¼ teaspoon freshly ground black pepper

Rub:

2 teaspoons salt
2 teaspoons onion powder
1 teaspoon mustard powder
½ teaspoon freshly ground black pepper
½ teaspoon garlic powder

1. To make the barbecue sauce: Combine all the ingredients in a medium-size saucepan over medium heat and simmer for 5 to 6 minutes, until the mixture is smooth and well blended. Stir often and watch for burning. Remove from the heat and let the sauce cool at least 10 minutes before using.
2. To make the rub: Combine all the rub ingredients in a small bowl.
3. Pat the chicken dry inside and out with paper towels. Apply the rub all over the bird, under the breast skin, and inside the body cavity.
4. Truss the chicken with kitchen twine. Run the rotisserie spit through the onion and insert it into the chicken cavity. Use a paring knife to cut a pilot hole in the onion to make this easier. Continue to run the spit through the chicken and secure with the rotisserie forks.
5. Select Grill, set the temperature to 400ºF (205ºC), and set the time to 70 minutes.
6. Place the chicken in the grill and set a drip tray underneath. Roast until the meat in the thighs and legs reaches 175ºF (79ºC). The breasts should be 165ºF (74ºC). Baste the chicken with the barbecue sauce during the last half of the cooking time. Do so every 7 to 10 minutes, until the bird is nearly done and well coated with the sauce.
7. Remove from the heat, carefully remove the rotisserie forks and slide the spit out, and then set the chicken on a large cutting board. Tent the chicken with aluminum foil and let it rest for 10 to 15 minutes before cutting off the twine and carving.

500.Pork Loin Roast with Spice Rub

Prep time: 10 minutes | Cook time: 45 minutes | Serves 4

1 (4-pound / 1.8-kg) bone-in pork loin roast

Brine:

3 quarts water
½ cup table salt (or 1 cup kosher salt)
¼ cup brown sugar

Spice Rub:

4 cloves garlic, minced or pressed through a garlic press
1 teaspoon minced rosemary
1 teaspoon fresh ground black pepper
½ teaspoon hot red pepper flakes

1. Combine the brine ingredients in a large container and stir until the salt and sugar dissolve. Submerge the pork in the brine. Store in the refrigerator for four to eight hours.
2. One hour before cooking, remove the pork from the brine and pat dry with paper towels. Mix the rub ingredients in a small bowl, then rub over the pork shoulder, working the rub into any natural seams in the meat. Truss the pork roast, skewer it on the rotisserie spit, and secure it with the rotisserie forks. Let the pork rest at room temperature.
3. Select Grill, set the temperature to 450ºF (235ºC), and set the time to 45 minutes. Set a drip tray in the middle of the grill.
4. Put the spit in the grill and make sure the drip tray is centered beneath the pork roast. Cook the pork until it reaches 135ºF (57ºC) in its thickest part.
5. Remove the pork from the rotisserie spit and remove the twine trussing the roast. Be careful - the spit and forks are blazing hot. Let the pork rest for 15 minutes, then slice and serve.

Appendix 1 Measurement Conversion Chart

VOLUME EQUIVALENTS(DRY)

US STANDARD	METRIC (APPROXIMATE)
1/8 teaspoon	0.5 mL
1/4 teaspoon	1 mL
1/2 teaspoon	2 mL
3/4 teaspoon	4 mL
1 teaspoon	5 mL
1 tablespoon	15 mL
1/4 cup	59 mL
1/2 cup	118 mL
3/4 cup	177 mL
1 cup	235 mL
2 cups	475 mL
3 cups	700 mL
4 cups	1 L

VOLUME EQUIVALENTS(LIQUID)

US STANDARD	US STANDARD (OUNCES)	METRIC (APPROXIMATE)
2 tablespoons	1 fl.oz.	30 mL
1/4 cup	2 fl.oz.	60 mL
1/2 cup	4 fl.oz.	120 mL
1 cup	8 fl.oz.	240 mL
1 1/2 cup	12 fl.oz.	355 mL
2 cups or 1 pint	16 fl.oz.	475 mL
4 cups or 1 quart	32 fl.oz.	1 L
1 gallon	128 fl.oz.	4 L

WEIGHT EQUIVALENTS

US STANDARD	METRIC (APPROXIMATE)
1 ounce	28 g
2 ounces	57 g
5 ounces	142 g
10 ounces	284 g
15 ounces	425 g
16 ounces (1 pound)	455 g
1.5 pounds	680 g
2 pounds	907 g

TEMPERATURES EQUIVALENTS

FAHRENHEIT(F)	CELSIUS(C) (APPROXIMATE)
225 °F	107 °C
250 °F	120 °C
275 °F	135 °C
300 °F	150 °C
325 °F	160 °C
350 °F	180 °C
375 °F	190 °C
400 °F	205 °C
425 °F	220 °C
450 °F	235 °C
475 °F	245 °C
500 °F	260 °C

Appendix 2 Air Fryer Cooking Timetable

Beef

Item	Temp (°F)	Time (mins)	Item	Temp (°F)	Time (mins)
Beef Eye Round Roast (4 lbs.)	400 °F	45 to 55	Meatballs (1-inch)	370 °F	7
Burger Patty (4 oz.)	370 °F	16 to 20	Meatballs (3-inch)	380 °F	10
Filet Mignon (8 oz.)	400 °F	18	Ribeye, bone-in (1-inch, 8 oz)	400 °F	10 to 15
Flank Steak (1.5 lbs.)	400 °F	12	Sirloin steaks (1-inch, 12 oz)	400 °F	9 to 14
Flank Steak (2 lbs.)	400 °F	20 to 28			

Chicken

Item	Temp (°F)	Time (mins)	Item	Temp (°F)	Time (mins)
Breasts, bone in (1 ¼ lb.)	370 °F	25	Legs, bone-in (1 ¾ lb.)	380 °F	30
Breasts, boneless (4 oz)	380 °F	12	Thighs, boneless (1 ½ lb.)	380 °F	18 to 20
Drumsticks (2 ½ lb.)	370 °F	20	Wings (2 lb.)	400 °F	12
Game Hen (halved 2 lb.)	390 °F	20	Whole Chicken	360 °F	75
Thighs, bone-in (2 lb.)	380 °F	22	Tenders	360 °F	8 to 10

Pork & Lamb

Item	Temp (°F)	Time (mins)	Item	Temp (°F)	Time (mins)
Bacon (regular)	400 °F	5 to 7	Pork Tenderloin	370 °F	15
Bacon (thick cut)	400 °F	6 to 10	Sausages	380 °F	15
Pork Loin (2 lb.)	360 °F	55	Lamb Loin Chops (1-inch thick)	400 °F	8 to 12
Pork Chops, bone in (1-inch, 6.5 oz)	400 °F	12	Rack of Lamb (1.5 – 2 lb.)	380 °F	22

Fish & Seafood

Item	Temp (°F)	Time (mins)	Item	Temp (°F)	Time (mins)
Calamari (8 oz)	400 °F	4	Tuna Steak	400 °F	7 to 10
Fish Fillet (1-inch, 8 oz)	400 °F	10	Scallops	400 °F	5 to 7
Salmon, fillet (6 oz)	380 °F	12	Shrimp	400 °F	5
Swordfish steak	400 °F	10			

Vegetables

INGREDIENT	AMOUNT	PREPARATION	OIL	TEMP	COOK TIME
Asparagus	2 bunches	Cut in half, trim stems	2 Tbsp	420°F	12-15 mins
Beets	1½ lbs	Peel, cut in ½-inch cubes	1Tbsp	390°F	28-30 mins
Bell peppers (for roasting)	4 peppers	Cut in quarters, remove seeds	1Tbsp	400°F	15-20 mins
Broccoli	1 large head	Cut in 1-2-inch florets	1Tbsp	400°F	15-20 mins
Brussels sprouts	1lb	Cut in half, remove stems	1Tbsp	425°F	15-20 mins
Carrots	1lb	Peel, cut in ¼-inch rounds	1 Tbsp	425°F	10-15 mins
Cauliflower	1 head	Cut in 1-2-inch florets	2 Tbsp	400°F	20-22 mins
Corn on the cob	7 ears	Whole ears, remove husks	1 Tbps	400°F	14-17 mins
Green beans	1 bag (12 oz)	Trim	1 Tbps	420°F	18-20 mins
Kale (for chips)	4 oz	Tear into pieces,remove stems	None	325°F	5-8 mins
Mushrooms	16 oz	Rinse, slice thinly	1 Tbps	390°F	25-30 mins
Potatoes, russet	1½ lbs	Cut in 1-inch wedges	1 Tbps	390°F	25-30 mins
Potatoes, russet	1lb	Hand-cut fries, soak 30 mins in cold water, then pat dry	½ -3 Tbps	400°F	25-28 mins
Potatoes, sweet	1lb	Hand-cut fries, soak 30 mins in cold water, then pat dry	1 Tbps	400°F	25-28 mins
Zucchini	1lb	Cut in eighths lengthwise, then cut in half	1 Tbps	400°F	15-20 mins

Appendix 3 Recipe Index